Weather in Texas

Weather

in Texas

The Essential Handbook

THIRD EDITION

George W. Bomar

UNIVERSITY OF TEXAS PRESS AUSTIN

Support for this book comes from an endowment for environmental studies made possible by generous contributions from Richard C. Bartlett, Susan Aspinall Block, and the National Endowment for the Humanities.

Printed in USA
Third edition, 2017

Portions of this text were previously published under the titles *Texas Weather* (1983) and *Texas Weather: Second Edition, Revised* (1995).

Photographs that appear on the pages indicated below are credited as follows: page iv, © Wyman Meinzer; page vi, © Kenny Braun; page viii, © Kenny Braun; page xiv, Photograph by Susan Cobb; page 22, National Weather Service Collection; page 36, © Kenny Braun; page 78, Photograph by Shawn Newsom; page 132, Texas Department of Transportation; page 152, © Kenny Braun; page 194, Photograph by GalgenTX; and page 214, © Kenny Braun.

The paper used in this book meets the minimum requirements of ANSI/NISO Z39.48-1992 (R1997) (Permanence of Paper). ♾

Library of Congress Cataloging-in-Publication Data

Names: Bomar, George W., author.
Title: Weather in Texas: the essential handbook / George W. Bomar.
Other titles: Texas weather
Description: Third edition. | Austin: University of Texas Press, 2017. | "Portions of this text were previously published under the titles Texas Weather (1983) and Texas Weather: Second Edition, Revised (1995)." | Includes index.
Identifiers: LCCN 2016048673
ISBN 978-1-4773-1329-9 (pbk.: alk. paper)
ISBN 978-1-4773-1501-9 (library e-book)
ISBN 978-1-4773-1502-6 (non-library e-book)
Subjects: LCSH: Texas—Climate.
Classification: LCC QC984.T4 W67 2017 | DDC 551.69764—dc23
LC record available at https://lccn.loc.gov/2016048673

doi:10.7560/313299

In memory of E. L. Bomar, my grandfather and my inspiration to be a student of Texas weather, and dedicated to all Texas volunteer weather observers, storm trackers, and first responders who help us cope with the effects of bad weather.

Contents

Preface

Few subjects evoke as many tall tales and jokes as the weather, especially the varieties that legitimize Texas as one of the more interesting places on Earth to visit—or live. In many respects, Texas is truly a land of contrasts, and exceedingly often the extent of the state's diversity is punctuated by extreme and abrupt changes in its weather. Every winter ushers in bursts of biting cold from the Arctic Circle, occasionally in the form of blinding blizzards or paralyzing ice storms. Spring is reliably tumultuous, raking communities seemingly at random with tornadoes, vicious hailstorms, and overwhelming floods. Although notorious for its monotonous heat and humidity, summer is often rich with surprises, interrupting a debilitating drought with a water-laden tropical cyclone or letting in a dose of momentarily refreshing Canadian air. The autumn, while heartily welcomed for the relief it affords from heat and drought, can be exceptionally capricious with its propensity to spawn flash floods and premature frosts. Every year is unique, and in any year the fate of some Texans is diametrically opposite to the good fortunes of others. More the rule than the exception is the prevalence of drought in one region while other sectors have more rainwater than they can capture and hold. It is no stretch to say, on most any early-spring or late-autumn day, a weather observer can observe a snowstorm pelting the Panhandle at the very moment abrasive dust is scouring the Permian Basin and searing heat is wilting the Winter Garden region in the south. For every region of Texas, the utter dominance of drought one year is no assurance that rising floodwaters will not be a concern in the year that follows.

Texas weather is also a target for an inordinate amount of praise, and blame, that folks habitually assign for the favors and misfortunes they experience at the hands of Mother Nature. We boast about the intermittent balminess of our winters when folks elsewhere complain about the ever-present snow cover and lack of sunny skies in northern climes. We excuse having to endure weeks of torrid temperatures and absence of rain clouds in summer by asserting how the mildness of winters more than compensates for the momentary discomfort. Likewise, the weather absorbs much of the blame for what often goes wrong. Whereas some of that blame is justifiable, a lot of the time the unfavorable outcome has more to do with our carelessness or lack of understanding on how to cope when adverse weather happens.

This book attempts to capitalize on our unending quest to know more of what is the most prudent course to take when we face challenging weather. Knowledge often begets confidence, so the more we understand the capabilities and limitations of various weather threats, the less fearful we tend to be. In this edition, an enlarged portion of most chapters is devoted to the precautions and proactive steps the reader can take to ensure a most favorable outcome once the weather threat has passed. While some long-held notions about the weather are debunked, new ideas on how best to cope have evolved to help protect humans—and our cherished pets—as well as prized possessions.

Great strides have been made in recent years in understanding how the weather affects the populace—and marked improvements have occurred in the abilities of weather observers and specialists to warn the public when danger is imminent. It is today a well-worn joke that forecasting is the one occupation for which predictions of future weather can be wrong half the time while the prognosticator gets to keep his or her job. The fact is, weather forecasting in the twenty-first century is more precise than ever—and the accuracy of those forecasts now extends well beyond the 24- to 48-hour time frame with which previous generations were familiar. This volume seeks to inform the reader on what we know about various weather threats, why they happen, and the extent of their effect on life in Texas. Its contents are geared to meet the needs of those working in fields such as engineering, building and highway construction, and disaster preparedness. The material also will serve to enlighten readers whose work, and hobbies, center upon farming, ranching, gardening, outdoor sports, and recreation.

While this book can serve as a text for students of Texas weather, it is designed to address the needs of an audience with wide-ranging interests. Consequently, in-depth treatment of physical concepts underlying particular weather phenomena, including mathematical and theoretical considerations, will be left to other books. Many readers will discover some chapters to be of greater interest and utility than others. Some readers will search, unsuccessfully, for mention of a particular weather event that made a lasting imprint on them. Though the book is devoted to describing a plethora of weather episodes affecting a significant portion of the populace over many years, far more incidents have to be left unmentioned because of constraints on space. The federal government maintains an elaborate file of "storm events" that can be accessed to fill in details on specific weather occurrences, no matter how localized they may have been at the time.

Interest in the vagaries of Texas weather is keen and abiding, in part because of the potential of a type of weather to do *for* us as well as *to* us. This interest is acknowledged at the beginning of most chapters by an anecdotal description of some of Texas's most calamitous events in history. The intent is not so much to frighten as it is to cultivate an awareness of potential hazards that history warns are repeatable—so we can take the necessary steps to remain out of the line of fire when something similar recurs in our neighborhood in the future. It is true that lightning does strike twice in the same place.

Unusual features of the weather leave indelible imprints on our hard drives, so in the chapters a concerted effort is made to include more than a few of the most unforgettable incidents. The voluminous cache of weather data that is the National Climatic Data Center was accessed to create various tables featuring events, and periods of time, so that the reader might have a better perspective of how those events rank in the historical narrative.

The introductory chapter is geared to identifying the framework within which our weather functions. Weather is a key manifestation of the ways our Earth interacts with the sun, the supplier of the energy that fuels the engine that is our atmosphere. Chapter 2 gives a history of how Texans have paid attention to the capricious nature of that atmosphere, including the way the National Weather Service has transformed its way of measuring, predicting, and warning of the more deleterious elements of the weather. There is an appreciable percentage of the populace with an affinity for keeping account of the weather, so the reader will find guidance on how to maintain a personal weather station. Chapter 3 takes a measure on the large-scale movers and shakers of our weather, including the jet stream and frontal boundaries that are the catalysts for the changes we expect in every season of the year. A nod is given as well to the role that El Niño, and his counterpart, La Niña, play in skewing our weather away from normal in most years. Chapters 4 and 5 discuss the excessive heat and chill, respectively, that create hardship for many Texans in some years.

Beginning with chapter 6, the focus of the book shifts to specific weather phenomena, outbreaks of which warrant close attention and a readiness to react. Too much rain over short intervals spawns floods, often with precious little time to take refuge—though the National Weather Service is more adept than ever at alerting the public to imminent danger. In chapter 7, the thunderstorm is appreciated for its life-giving rains, though recipients of those showers must be wary of what too often accompanies the deluges: flash floods, lightning, and hail qualify the stormy weather as a bittersweet experience. For several months during the warmest part of the year the threat of a tropical cyclone, most notably a named storm as serious as a hurricane, looms for coastal residents, as illustrated in chapter 8. Yet hurricanes of a different sort—from the eastern Pacific that careen into the Mexican coastline—supply semi-arid West Texas with the bulk of its rainfall in some years. A much more localized swirling of the wind, the tornado, is presented in chapter 9 as perhaps the most feared of all atmospheric eruptions. Although the likelihood of a "twister" hitting a specific target is remote at best, the tornado's legacy of occasional bizarre fallout is enough to foster a disproportionate angst in some people. A wind of far less velocity is the focus of chapter 10, the kind of air movement that can bring relief to some (sea breeze) while annoying others (dust storm, dust devil).

With so much to read and talk about, it can no longer be said that no one ever does anything about the weather. To be sure, efforts to change our weather misfortunes are feeble—and some would assert strictly wishful thinking. Yet for several decades now, a well-orchestrated effort has been underway to extract more water out of the typically inefficient thunderstorm, as chapter 11 describes. There is evidence that working with Mother Nature has a payoff, though quantifying the benefit remains elusive. Even with a growing confidence that small steps can help us nullify the ravages of drought, we are sure to see, for years to come, much of our energy still being devoted to coping with the distasteful aspects of the weather, if not avoiding them altogether.

Weather in Texas

1.

Our Ocean of Air

The very instant you took your first breath, you locked in an unbreakable bond with Earth's atmosphere. The immediate and involuntary interaction you had with your environment activated your lungs and fomented other biological adjustments within you that ensured you would irrevocably be changed—and bound inextricably to that atmosphere. The ocean of air in which you were immersed would now be an allegiant companion, with whom you would have a give-and-take relationship. In an imperceptibly small way, your presence in the world would forever alter the atmosphere as well. At this very moment, as you read these words, you are making a donation to the water supply in the air around you. This involuntary offering comes in the form of moisture evaporating from the pores of your skin and water emitted into the air with each breath you take. The approximate one quart of water you supply each day, when combined with exhalations from others around you, feeds nature's hydrologic cycle, which ensures that water will return in a week's time in the form of precipitation—to be consumed by creatures like you. To be sure, because the total global precipitation is some one quadrillion times (10^{15}) more than any one individual's contribution, your effect is infinitesimally minute. Nonetheless, those 1,000 molecules of water you supply daily serve as fodder for the cloud cover you observe, possibly even the rain shower or dusting of snow that occurred a fortnight ago. Perhaps months before you were born, your parents were advised that your arrival would "change their world," and the instant you were born, you began to do precisely that—in more ways than one.

The symbiotic relationship you maintain with your atmosphere explains, only in part, why no other item of human interest is so much the subject of more insipid conversation on street corners and in coffee shops than the vagaries of Texas weather. Because of its diversity, severity, and—all too often—its unpredictability, Texas's brand of weather produces a disproportionate share of disappointments, both minor and major. It is the object of hilarious jokes and hyperbolic claims. With few exceptions, it is the focal point of intense and immediate daily interest.

The innumerable gradations of heat and cold, of drought and downpours, of wind and calm, do far more, however, than serve as topics of popular conversation. They mold and shape the citizenry to fit the environment; the never-ending skirmishes between competing masses of polar and tropical air hold the populace in their embrace. Of course, the extent of influence is not nearly as acute now as in the past when nearly all our ancestors lived directly off the land, fishing, hunting, caring for their herds, and literally raising cane. Today we live in predominantly centrally heated or cooled environments. Still, our dependency on the demeanor of the atmosphere is never more clearly understood than when the absence of rain shrinks the water supply to alarming levels or when too much heat or cold inhibits the production of food and fiber. We take solace in the fact that the fortitude and vitality that allowed our ancestors to persevere in the midst of storms, flood, and drought remain as the inspiration we will need to endure what many experts say is a more foreboding environment that awaits us because of climate change.

The oft-expressed assertion that "if you don't like the weather right now, just wait a moment and it will change" is not unique to Texas. Folks in other parts of the United States make the identical claim. The truth is, Texas weather, particularly in summertime, often becomes downright monotonous. If you hardly can stand the heat and high humidity that evidences the shift from spring to summer, hunker down—or make plans to visit Colorado. Summer's heat becomes entrenched around the solstice in late June, and only a haphazard tropical cyclone is likely to afford any relief for weeks and weeks. Get beyond the wearisome uniformity of summer, and you just might thrive amidst the heterogeneity of nature's often irrational ways. It matters not that you live in the vast expanses of the Trans Pecos, the undulating prairies of the Low Rolling Plains, or the dense thickets of East Texas, the one constant about Texas weather is its mutability (fig. 1.1). The weather's proclivity to be different from one week to the next—if not from day to day—is occasionally punctuated by the occurrence of a dramatic event that earns inclusion in the almanac of Texas weather extremes (appendix 1 is a list of Texas weather extremes).

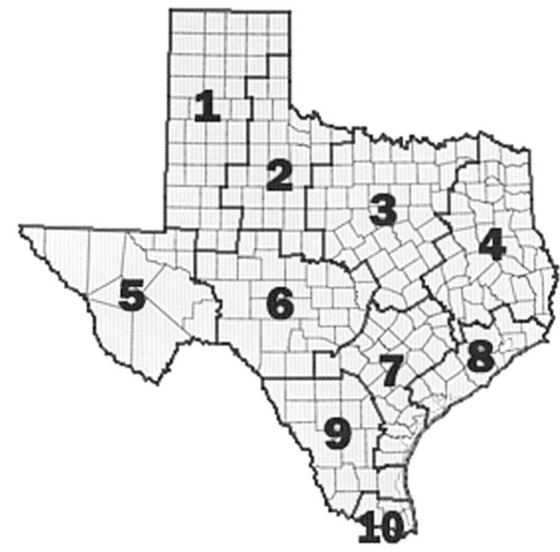

FIG. 1.1 Climatologically, Texas is segmented into ten climatic divisions, which are referred to often in this text. 1. High Plains; 2. Low Rolling Plains; 3. North Central; 4. East; 5. Trans Pecos; 6. Edwards Plateau; 7. South Central; 8. Upper Coast; 9. Southern; 10. Lower Valley. Source: Illinois State Water Survey

The same reversals in weather fortunes afflict most other regions of the country just as they confound Texans. After all, a change in the weather most often stems from the migration of air masses born thousands of miles to the north and west. What makes the shifting vagaries of weather so palpable—and popular—to residents of the Lone Star State is the state's location in the midlatitudes of North America and its multiplying concentrations of people, whose numbers make the Lone Star State today the second-most populous in the nation. The sequence of events in one September a few decades ago illustrates how vulnerable the state remains to the whims of Mother Nature.

To the dismay of those living on the plains and prairies of West Texas worn down by seemingly interminable heat, summer refused to take a back seat as the autumnal equinox approached. Afternoon temperatures soared yet again to near 100°F (38°C) as the cotton farmer adjusted the controls of his irrigation system and the oil-field worker inspected one in an array of seesawing pumps. Within hours, however, a recognizable omen appeared on the far northern horizon that signaled an abrupt and drastic alteration in the weather was in the offing. A bank of ominous dark clouds spread rapidly southward, yielding flashes of lightning, rumbles of thunder, and dashes of rain. The key to those watching was the sky was changing complexion to the north, a telltale indicator that the door to the Arctic Circle was about to open. Sure enough, all of a sudden the unfamiliar breath of Old Man Winter was whipping through the High Plains and across the Caprock. Readings that had lofted to triple digits plummeted to the 50s as the sun dropped below the western horizon. Winds picked up in speed as the evening grew longer, and a persistent overcast supplied welcome—if only intermittent—bursts of light rain throughout the night. For the next three days, a chilly northeast wind retained temperatures in the 50s even at midday. The abrupt and marked change in the weather was due to none other than a bona fide "blue norther."

As delectable as the abrupt reversal in the weather pattern was to plainspeople ready for summer to be discarded into the dust bin of history, the hemisphere's weather engine had more surprises in store. Once the wind veered from the northeast back into the southwest, temperatures shot skyward again. The 3-day spell of chilly, damp, and windy weather, then supplanted by a rapid warm-up, placed excessive stress on tens of thousands of acres of burgeoning cotton. This time around, the culprit was not the usual untimely pounding by pea-to-marble-size hail. Rather, a war between frigid and simmering air masses that originated in such diverse areas of the globe as the North Pole and the Chihuahuan Desert was responsible for a loss of $40–50 million wrought on a cotton crop that is perennially the treasure of a 25-county area of the southern and central High Plains.

Our Weather's Point of Origin

Like every other part of the world, Texas weather begins with activity on the sun, which supplies the planet with the energy needed to drive weather systems that shape our climate from year to year. While the Earth is dwarfed by the sun (a third of a million Earths would fit inside it), the source of our energy is itself a yellow dwarf star, one of many millions that adorn our universe. It is, by far, the closest star to Earth, the next nearest being Alpha Centauri, over 250,000 times farther away from Earth than the sun. The amount of matter used by the sun to generate light and heat continuously is gargantuan—some 4.4 million tons each second! That activity reveals the sun has a surface temperature of about 10,800° Fahrenheit (6,000° Celsius), which pales in relation to the estimated temperature at the core—a mind-boggling 25,000° Fahrenheit (14,000° Celsius)! The engine that is the sun is constantly in a state of violent flux: large "flares" of energy intermittently eject from the sun's surface far into outer space. At other times, and sometimes coincident with flare activity, darker, relatively "cooler" areas called sunspots wax and wane in cycles that last around 11 years each.

Strictly speaking, we survive—and thrive—in one gigantic greenhouse whose transparent ceiling encircles the globe at an altitude of 8–10 miles (13–16 kilometers). Within this gaseous envelope, a mixture of gases protects all living things from the deep cold and the lethal radiation of outer space. The biosphere in which we function is far from self-sustaining, however. Rather, life on Earth is at the mercy of a colossal, incandescent cauldron of gas known as the sun. Without heat energy from the sun, life on this planet could be maintained for only a few fleeting moments. But our atmosphere gets credit as well. Without its capacity for transforming and distributing energy from the sun around the globe, life as we know it could not flourish.

An Atmosphere Gassed for Action

The relatively thin atmosphere enveloping Earth is made up of a uniform mixture of permanent gases known as dry air, which contains varying amounts of other materials, such as water vapor and organic and inorganic impurities. Four gases—nitrogen (78 percent by volume), oxygen (21 percent), argon (1 percent), and carbon dioxide (0.03 percent)—account for more than 99 percent of the pure, invisible, and odorless dry air that we depend upon for survival. Oxygen is the most crucial gas for the sustenance of animal life, whereas carbon dioxide is vital for the plant world. However, carbon dioxide is also of monumental climatic significance mainly because it effectively, and selectively, absorbs appreciable amounts of radiation emitted by Earth that would otherwise be lost to space. In the absence of this capacity to capture warmth, nighttime temperatures would be markedly lower. Of greatest importance to our weather and climate, however, is the presence in the atmosphere of water vapor, also an invisible and odorless gas that is highly variable in amount but usually accounts for about 3 or 4 percent of the total volume of air. Its value to us far outweighs its percentage contribution to the total volume of air, for it not only provides the ingredients for clouds and precipitation but also absorbs certain types of solar and terrestrial radiation. Water vapor also possesses the unique characteristic of being able to change its state from solid to liquid to gas while remaining an integral component of the atmosphere. It is while water vapor is undergoing a transition—from vapor to liquid to form clouds, for example—that it serves as a major source of atmospheric energy.

What constitutes Earth's atmosphere in the lowest 50–60 miles (80–97 kilometers) remains rather constant. The concentration of ozone (O_3) increases with altitude to a maximum 15 miles (24 kilometers) above the surface. Ozone is for us a bulwark, an important regulator of the types and amounts of solar energy that reach the land and water surfaces of Earth. It shields terrestrial life from the lethal effects of ultraviolet radiation emanating from the sun. Hundreds of dust particles per cubic inch fill the atmosphere and play an important role in the formation of clouds and precipitation by acting as nuclei upon which atmospheric moisture collects to form droplets. It is the presence of these myriads of submicroscopic dust particles, along with certain molecules of gas, that give us the blue color of the sky and the brilliant red hues of sunsets by selectively scattering the sun's rays. Though some of this dust is washed to Earth's surface by the rainfall it helps to generate, the atmosphere's supply of dust particles constantly is being replenished. Of increasing concern these days is the massive introduction of many impurities, especially those that result from the burning of fossil fuels, which are decidedly harmful to humanity. Because of the state's blossoming population—and a concomitant explosive growth of industrial activity and use of automobiles—atmospheric pollution has become a principal concern for Texans living in the state's biggest cities.

A Layered Look

The Texas atmosphere manifests four fairly distinct layers that are differentiated mainly on the basis of how temperature varies with elevation. The layer adjacent to Earth's surface, and the sphere in which virtually all of humanity operates (except for astronauts living in the space station), is the troposphere. Extending to about 8–9 miles (13–14 kilometers) above the ground, it is the domain within which variations in the weather are most pronounced. This is so because the troposphere contains about three-fourths of the atmosphere's total mass and practically all of its water vapor (and clouds). Throughout the troposphere, the upper limit of which is called the *tropopause*, temperature for the most part on most days decreases with increasing height.

In contrast to the troposphere, the stratosphere exhibits very little, if any, change in temperature with increasing height. Relatively warm temperatures may be found near the top of this layer, resulting from the concentration of ozone, the highly efficient absorber of solar energy. Above the top of the stratosphere, at an altitude of about 16 miles (26 kilometers), is the mesosphere, where temperature increases and then decreases with greater elevation. It is in the upper limit of the mesosphere, at an altitude of about 50 miles, that most meteors burn and disintegrate. At the top of the heap, the layer from 50 to 300 miles high (80–480 kilometers), known as the ionosphere, has a pivotal role to play as well. Particles that make up this slice of the atmosphere reflect certain radio waves, allowing humans to communicate with one another. While changes in the density and composition of the upper layers of Earth's atmosphere conceivably affect the weather near Earth's surface, our greatest concern is with the behavior of the lowest layer of the atmosphere, for the troposphere is the sphere of our weather.

Checks and Balances

An incessant and immense stream of energy from the sun enters this envelope of air we call our atmosphere. Energy gained from the visible segment of solar radiation (also known as insolation) supplies the fuel necessary for the multitude of machinations that make up Earth's weather and climate. Because Earth, in the short term, is not warming up or cooling off substantially, it must return about as much energy to space as it receives from the sun. However, some parts of Earth's atmosphere—the tropics and subtropics—collect more solar energy than they give back to space, whereas other parts—mainly the Arctic and Antarctic Circles—give off much more than they receive directly from the sun. This continual transfer of heat energy, both horizontally and vertically, keeps the whole mechanism known as the atmosphere in balance. It is this perpetual exchange that sets up a host of temperature variations.

While much of the sun's energy is absorbed (one-half by the Earth's crust, either directly or indirectly, and about one-fifth by the atmosphere), the leftovers are reflected back into space by clouds and Earth's surface—or they get scattered elsewhere in the atmosphere. Heat energy is transferred between the Earth's surface and the air—or from one portion of the atmosphere to another—by one of three processes: (a) convection, (b) conduction, or (c) radiation. The processes of condensation and evaporation of water also bring about exchanges of heat energy between various surfaces and the atmosphere. These various methods of transferring heat energy maintain a fairly stable global-heat budget over relatively long periods of time. The amount of insolation received at any point on Earth depends upon such factors as the output of energy from the sun, the distance between Earth and the sun, the angle at which the sun's rays strike Earth's surface, the duration of the daylight period, and the constituency of the atmosphere itself. The varying angle at which the sun's rays hit Earth's surface is responsible for the unequal distribution of solar energy over this planet, which in turn determines the seasons of the year and the degree of variability of our weather. Table 1.1 shows the orientation of the arc that the sun traces across the sky for each season of the year. At the start of summer, because Brownsville is at latitude 25°54' N (or a little more than 2° from 23.5°, the Tropic of Cancer), the sun at noon over the city is virtually directly overhead (87.5°), while 785 miles (1,264 kilometers) to the north in Amarillo, the sun is 12° to the south from overhead. By contrast, with winter beginning just days before Christmas, the path the sun takes from sunrise to sunset is only one-third (31°) of the distance above the horizon toward vertical. Even in Brownsville, shadows are long because at midday, the sun is almost equidistant (41°) between the horizon and vertical. These stark differentials in the sun's orientation between summer and winter explain why the two seasons are so drastically different temperature-wise—from one end of Texas to the other.

The huge disparity in temperatures from summer to winter is also attributable to the amount of time the sun's rays are reaching the surface. In summer, it is the nearly vertical position the sun takes as it traverses the sky, combined with the amount of time its rays are penetrating the atmosphere, that makes the season a torrid one. As shown in table 1.2, on a

TABLE 1.1

Declination of the Sun

	Sun's arc (°) above the horizon			
TIME OF YEAR	AMARILLO	DALLAS	SAN ANTONIO	BROWNSVILLE
Vernal equinox (Mar)	55°	58°	61°	64°
Summer solstice (Jun)	78°	81°	84°	88°
Autumnal equinox (Sep)	55°	57°	61°	64°
Winter solstice (Dec)	31°	34°	37°	41°

cloud-free early summer day, the sun shines for more than 14½ hours in Amarillo, nearly an hour more than in Brownsville. On the other hand, at the start of winter, daylight lasts for only 9¾ hours in the Panhandle, almost an hour less than in the state's southern tip. No wonder, then, that the average annual temperature increases almost linearly (and latitudinally) from the northern tip of Texas to the state's southern extremity (fig. 1.2).

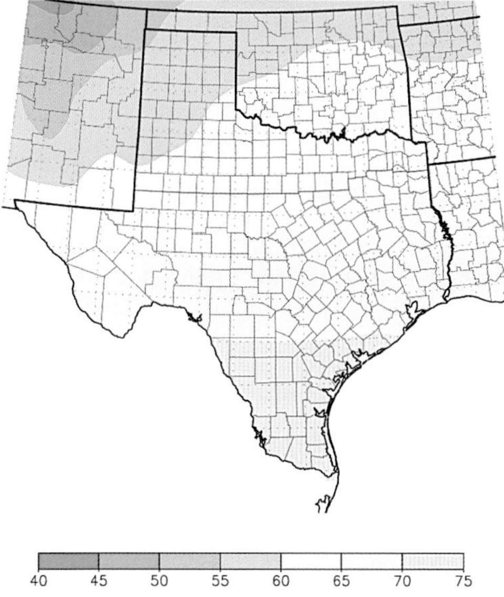

FIG. 1.2 Average annual temperature (°F) across Texas. Source: Illinois State Water Survey

The Atmosphere's Autograph

The best measure of this uneven distribution of incoming radiation from the sun is the temperature. The word "temperature" is a relative term indicating the degree of molecular activity, or simply the measure of warmth—or lack of same—of a substance. As the molecules move more rapidly, the temperature climbs. To measure the degree of coldness or hotness, an arbitrary scale is used. In the United States, temperature is commonly expressed in degrees Fahrenheit (°F); the boiling point of water at sea level is 212°F and the freezing point is 32°F. Another temperature scale, one that is used in nearly every other country, is Celsius (formerly known as Centigrade). In this system of units, the boiling point is 100°C and the freezing point is 0°C. One scale may be converted to the other using the following formulas:

$$°F = 32° + 9/5°C$$
$$°C = (°F - 32°) \times 5/9$$

Values of temperature throughout this text are expressed in degrees Fahrenheit, with degrees Celsius included parenthetically (except in the appendixes). A few decades ago, an attempt was made to wean the United States from the use of English units such as Fahrenheit and miles, but to no avail. Somehow, a temperature of 40°C is not nearly as enchanting as 104°F!

TABLE 1.2

Length of Daylight by Season

	Amount of time (hours:minutes) from sunrise to sunset			
TIME OF YEAR	AMARILLO	DALLAS	SAN ANTONIO	BROWNSVILLE
Vernal equinox (Mar)	12:09	12:08	12:08	12:08
Summer solstice (Jun)	14:32	14:19	14:01	13:46
Autumnal equinox (Sep)	12:07	12:07	12:07	12:07
Winter solstice (Dec)	9:47	9:59	10:15	10:31

With the Fahrenheit scale sacrosanct for at least another generation or so, a variety of temperature statistics—in degrees Fahrenheit—is used to describe the "personality" of a region's "average," or long-term, weather. The most frequently used value is the daily mean, or average, temperature. It is computed by taking the lowest and highest readings for a 24-hour period, summing them, then dividing that sum by two to get the mean. Actually, hourly readings of temperature measured throughout the 24-hour period would serve as a better basis for deriving a daily mean temperature, but the number of locations where the temperature is read only once a day far exceeds the sites where readings are recorded electronically on the hour. Besides, statistical studies have shown that on most days the average of the extremes and the average of hourly observations do not differ significantly. The difference between the minimum and maximum temperatures for the 24-hour period is the diurnal (or daily) range. The vast majority of local weather forecasts identify the diurnal range by providing predictions of overnight low and afternoon high temperatures for a given locale. The average (or mean) monthly temperature is derived by adding the daily means and dividing by the number of days in the month. Average monthly low and high temperatures, when grouped in threes (December through February for winter, March through May for spring, and so on), quantify variations in temperature from one season to another. Though they are of less interest, average annual temperatures, both minimum and maximum, consist of the average values of either mean monthly or seasonal temperatures.

Texas's patterns of temperature are influenced to a great degree by the amount of insolation reaching the surface, a quantity of considerable import because the range in latitude (from 26°N in the extreme south to 36°N in the northern fringe) places Texas on the equatorial side of the midlatitude regions. But its subtropical latitude is not the only controlling factor related to the receipt of solar radiation. On the majority of days no matter the season, the Gulf of Mexico has a profound bearing upon weather throughout Texas—and especially in the coastal plain—because prevailing winds for much of the year blow from the sea onto the land. Cold spells, the kind ushered by north winds from Canada and the Arctic Circle, usually last no more than a few days at a time near the Texas coastline because of the warming effect of Gulf waters, which becomes pronounced once the wind shifts from the north back into the southeast. Still another, albeit less prominent, influence on the variation of temperature across Texas is the presence of mountain barriers. This insulating effect from mountain ranges is sometimes evident in the Trans Pecos in winter. Cold polar or Arctic air surging southward out of the Great Plains sometimes piles up on the lee side of such ranges as the Guadalupe, Chisos, Davis, Delaware, and Chinati Mountains, sheltering the area from the Big Bend upstream to El Paso from the stiff north winds and plummeting temperatures that accompany cold-air intrusions elsewhere in the state.

The Diurnal Cycle

On the vast majority of days in every season, day-to-night variations in temperature across Texas are almost always appreciable. With the setting of the sun, the amount of incoming solar radiation quickly drops, and the outgoing terrestrial radiation increases markedly. Evaporation plummets and, if Earth's surface cools sufficiently and the dew point is attainable,

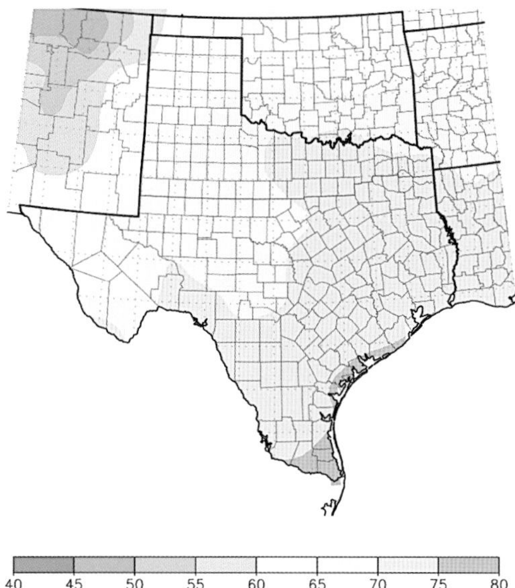

FIG. 1.3 Average summer morning low temperature (°F). Source: Illinois State Water Survey

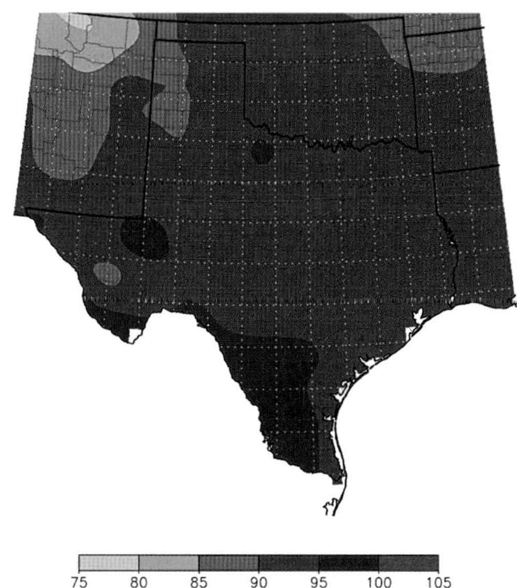

FIG. 1.4 Average summer afternoon high temperature (°F). Source: Illinois State Water Survey

condensation in the form of dew or frost occurs. Depending upon the amount of moisture in the air, the difference between daytime high and nighttime low temperatures may be as much as 30°–40°F (17°–22°C). There is a smattering of days in Texas, particularly in winter, when the air may be so laden with moisture that the diurnal range in temperature is only a few degrees. On most days, the temperature will bottom out within about an hour or two of daybreak, the point at which absorbed incoming solar radiation begins to counteract the removal of heat energy by radiative processes that have been going on all night at the Earth's surface. Though incoming solar radiation ordinarily reaches a maximum at midday, daytime high temperatures usually occur a few hours later, in mid or late afternoon. In the same way a room remains warm for a while after the stove is turned off, this lag is mainly due to the capacity of the atmosphere to store heat.

The diurnal temperature range is invariably larger on clear days than on cloudy ones because an overcast sky reduces substantially the escape of terrestrial radiation at night. Conversely, with clear skies, a maximum of solar radiation penetrates the atmosphere to Earth's surface during the day, and at night the outgoing radiation is not impeded by clouds. How much moisture there is in the air also dictates day-to-night temperature fluctuations. Because moisture in the air is most often more abundant in areas along and near the Texas coastline, diurnal ranges in temperature are much smaller than in areas that are more distant from the Gulf. For instance, on a typical summer day, the diurnal temperature range at Galveston is 80°F (27°C) to 86°F (30°C), while up on the High Plains the temperature at Amarillo varies from a low of 65°F (18°C) to a daytime high of 94°F (34°C) (figs. 1.3, 1.4).

Another key influence on the daily range of air temperature is the type of soil absorbing, and releasing, heat from the sun. The air above a sandy, loosely packed soil likely will have a greater diurnal range in temperature than that over a tightly packed clay soil. Hence, frost is a bit more prone to occur in a sandy area than in one dominated by clay. Also, daily temperature ranges are larger over dry soils than over wet ones. In the coldest months of the year, a snow cover induces the air temperature to fall lower at night.

More than ever before, the urban heat-island effect has a discernible effect on how the temperature varies, especially in Texas's larger metropolitan areas. On many nights, variations in the heat energy budgets of the large cities and the surrounding countryside may be as much as 5°F (3°C) to 8°F (5°C). Indeed, on some nights that are especially clear and calm, the temperature at a street intersection in an urban area may be 12°F (8°C) or warmer than at the same elevation on the outskirts of the urban area. Vast areas consisting of concrete, asphalt, and brick are responsible for storing a lot of heat energy, which prevents nighttime cooling from reducing the temperature as much as in open, grassy rural areas. The heat—and pollution—given off by industry, auto traffic, and residences in cities contributes to greater retention of heat by the lower atmosphere at night.

In the same way that day-to-night variations in the amount of solar radiation reaching Earth's surface affect the short-term distribution of temperature, variations in insolation from season to season affect the annual march of temperature. The perennial shift in seasonal temperatures reflects the gradual increase in solar energy from midwinter to midsummer, and the gradual diminution from midsummer to midwinter. The consistent angle at which Earth tilts toward and away from the sun provides the rhythm of the changing seasons so familiar to all (fig. 1.5). Because the ground is slower to conduct heat than the atmosphere above it, the air temperature usually lags from one to two months behind the periods of minimum and maximum solar radiation. Thus, even though the sun's rays are striking the Texas atmosphere at the greatest angle in mid-December, the state usually does not sustain its coldest weather until sometime in January—and every so often, in February. This lag is also responsible for the peak heating period

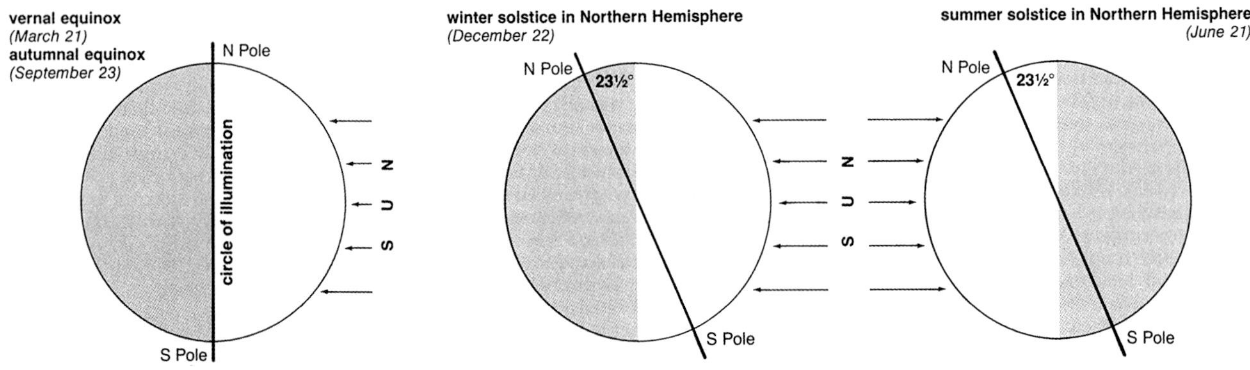

FIG. 1.5 Orientation of Earth relative to the sun at the beginning of each season of the year. Source: George W. Bomar

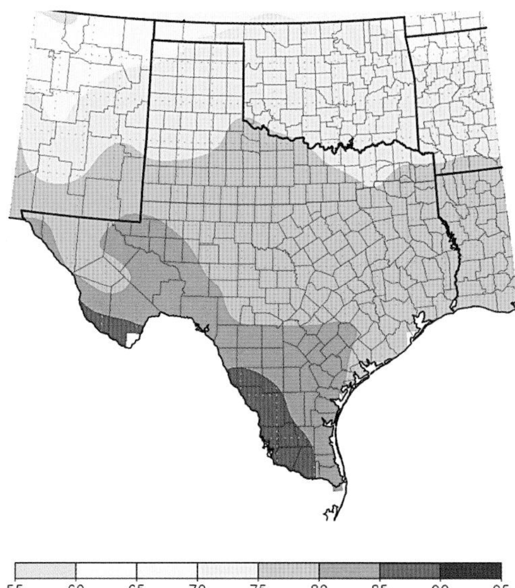

FIG. 1.6 Average spring afternoon high temperature (°F). Source: Illinois State Water Survey

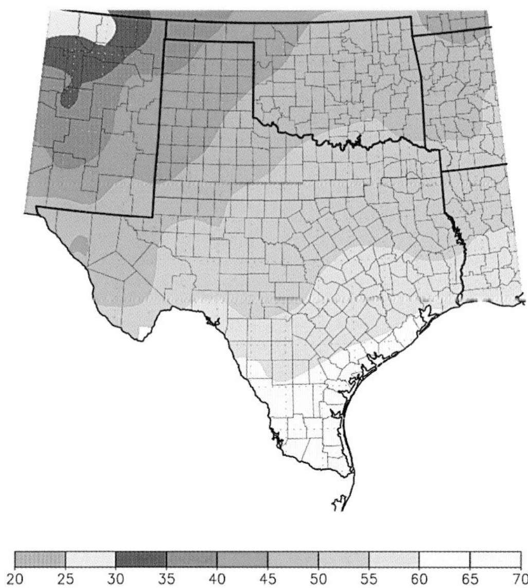

FIG. 1.7 Average spring morning low temperature (°F). Source: Illinois State Water Survey

in summer coming in July or August, not when the sun is at its highest angle in June. The effect that the Earth-sun configuration has upon the seasonal variation of temperature across Texas is discussed on the following pages, with emphasis given to the occurrence of abnormally cold weather during winter—the type that results in hard frosts and freezes. The opposite condition—a searing heat wave with its associated drought—is treated extensively in chapter 4.

Spring

With the rays of the sun striking the Equator directly from above on or about March 20 or 21, an event called the vernal equinox (because night and day are of equal length), a thawing from the winter cold already has taken place in the southern half of the state. Along with the turbulence that makes spring the most nerve-racking season of the year, the humidity increases, as do daytime temperatures. By the middle of spring (April), daytime high temperatures vary from the low 70s in the Texas Panhandle to the low- and mid-80s in the southern extremity (fig. 1.6). Of course, cold fronts continue pushing through Texas with considerable vigor at this time of the year, and differences between low and high temperatures for several days after frontal passage usually are large. The exchange between polar and subtropical air ensures nighttime low temperatures remain pleasant, with nighttime lows consistently dipping into the 60s in all but extreme South Texas (fig. 1.7). But once a "norther" runs its course, a process that often takes only a couple of days, strong southerly flow enriches the atmosphere with abundant moisture and elevates the temperature almost to summer-like levels.

For much of Texas, the season's last freeze signals the onset of the "frost-free" period. More realistically, for agricultural purposes, the interval between the last killing frost of spring and the initial killing frost of autumn is the most useful indicator of the growing season. A freeze, with or without frost, that kills happens when the temperature drops into the 20s and remains there for enough hours to seriously injure or destroy plant life. The length of the freeze-free season decreases in duration with the northward progression of latitude, the only exception occurring in the mountains of the Trans Pecos, where the high elevations often allow an uncommonly late freeze. The "normal" last spring freeze on or about April 25 in the northern Panhandle marks the start of a freeze-free period that will usually last about 175 days. Near the center of the state—in the vicinity of Brownwood—the freeze-free period lasts about 225 days, beginning with the average last spring freeze on March 25. By that time, the wildflowers in the Texas Hill Country are in full splendor, particularly so if the previous winter has provided ample moisture. In some years in the southern tip of Texas, the freeze-free period has no beginning or ending because the temperature never dips low enough to affect plant life. A comprehensive listing of last spring and first fall freeze dates for dozens of Texas communities, as well as the typical length of the freeze-free (or growing) season is given in appendix 2.

The season of freezes earns undue attention when it extends substantially longer than expected. In mid or late spring, an untimely freeze may catch field crops in the seedling stage or trees and shrubs that are budding or blossoming. The hard freeze that gripped the southern half of Texas on the morning of March 2, 1980, was especially nocuous because it struck peach and plum trees that had budded just a week earlier in the midst of 80°F (27°C) heat. About half of the peach crop, valued at more than $3 million, was lost in several counties in the Texas Hill Country. Morning temperatures in the low 20s also destroyed sprouting cotton, grain sorghum, and vegetables in the coastal bend section of the state.

Summer

For the whole of the season, which in climatological terms begins with the start of June—or some three weeks ahead of the summer solstice—summer is consistently hot in Texas. On the vast majority of days in June, July, and August, temperatures in every sector of the state—except for some of the offshore islands—peak somewhere in the 90s or low 100s. Where the humidity is dependably low, relief is afforded at night as the air loses enough heat to make the evenings and early mornings delightfully cool. This cooling down is punctuated most obviously in the mountainous portions of the Trans Pecos, where temperatures frequently drop into the 50s around daybreak before skyrocketing back into the 90s by midafternoon. Farther east, however, and especially in the coastal plains, enough moisture from the Gulf is usually present to prevent temperatures from dropping much below 70°F (21°C) before sunrise. That same moisture contributes to sultry, sometimes sweltering, afternoons.

The day-to-day variation in temperature across Texas is much more subdued in summer than at any other time of the year. By the time of the summer solstice, which occurs on or about June 21, temperature variations from daybreak to nearly dusk are about the same day upon day and, in some years, week after week. The constancy of summer temperatures is largely due to the absence of weather-changing frontal systems from the higher latitudes. Cool fronts occasionally ease into the northern fringe of Texas in summer, but they seldom penetrate far beyond the Red River. Even when they do, the polar air infused into the state behind the front is so diffuse that it rarely causes drops in the temperature of more than 5°–10°F (3°–6°C). In addition, relatively high relative humidities, ranging from noontime readings of 45 percent in North Central Texas to 65 percent in the Upper Coast, prevents the diurnal temperature variation from fluctuating more than 20°–30°F (11°–17°C). Morning lows in midsummer (July) range from the upper 60s in the northern High Plains to the upper 70s in more than half of the remainder of Texas (fig. 1.3). Daytime highs, on the average, are in the 90s statewide (fig. 1.4).

The heat keeps on building until it attains a peak usually in late July or sometime in August in all but the two westernmost regions, where the hottest temperatures in many years occur in late June or early July. With few exceptions, hottest daytime temperatures with numbing consistency are found in Southern Texas near the Rio Grande between Del Rio and Laredo, along the Rio Grande between El Paso and Big Bend National Park, or in the northern Low Rolling Plains within the triangle bounded by Childress, San Angelo, and Gainesville.

Autumn

With the angle at which the sun's rays reach the surface of Texas increasing to the point that the lengths of daylight and darkness are approximately the same, the onset of the autumnal equinox occurs. By this juncture, on or about September 22 each year, the length of the day is slightly over 12 hours long. The state's weather will have begun to cool down, as one or more polar air masses will have penetrated most, if not all, of the state, ensuring that the drier continental air that ensues will have brought about a wider

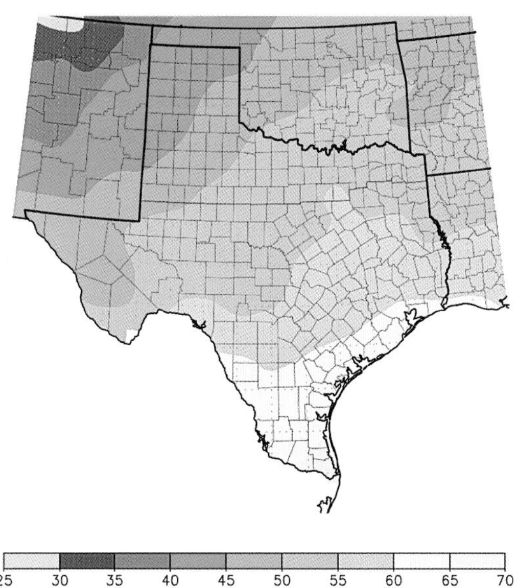

FIG. 1.8 Average autumn morning low temperature (°F). Source: Illinois State Water Survey

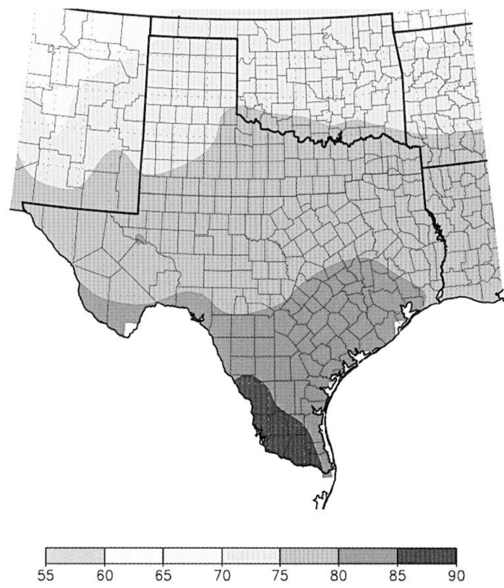

FIG. 1.9 Average autumn afternoon high temperature (°F). Source: Illinois State Water Survey

range between morning low and afternoon high temperatures. Relative humidities statewide on many autumn days—and even nights—are significantly lower by midautumn (October) than those that typified summer. During October, morning low temperatures range from the low 40s in the northern reaches of the Panhandle to the 60s in the southern quarter of the state (fig. 1.8), while afternoon highs vary from the low 70s in the Panhandle to the high 80s in the Lower Valley (fig. 1.9).

As in much of the United States, autumn arrests the growing (or freeze-free) season in most of Texas. Canadian air cold enough to promote a frost will have encased the Panhandle before October is finished. Then there is the usual progression southward of the freeze line with each entry of more cold polar air. The frost that is inevitable may be one of two varieties: (a) advection, or air-mass, frost, which occurs when the surface temperature drops to the freeze mark because of the influence of a passing cold front; or (b) radiation frost, which results on clear, calm nights when ice crystals form on cold objects. Air-mass frosts, known commonly as freezes, can be especially harmful when they occur prematurely in autumn before plants, including many kinds of crops, have had time to make the necessary seasonal physiological adjustments. Plants killed by a general (widespread) freeze may be damaged only partially by a radiation frost, which tends to be spottier, although the economic effect of one may be as great as the other. For instance, a berry or fruit crop may be eradicated by one hard frost, but the plants themselves may not be hurt so severely as to be unable to produce again at a later time.

Winter

As the shadows cast by a declining arc of the sun across the sky reach their peak, on or about December 22, the Earth's northern pole is tilted away from the sun by a 23.5° angle. Because of Earth's orientation at the time of the winter solstice, the intensity of light from the sun is at a minimum resulting from the longer path it must traverse through Earth's atmosphere. Normally by now, both day and nighttime temperatures have been steadily dropping, approaching a season minimum sometime in late December or in January. In midwinter (January) temperatures often fall to near, or below, the freezing level in the northwestern half of the state, while lows in the 40s are common farther south (fig. 1.10). Meanwhile, daytime highs are frequently no higher than the 50s in the northern half of the state and in the 60s everywhere else (fig. 1.11). The day-to-day deviation of low and high temperatures from normal is often drastic, however. During nearly every winter, the temperature will dip to near 0°F (−18°C), or even lower, on one or a few occasions in the northern fringe of the Panhandle. In fact, subzero temperatures have abounded in the Texas Panhandle and in scattered other spots in northern Texas on more than a few occasions over the past several decades. A reading of −10°F (−23°C) or lower can be expected somewhere in the High Plains once every two years. (See appendixes 3–5 for statistics on the distribution and extent of freezes in Texas.)

It is in winter when temperatures pose the greatest risk to the agricultural sector of the Texas economy. Freezing temperatures are most numerous in the colder half of the year in the Texas Panhandle, where an average of five out of every six mornings features low readings at or below 32°F

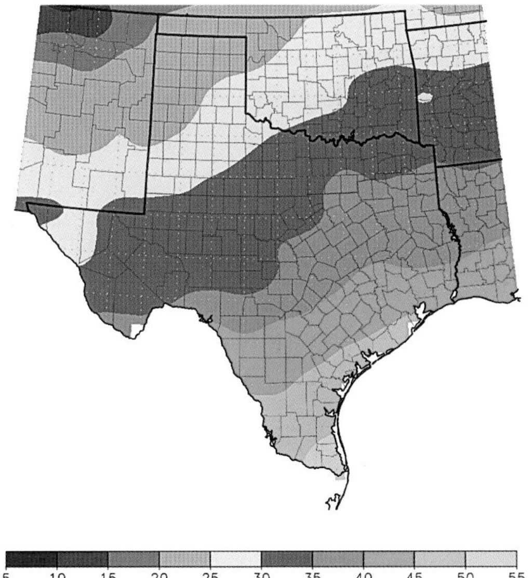

FIG. 1.10 Average winter morning low temperature (°F). Source: Illinois State Water Survey

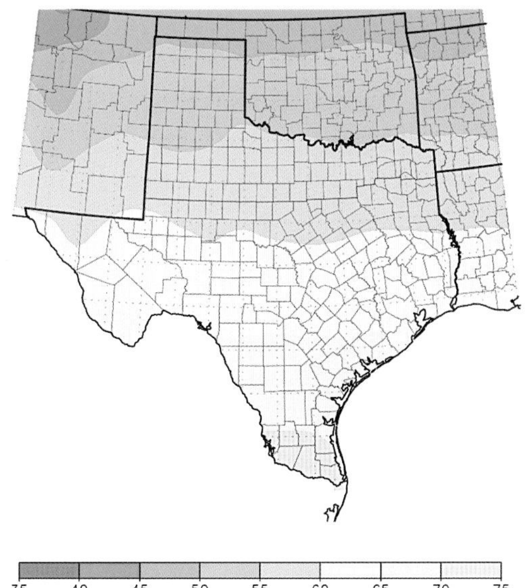

FIG. 1.11 Average winter afternoon high temperature (°F). Source: Illinois State Water Survey

(0°C) (appendix 3). Freezes are least common in the southern extremity of the state, where an average of one freeze is experienced every winter. Even farther north, in a strip of coastal plain closest to the Gulf that includes Houston, Victoria, and Corpus Christi, the number of freezes in a typical year is less than a dozen.

Whenever growing plants are subjected to freezing temperatures for any substantial length of time, damage or even death is to be expected unless a concerted effort is made to protect them. Even then, the most devoted effort to shelter orchards, vineyards, and gardens is to no avail. Every few years a mass of Arctic air will plunge temperatures to unseasonable, and unreasonable, levels—enough to devastate the winter crop in the southern quarter of Texas. For instance, the hard freeze that gripped all of Texas on January 9–12, 1962, totally destroyed the unharvested citrus crop in southernmost Texas except for a small quantity salvaged for juice processing. Growers sustained a loss amounting to $9.5 million, and vegetable producers suffered a loss of $8 million. While temperatures hovered around −15°F (−26°C) in the Panhandle, the deep freeze held the Lower Valley in its grasp for 65 hours! Readings one morning dipped to 10°F (−12°C) at Rio Grande City, and Brownsville recorded a minimum of 19°F (−7°C), the lowest temperature in that southernmost city in recorded history. The freeze was so severe, pervasive, and persistent that young citrus trees suffered extensive damage and older trees had their bark split. The state's flax crop was virtually destroyed, and nearly all of the oat crop was lost.

An historically frigid blast of Arctic air caused very heavy crop damage in Southern Texas on January 2–3, 1979. The Arctic cold wave forced temperatures throughout the Lower Valley below the freezing level for nearly 12 hours and resulted in a citrus loss of approximately $25 million. Many other kinds of crops also sustained extensive damage because temperatures remained too low for too long. (Critical temperatures for various crops are 27°F [−3°C], avocado leaves; 26°F [−3°C], oranges; 25°F [−4°C], grapefruits and young cabbage; 24°F [−4°C], citrus leaves, mature cabbage, lettuce, and most other winter vegetables; 22°F [−6°C], citrus twigs.)

For a ruinous freeze like that which hit the Lower Valley at the dawn of 1979, the recurrence interval is once every 6 years. More severe freezes, like that which ravaged Texas's southern extremity in January 1962, when temperatures dropped into the teens in the Lower Valley, occur about once every 10 to 12 years. Rural agricultural areas are nearly always several degrees colder on nights of major freezes than are nearby cities. As a rule, temperatures throughout the Lower Valley average about 3°F (2°C) colder than the "official" National Weather Service temperature measurement made at Brownsville's airport. So, with a reported low temperature at Brownsville of 26°F (−3°C), many of the crop-growing areas in the Lower Valley sustain readings in the neighborhood of 23°F (−5°C), which is the threshold for a major freeze. A low of 22°F (−6°C) at Brownsville suggests readings in the teens elsewhere in the Lower Valley, or a severe or catastrophic freeze in which profound and extensive damage is done to most citrus and winter vegetables.

These more modern serious freeze episodes pale in comparison to a few that inflicted severe hardship on the Lower Valley more than a century ago. Reliable, albeit spotty, weather records reveal that the decade leading up to the turn of the twentieth century furnished several extremely hurtful freezes. The most injurious hit Brownsville in February 1895, when freezing temperatures prevailed for *six straight days*, and readings plummeted to the upper teens and low 20s. During that time, more than 6 inches of snow fell in the Lower Valley! The same area also endured a disastrous freeze in February 1951, when temperatures again plunged into the teens and low 20s. It was on that occasion that a heavy glaze struck the state's southern tip, with ice accumulations amounting to a stunning inch or two in many places.

Our Changing Climate

Indeed, the seasons account for the ever-changing nature of Texas weather. But the climate of Texas changes too, yet much more slowly and far less perceptibly. While the weather describes day-to-day aspects of our atmosphere's behavior, the climate of the Lone Star State is a measure of average conditions in a particular sector over decades, even centuries. (See appendixes 6–9 for data on averages and historic extremes of Texas weather.) The weather is always going to change more from one day to the next than the climate will change from year to year. The difference between the weather and climate explains why a lone weather event cannot be relied upon to validate, or disprove, the existence of climate change. A prolonged heat wave that sponsors 100-degree temperatures for several weeks at a time does not mean the climate of the Edwards Plateau, for example, is warming. Likewise, an Arctic outbreak around Christmas that plunges temperatures below 0°F in the Panhandle is not to be construed as an argument against climate change. If heat waves, or cold waves, recurred with increasing frequency in many years over several decades, then the climate could be said to be changing.

The complexion of Texas's climate has been changing, albeit subtly, for generations. The best documentation available to substantiate these gradual changes lies within temperature data collected at scores of locations across Texas over the previous 120 years. Daily temperature extremes are known for a few dozen locations as long ago as the Civil War, and before then at military outposts maintained prior to, and following, Texas's annexation into the United States in 1845. The data are sparse, however, and often discontinuous at these locations. So, we are left to infer from other, more obscure sources the types of weather that prevailed in the early nineteenth century—and for several centuries preceding it. These inferences are important, because without an overview of Texas extending beyond a century or so, we cannot place current climate change in its proper context. For example, to what extent is the recent warming of the temperature in Texas due to human-induced activity and how much is attributable to natural variations within the climate cycle? That cycle may well extend over many hundreds of years, if not a millennium or two. Our rich data base derived from strategically placed thermometers is much too short to assess the magnitude and frequency of those natural variations.

Thus, we look to other sources, or proxy records, to reconstruct past changes in temperature or rainfall. These records are ensconced in a multitude of natural archives, the most notable being tree rings. While not direct measures of temperature and rainfall, rings are inextricably linked to prolonged spells of heat, drought, and excessively wet spells, giving us some clues to changes in past climate. Rings are particularly responsive to abnormal fluctuations in temperature: the light, low-density layers reflect growth in the warm season, and dense, dark layers highlight the end of the growing season with the onset of cold weather. Some trees thrive for hundreds of years, so small borings from a selection of trees can be used to construct a single, composite tree-ring record that sheds light on how the climate changed over a long period. Sampling in Texas suggests the mean temperatures in the most recent decades are the warmest they have been in at least the last 400 years. Extrapolating the warmth of our weather prior to 1600 is quite difficult primarily because few, if any, trees have existed long enough.

If we confine ourselves to the frame of history when reliable temperature statistics were collected at specific locations continuously over many decades, the warming trend is obvious in a graph of the mean annual temperature for Dallas (fig. 1.12). From year to year the changes appear random, substantially above normal for several straight years, for example, in the 1950s, then subnormal for much of a later decade, such as nearly all of the 1970s. But when all the fluctuations, from year to year and decade to decade, are "smoothed," the slant of the solid line is unmistakably upward, attesting to an increase in mean annual temperature of about 1.5°F from beginning to end of the twentieth century. Each decade was warmer than the one preceding it. There are exceptions, most notably the decade of the 1970s, which was generally cooler than any other decade before or after it. One takeaway from plotting the mean annual temperature for a location is that one or a few unusually warm or cool years does not mean climate change is intensifying. Rather, we look to the longer-term trend to see if the change is appreciable. If the period of record is extended back as far as the late-nineteenth century, as with the mean

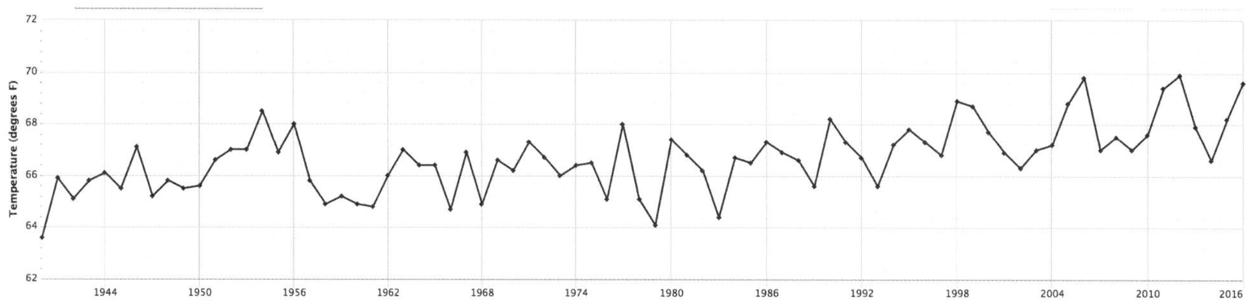

FIG. 1.12 Mean annual temperature (°F) at Dallas, 1940-2016. Source: National Climatic Data Center

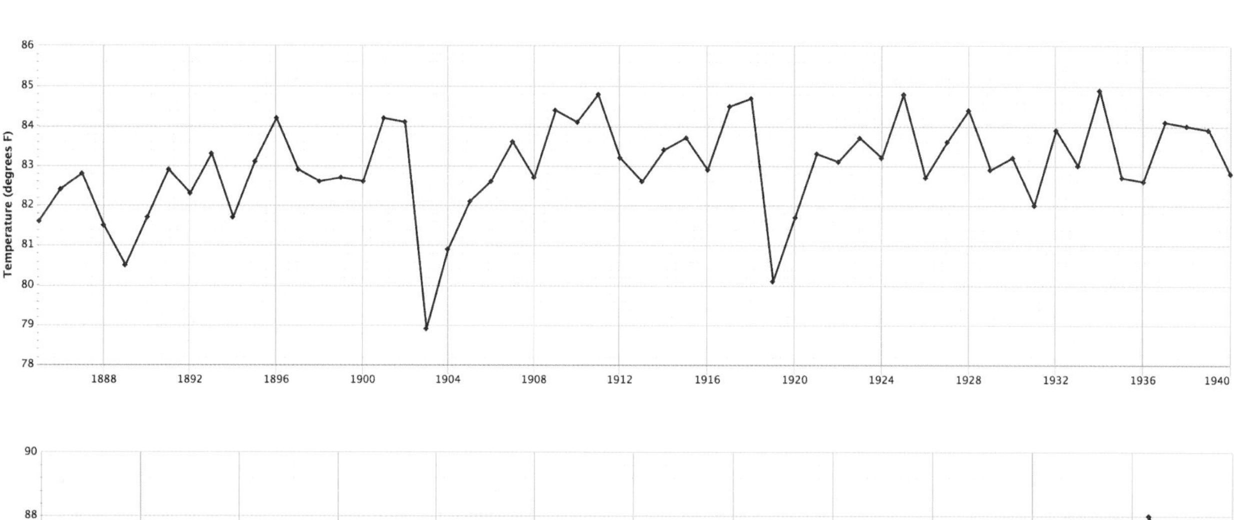

FIG. 1.13 Mean summer temperature (°F) at San Antonio, 1885-2016. Source: National Climatic Data Center

summer temperature for San Antonio (fig. 1.13), an even longer increasing trend is evident.

Another indication that the Texas climate has warmed significantly is the prevalence of extraordinarily warm years in very recent decades (table 1.3). Of the 10 warmest years on record (or since 1895), 6 of them occurred after 1997. The 3 warmest years, all with a mean annual temperature of 2.0°F or greater than normal, took place more recently than 2005. On the contrary, of the 10 coldest years, 6 occurred earlier than 1920. The 2 coolest years, averaging 2.5°F or colder than normal, took place in 1895 and 1903. To be sure, one can find exceptions to these generalizations: Both 1933 and 1934 rank among the 10 warmest years, and 1979 and 1983 are among the 10 coolest years. What might explain individual years that appear to disrupt the trend? Plenty of factors shape our climate, including cyclical features like El Niño (and La Niña) that exert abnormal warming (or cooling) over periods lasting a number of months. But these short-term anomalies say very little about long-term trends. A "most valuable player" may have a "slump," during which he goes hitless over a dozen at-bats, but his value to the team is best evidenced by a batting average—and slugging percentage—over an entire season.

Another manifestation that the climate is continuing to warm is the lengthening of the growing season, defined as the stretch of time between a point in spring (or late winter) and one in autumn when the temperature remains above 32°F around the clock. Over the twentieth century, the growing season across Texas lengthened by an average of one to two weeks. Most of the days added to the growing season came in the most recent three or four decades—when the season lengthened at a rate faster than the increase in average annual temperature. This is primarily attributable to the diminution of the difference between daytime high temperature and nighttime low temperature, a development one would expect from the presence of more greenhouse gases that entrap heat, elevating nighttime temperatures. As a consequence, this earlier "thaw" leads to changes in the blooming history of plant life, and the shorter freeze season evokes adjustments in the breeding, nesting, and migration of a whole host of birds, mammals, and insects.

TABLE 1.3

Texas's Warmest and Coolest Years

Given are the average annual temperature (°F), 1895-2015, and the departure from normal (65.0°F; based on data for 1901-2000).

RANK	YEAR	AVERAGE	DEPARTURE
Warmest years			
1st	2012	67.8	2.8
2nd	2011	67.3	2.3
3rd	2006	67.1	2.1
4th	1998	67.0	2.0
5th	1954	66.6	1.6
	1999	66.6	1.6
	1933	66.6	1.6
8th	1934	66.5	1.5
	2000	66.5	1.5
	1921	66.5	1.5
Coolest years			
1st	1895	62.3	−2.7
2nd	1903	62.7	−2.3
3rd	1976	62.8	−2.2
4th	1979	62.9	−2.1
5th	1968	63.1	−1.9
	1912	63.1	−1.9
7th	1905	63.2	−1.8
	1913	63.2	−1.8
9th	1919	63.3	−1.7
10th	1983	63.4	−1.6

Overall warming Texas temperatures for decades now is consistent with what climate scientists from around the world have been saying about a general warming of temperatures worldwide. A multitude of experts from around the world, known as the Intergovernmental Panel on Climate Change (IPCC), which was formed in 1989, issues reports periodically that assess the state of our understanding of climate change. Because each report goes through multiple levels of open and expert review before being finalized, the IPCC assessments are construed as the consensus of the scientific community and thus are relied upon by various governments for direction in formulating policies to deal with the threat of climate change. The panel's most recent summary of the state of Earth's climate in 2007 asserts that "warming of the climate system is unequivocal" and "there is very high confidence that the net effect of human activities since 1750 has been one of warming." Looking into the future, the IPCC projects an overall warming of between 3.2°F and 7.2°F during the twenty-first century, depending upon the extent that carbon dioxide (CO_2) emissions are curtailed.

With a plethora of sound scientific research from reputable institutions around the globe corroborating the changes, it is rather remarkable that the public remains divided over the reality, and extent, of those changes. To be sure, much is yet to be learned about Earth's climate system—and the causes and effects of climate change. What we do know is that some warming, or cooling, is due to natural changes caused by the sun and volcanoes on Earth. In fact, solar factors such as sunspot activity may play a bigger role in current and former climate on Earth than previously had been thought. Greater clarity is needed on just how much the climate is warming in some parts of the world—and perhaps cooling in other sectors. Climatology, after all, is relatively new and a rapidly evolving field of study. Skepticism about scientists' ability to forecast accurately the weather a few weeks in advance lends itself to a greater doubt that anyone can reliably foretell what the climate of Texas will be in 50 years.

Having much to learn, however, does not mean we can surmise little or nothing about the probable climate of the future. Some facts about our atmosphere are irrefutable. We know that CO_2 in the atmosphere entraps heat from the sun, and we can measure how much CO_2 is being added to the atmosphere from the burning of fossil fuels, such as coal, oil, and natural gas. It is known that more fossil fuels have been consumed since the dawn of the Industrial Revolution, with a resulting one-third rise in CO_2 in the past couple hundred years. There is widespread agreement among climate experts that an increase in CO_2 and a concomitant warming of the atmosphere melts ice caps and glaciers and leads to expanding ocean waters and a rise in sea levels. Since 1900, oceans are some 8 inches higher while the air temperature near Earth's surface is, on average, 1.3°F hotter.

Earth reacts to increasing temperatures—but in a myriad of ways, some very predictable and others unforeseen, some exacerbating the rise in average global temperature while others restrain it. Droughts, torrential rainstorms, and other weather extremes seem to be happening more often now than a century ago. That is a reasonable assumption given that warming, according to computations from atmospheric scientists, has already put about five percent more water vapor into the atmosphere today, on average, than there was in 1900. On the other hand, the warming that would seem to promote greater cloud cover could, in turn, reflect more solar energy back into space, thereby mitigating to some extent a continuing rise in temperature. The opposite effect could occur as the ice cover in the Arctic shrinks. The Arctic's permafrost, responding to warming temperatures, could release carbon that has been encased in the ice for millennia, thereby aggravating the upward trend in temperatures.

Discerning any trend toward warmer climate is much less a challenge than identifying the root causes of higher temperatures—and specifying what human beings can do, if anything, to slow the momentum. Various approaches have been taken, and others are being proposed, to afford consumers an opportunity to try and mitigate the effect of a warming climate. The benefits of many of these tactics appear to be a mixed bag, however. For instance, greater use of ethanol in autos, it is argued, would lessen our dependency on resources like coal and oil, resulting in a reduction of CO_2 into our atmosphere. But producing more ethanol (from corn) requires energy from fossil fuels, leaving consumers with the likelihood that the total emissions from the use of corn ethanol may not be substantially different from those generated by using gasoline in cars. Using more "clean coal," a product of a process known as carbon capture and storage, requires a lot of energy to remove the CO_2 and liquefy it, leaving producers with the reality that no appreciable reduction in CO_2 emissions actually was realized. Solar energy is superabundant, but existing technology can convert only a small percentage of the energy falling on panels, calling into question the cost-effectiveness of those panels until they can be made more efficient. Like solar, wind is variable and unpredictable, leaving producers of wind energy with challenges of storage and transport.

If the assumption that a warmer climate will be disruptive to life as we know it has validity, then we cannot afford to ignore the problem. On the other hand, if the effects of climate change are inconsequential, then we risk wasting a lot of resources for no reason. The dilemma we share is, if we wait until the fog about climate change has sufficiently cleared for us to know what, if any, threat we face, we may well have waited too long to unravel the damage, whatever it turns out to be.

2.

Eyes to the Skies

For many generations, a proud tradition of measuring the elements and idiosyncrasies of Texas weather has endured, even as technological advances have given us remote sensing tools that negate the need for human beings to be on station to document every nuance of nature. With a regularity matching that of the four seasons themselves, a ritual with deep roots in the distant past is repeated hundreds of times in Texas every day of the year: A person ambles a short distance from a house or business establishment to a shiny cylinder positioned in the middle of an open space, centered perhaps in the middle of a backyard or near the edge of a vacant lot. Clasping a black measuring stick, the observer peers into the top of the canister, then lowers the stick through an opening before withdrawing it an instant later. The stick is raised to eye level, and a mental notation is made of where the moistened section of the stick ends. Then, he or she removes the funnel that caps the cylindrical container and empties the rain water captured inside. Finally, satisfied that all systems are set for the next round of measurements, the observer strolls from the scene and upon entering his or her house or business consults an electronic display of minimum and maximum temperatures for the previous 24-hour period. Armed with both rain gauge and thermometer readings, the observer then enters both on a tablet or sits in front of a desktop computer, maybe even a laptop, and electronically stores—and sends—the data for later publication and transmission by the National Weather Service (NWS).

In this most modern of eras, with the prevalence of and access to electronic gadgetry, a weather observer no longer needs even to leave the house to gather metrics on changes in temperature. For more than a century, the white Cotton Region Instrument Shelter served as the destination of hundreds of volunteer weather observers, who dutifully peered at thermometers mounted inside the structure to gauge the temperature every morning or evening (fig. 2.1).

In recent years, what appears to be a habitat for bees has been replaced by the NWS with a smaller, louvered unit containing a thermistor that is connected by underground cable to an observer's house. This minimum-maximum temperature system provides a continuous digital read-out of current temperature, as well as a record of minimum and maximum temperatures for the day, calibrated to one-tenth of a degree Fahrenheit. Observers can note temperature extremes at the appointed time (usually around sunrise or sunset) without ever having to walk outside. (They still must venture out to the rain gauge, however, to measure rainfall by means of a dipstick.)

FIG. 2.1 The ageless Cotton Region Instrument Shelter served as the sanctuary for thermometers used by volunteer weather observers for generations in Texas. Source: George W. Bomar

While technology has made the chore of weather observing more accommodating for the volunteer weather watcher, the data routinely collected and filed with the NWS remain valuable. It is these pieces of data that enhance our understanding of the disposition of the sea of air that swirls incessantly around us—and in what ways the climate may have changed over many decades. Since the late-nineteenth century, hundreds of public servants have dutifully preserved their observations, filing them with appropriate government authorities for permanent archive. The diligent documenting of the weather day upon day has been sustained within some families over several generations. Thanks to these indefatigable observers, some localities in Texas have complete weather histories spanning 50 years or longer.

The growing repository of weather data is of immense value to many in our increasingly mobile society. Prior to their arrival, outsiders contemplating a visit or move to the state can tap this storehouse for information on what to expect from the weather—and hence what to wear or plan for, even the type of home to build and where to situate it. With climate now a prime consideration in many business decisions, a planner or investor can know about wind or moisture conditions for virtually any area of interest. As has been true for centuries, an analysis and understanding of weather are of critical significance to any successful agricultural endeavor. Adequate planning for developing water resources and for highway design and construction also must be based upon reliable climatological data. Indubitably, many and varied facets of the Texas economy have prospered greatly from an awareness of the tendencies, excesses, and limitations of Texas weather. The hundreds of volunteer weather observers who faithfully stay on task have contributed immeasurably to one of the healthiest economies on Earth.

Eyes of Texas on the Weather

Though not nearly as exhaustive in range or detail, the first known weather records for Texas were kept by Spanish settlers, who established and maintained numerous missions around the state from 1682 until the early decades of the 1800s. Anglo-American settlers, who later supplanted the Spaniards and colonized the same areas, also kept records of significant weather developments in the decades leading up to the American Civil War. The earliest Texas weather record on file in the national climatic archives in North Carolina consists of data recorded at Camp Nacogdoches in September 1836—the year Texas won its independence from Mexico. Most of the documentation, found mainly in logs, diaries, and journals, is piecemeal and deals only with severe or other unusual weather events. Nonetheless, these weather records are of indispensable value to climatologists seeking to understand general weather trends in the pre–Civil War era.

Likely the first systematic approach to collecting and recording weather information started with the establishment of numerous military outposts on the Texas frontier between 1840 and 1860. The earliest such military weather station was maintained at Fort Houston in Anderson County, near the present site of Palestine. As with many other military outposts devoted to documenting the weather, observations lasted until the outbreak of the Civil War in the early 1860s. In some instances, though, weather records were maintained after the war by civilian observers who lived near the outpost and assumed the task of making the observations and storing the data on a daily basis. For instance, Fort Bliss (El Paso) maintained weather observations through and after the Civil War, though the 26-year record ending in 1876 is only 70 percent complete. Fort Davis is second only to Fort Bliss in length of history, with records beginning in 1855—but the archive is only 60 percent complete. Thanks to the diligence in keeping accurate records by conscientious nonmilitary personnel, some locales (e.g., Fort Stockton) have a nearly complete weather history spanning more than a century.

Civilians were also at work observing the weather prior to the Civil War in areas without military bases. Weather annals containing rainfall data as early as 1846 were kept by a resident of San Jose Island (the original name restored by the legislature in 1973 to the land long known as St. Joseph Island), a settlement offshore from Rockport. A settler at Fredericksburg began a systematic record of both temperature and precipitation in August 1849. Texas A&M University, known at the time as the Texas Agricultural and Mechanical College, began temperature and rainfall measurements in May 1882, ensuring that, except for a few brief breaks, College Station has a virtually complete weather history covering a whole century. A nearly complete chronicle of the weather is also available for the state's capital city; both temperature and precipitation measurements were begun in Austin in January 1856 and, except for five missing months in 1882–1883, the record is stunningly complete for an entire 160-year period. No other locale in Texas is known to have as thorough a weather record for as long as that belonging to Austin, although more than a dozen other sites have an almost complete record covering the period from the Civil War era to the present. While

El Paso's weather archive began 6 years earlier than Austin's, it is not nearly as continuous, with about one-fifth of data missing between 1850 and 1900. Two localities, including Galveston Island, have perfect (continuous) records for the several decades after the Civil War; the other, Indianola, has a 14-year complete record that ends in 1886, when the community was buried by a hurricane—the second hurricane to destroy it over an 11-year period!

A Legion of Volunteers

The US Congress established the taking of weather observations as part of the Army Signal Service in 1870. Twenty years later, in 1890, when the mission was transferred to the US Department of Agriculture and named the US Weather Bureau, daily weather measurements were being made at seventy-eight locations within Texas, and volunteer (unpaid) civilian observers were making more than three-fourths of all the recordings. Today the NWS measures precipitation (primarily rainfall) on every day of its occurrence at approximately 650 locations within the state, and private citizens (cooperative observers) account for about 90 percent of those observations. The vast majority of daily readings are made around daybreak (at 7 or 8 a.m.) on every day of the year. A very few stations, including that of this author, have readings made prior to sunset, or around 5:00 or 6:00 in the evening. Practically every one of Texas's 254 counties has at least one weather station (mainly county seats) where a volunteer observer makes daily precipitation and temperature observations. Many counties have several data collection points, and with very few exceptions, minimum and maximum temperatures are measured in addition to daily precipitation in each county seat.

Each cooperative weather observer is furnished a standard 8-inch (in diameter) rain gauge—one capable of holding 20 inches of rainwater and which comes with a calibrated dipstick (fig. 2.2). The majority of these stations also are equipped with an instrument shelter that houses an electronic sensor for measuring daily extremes in temperature (fig. 2.3). A secondary network, consisting of "recording" rain-gauge stations, uses a more sophisticated rain-measuring device to quantify the rate and the amount of rain that falls. In all, some type of rainfall data is gathered on a daily basis at more than a thousand different locations in Texas.

The daily data from these volunteer observers are filed with the NWS and the National Center for Environmental Information (NCEI), which is a federal facility in Asheville, North Carolina. Personnel of NCEI apply quality-control measures to ensure accuracy in the data before they are eventually published. These data can be obtained online free of charge—unless the data are needed in certified form for legal, insurance, or business purposes, a procedure that costs the user a fee. The quality-controlled final data are usually available only a few months after the data are collected and filed by the observer. Unedited data can be had almost instantaneously, however, as many cooperative observers now use software that gives them the capability to enter their precipitation and temperature measurements electronically into the NCEI system immediately upon making the observations. Anyone with internet access can retrieve NCEI information on a virtual, real-time basis. With these unedited data, the NWS cautions the user that the measurements have not been examined for errors.

During much of the year, when convective clouds are responsible for the bulk of an area's precipitation, rainfall can vary dramatically over

FIG. 2.2 The 8-inch standard rain gauge, which holds up to 20 inches of rainwater, is still used to measure precipitation by hundreds of volunteer weather observers. Source: George W. Bomar

FIG. 2.3 The Minimum-Maximum Temperature System (MMTS) today allows volunteer weather watchers to monitor the temperature on an around-the-clock basis. Source: George W. Bomar

short distances—even within neighborhoods. To fill in the gaps where cooperative weather observers with electronic gear do not reside, the NWS collaborates with a grassroot network of volunteers known as the Community Collaborative Rain, Hail, and Snow (CoCoRaHS) Network. These volunteers are armed with smaller 4-inch diameter—but highly accurate—rain gauges to collect daily rainfall readings that are entered into a website (www.cocorahs.org) where interactive maps can be accessed. The observers also serve as a plentiful source of "eyes" to identify severe weather, such as a tornado, damaging hail, or destructive straight-line winds, and thereby enable the NWS to pinpoint locations for severe-weather warnings. The number of CoCoRaHS observers in Texas now numbers nearly 4,800, with many of them farmers, ranchers, teachers, and schoolchildren. Offices of the NWS around the state continually enroll these volunteers in the network. It is estimated that as many as 25,000 observers are needed to supply saturated coverage for the whole of the state.

Another huge cadre of volunteers are storm-spotter teams, who monitor hazardous weather conditions around the state. These men and women attend annual training sessions, known as SKYWARN conferences, to be trained or given refresher courses that cultivate skills in identifying severe thunderstorms, flash flooding, tornadoes, and other extreme forms of threatening weather. Many of these people serve the public as police officers, firefighters, dispatchers, utility workers, and amateur radio operators. Others are interested citizens devoted to protecting their neighborhoods and communities. The spotters learn how to recognize the difference between actual funnel clouds and other low-hanging cloud formations—a critical distinction that helps minimize the chance that the public is unnecessarily mobilized. Too many false alarms can inure the public to legitimate warnings. Professional meteorologists, many of whom work at various NWS forecast offices in Texas, conduct the training sessions, often on weekends, to hone spotters' skills but also to instruct them on how to stay safe while spotting and reporting on storm events. Training at SKYWARN conferences is usually open to the public, and anyone properly trained can be certified as a spotter.

Even with countless volunteers routinely collecting rainfall and temperature data on a daily basis, or on occasions when adverse weather threatens, the trend in weather observing today involves the deployment of automated equipment that provides very reliable and almost continuous data without the engagement of a human observer in the process. These mesonets, or concentrations of stations within a river basin or watershed, yield a plethora of valuable data around the clock on several variables in addition to precipitation and temperature. Two of the more notable networks are the "West Texas Mesonet," a far-reaching array of nearly 100 stations maintained by the NWS in the vast High Plains region, and the "Hydromet" of the Lower Colorado River Authority (LCRA), a dense collection of some 275 river and weather gauges within the lower Colorado River basin. The High Plains mesonet as of this writing has been in operation over 10 years; at five-minute intervals data are collected on wind speed and direction, atmospheric pressure, solar radiation, dew point, and soil temperature. Networks like that operated by the LCRA provide near-real-time data on stream flow, river stages, precipitation amounts, temperature extremes, and relative humidities. Each station has telemetry that allows the data to be transmitted almost continuously to a centralized data depository, where the data can then be accessed via the internet. One obvious advantage afforded by these networks is the uninterrupted flow of key information, night or day, that alerts, observers to threats on human safety caused by heavy rain events.

An unknown number of residents document the weather without ever submitting their records to the government for quality control and publication. The ritual of setting out rather primitive instruments like buckets to catch rainfall, then measuring the catch with nothing more sophisticated than a ruler, has continued for generations all over the state. Volumes of notes pertaining to weather phenomena like hail and ice storms have been maintained for dozens of years, then get handed down to younger members of the family. Undoubtedly, an untold amount of records made by these citizen observers has been displaced or destroyed over several generations. The observations are invaluable to NWS officials who conduct "bucket surveys" in the wake of an extreme heavy-rain or flood event. The data can be incorporated into computer models to help the NWS improve its capacity to forecast these episodes with greater precision, thereby giving communities more advance notice and ensuring public safety.

The National Weather Service

There is also a cadre of paid professional weather observers who work for the NWS around the clock every day of the year, monitoring evolving weather conditions and giving the public timely advance word of possibly threatening situations. Monumental changes in the way Texas weather is observed and documented have been made since money was first appropriated by the US Congress in the late-nineteenth century to run the US Weather Bureau, now the NWS. At that time the Weather Bureau was an element of the US Army Signal Service. More recently, particularly after World War II, immense strides have been made in improving forecasting skills. Today, NWS supercomputers located near Washington, DC, process voluminous weather observations made in every hour on each day by sensors at land-based stations, on ships at sea, and from satellites, weather balloons, and aircraft. Methods for disseminating massive collections of processed weather data have been transformed radically in the past few decades: raw material for forecasters today consists of satellite imagery, analyzed surface and upper-air weather data, radar images, and computerized forecasts containing projections of storm movement and growth. Weather forecasts almost universally are more reliable today than ever before, not just because the quantity and diversity of useful weather data have expanded in phenomenal ways but also because techniques for handling the data and formulating projections have undergone repeated refinements and modernization. No longer are daily forecasts dependent largely upon surface weather observations; emphasis now is given to detecting more subtle changes that constantly occur higher in the atmosphere and have a major effect on conditions at the surface.

The capability to detect and anticipate an evolving weather threat was augmented in dramatic fashion once the NWS completed the modernization of its facilities and tools in the 1990s. The centerpiece of the massive federal initiative to incorporate the latest and finest in electronic surveillance technologies into weather detection and prediction has been the Doppler radar, also known as NEXRAD (an acronym for "next-generation weather radar"). Doppler radar was pioneered by the US military during the 1950s as a guide for ground-to-air missiles. It later came into civilian use as a navigation aid on commercial aircraft. Now Doppler radar is being used by the NWS to detect and track both storm clouds and cloud-free frontal systems. Tracking the "invisible" forcing mechanisms (dry lines and gusts and cold fronts) that produce the storms, along with their concomitant hail, damaging winds, and tornadoes, enhances the professional meteorologist's ability to predict their evolution and impact. Doppler radar allows forecasters to discern the distribution and intensity of wind flow within and around storm systems, as well as the types of precipitation (chiefly rain and hail) generated by them. Each Doppler radar is able to depict instantaneously, lucidly, and in minute detail, weather phenomena up to 125 miles (200 kilometers) away from the radar site, with considerable detection capacity of other phenomena up to 250 miles (400 kilometers) away. More than one dozen of the Doppler systems, some maintained by the US Department of Defense, are situated in Texas, with additional coverage afforded by identical systems located in adjacent states but near the Texas border. They have demonstrated their value in saving lives and protecting property by providing earlier and more precise warnings of severe weather events such as flash floods, tornadoes, and thunderstorms.

Doppler radar has reduced dramatically the time frame between recognition and issuance of warnings, including those for tornadoes. The precursors to the Doppler radar, the C-band radars of the 1970s and 1980s, enabled forecasters to detect and warn the public an average of only about six minutes before a twister struck a populated area. Virtually all of Texas is under constant radar surveillance. Network radar units (WSR-88Ds), stationed at Amarillo, Midland, El Paso, San Angelo, Dallas, New Braunfels, Laughlin Air Force Base near Del Rio, Dickinson, Granger, Corpus Christi, Lubbock, and Brownsville, provide an electronic view of precipitation patterns in practically every corner of the state every hour of the day. Not only has Doppler radar greatly expanded the lead time for issuance of warnings, it also has reduced substantially the number of false alarms issued by the NWS. Some studies have indicated that the frequency of "crying wolf" has been shaved by more than half by use of Doppler radar. Additionally, Doppler radar has contributed immeasurably to ongoing research in understanding and quantifying cloud behavior and its interaction with the environment. The NWS continues to upgrade the Doppler system: adding a "dual polarization" capability to all the Texas radars now affords NWS staff and other researchers an opportunity to dissect more effectively the core of a thunderstorm to detect and measure the kinds of meteors (e.g., hailstones, ice, graupel) existent within the cloud body.

In addition to Doppler radar, other modern and integral weather-observing components of the NWS modernization effort led to the automation of virtually all surface weather observations. The Automated Surface Observing System (ASOS) is now a fixture at dozens of airports serving Texas cities (fig. 2.4). An array of sensors allows weather data to be served to the public more accurately, continuously, and automatically around the clock without human intervention. Before the advent of ASOS, and related but less-sophisticated companion systems, data on temperature, humidity, wind, pressure, and sky condition had to be discerned with the human eye and then inserted into rather primitive communication tools like radios and teletype. Along with other automated detection systems now in use by the NWS, ASOS supplies wind data to air-traffic controllers by the hour or by the minute, with updated wind reports every few minutes. The automated systems archive an assortment of weather data (air temperature, dew point, air pressure, visibility, cloud height, and the amount and intensity of rain, freezing rain, snow, and drizzle) at least on an hourly basis—and much more frequently when developing weather warrants it. The weather charts now accessible online, and those seen by television viewers, are based upon these routine observations.

FIG. 2.4 Automated weather-observing installations of the National Weather Service at many Texas airports now provide a continual flow of valuable information about wind, temperature, humidity, pressure, and visibility. Source: George W. Bomar

Weather conditions aloft in the atmosphere are quantified twice daily at an array of "upper air" observatories across the country, seven of which are located in Texas. An instrument package borne by a large hydrogen-filled balloon is released each morning around dawn and each evening around dusk. The instrument package, consisting of temperature, pressure, and humidity sensors, collects data as the package is lifted through the atmosphere to altitudes of 120,000 feet (37 kilometers) or higher and transmits the data back to a receiving unit on the ground. Tracking the movement of the balloon with its instrument package as it ascends provides the direction and speed of winds at all levels of the atmosphere. These invaluable data are supplemented by a continuous flow of satellite imagery, in both visible and infrared spectra, affording forecasters a "bird's eye" view of evolving weather systems.

The interminable flow of weather data feeds computers that generate forecasts covering all of Texas's 254 counties. A growing array of short and longer-range forecasts is loaded onto websites, easily and readily available to the public. A broad variety of forecast products, along with timely observations, is disseminated to the public via social media and by the National Oceanic and Atmospheric Administration (NOAA) Weather Radio. These outlooks are companion pieces to warning services that also are provided by staffs of professional meteorologists when conditions warrant the publication of those alerts. The well-trained analysts use all the tools available to them to recognize every threatening weather situation, then formulate appropriate warnings and ensure they are disseminated. The men and women of the NWS work around the clock at Weather Forecast Offices in Amarillo, Lubbock, Midland, El Paso, San Angelo, Fort Worth, New Braunfels, Houston, Corpus Christi, and Brownsville. When a hazardous weather alert, such as a tornado or severe thunderstorm warning, is issued, a signal sent from the NWS office activates NOAA Weather Radio receivers specially designed to activate an alarm. Sounding of the alarm (or siren) notifies the listener that a weather emergency exists, and the system then furnishes information to enable the listener to take appropriate measures.

Weather Detection from Home

The desire to have more "personalized" weather observations has led countless Texans to invest in a wide assortment of weather tools and instruments. The availability of a diversity of devices, many of which are quite affordable, has cultivated a growing appreciation for the uniqueness of Texas weather. Most communities now consist of a spate of homeowners with their own means of quantifying rainfall and measuring the temperature, if not the speed and direction of the wind among other variables. In some instances, however, the readings obtained from homemade weather stations are not sufficiently accurate because the observer has not taken care to position the sensors properly. The following is intended to help the amateur weather observer set up and maintain a reliable and properly exposed home weather unit.

A key element of weather information for any weather observer is the amount of rainfall. The most common type of rain gauge in use by the public today is the fence-post variety consisting of a glass tube with gradations usually of 0.1 inch. If properly exposed, the gauge can give the observer a reasonably approximate measure of how much rain fell since the gauge was last emptied. Obviously, if precision is critical to the observer, a larger, more sophisticated rain-collecting device is a must. Some plastic rain gauges available in hardware and other stores afford measurements in hundredths of an inch, but this type of gauge is vulnerable to cracking in freezing weather. A more expensive type of rain gauge—that used by cooperative weather observers all over Texas—is an excellent choice, for it not only provides precise measurements (in hundredths of an inch) but also is easy to install and maintain, and it is more durable. In addition, this "8-inch standard National Weather Service" rain gauge will collect as much as 10 inches of rain before overflowing. The accuracy of these gauges is unassailable, and some observers who are diligent in using them make the data from these gauges available to their communities as "official" statements about rainfall occurrences (fig. 2.5). If observers desire to have a truly elaborate home weather station, they may obtain a remote-reading rain gauge (one that allows them to read the amount of rainfall by means of a resettable counter in their homes or offices) or a tipping-bucket rain gauge (a recording device complete with strip chart that indicates rainfall intensity as well as amount for a period lasting as long as one week).

It is extremely important for the observer's rain gauge to be properly exposed. The mouth or top of the gauge should stand at least 3 feet above ground level. Be sure not to use a container with sloping sides; ideally the container should be a perfect cylinder. Position the gauge as far away as possible from trees, fences, buildings, or any other obstructions that might have a bearing on how much water falls into the gauge. Remember that good exposures are not always permanent; the growth of vegetation and other alterations to the surroundings can transform an excellent exposure into an undesirable one in a relatively brief spell of time.

A secondary measure of precipitation during the cold season is the amount of snowfall observed, especially in those regions of Texas where snow accumulations are common. The amount of snow that collects in a rain gauge is not indicative of the actual snow accumulation because some of the snow catch may melt in the gauge before the observer is able to make a reading. Instead, the weather observer should select a flat, smooth surface (such as a concrete slab) away from an obstruction, where drifts tend to occur. To get a representative snowfall reading, it is best to make at least three measurements—by thrusting a ruler or yardstick through

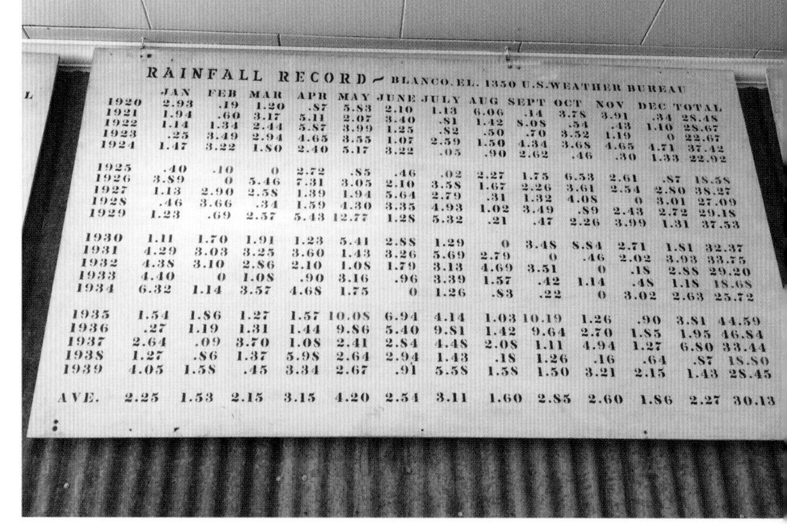

RAINFALL RECORD ~ BLANCO. EL. 1350 U.S. WEATHER BUREAU

	JAN	FEB	MAR	APR	MAY	JUNE	JULY	AUG	SEPT	OCT	NOV	DEC	TOTAL
1920	2.93	.19	1.20	.87	5.83	2.10	1.13	6.06	.14	3.78	3.91	.34	28.48
1921	1.94	.60	3.17	5.11	2.07	3.40	.81	1.42	8.08	.54	.43	1.10	28.67
1922	1.14	1.34	2.44	5.87	3.99	1.25	.82	.50	.70	3.52	1.19	0	22.67
1923	.25	3.49	2.94	4.65	3.55	1.07	2.59	1.50	4.34	3.68	4.65	4.71	37.42
1924	1.47	3.22	1.80	2.40	5.17	3.22	.05	.90	2.62	.46	.30	1.33	22.92
1925	.40	.10	0	2.72	.85	.46	.02	2.27	1.75	6.53	2.61	.87	18.58
1926	3.89	0	5.46	7.31	3.05	2.10	3.58	1.67	2.26	3.61	2.54	2.80	38.27
1927	1.13	2.90	2.58	1.39	1.94	5.64	2.79	.31	1.32	4.08	0	3.01	27.09
1928	.46	3.66	.34	1.59	4.30	3.35	4.93	1.02	3.49	.89	2.43	2.72	29.18
1929	1.23	.69	2.57	5.43	12.77	1.28	5.32	.21	.47	2.26	3.99	1.31	37.53
1930	1.11	1.70	1.91	1.23	5.41	2.88	1.29	0	3.48	8.84	2.71	1.81	32.37
1931	4.29	3.03	3.25	3.60	1.43	3.26	5.69	2.79	0	.46	2.02	3.93	33.75
1932	4.38	3.10	2.86	2.10	1.08	1.79	3.13	4.69	3.51	0	.18	2.88	29.20
1933	4.40	0	1.08	.90	3.16	.96	3.39	1.57	.42	1.14	.48	1.18	18.68
1934	6.32	1.14	3.57	4.68	1.75	0	1.26	.83	.22	0	3.02	2.63	25.72
1935	1.54	1.86	1.27	1.57	10.08	6.94	4.14	1.03	10.19	1.26	.90	3.81	44.59
1936	.27	1.19	1.31	1.44	9.86	5.40	9.81	1.42	9.64	2.70	1.85	1.95	46.84
1937	2.64	.09	3.70	1.08	2.41	2.84	4.48	2.08	1.11	4.94	1.27	6.80	33.44
1938	1.27	.86	1.37	5.98	2.64	2.94	1.43	.18	1.26	.16	.64	.87	18.80
1939	4.05	1.58	.45	3.34	2.67	.91	5.58	1.58	1.50	3.21	2.15	1.43	28.45
AVE.	2.25	1.53	2.15	3.15	4.20	2.54	3.11	1.60	2.85	2.60	1.86	2.27	30.13

FIG. 2.5 A 100-year tabulation of observed rainfall for Blanco is displayed at one of the town's restaurants. Source: George W. Bomar

the snow until the measuring device makes contact with the underlying surface—in different locations and then average the values. As a very general rule, the depth of snow can be converted to equivalent inches of rain by dividing that depth by 10. Yet, in some instances when the air is especially dry or moist, more or less than 10 inches of snow is required to equal 1 inch of rain. It is best for the observer to allow the snow catch to melt in the gauge before measuring the liquid content. You may want to remove the gauge from its support and melt the snow catch in the house to obtain an accurate measurement of liquid precipitation.

If the amount of precipitation is not of pre-eminent concern to the amateur observer, then the variation in temperature during the day, or from day to day, is likely to be the focus. Since it is dependent upon the amount of wind and sunshine, as well as precipitation when it occurs, the temperature of the air is the single best indicator of overall weather conditions in a particular locale. By using temperature data collected each day in conjunction with observations of precipitation, the amateur observer can be well on the way toward quantifying the effects of weather on such domestic enterprises as farming, gardening, and yard work.

To get an accurate reading of temperature, be certain not to locate a thermometer where it will be struck by direct sunlight at any time of the day. This precludes positioning the instrument in most places on the east, south, or west sides of the home. Ideally, thermometers should be located away from a large structure, such as a house, for by radiating heat or sheltering the instrument from the wind the structure contributes to bias in the temperature reading. As a result, a thermometer that is on the north side of a house, in the shade, and protected from the prevailing southerly breeze in the summer will give unrealistically low readings. Also, a home—especially one made of brick or stone—absorbs a great amount of heat from the summer sun, such that in the evenings the house emits some of that heat, which in turn can contribute to an unrepresentative temperature reading.

The key to measuring temperature accurately is to place your thermometer(s) in a shielded but well-ventilated structure. Specially constructed instrument shelters used by cooperative weather observers for the NWS may not be affordable, so the home-based weather observer may elect to build a shelter. Remember that such a home-made structure should be made of wood and painted white (to allow a minimum amount of solar heat to be absorbed by the device); it must protect the instruments contained within it from sunlight; and it should provide for sufficient ventilation: the sides should be louvered to permit air to circulate freely. Make certain also that the ground over which the shelter is located is representative of the surrounding area: avoid installing a shelter on a steep slope or in a sheltered hollow (unless, of course, you want temperature data for such an environment). Keep the shelter as far away from any obstruction as is practicable and displace it as much as possible from extensive concrete or paved surfaces. One more key piece of advice: the thermometers should be positioned in the shelter at a height of about 5 feet—or approximately eye level.

Many homeowners have an aneroid barometer hanging on the wall somewhere in the house. In many instances, the instrument serves only as a decorative addition to the room. Yet, some homeowners with barometers know the pressure of one's immediate environment can be a good source for supplemental information, such as an abrupt change in the weather brought by a cold front or squall line of heavy thunderstorms. To make good use of an aneroid (or dial) barometer, leave it inside the house and at eye level for ease of reading the scale. It is not necessary to place your barometer outdoors—particularly in an instrument shelter—to get a representative pressure reading of your environment.

To have a record of wind movement you will need both a wind vane (to measure wind direction) and an anemometer (to measure wind speed). Precision wind-recording instruments may be purchased from most manufacturers of meteorological equipment. Some of the more expensive varieties provide a digital readout of continuous measurements of wind speed and direction. The industrious observer may elect to forego the expenditure of a sizable amount of money for a wind-measuring device and instead construct one. You can fashion a homemade wind vane with a few pieces of wood and a metal plate (such as a license plate) for a fin and obtain a highly satisfactory indication of the direction from which the wind is blowing. A homemade wind sock resembling those used at airports also suffices as an accurate indicator of wind direction. As with most other types of weather equipment, wind instruments should be as far removed as possible from any obstructions.

Signs from Mother Nature

For millennia, human beings have used their practical knowledge of the weather to grow or otherwise secure food, defend family and country, sail the seas, and capture energy. Seasoned mariners have used their knack of scanning the distant horizon to ascertain if it is timely to venture out to sea. Fruit growers note the shift in the wind and ready their smudge pots for use on a night sure to bring a killing frost. This intuitive feel for weather on the part of many veteran weather watchers has given rise to numerous credible and practical observations that are both helpful and enlightening:

- A shift in the wind invariably means a significant change in temperature; most often, a southerly wind brings warmer temperatures, while a northerly wind causes the temperature to fall.
- Dew rarely forms on a night when skies are overcast.
- Frost can occur even though "reported" temperatures go no lower than the upper 30s.
- The humidity declines notably when winds veer from a southerly direction to a westerly or northerly direction; conversely, in most areas of Texas, a wind coming from the east or southeast means an increase in moisture.
- A shift toward inclement weather (rain or even snow) sometimes is forewarned by a ring, or halo, around the moon.
- Clearing skies are in the offing when dark clouds grow lighter and lift to high altitudes, and when the barometer reveals the air pressure to be rising rapidly.

The sky, or atmosphere, is not the only giver of clues about impending weather developments. The behavior of many members of the animal world suggests a predictable change in the weather as well. Hunters have long been aware that prey react in consistent ways to major fluctuations in the weather pattern. Adept fishers can testify of the effect of weather on the volume of the catch. While some of the observations formulated over the years by veteran weather watchers amount to little more than thinly disguised "folk tales," numerous practical observations made from the animal world contain considerable veracity:

- Insects are more active prior to a storm because the warm, moist air prevalent beforehand is more comfortable to them.
- Joints in the human body are more likely to ache before a change to colder, wetter weather (resulting from low pressure in advance of the storm allowing the gas in one's joints to expand and create pain).
- Frogs croak more often before a storm, for the air is more humid at that time, thus allowing them to stay out of the water longer without their skin drying out.
- Birds fly lower before a storm arrives, for lower pressure signaling a forthcoming storm creates pain in their pressure-sensitive ears; the lower they fly, the less the pain.

Undoubtedly, there is much yet to be discovered about the forecasting potential inherent in the activities of nature. With our complex and sophisticated array of modern instruments, we have made a quantum leap in gathering a wealth of information about the vagaries of Earth's atmosphere. At the same time, we have been made aware of the fact that the atmosphere is fundamentally unpredictable to a significant degree and that this innate inconsistency is independent of the amount of knowledge we gain about the atmosphere's behavior or the extent to which we devote our resources to the forecast problem. We can be encouraged by the realization that we are not yet near the limit of our ability to predict the weather. Still more improvements in forecasting methodology are in the offing.

Those advances just might derive, in part, from a closer scrutiny of how other constituents of the animal world respond to nature's seemingly whimsical behavior. Certainly, our ability to anticipate nature's next move on the weather front can be enhanced as we attain greater skill in using efficiently and thoroughly the myriads of weather data now being amassed. With improved computer technology and a growing awareness of the inner workings of our intricate and sensitive atmosphere, giant strides in formulating and communicating better and longer-range forecasts just might be as anticipated as the rising of tomorrow's sun.

3.

Weather's Change Agents

There was good reason to scoff at the revelation that the groundhog, in Pennsylvania, had seen his shadow the morning of February 2, 1899. That assumes, in the long-ago era of the telegraph, that even a few Texans were aware of the prediction, made by the caretakers of the furry critter whose exit from his hole is scrutinized carefully every winter, that the cold weather of winter still had six weeks to run. Temperatures in South Texas on that late-winter day were creeping into the 90s by early afternoon. In fact, the day following the groundhog's ballyhooed appearance, the temperature along the Rio Grande almost hit the 100°F (38°C) mark. However, as is almost common in late winter and early spring, the weather scene in Texas underwent a sudden about-face. With nothing but strands of barbed wire separating the plains and prairies of Texas from the frozen tundra of the Arctic region, a ponderous mass of glacial air poured through the state, forcing temperatures to unparalleled depths. By the time the Arctic air settled in over Texas on the morning of Lincoln's Birthday, the scales on some thermometers were nearly inadequate to gauge the intensity of the extreme severe cold. Readings bottomed out below 0°F (−18°C) in virtually all the northern two-thirds of Texas, while in the usually tepid southern extremity of the state temperatures skidded just short of 10°F (−12°C) (fig. 3.1). No corner of the state—not even the partially insulated offshore islands—escaped the bone-numbing chill of this cold snap.

A writer who chronicled the event offered the most colossal of understatements: a cold-weather spell of "marked intensity" that made the month as a whole "very unfavorable for farming operations." The most severe of Texas's legendary cold fronts destroyed all but those winter vegetables that had been heavily protected. Damage to fruit and vegetable crops was extensive and severe. The total dollar loss amounted to "many thousands of dollars," no small sum in pre-twentieth-century terms. The extraordinarily large mound of Arctic air produced a barometric

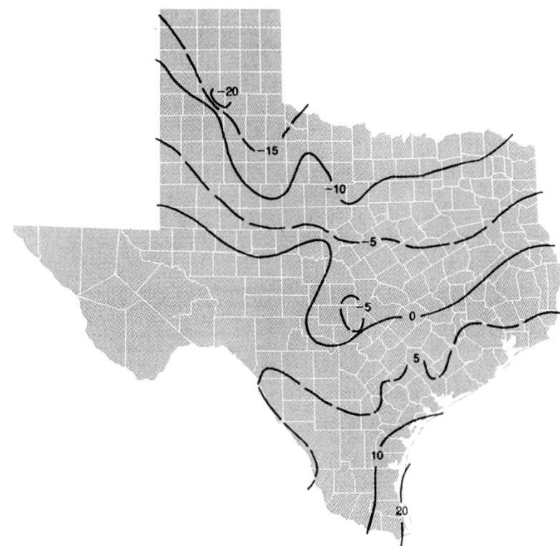

FIG. 3.1 Lowest temperatures (°F) during the historic cold spell of February 11–13, 1899. Source: George W. Bomar

pressure reading of 31.06 inches (of mercury) at Abilene. Its chill lowered the temperature to −23°F (−31°C) at Tulia in the Southern Texas Panhandle, while morning minimums from −10°F (−23°C) to −15°F (−26°C) were common in the Red River valley. Largely owing to this historic cold front, the average statewide temperature for the shortest month of 1899 was more than 11°F (6°C) below normal.

The Clash of Air Masses

Folks commiserating about the weather invariably evoke the term "front." This is because most notable and abrupt changes in the weather—like that of late-winter 1899—come about as a consequence of the intrusion of a fresh air mass, the leading edge of which is like an advancing blade on a road grader. The term "front" is believed to have originated with Vilhelm Bjerknes, who established the renowned Norwegian School of meteorology that led the way in developing synoptic weather theory and analysis in the early twentieth century. Bjerknes envisioned air masses engaging one another much like the battlefronts of World War I, coining the term front to connote the leading edge of the advancing air mass.

Much of the time a front's arrival is signaled by something dramatic, such as a clap of thunder, rain, or a sudden, chilling wind too harsh to be ignored. A front is not some thin, discrete line like that depicted on most television weather charts. Instead, it is a pronounced transition zone that lies between two masses of air having different temperatures and, hence, differing densities. Confront one air mass with another that is cooler and heavier, for instance, and the clash that ensues takes place in a narrow zone separating the two antagonists. How pronounced the change in temperature is within the frontal zone depends upon the season of the year and, more specifically, the source region of the air mass that is advancing—and replacing the air mass antecedent to it.

At times in winter frontal boundaries will be as narrow as 15–25 miles (25–40 kilometers), though more commonly they are thicker than that. In summer, when fronts tend to be weak and diffuse, the zone where competing air masses joust with each other may be more than 100 miles (160 kilometers) across. Though weather charts depict fronts as two-dimensional features, they are in fact three-dimensional (fig. 3.2). In advance of the front, temperatures vary little over great distances; this is denoted by isotherms—lines connecting points of equal (iso) temperature (therm)—that are essentially parallel to the ground. Within the frontal zone, however, temperatures change substantially over short distances, as denoted by the isotherms that run vertically and close together in the figure. Behind the frontal zone and deeper into the advancing cold air mass, temperatures continue to fall but not quite as dramatically as within the frontal boundary itself. Another aspect of a cold frontal zone is the fairly uniform temperature throughout the frontal boundary from top to bottom.

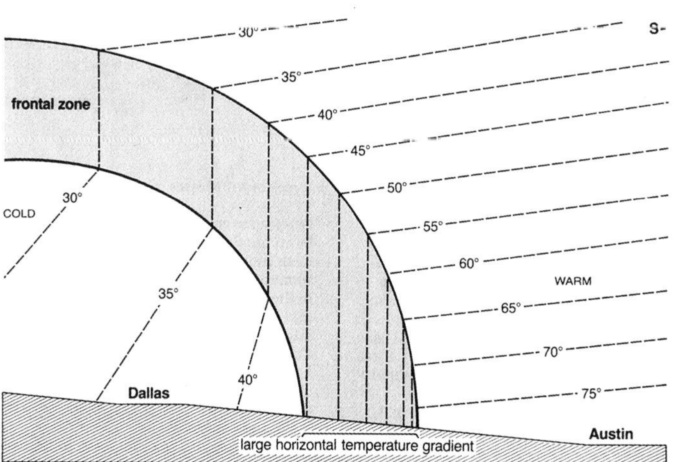

FIG. 3.2 Vertical cross section showing a large horizontal temperature gradient (depicted by isotherms—dashed lines) within a frontal zone during winter. Source: George W. Bomar

Relief for Texans baked by an unrelenting summer heat wave is spelled f-r-o-n-t, as in a fresh surge of cool Canadian air. There is something invigorating about a sudden shift in the wind that brings in the flow of air that is noticeably cooler and drier, the most prominent characteristics of a vintage Canadian air mass. While the relief may have seemed slow in coming to those residents who long for the crisp days of autumn, the infiltration of Canadian polar air takes place rather quickly. The time required to transport the cool air more than a thousand miles across the US-Canadian border and as far south as the northern limit of the Gulf of Mexico pales in comparison to the time taken for the air mass to form. An air mass is an extensive portion of the lower atmosphere typified by a fairly uniform distribution of temperature and moisture, and it comes about only after air has resided in a particular area within or near the northern polar region for many days—and sometimes for several weeks.

Climatologists assign names to air masses that identify the source regions within which they were constituted. With the surface of Earth consisting of low and high latitudes that are either continental or oceanic (or maritime) in nature, fronts entering Texas usher in one of the following four varieties of air masses: (a) continental polar (or Arctic), designated as cP (or cA); (b) maritime polar (mP); (c) continental tropical (cT); or (d) maritime tropical (mT) (fig. 3.3). Many of the cold fronts that invade Texas in winter introduce continental polar or Arctic air, though the former is much more common than the latter. True continental Arctic air reaches Texas only occasionally and is responsible for the especially frigid spells when the temperature dives to near or below 0°F (−18°C) in the Panhandle and freezes occur in the Lower Valley. By contrast, maritime polar air, because its source region is the relatively warmer waters of the northern Pacific Ocean, is almost always milder than the air that develops over the more frigid interior continental regions of Canada. Penetration of maritime polar air is more common in Texas in spring and autumn than that of continental polar air. Intrusions of tropical air are common throughout the year in Texas, though the eastern half of the state is enveloped more often by maritime tropical air than is West Texas.

In the absence of any exchange among these air masses, Texas would be without most of the sudden, drastic fluctuations in wind, cloudiness, temperature, humidity, and precipitation that make the climate of the state so diverse, intriguing, and unpredictable. Because basically the same types of air masses enter Texas intermittently throughout most of the year, there are distinct patterns of weather associated with them that an experienced observer of the sky can, on most occasions, readily identify.

Polar Invasions

Cool, even cold, air masses from higher latitudes that move south and east through Texas act as wedges that thrust warmer, resident air above them, lifting the less dense air and usually causing cloud cover (fig. 3.4). Passage of a cold front is invariably typified by a shift in the wind from the south or east. Far less often, cold air from Canada can "back" into Texas from the mid-Mississippi River valley, causing surface winds to shift from the south into the east, then northeast.

Most cold frontal passages spawn, in addition to a palpable shift in wind direction and speed, some type of cloud cover and, quite often, one or more varieties of precipitation. The kind of cloudiness—and moisture—produced by a cold front depends on the stability and the moisture

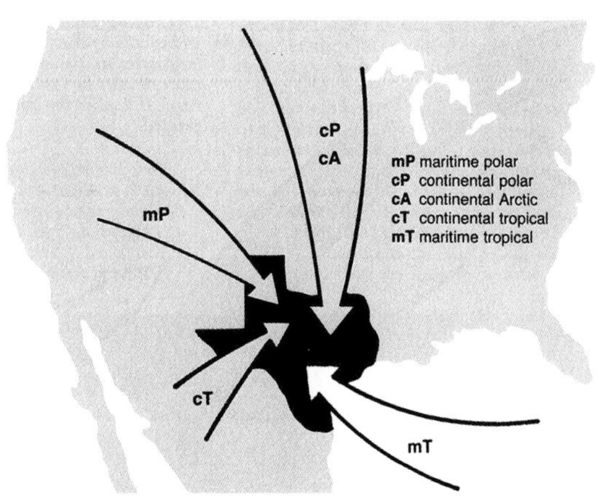

FIG. 3.3 Types of cold and warm air masses that infiltrate Texas every year. Source: George W. Bomar

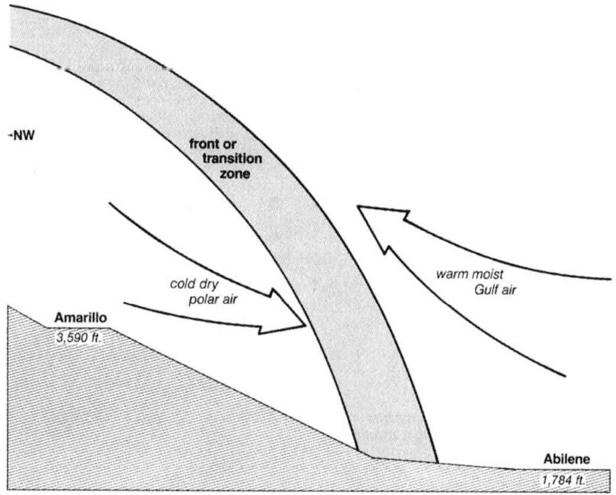

FIG. 3.4 Cross-sectional view of a cold front, where advancing cold polar air lifts warmer Gulf air. Source: George W. Bomar

content of the two interacting air masses, especially that of the air mass being replaced, as well as the degree to which the incumbent air mass is forced to rise. Cold fronts are designated on weather charts as solid lines (usually blue) with barbs pointing in the direction toward which the cool air is moving. Most of the time when a cold front whips into Texas, the mild or warm air that is forced to ascend ahead of it flows in a fairly narrow zone almost parallel to the incoming front. In the colder half of the year, most cold fronts entering Texas have fairly steep slopes and move rapidly; any precipitation associated with their movement is most often short-lived and confined to a zone 25–50 miles (40–80 kilometers) on either side of the front. If a cold front moves rapidly, thereby forcing the resident air to rise vigorously, then one or more bands of large convective clouds, or thunderstorms, form in the frontal region. A fast-moving cold front may so disturb the air in advance of it that one or several lines of intense thunderstorms, or squall lines, may either precede or accompany it. On the other hand, in late spring and early autumn, and occasionally in summer, a cool front sometimes will stall before penetrating the whole state. With "steering" winds aloft quite weak, and because the dome of cool air is shallow, warm, moist air surges up over the cool air and extends for many miles behind the cold front. In this instance, cloudiness caused by the front is much broader, extending at times for hundreds of miles behind the front, and precipitation produced by the clouds usually lasts longer and also extends well behind the cold front.

Cold fronts potent enough to traverse most if not all of Texas are common from early autumn through the middle of spring. Sometimes during this October to May interval, the fronts push through the state without triggering significant precipitation, a happenstance that may be attributed to the absence of enough moisture in the warm air mass being replaced by the invading cool air. The average number of cold fronts for most sections of Texas is seven or eight in April, while six cold fronts normally infiltrate the state in each of the months of January, February, and March. Average frequency of cold fronts progressively drops off, from north to south across Texas, as summer approaches. Whereas at least a half-dozen cold fronts customarily enter the Panhandle in July and August, no more than two of them ever reach the southern quarter of Texas in those months. In many years, cold fronts fizzle out long before they reach the Texas coastline. Especially hot seasons attest to the utter absence of any Canadian air invading any sector of Texas (table 3.1).

TABLE 3.1

Texas's Warmest Seasons in History

RANK	SEASON	DEPARTURE[1]
1st	Summer 2011	+5.3°
2nd	Winter 1907	+5.1°
3rd	Winter 1952	+4.6°
4th	Autumn 1931	+4.5°
	Spring 2012	+4.5°

[1] Based on the mean for 1981-2010.

The Tropical Rebound

The typical cold front is rambunctious compared with air mass movements from the warmer tropics northward into Texas. With Texas being on the underside of the midlatitudes, Canadian air masses that surge southward with usual regularity in the colder half of the year do not linger but for only a day or a few at most. The anticyclonic (clockwise) circulation of these cool or cold air masses, when nudged into the Gulf of Mexico, soon begin sending air into Texas, known as "return flow," that has been modified by the relatively warmer waters of the Gulf (fig. 3.5). As this compromised air surges northwestward out of the Gulf, its leading edge becomes a warm front. One of the first clues of an impending warm-frontal passage is the migration at high levels in the atmosphere of thin, wispy, ice clouds known as cirrus. The thin strands of cirrus clouds thicken gradually into an overcast, which within hours lowers to the extent that light precipitation begins falling. Because the rain falls through the shallow layer of cool air about to be replaced by the warm front, the cool air often becomes saturated and fog develops. Once the warm front passes, the fog dissipates, the sky lightens, and the precipitation ceases. Well behind the warm front, in the midst of the warm, moist tropical air, only scattered middle clouds are seen.

Warm frontal passage, unlike its cold counterpart, is the culmination of the series of progressively worsening weather events described earlier. Initially, the warm moist air from the Gulf streams up over the shallow dome of cool (or cold) air long before the leading edge of the warm air mass is felt at the surface. This is because the invading warm air is less dense than the air it is trying to supplant, and it overrides the shallow cool air that hovers near the ground. During its ascent, as the warm air is chilled, condensation in the form of cloudiness takes place. Slowly the incoming warm air erodes away the edge of the cool air, or the cool air mass retreats, allowing the warm air to advance at the surface as well as aloft. Distinguishing marks of the passage of a warm front in Texas are a wind shift, whereby winds veer from the north or northeast into the east or southeast, a sharp increase in humidity (usually expressed on a weather chart as sizable jumps in the dew-point temperature), and sometimes notable rises in air temperature. Of course, changes in the amount and type of cloud cover, and any resulting precipitation, are sure tip-offs to the arrival of a warm front.

Thunderstorms sometimes are spawned from the movement of warm air from the Gulf back into Texas, though the incidence of substantive rains from them is markedly less than storms triggered by advancing cold fronts. The type and amount of precipitation that precedes the arrival of a warm front at the ground depends upon the moisture content and stability, or lack of it, within the oncoming warm air mass. The slope of the frontal zone between the residual cool air next to the surface and the overriding warm, moist air is also a key determinant to the rate of precipitation. If the warm air surging northward out of the Gulf of Mexico is highly unstable (and it often is in autumn, late winter, and early spring), then towering thunderheads may form. Most of the

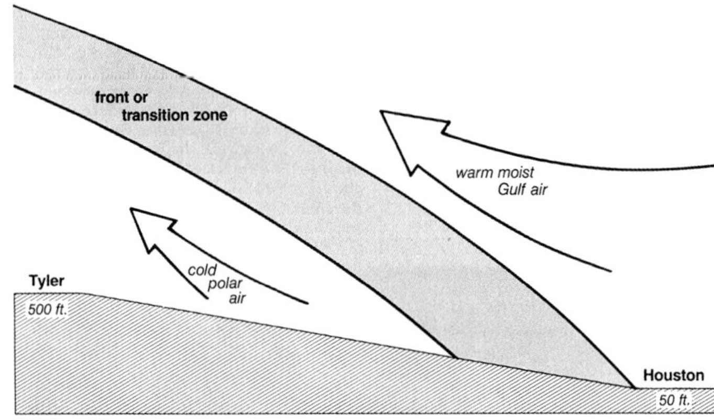

FIG. 3.5 Cross-sectional view of a warm front, where advancing warm, moist Gulf air runs over a more dense dome of cold polar air. Source: George W. Bomar

time an Earth-bound observer cannot discern these thunderclouds because a low overcast obscures them, but their presence is unmistakable. Downpours that give substantial amounts of rainfall usually are the fallout from these large thunderstorms, which are not uncommon in the coastal plain during winter. Occasionally, warm, moist air may slide up over a shallow dome of cold air as far inland as the Texas Panhandle and, with the aid of some upper-atmospheric disturbance that gives added lift to that moisture, form thunderstorms that release a combination of rain, sleet, and snow. Thunder-snow showers, the result of precipitation shed by a thunderstorm falling through a subfreezing atmosphere, are not that rare in far northern Texas in winter.

Warm fronts garner much less publicity than cold ones during television weathercasts, even though they can be prolific rain producers during the cold season in Texas. After all, there is seldom any "bang" from them like the radical alterations in weather brought by the usually boisterous cold fronts. When warm fronts occur, they are more distinguishable in the coastal plain and East Texas than in any other sector. One or a pair of pronounced warm fronts push into the heart of Texas, on average, in April, but they seldom reach the higher elevations out west. Clearly defined warm fronts are almost nonexistent in summer in Texas, an absence explained by the warm, moist air that almost constantly covers the state at this time of the year. Warm fronts appear on weather maps as solid, red lines to which are appended half circles "pointing" in the direction to which the warm air is moving.

A Frontal Stall

An unmistakable clue that summer is angling for influence is the diminishing number of cool fronts that extend deep into Texas. Quite a few of the cool fronts that penetrate the Panhandle and Red River valley from May into June fail to reach interior portions of the state. Rather, these fronts bog down somewhere south of the Panhandle or Red River and either retreat later as a warm front or dissipate altogether. Nonetheless, though feeble and fragile when they become stationary, these boundary zones, where the cold air from the north mixes with warmer air from the south, serve as incubators for occasionally bountiful rains. Actually, these transition zones never completely stall; instead, they oscillate back and forth over short distances, allowing moist Gulf air and drier Canadian air to interact, thereby fomenting rainstorms. The storms, in turn, dump rainfall and, in doing so, chill the near-surface layer of air, which then spreads out and acts as a cold front. Labeled outflow boundaries, the advancing chilled air triggers a wave of more distant rainstorms. These new boundaries are recognized by the clusters, or bands, of rain showers that follow a path often parallel with the front. These seemingly dormant weather systems are more appropriately called "quasi-stationary." If the air to the south of the nearly stationary front is highly moist and unstable, and if the front lingers in the same area for several days, the precipitation is likely to be persistent and steady, with flooding a common consequence. A quasi-stationary front that lay along the Red River for several days in October 1981, allowed bands of heavy rain to form and caused extensive flooding in much of the region bounded on the north by the Red River and on the south by

Abilene and Fort Worth. These massive areas of persistent rain moved very little over a period of four days and dumped rains of 5–15 inches, which caused more than $105 million in flood damage to property.

Over the course of a year, stationary fronts contribute more of the total annual rainfall of the Panhandle region than any other section of the state. During each of the months of May, June, and July, an average of ten fronts will extend into northernmost Texas, then stall and ultimately disintegrate. The resident air destabilized by these frontal boundaries spawns thunderstorms that furnish noteworthy rains, especially when a boundary fluctuates back and forth over small distances before it loses its identity. On the other hand, quasi-stationary fronts are seldom seen in the state's southern extremity in June and July, principally because very few, if any, fronts ever survive a southward trek across Texas in the year's hottest period. Fronts are least likely to go stationary in the six colder months of the year, when the upper-air wind flow over Texas is potent. Most cool fronts entering from the north or northwest are pushed completely through the state without slowing down appreciably.

Weather's High-Level Engineers

Other than pilots and meteorologists, few Earth-bound people pay a lot of attention to the behavior of Earth's upper atmosphere. After all, those weather elements with which humans have direct interaction are the fronts and low- and high-pressure cells that make contact with Earth's surface. Yet, the ebb and flow of air high in the atmosphere are linked inextricably with the weather systems that shape our environment next to that surface. To be able to predict when, where, and at what speed fronts will enter and exit Texas, for instance, demands that one be aware of changes that are constantly taking place at 10-, 20-, even 30-thousand feet up in the atmosphere.

A key measure of the ocean of air in which we exist is the barometric pressure, simply the weight of all the air above the level at which the pressure is being measured. Obviously, then, pressure is greatest at Earth's surface, though even at that level the atmospheric pressure varies from spot to spot and from hour to hour. Pressure decreases rather rapidly with height, especially in the lowest 10,000 feet (3 kilometers) of the atmosphere (fig. 3.6). In this nearest-to-Earth layer, the pressure typically drops some 3 millibars, which is the equivalent of about 0.10 inch of mercury, for each 1,000-foot increase in elevation.

Across the surface of Texas, the rate of change of pressure, or gradient, is much less in the horizontal than in the vertical direction. Nonetheless, these relatively minor horizontal differences are vitally important in that they explain why, at any particular point in time, wind speed and direction differ from one area of the state to another. Surface atmospheric pressure is depicted on standard weather maps by isobars, which are lines connecting points having the same pressure. Weather reports issued to the public give the measure of air pressure in "inches of mercury": a weather report stating that the barometric pressure is 29.90 inches of mercury means the atmospheric pressure is sufficient to support a column of mercury, such as in a mercurial barometer, 29.90 inches high. (One inch of mercury is the equivalent of 33.86 millibars [mb], the quantifier of air pressure preferred by meteorologists.)

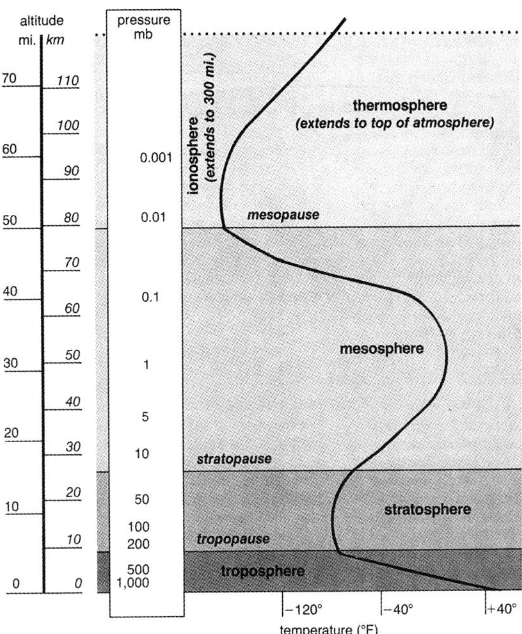

FIG. 3.6 Change of atmospheric pressure with height on a typical warm-season day. Source: George W. Bomar

Every day, while tuned in to weathercasters' descriptions of current and expected weather conditions, we hear references to highs and lows. A low-pressure area is one in which the pressure is lower than that of surrounding areas at the same elevation. It is also referred to simply as a "low," or less-often a "cyclone," and it is designated as an L on a weather map. If there is no recognizable center of low pressure but rather an elongated region (or valley) of low pressure, the feature is called a "trough." Conversely, an area with a higher pressure than its surroundings is called a high-pressure cell. It is also identified by the terms "high" and "anticyclone." If there is no identifiable center of high pressure but only an elongated pattern of higher pressure, the feature is known as a "ridge."

These upper-level features are readily identifiable every day because sensors are launched from National Weather Service installations around Texas to record temperature, moisture content, and wind flow from near the surface almost to the top of the atmosphere. Radiosondes, lifted by helium-filled balloons launched every morning and again every evening from sites in El Paso, Midland, Amarillo, Fort Worth, Corpus Christi, and Brownsville (as well as others in adjacent states), send back data for dozens of levels in the atmosphere that allow the ridges and troughs to be pinpointed for forecasting purposes. From these data, the total amount of water vapor in the atmosphere can be calculated—a key indicator of whether enough "fuel" exists to feed thunderstorms that might develop on a given day. A compilation of precipitable water, for example, illustrates how the atmosphere customarily loads up with water as the warm season matures (fig. 3.7). On many summer days, if all the water vapor in a column of air, say 4 inches in diameter, from the surface to the top of the atmosphere above Corpus Christi could be congealed into liquid water, the amount would exceed 1.5 inches in that 4-inch column! That number drops off significantly in the coldest months of the year, to about half that value. Amarillo's atmospheric moisture peaks in the summer as well, but the total content is barely 1 inch on any given day.

High-pressure systems that enter Texas in autumn, winter, and spring are more substantive than those that prevail in summer. They consist of colder and usually drier air with brisk winds on the periphery but calm conditions at the core of the high. When these massive domes of polar air follow in the wake of a cold front, they initially bring strong winds (which rotate

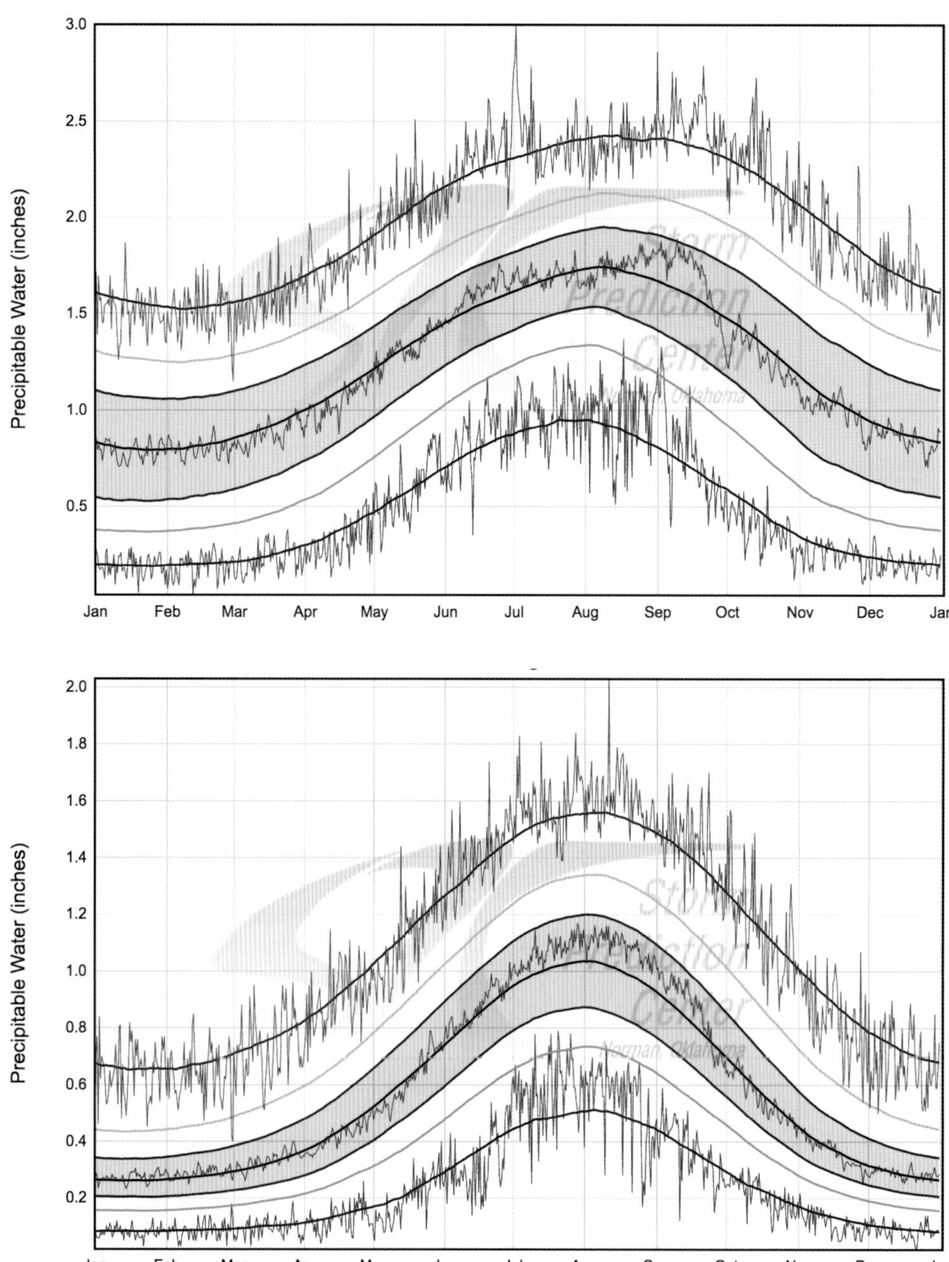

FIG. 3.7A & 3.7B Average daily precipitable water in the atmosphere at (upper) Corpus Christi and (lower) Amarillo. Source: National Oceanic and Atmospheric Administration

TABLE 3.2
Extremes in Barometric Pressure Dallas-Fort Worth

SEASON	MAXIMUM (YEAR)	MINIMUM (YEAR)
Winter	31.06 (1983)	28.97 (1960)
Spring	30.77 (1996)	29.14 (1953)
Summer	30.32 (1979)	29.37 (1974)
Autumn	30.84 (1986)	28.94 (1961)

in a clockwise—or anticyclonic—direction) and rapidly plunging temperatures. As the center of the high approaches a particular locale, winds slow down and eventually cease to blow when the core of the high draws near. The clockwise flow of air around the western edge of a summer high (known commonly as the "Bermuda high," so called because its core is situated well off the eastern coast of the United States) is weaker, warmer, more stagnant, and likely to produce haze. Most of the time, high pressure near the surface connotes fair weather, although if a trough of low pressure in the upper atmosphere is also at play, the weather can be cloudy and wet even though high pressure prevails at the surface.

The air is heaviest in winter—when air masses originating as far away as Siberia spill eastward, then down the lee side of the spine of the Rockies into the Gulf of Mexico. A typical winter ushers several of these continental Arctic air masses that completely smother Texas, forcing the barometric pressure to 30.75 inches or more. The coldest temperatures of the decade are invariably produced by these immense piles of dense air. Table 3.2 illustrates how the density of these air masses from the Arctic Circle varies among the seasons. The mound of Arctic air in summertime, on those infrequent occasions when it survives the trek across the US Great Plains, is greatly diluted by the time it reaches Texas: the greatest barometer reading in the summer for Dallas-Fort Worth (30.32 inches) pales in comparison with the all-time maximum reading (31.06 inches) that occurred in winter. Conversely, lowest barometric pressure usually occurs in the spring—unless a tropical cyclone invades the state in the summer or autumn. Some of the lowest barometer readings ever observed (below 29.00 inches) were caused by the arrival of Hurricane Carla in 1961.

By contrast, and as a general rule, low pressure usually spawns foul weather. In the cooler half of the year, the counterclockwise winds that characterize a low may be quite strong, whereas in summer the lows of nontropical origin feature rather weak circulation. As long as a low remains connected with the belt of strongest upper-atmospheric winds (commonly referred to as the jet stream), the weather generated by it usually is fairly predictable. However, if the low becomes detached and drifts irregularly, its behavior becomes much more unpredictable.

The Real Jet Stream

Sports fans often like to blame the outcome of games on balls knocked out of the park—or those not caught within the playing field—on the jet stream surging through a stadium. While the role of blustery low-level winds on deciding game results may not be up for discussion, the real jet stream surely cannot be culpable. After all, that broad belt of westerly winds for much of the year incessantly blows high in the atmosphere, 25,000 or even 30,000 feet (6–9 kilometers) above ground level. Within this belt there is usually at least one relatively narrow channel of winds having much stronger speeds, of at least 50–75

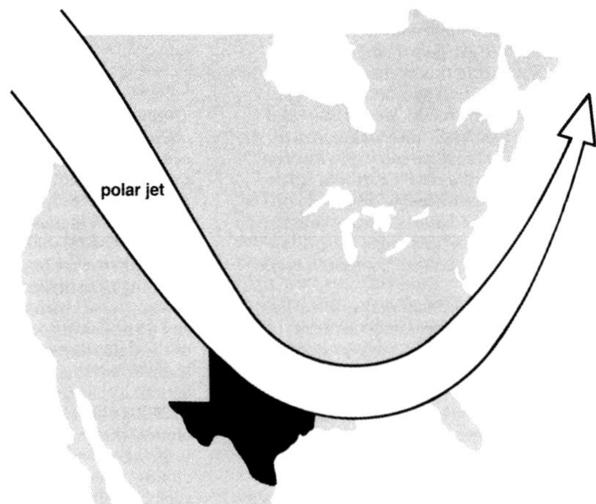

FIG. 3.8 Typical orientation of the polar jet stream in winter, when piles of cold air from the Arctic Circle are ushered into Texas on occasion. Source: George W. Bomar

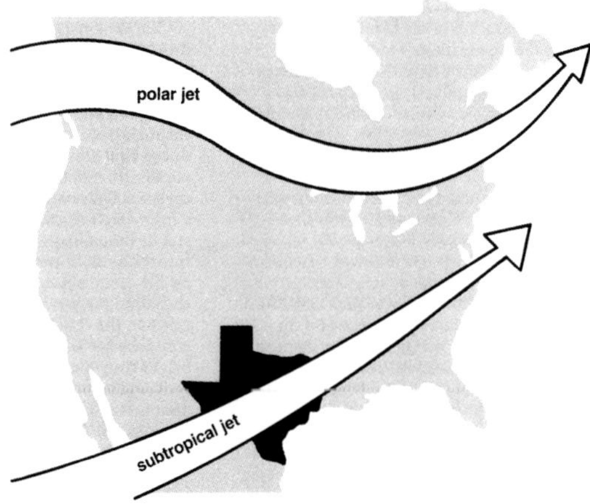

FIG. 3.9 Typical orientation of the warm subtropical jet stream in spring and autumn, when the polar jet has retreated into Canada and moisture is pumped into Texas from the Pacific Ocean. Source: George W. Bomar

miles per hour (mph) during the colder half of the year. The jet stream is a key element of the large-scale weather pattern over Texas because it often serves to move air masses into and out of the state and it also sponsors the formation of cyclones, or low-pressure centers, along fronts at Earth's surface. Actually, there are two types of jet streams that affect the weather over Texas: the polar jet and the subtropical jet. The polar jet, at an altitude of about 30,000 feet (9 kilometers) above mean sea level, is commonly found in the Texas atmosphere only in the colder half of the year (fig. 3.8). The rest of the year, it is too far north to have any pronounced effect on conditions in Texas. The subtropical jet, on the other hand, is far more influential (fig. 3.9). It is a frequent feature of the upper-level wind flow over Texas in spring and autumn and, at times, in summer and winter.

Dangerous snowstorms and abrasive windstorms in winter and in spring are assembled and set in motion by a strong jet stream high in the atmosphere over the southern Rockies. Indeed, the lee side of the Rockies, in an area that encompasses the Texas Panhandle, is a prime location for the development of these intense surface storms, a process also known as cyclogenesis. Jet-speed winds with velocities of 150–250 mph some 25,000–35,000 feet (6–11 kilometers) high above the surface induce tons of lower-level Gulf moisture to flow across Texas into this area of deepening low pressure just above the surface. The low-pressure center customarily undergoes rapid intensification and surges eastward across the Texas Panhandle into Oklahoma, most often spreading snow in winter and early spring in Texas's northern fringe and providing meaningful rain farther south in the state.

Major changes in the routine weather in Texas's coastal plain during the cooler half of the year are also attributable to the polar jet stream. Frequently, cold fronts that traverse the state sag and then stall either along the Texas coastline or a short distance offshore. When these fronts bog down, the rapid clearing that often takes place after frontal passage does not occur. Rather, low overcasts with intermittent light rain or drizzle coupled with dense fog may linger along the Texas coast and for many miles inland for several days. Skies eventually break up only when a "wave," or low-pressure center, is manufactured somewhere along the stalled front and moves toward the central Gulf coast. Before these low centers get fully organized and then move away from the Texas coastline toward the central Gulf coast, they usually shed very appreciable rains on the Texas coastal plain. A large percentage of the 3-to-5-inch rains that typically occur in each month of winter in the Upper Coast stems from these maritime lows that spin into being not far offshore.

A Clue Is in the Water

As vast and potent as the polar jet stream and its cousin, the subtropical jet, are as influences on Texas weather, even they are shaped and fueled by changes in the temperature of surface waters far beyond Texas, especially in the equatorial Pacific Ocean. Most folks now have a degree of familiarity with El Niño, a pronounced warming of the ocean surface (and to a significant depth in the ocean itself) that fosters changes in the behavior of the atmosphere over North America. El Niño, and its counterpart, La Niña, have been factors in the world's climate for ages: something abnormal about the seas off the coast of South America was noted by Spanish explorers some 400 years ago. But it was not until the mid-twentieth century that oceanographers and atmospheric scientists began to view the phenomenon as a key ingredient of the global weather system that brought periodic drought and excessive rainstorms to many disparate parts of the globe. Even today, scientists nurture various notions on what initiates the process that leads to an El Niño, or a La Niña. It is known that a correlation exists between the oceanic circulation that produces El Niño and the Southern Oscillation, a seesaw-like pattern of fluctuating atmospheric pressure between the western and eastern sectors of the Pacific.

When an El Niño is underway, the equatorial trade winds that normally blow west diminish and change direction, flowing east instead and allowing warm water to the west to slosh eastward. This exchange takes months to unfold, and a hot tropical sun warms the water further, so that by the time it reaches South America, it displaces the cold, upwelling water that usually dominates during the North American winter. That is why fishermen operating off the coasts of Ecuador and Peru centuries ago coined the term "El Niño," or "boy child" (a reference to the Christ-child), to refer to this unusually warm water and to the type of fish they were unaccustomed to harvesting, which peaked around the end of the year. This pronounced movement of warm water has repercussions for Texas weather, even months after the El Niño has vanished. The additional warmth from El Niño waters energizes both polar and subtropical jet streams, which in turn bring changes, often dramatic ones, to the Lone Star State. More often than not, an El Niño, particularly a moderate or strong episode, invigorates the subtropical branch of the jet stream to the extent that rain events are more numerous and significant. El Niño's effect is most often felt in late autumn and winter, but some spring seasons also reflect El Niño's influence.

El Niño episodes occur every few years and last, on average, about 12 to 18 months—somewhat less in duration than their counterparts, the La Niña events (fig. 3.10). From 1950 to 2016, there have been 18 distinct El Niño events, the longest one (23 months) occurring at the end of the infamous drought of the 1950s, or from the spring of 1957 to the spring of 1959. A pair of El Niño events, in 1979–1980 and 2006–2007, lasted only 5 months, and neither was very intense. Curiously, a lengthy El Niño occurred during the early years of the 1950s drought (from 1951 through 1953), but it was a weak episode, disintegrating during the summer of 1952 only to post a resurgence the following autumn. It obviously was not potent enough to dent significantly the landmark drought, thereby illustrating how other atmospheric (or oceanographic) influences must have been dominant. The two strongest events, in 1997–1998 and 2015–2016, led to several seasons in which Texas's precipitation statewide ranked in the top ten (table 3.3). Three of the other top six El Niño episodes since 1950 contributed to exceptionally wet autumns or winters.

The antithesis of El Niño, conveniently labeled La Niña, also has an indelible bearing on Texas weather, especially in the warm season, or seasons, that ensue once it has materialized. The ever-changing nature of the surface waters in the Pacific leads to about as many episodes of La Niña as its counterpart. In fact, a La Niña can be counted on to appear about every 4 to 8 years, and sometimes it can have more than one phase, each lasting from about 12 to as many as 18 months. A La Niña is evidenced by pronounced cooling of the surface waters in the equatorial Pacific, at times as much as 3.0°F below the normal maximum sea-surface temperature of 82°F (28°C) off the South American coast. La Niña's effect on Texas is in ways dramatically different than El Niño's. Instead of torrential rains, a La Niña more often than not shuts down rain production for extended periods, invoking if not exacerbating drought. There is also a link between La Niña and the incidence of tropical weather disturbances in the Atlantic basin, with

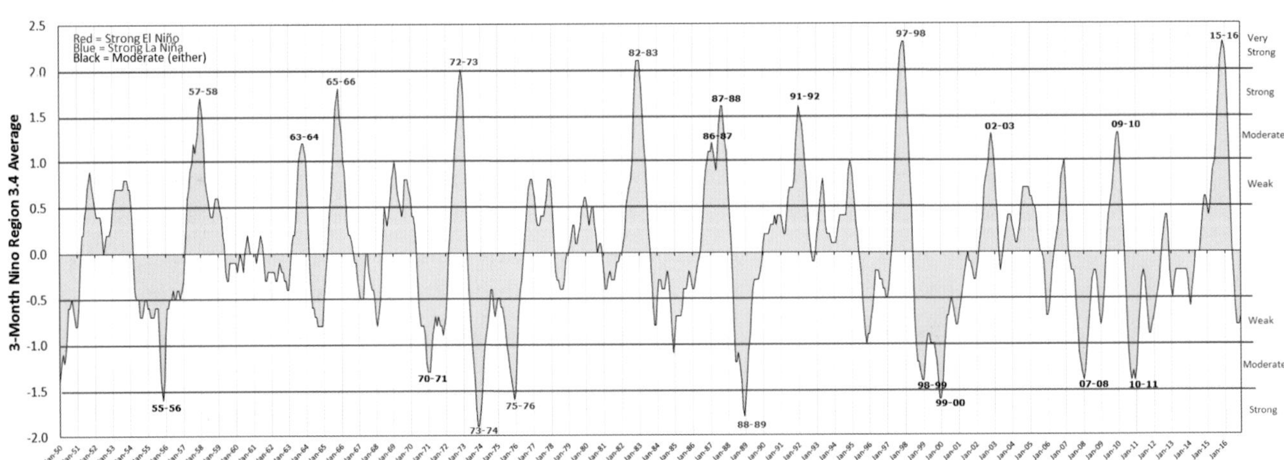

FIG. 3.10 Surface water temperature anomalies in the equatorial Pacific have oscillated in recent years between warm episodes (El Niño, with the index above zero) and cold ones (La Niña, with the index below zero). Source: National Oceanic and Atmospheric Administration

hurricanes and tropical storms more prone to form, or invigorate, in the Gulf of Mexico, thereby fomenting huge concern among Texas coastal residents.

With the El Niño-La Niña cycle so identifiable, it would seem that we need only to recognize which is taking place to prepare for harmful floods or debilitating drought. The fact is, these episodes of exaggerated warming and cooling of the equatorial Pacific do not always leave the same footprints. Since the capability to monitor and measure the evolution of both El Niño and La Niña effectively was devised in the years after World War II, there have been a dozen La Niña events observed in the central Pacific, all of them undoubtedly responsible for vagaries in the weather patterns observed in and near Texas. The typical La Niña has had a lifespan (24 months) notably longer than her brother, El Niño. Indeed, the two most intense episodes (1973-1976 and 1998-2001) lasted much longer (over 3 years), although one La Niña (1964-1965) lived barely a year.

The six most influential La Niña events (table 3.4) had a mixed effect on Texas. For example, the La Niña that formed midyear 2010 was accompanied by the driest summer (2011) in Texas weather history. But the most intense La Niña of modern times (1973-1976) appears to have delivered the coolest summer (1976) in history, as well as the sixth wettest summer the year before! In fact, all three summers bracketed around the La Niña of the early 1970s were remarkably cooler than normal, whereas the second most intense La Niña (1998-2001) occurred at a time when all three summers, ending in 2001, were substantially hotter than usual. Then there is the La Niña of the early 1950s, believed culpable for the landmark drought of the 1950s: the summer of 1950 turned significantly wetter than normal—before hot, dry summers resumed in 1951 and beyond. Sometimes a paradox like this can be explained by a hyper-active tropical storm season, within

TABLE 3.3
Major El Niño Episodes Affecting Texas

Index indicates average departure from normal, 1950-2017

RANK	YEARS	MONTHS	INDEX	EFFECT
1	1997-1998	13	+1.56	6th wettest winter 7th wettest autumn
2	2015-2016	16	+1.44	7th wettest spring 8th wettest autumn
3	1972-1973	11	+1.32	41st wettest winter
4	1982-1983	15	+1.30	18th wettest winter
5	1965-1966	11	+1.22	33rd wettest winter
6	1986-1988	18	+1.09	7th wettest winter

TABLE 3.4
Major La Niña Episodes Affecting Texas

Index indicates average departure from normal, 1950-2017

RANK	YEARS	MONTHS	INDEX	EFFECT
1	1973-1976	38	– 0.91	Coolest summer (1976) 6th wettest summer (1975)
2	1998-2001	37	– 0.90	14th hottest summer (2001)
3	1988-1989	21	– 0.87	18th coolest summer (1989)
4	1970-1972	21	– 0.83	30th driest summer (1971)
5	1950-1951	15	– 0.82	20th driest summer (1951)
6	2010-2012	25	– 0.75	Driest summer ever (2011)

which one or more wet tropical cyclones strike at or near the Texas coastline, dumping prodigious rainfall totals that skew precipitation totals for the entire summer (June 1–August 31).

Clouds—When Vapor Becomes Visible

Just as rustling leaves in a tree tell us the wind is blowing, the appearance of clouds in the sky inform us about the more complex processes, involving the jet stream, that are in play high above us. Indeed, clouds often tip off the professional meteorologist to significant weather changes taking place in the upper atmosphere that might not be discerned by using a thermometer or barometer.

Thanks to a continual stream of satellite imagery, both visible and infrared, the veteran weather watcher can give scrutiny to these cloud assemblages from above as well as ground level. In being able to identify certain types of clouds, even amateur weather watchers can be better informed about impending weather changes. The altitude of clouds is also significant, for each cloud type is formed differently—in a way that is related to the type of weather that it portends. When one understands the difference between high, wispy cirrus clouds and a lower and more ominous sheet of cirrostratus, for example, one can make a fair guess as to whether conditions will be fair or inclement and how soon a change can be expected.

All cloud types consist of multitudes of water droplets, ice crystals, or a combination of the two. When the cloud cover is high and thin enough to allow the sun, or moon, to shine through it, certain optical effects are produced that allow one to ascertain if the clouds are made of water droplets or ice crystals. Occasionally every winter, a halo—a narrow, bright ring around the sun or moon—is produced when rays of light from the sun or moon are refracted (or bent) by the cloud cover. The halo indicates that the cloud layer is high and made of ice crystals. On the other hand, if the cloud cover is composed of water droplets, a corona, or a bright ring made of various colors, may form to encompass the sun or moon. The diameter of the corona, which stems from the diffraction of light rays by spherically shaped water droplets making up the cloud layer, is considerably smaller than that of the halo. Usually a corona is observed around the moon and not the sun, whose beams of light may be too powerful for the ring surrounding it to be seen.

Even when the air becomes saturated (a relative humidity of 100 percent), a cloud will not form unless microscopic particles are present upon which tiny water vapor droplets can cluster. Fortuitously, the atmosphere is never lacking in these tiny substances. Their numbers are enormous, for they consist of soil raked up from the land surface by the wind, sea-salt particles from the evaporation of ocean spray, and a cornucopia of products of combustion (such as smoke). These materials may be found in every region of Texas on any day of the year, though the concentration of each type is usually greatest near its source region. They are referred to as condensation nuclei, and they are known to be hygroscopic in nature because, to one extent or another, they have an affinity for water. Indeed, a salt particle is such an effective hygroscopic nucleus that it will attract moisture even before the relative humidity of the air reaches 100 percent. Anyone who has had to contend with the clogging of a saltshaker in damp weather can attest to salt's propensity for drawing water vapor to it.

A

B

C

FIG. 3.11A, 3.11B & 3.11C Cloud types that occur most often in Texas are (a) fair-weather cumulus, (b) morning stratus, and (c) daytime stratocumulus. Source: George W. Bomar

Cloud Species

In general terms, clouds are formed in two ways: (a) by rising air currents and (b) by the condensation of water vapor in the air into a visible cloud (fig. 3.11). The first method leads to the development of cumulus (or cumuli-form) clouds, so named because the term cumulus means "accumulated or piled up." Cumulus clouds, because they form in air that is buoyant, have significant vertical development and consist of elements that normally are individual heaps. The second method results in the development of stratus (or stratiform) clouds; the word stratus stands for "layered or sheet-like." This type of cloud is found in air that is ascending very gently and uniformly as a result of large-scale convergence of air near Earth's surface. The vertical movement of air associated with cumuliform clouds is nearly always much more vigorous but far less uniform than that of stratiform clouds. Of the ten basic forms, or genera, of clouds that occur in the atmosphere, nine of them contain either the term stratus or the term cumulus.

The ten genera of clouds are classified according to height: (a) high, (b) middle, (c) low, and (d) clouds having great vertical extent. As a rule, high clouds consist entirely of ice crystals, whereas the middle and low cloud varieties are composed primarily of water droplets. However, the upper segments of middle clouds may feature the coexistence of water droplets and ice crystals. Clouds with large vertical dimensions—such as the thunderhead—usually have lower portions made up solely of water droplets, middle segments consisting of both water and ice, and upper sections composed entirely of ice. The average height of the bases of low clouds ranges from the surface of Earth to about 6,500 feet (2 kilometers), middle clouds from 6,500 to 16,500 feet (2–5 kilometers), and high clouds between 16,500 and 45,000 feet (5–14 kilometers). The cumuliform clouds having much vertical extent, often referred to as "towering cumuli," are in a class by themselves, for their bases may be only a few thousand feet above ground level while their tops on a few occasions may extend as high as 70,000 feet (21 kilometers).

The high cloud that is most familiar is cirrus, often observed in the "mare's tails" pattern, or as wisps that are thicker at one end than the other. Cirrus clouds, when unattached and arranged irregularly in the sky, usually hint of fair weather, but if they are systematically arranged in bands, a spell of inclement weather is in the offing. Cirrostratus clouds consist of thin sheets or layers of ice crystals that give the sky a milky appearance. This is the type of cloud that sometimes produces halos around the sun or moon and, in the process, suggests a deterioration in the weather that often leads to rain. As an arrangement sometimes labeled a "mackerel" or "buttermilk" sky, cirrocumulus clouds appear as thin, white patches of clouds having a rippled appearance. None of the three types of high clouds is capable of supplying rain, or any other form of precipitation, to Earth's surface. Yet they provide clues as to whether fair weather or a spell of rainy conditions is imminent. If cirrocumulus clouds thicken and merge together to form a solid layer or sheet, then wet weather is probably on the way. Cirriform clouds are seen in Texas in every season of the year, though with greater frequency in winter than in summer.

Of the three main categories of clouds, middle clouds are observed least often in the Texas sky. Still, they are not uncommon in every season of the year, though their frequency of occurrence is less in summer than in winter. The most prevalent of the three types of middle clouds is the altostratus variety, a uniform, fairly dense sheet of gray or bluish color that often covers the entire sky. The composition of altostratus clouds is complex; they usually are several thousand feet thick and transcend the freezing level. Altostratus clouds look somewhat like cirrostratus, but they are thicker, and one can distinguish the two by remembering that though the sun or moon may shine wanly through altostratus, the sunlight or moonlight does not create a halo. Altostratus clouds frequently come after the formation of cirrostratus and are followed by widespread and fairly continuous precipitation. Altocumulus clouds occur as waves or patches of puffy or globular clouds and are white or gray in appearance. They consist of small liquid water droplets and closely resemble their cousins of a higher altitude—the cirrocumulus. Altocumulus can be differentiated from cirrocumulus by keeping in mind that the former sometimes casts shadows. A third species of middle cloud is the nimbostratus, a dense, shapeless, and gray-colored or dark cloud from which continuous, and sometimes heavy, rain often falls. It is made up of large water droplets and sometimes a mixture of falling raindrops and snowflakes. Virga, or rain that falls out of a cloud but never reaches the ground, may be seen with nimbostratus and sometimes serves as a prism by diffracting sunlight into its many constituent colors. If winds are strong, fractostratus, or low scud clouds, often accompany nimbostratus clouds.

No matter the region, Texans see more low clouds than any other genera throughout the year. The most easily recognized and often observed cloud type is the cumulus, a puffy, white cloud whose top is usually dome shaped with a cauliflower structure and whose bottom is nearly horizontal. Cumulus clouds are the product of rising currents of air from the layer of atmosphere near the ground, and so their shape is constantly undergoing changes. As a rule, if they do not grow together or to great heights, cumulus clouds connote fair weather. If they sustain considerable vertical development, however, they often grow into cumulonimbus clouds, the most spectacular of all the cloud genera, whose summits invariably reach great altitudes (fig. 3.12). These mountainous clouds, known commonly as thunderheads, fit all three cloud classifications because they have bases only a few thousand feet above the surface (as much as 8,000 to 10,000 feet [2–3 kilometers] in the semi-arid plains of West Texas) and tops that invariably extend as high as several tens of thousands of feet.

What dictates how tall thunderheads grow is the ceiling of the troposphere. At that level, the temperature of the air stops cooling with increasing height, and relatively warmer air that constitutes the stratosphere takes over. The top portion of the thunderhead then flattens out, leaving the classic anvil shape that is the signature of the full-fledged thunderhead. When this "capping" takes place, the thunderstorm, having reached maturity, will soon begin to decay. Cumulonimbus clouds are the instigators of much of the severe-storm phenomena that pose a threat to human safety: high winds, hail, lightning, flash-flooding rains, and tornadoes. They occur in every region, though the frequency of occurrence is greatest along the upper Texas coast, where the blossoming towers can tap into an abundant supply of Gulf moisture. Though somewhat fewer in number, the cumulonimbus clouds that erupt at higher elevations out west are much more prone to produce damaging hail and strong downburst winds (table 3.5). Cumuliform clouds, including the smaller cumulus and the larger cumulonimbus, are very common in every season except winter. Even in the coldest quarter of the year, thunderstorms occasionally erupt.

Stratus and stratocumulus are other types of low clouds that occur often—in every season of the year in all regions of Texas. Stratus is a low, uniform, gray layer of cloud that resembles fog, but it does not rest on the ground. As the lowest of all cloud types, it is made up of widely

FIG. 3.12 The cumulonimbus, or thunderhead, is the cloud type producing the bulk of rainwater observed in Texas in a typical year. Source: Texas Department of Transportation

TABLE 3.5
Stormiest Major Cities in Texas

Shown are the number of days with a thunderstorm in a typical year, which is based on data for the period 1981-2010.

LOCATION	DAYS
Beaumont	66
Houston	63
Victoria	56
Amarillo, Wichita Falls	49
Lubbock	47
Dallas-Fort Worth	46
Austin	43
Waco	41

dispersed water droplets. The bases of stratus clouds may be as low as a few hundred feet above the ground and as high as several thousand feet. They seldom produce anything more substantive than a fine light rain and often yield nothing more substantive than drizzle. They are distinguished from stratocumulus in that they are grayer and are more uniform at the base. Stratocumulus clouds, on the other hand, have a rounded appearance and nonuniform bases. They do not produce rain, but they may be transformed into nimbostratus, which are capable of generating good rains. Stratus clouds are very common in winter, particularly in the coastal plain. Stratocumulus clouds are found frequently in the warm season in the southeastern quadrant of Texas; they make up the low cloud cover that forms on many mornings in late spring, summer, and early autumn before dawn but then dissipate when the sun sufficiently warms up the layer of air near the ground.

Another indicator of the types of air masses and clouds that predominate in various regions of Texas is the amount of sunshine received (table 3.6). Sunshine enthusiasts will find the western tip of Texas to be the most appealing place, for it is the Trans Pecos that customarily sustains the least amount of cloud cover, regardless of the season of the year. Only 1 out of every 6 to 10 days is overcast in spring, summer, and autumn in El Paso. Even in winter, cloudy skies typically occur on only 1 out of every 7 days, while half of the days in the month of January are clear. Autumn is even more cloud free than winter in the Trans Pecos, with an average of 2 out of every 3 days categorized as clear. For the year as a whole, El Paso surpasses all other big cities in Texas in receiving sunshine: the mean annual amount of sunshine there is 84 percent of the total possible, with both May and June providing an average of 90 percent. By contrast, because of its proximity to the state's primary source of moisture, the coastal plain is traditionally the cloudiest region of all. A bit more than half of the days in winter and spring are marked by a substantial cloud cover not only in the Upper Coast but elsewhere throughout the eastern half of Texas as well. Beaumont, Corpus Christi, and Brownsville get less than 60 percent of the total possible sunshine on an average, year-round basis. In fact, the sun shines only an average of 41 percent during December and January in Brownsville and only 43 percent in December in Corpus Christi. Taking the year as a whole, the amount of cloudiness in North Central and East Texas is only slightly less than that in South Central Texas. Elevations in much of these regions do not differ greatly, and with the prevailing wind much of the time being from the south, low-level moisture is usually spread fairly uniformly over all of these three regions. There are more cloud-free days in autumn than in any other season of the year in virtually all of Texas.

TABLE 3.6

Sunniest Major Cities in Texas

Shown is the average annual sunshine (percent of total possible). Sunshine data for these locations span periods of up to 60 years.

CITY	PERCENT
El Paso	84
Amarillo, Midland	74
Lubbock	72
Abilene	70
Dallas-Fort Worth	61
Austin, Corpus Christi	60

Clouds That Lie Low

One type of low cloud that complicates human activity quite often is fog. As the aggregate of many millions of minute water droplets that break the path of light rays, fog can be a nuisance if not a hazard, especially to people traveling in it. A thick, "pea-soup" fog can so enshroud an airport as to put it temporarily out of commission; it can make navigation on inland and coastal waterways difficult and treacherous; and it can slow highway motor traffic and sometimes contribute to serious auto accidents. Not everything about fog is adversarial, however. It can be an asset to folks attempting to protect certain crops or vegetation. By retarding the rate at which air cools radiationally at night, a thick fog can spare an area from what might otherwise be an untimely killing frost.

Fog simply is a type of stratus cloud consisting of visible water droplets, the bottom of which touches the ground (fig. 3.13). Much of the time fog is formed by the cooling of the humid layer of air next to the surface below its dew-point temperature. As long as the temperature of the air remains above its dew-point temperature, the air continues to be unsaturated and is capable of holding additional water vapor until it becomes overloaded and must give up some of its moisture in the form of visible water droplets. If additional water vapor is not supplied, then condensation of some of the vapor in the air will not occur until the temperature of the air drops to the dew-point level. Moreover, when air that is unsaturated cools, its relative humidity increases. When the temperature reaches the dew point, the air is saturated and the relative humidity becomes 100 percent. For instance, it is known that air having a temperature of 75°F (24°C) and a dew-point temperature of 55°F (13°C) has a relative humidity of 50 percent. It follows, then, that for the air to become saturated and a mist or fog to occur, the temperature must drop to 55°F (assuming no additional moisture is pumped in or is withdrawn during this time). The astute weather watcher can make a good estimate of the likelihood of fog at night by determining the dew-point temperature and comparing it with the projected drop in air temperature. If the two readings are expected to coincide, then fog is likely.

FIG. 3.13 Fog, a type of cloud at or near the ground, is much more common in Beaumont (90 days a year, on average) than in far West Texas (2 days a year). Source: Texas Department of Transportation

Much of the fog that occurs in Texas is radiational in nature. It is observed on a year-round basis, when skies are clear, the wind is nearly—but not entirely—calm, and the near-surface layer of air is rich in moisture. A sky devoid of clouds aids the formation of radiational fog by allowing Earth's surface to cool itself quickly—a process accomplished by Earth emitting heat energy gained during the daytime into space without interference from cloud cover. A light breeze helps fog to form by mixing the coldest air next to the surface with warmer air immediately above it. Without this mixing, only dew is likely to form. On the other hand, if winds are blustery, too much mixing of the lowest layer of air takes place and, as a consequence, a layer of air cold enough to produce fog is never allowed to form.

Radiational fog, particularly in summer, often will burn off and dissipate not long after daybreak. The layer of fog, which may be as little as 50 feet (15 meters) thick or as much as several hundred feet thick, is eroded away from beneath, not from above. Much of the sun's warmth penetrates the fog layer and warms the ground, thereby setting up thermal currents that punch up through the fog layer and mix enough dry air with the foggy air to eradicate it. The day's initial bursts of sunlight were not sufficient to burn off a fog that formed on Interstate Highway 10 near Winnie on Thanksgiving morning in 2012. A collision involving a car that abruptly slowed because of the fog set off a chain reaction that led to wrecks on both sides of the divided freeway, involving nearly 150 vehicles and shutting down the vital artery for much of the holiday. Some 80 occupants of autos were injured, a dozen seriously, and two people, riding in a Suburban that was crushed by a tractor trailer rig, were killed. On a localized basis, radiational fog is far more prevalent in valleys than on hillsides. Depressions serve as reservoirs for the drainage of the coldest, and hence heaviest, air. Where the landscape is characterized by rolling hills and plains, it is not uncommon for the upland areas to be clear while nearby lowlands are enshrouded in fog. Valley fog usually is not thick and evaporates rapidly after daybreak.

A different type of fog, known as advection fog, is quite common in the Texas coastal plain, especially in the cooler segment of the year. Its development is dependent upon the horizontal movement of moist and relatively warm air from the Gulf of Mexico over a cooler land surface. From September until May it appears all along the Texas coastline and sometimes up to 100 miles (160 kilometers) inland. As humid subtropical air drifts farther inland over a progressively colder land surface at night, it is chilled to its dew point, at which moment it becomes saturated, and a thick fog ensues. Quite often, a light drizzle will accompany advection fog. The fog grows thick enough to restrict visibilities to a small fraction of a mile; indeed, it is not uncommon for visibilities to be lowered to only a few feet—or near zero in observer terminology.

Motorists are familiar with a highly localized brand of fog that occurs, often in winter, when cold polar or Arctic air invades an area and passes over the much warmer water surface of a lake or reservoir. This incoming cold air is warmed at its bottom by interacting with the water, while at the same time some of the water from the river or lake evaporates into the cold air. The few feet of cold air next to the water surface then becomes saturated, and condensation of the vapor in the cold air leads to the formation of steam fog. Texans can see the rising tufts of steam fog on cold, crisp winter mornings as they drive near lakes. In fact, in big cities with heavy traffic flow, the steam fog can be hazardous to drivers who encounter greatly reduced visibilities as they approach a river that courses through town: a failure to anticipate abrupt slowdowns near a bridge traversing the river can lead to vehicle pileups.

Upslope fog is common, especially in winter, at higher elevations in Texas. As moist air having a fairly high dew point advances far inland, it is lifted by the terrain and cools to the higher terrain's dew point, forming a fog that becomes so dense as to drop the visibility to a mile or less. This variety of fog commonly is seen in the Edwards Plateau, as well as farther north in the High and Low Rolling Plains. The fog, when very dense, can paralyze airport operations and make flying treacherous. A vintage 1946 Stinson aircraft encountered thick fog just after take-off from a private airfield in Dickens County before daybreak one March morning in 2011. Flying low enough to become entangled in barbed wire along a fence line, the airplane nose-dived into the ground and burst into flames, killing all three people aboard. Yet another type of fog that at times plagues large portions of Texas, usually in the coldest months of the year, is rain fog, also known as frontal fog, which is the result of air being saturated by falling rain. The rain, usually triggered by a slow-moving cold front, falls into a mass of relatively dry air, thereby increasing the moisture content of the air and lowering the temperature at the same time.

No region of Texas escapes being socked in by dense fog at least a few times every year. The majority of incidences of "heavy" fog—dense enough to lower the visibility to one-quarter mile or less—take place in winter. The foggiest area of Texas is the stretch of coastal plain extending from the coastal bend near Corpus Christi up the coast to the mouth of the Sabine River (table 3.7). In winter, fog beclouds the lower atmosphere on more than half the days in places such as Houston, Beaumont-Port Arthur, and Victoria. In fact, heavy fog typically occurs on one out of every four days in these locales in winter. The Upper Coast also experiences the greatest frequency of occurrence of heavy fog in each of the other three seasons of the year. Very thick fog hampers activity in South Central Texas and in the Lower Valley on at least a few days each month in spring and in late autumn. In all the state except the upper half of the coastal plain, heavy fog is quite infrequent in summer.

The Trans Pecos region west of the Guadalupe, Davis, and Chisos Mountains is spared dense fog more than any other area of Texas. Low-level moisture from the Gulf of Mexico rarely reaches this westernmost periphery of the state in amounts sufficient to allow fog to form. Thick fog at El Paso in summer is about as scarce as a snow cover in the lower Rio Grande valley in January. Even in winter, fog in the far west seldom thickens enough to plunge visibilities to less than one or a few miles. Occasionally, however, a dense fog can so restrict the visibility that air and ground traffic are hampered momentarily.

TABLE 3.7
Foggiest Major Cities in Texas

Shown is the number of days with dense fog in a typical year, which is based on data for the period 1981-2010. Dense fog occurs when the visibility is ¼ mile or less.

CITY	DAYS
Victoria	45
Beaumont	40
Corpus Christi	30
Amarillo	27
Brownsville	27
Houston	25

Clouds That Make Contact

The same radiational cooling responsible for fog also leads to the formation of dew and frost. Dew occurs on clear nights with little or no wind when the air temperature near the ground drops to its dew point. At that instant the water vapor in the air condenses to form water drops on objects like chilled blades of grass. The amount of water produced is largely inconsequential, though in semi-arid West Texas during long spells without rainfall the dew may be enough to aid the growth of plants that are able to absorb water on their leaves. If the temperature at ground level drops to the freezing point, white frost, instead of dew, forms. This frozen type of condensation is known as hoarfrost if it forms rather slowly during a crisp autumn, winter, or early spring night. If, on the other hand, a transparent, smooth coating of ice forms on the ground quickly, usually on a damp surface whose temperature plunges rapidly below freezing, then glazed frost is observed. Regardless of the rate at which they form, these two kinds of frost usually seriously affect the growth of grasses and other plants.

Frost makes its inaugural appearance in the northern half of Texas usually in October—though frost has been known to show up as early as around the autumnal equinox (late September). The first date of frost is not always coincident with the first freeze day, however. Indeed, frost can occur with reported minimum temperatures several degrees above the freezing mark because official temperature reports stem from a thermometer exposed to the air at eye level, some 5 feet above the ground. If frost is seen covering the ground, you can be certain that the temperature at ground level reached the freeze mark.

4. The Hardships of Summer

Veteran weather watchers had to suspect the approaching summer of 2011 would be more stultifying than usual. A mature La Niña in the equatorial Pacific was back for an encore, and such abnormal cooling of surface waters there often—but not always—serve as a harbinger of an usually hot and dry summer. More convincing evidence of a likely torrid summer came in the form of an extraordinarily warm spring and, worse, the driest spring season on record in Texas. The almost rainless spring followed an abnormally dry autumn and a very dry winter, so the Texas landscape ached for a long, sumptuous drink from the heavens long before the sun climbed higher and higher in its arc across the largely cloud-free sky as the solstice approached (June 21). No one, however, could have imagined the degree of brutality the summer of 2011 would inflict on the Lone Star State.

Summer-like heat in the triple digits was already entrenched in much of Texas weeks before school had been dismissed for the year. Daytime temperatures soared to levels never before seen in May, and the unbearable heat continued unrelentingly into summer, then into autumn (figs. 4.1, 4.2). In many areas, temperatures between Memorial Day and Labor Day were above normal for 95 percent of all days. The number of days with the temperature reaching 100°F (38°C) or greater not only broke records, it obliterated them in cities such as San Angelo (100 days, besting the previous record of 60 days), Wichita Falls (100, 79) Waco (90, 63), and Austin (90, 69). Triple-digit readings tortured residents of Del Rio for 50 straight days, and the string reached 44 in Waco and 42 in Dallas–Fort Worth (see appendix 9 for additional locations). Rain—all 0.37 inch of it—finally fell in Midland on August 11, after a record 83 days without any measurable precipitation, and for the first two-thirds of the year, the Permian Basin collected only 0.5 inch of rain, a mere 6 percent of what normally occurs. The hottest June on record in Texas (5.6°F above normal) gave way to an even hotter July

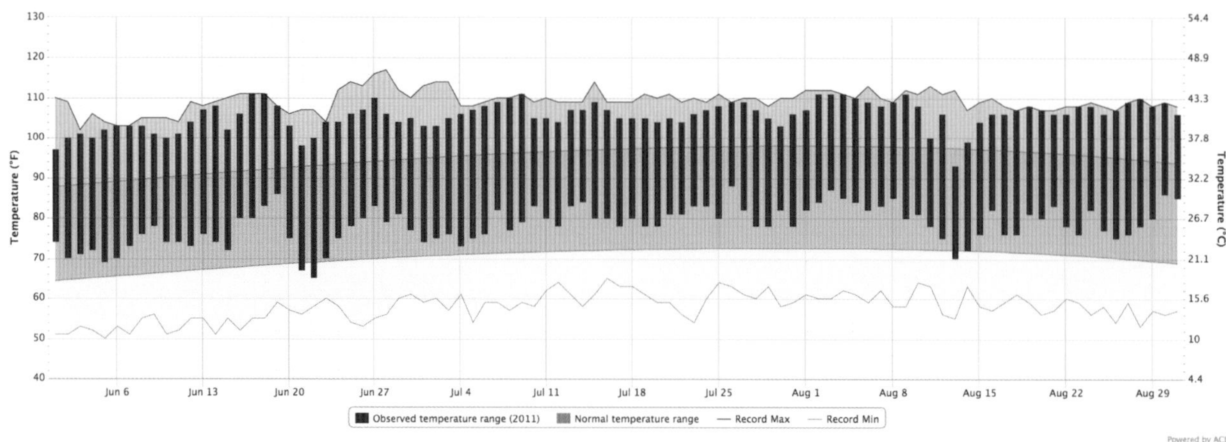

FIG. 4.1 During Texas's hottest summer (2011) in state history, cities set records for days with excessive heat: Wichita Falls suffered 52 straight days with 100°F heat, ending on August 12. Source: National Climatic Data Center

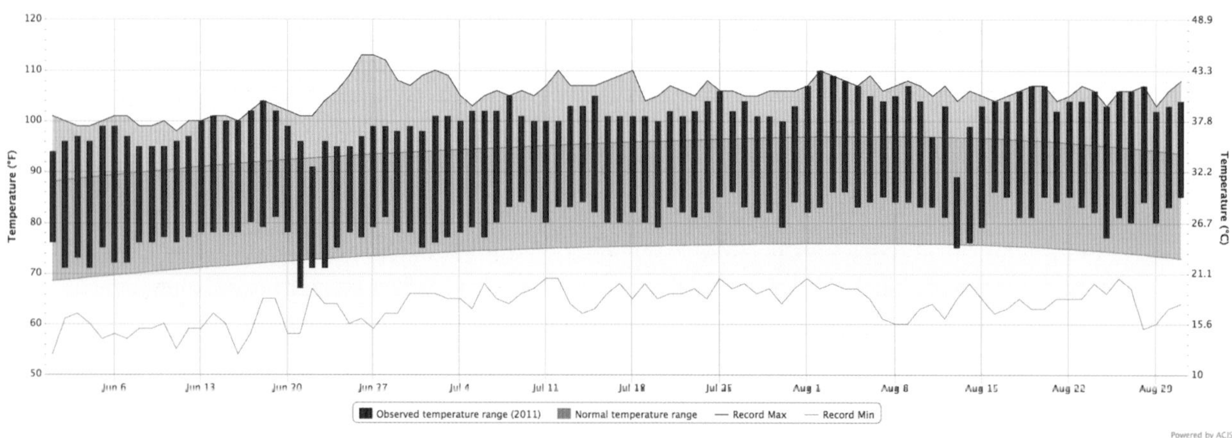

FIG. 4.2 One intolerable condition during the history-making summer of 2011 was excessive heat even at night: Dallas-Fort Worth had 37 consecutive days with the morning low temperature at or above 80°F—including 6 straight days of 85°F or hotter. Source: National Climatic Data Center

TABLE 4.1
Texas's Hottest Summers

RANK	YEAR	DEPARTURE[1]
1st	2011	+5.3°
2nd	1980	+2.9°
	1998	+2.9°
4th	1934	+2.8°
5th	1918	+2.1°
6th	1954	+2.0°
	1953	+2.0°
8th	1952	+1.8°
	1951	+1.8°

[1] Departure from twentieth-century average of 81.4°F.

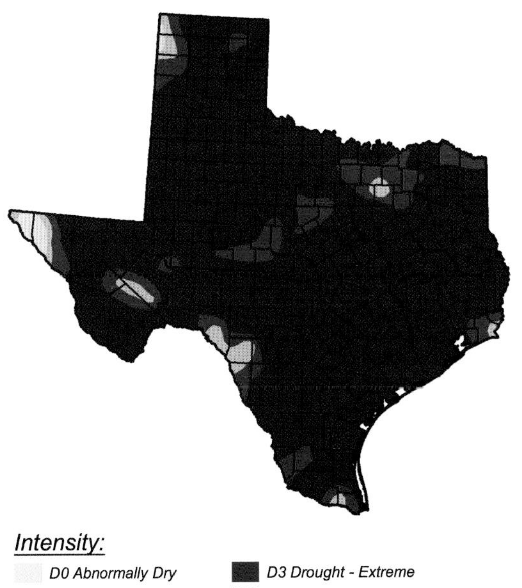

FIG. 4.3 During the killer heat wave of 2011, exceptional drought, the worst type measured, covered nearly 90 percent of the land area of Texas—by far more than in any recent year. Source: Office of Texas State Climatologist

(the hottest in history, or 4.7°F above normal), which yielded to an August that was the hottest of all (6.3°F above normal). Those three summer months combined in Texas matched the same summer in neighboring Oklahoma as the hottest season in any state in history! Not surprisingly, the mountain of hot air that resided over the whole of Texas for virtually the entire summer inhibited thunderstorms to the extent that the summer was also the driest in the state's history. The Gulf of Mexico stood helplessly by, furnishing no hope of relief until Tropical Storm Lee spun up on Labor Day weekend. But that storm bypassed Texas for the Louisiana coast, taking its moisture with it and leaving Texas to deal with a devastating wildfire near Bastrop. It is no wonder the summer left much of the northern half of Texas in the most intense drought ever witnessed.

The summer of 2011 was an historic scourge to Texas (table 4.1). It was so extremely hot that it stands far above all other unusually hot summers; its mean summer temperature was 5.3°F above the long-term average, easily topping the second hottest summer on record, the unforgettable summer of 1980. The drought it exacerbated grew to the point that nearly 90 percent of the entire state was afflicted with the highest (worst) classification of drought, an exceptional drought (fig. 4.3). It would have made the entire year the hottest calendar year on record, but its intensity was offset by a near-normal winter that preceded it. The drought aided by the implacable heat caused some $5.2 billion in economic losses, with more than half of that attributed to crop loss, especially cotton. In fact, the abandonment rate for cotton in Texas (which normally ranges between 15 and 20 percent each year) skyrocketed to 54 percent, and those farmers raising dry-land cotton saw a failure rate of 88 percent, with some 2.5 million acres (over 1 million hectares) of cotton lost. The heat-drought combination, piled on to the accumulated toll in agricultural losses due to drought in Texas since the turn of the twenty-first century, brought the total to more than $13 billion. With even more heat to come, by summer's midway point 94 percent of pasture and rangeland was rated poor or very poor, forcing ranchers to either sell their stock for slaughter or buy feed. The summer stole more water from both surface and underground sources than ever, leaving total storage in the state's 109 major reservoirs (19.99 million acre-feet) at an historic low. Nine of those reservoirs (including essentially dry lakes Spence, Fisher, Hords Creek, and Meredith) were less than 10 percent full (fig. 4.4). It is no stretch to label the summer of 2011 as, at a minimum, a 1-in-200-year event because (according to tree-ring data that extends back in history some 430 years) only one other summer (1789) appears to match the intensity of the horrific summer of 2011.

FIG. 4.4 Hubbard Creek Reservoir, near Breckenridge in Stephens County, was one of many lakes in North Texas that almost went totally dry during the summer of 2011. Source: George W. Bomar

Perennially Hot Summers

With Texas situated not far north of the Tropic of Cancer (where the sun's rays are truly vertical around June 21), summers here are destined to be hot. As the arc of the sun across the sky climbs higher once spring is spent and summer moves in, the amount of daylight steadily increases to about 14 hours a day across Texas. This ensures a gradual but steady warming of the lowest layer of the atmosphere and the crust of the Earth. The polar jet stream retreats northward toward and into Canada, and the infiltration of refreshingly cool and dry Canadian air diminishes. The parade of energetic midlatitude cyclones that usually brings uproarious spring rainstorms shifts poleward also, leaving Texas without any large-scale means of ventilating its atmosphere. With fewer cool Canadian air masses able to reach the Red River, warm, muggy air from the Gulf of Mexico becomes an immovable squatter. At times the Mexican desert heats up to the extent that hot air masses from there expand into Texas, inflating the temperature more while driving down the humidity, if only for a spell. In short, the traditional weather pattern of a Texas summer is one best described as monotonous: mild to warm muggy nights and repressively hot days.

The seemingly endless summer of 2011 notwithstanding, heat waves intense enough to scorch and kill are most common in Texas from early June through late August. Often the precursor to the onset of a heat wave occurs in the western sector of the state, where very hot temperatures well above 100°F (38°C) begin occurring frequently in May, if not April. By early or mid-June, intense heat will have gripped the region along and west of the Pecos River. In fact, in nearly every year, whether marked by a pronounced heat wave or not, the temperature in this westernmost region peaks sometime in late June or early July. In a typical summer the hottest daytime temperatures, averaged on a weekly basis, occur from about June 20 to July 4 at El Paso. Daytime highs then slowly tail off for the duration of summer, the end of which is characterized by daily maximums around 92°F (33°C) in Texas's westernmost metropolitan area. Elsewhere the hottest weather in summer takes place a few weeks later, from mid-July until mid-August. In a typical summer, daytime extremes usually peak in the low 90s in the High Plains sometime in July. From the Low Rolling Plains and Edwards Plateau to East and Southern Texas, the hottest summer weather, on average, occurs during the first 10 to 15 days of August, though occasionally the heat reaches a climax later in the month, near the end of the "climatological summer."

The scorching summer of 1980 fits the mold described above, but its intensity attained a level rarely experienced even in Texas. That summer's heat wave was slow to materialize, coming on the heels of an unusually mild spring—even a month of May that gave few clues of an approaching heat wave of historic proportions. Once the massive subtropical ridge of high pressure migrated northward out of Mexico early in June, as it always does, intense heat began building quickly. Then, for a solid two months, it never relaxed, causing human suffering of unimaginable intensity. At least 60 people within the state expired from heat stroke, and scores of others died from complications of other medical problems exacerbated by the extreme heat. Far greater numbers, in the thousands, suffered from heat cramps, heat shock, and heat exhaustion as daytime temperatures consistently shot into triple digits on successive days for weeks at a time. The absence of clouds on most days from mid-June into late July ensured a superabundance of sunshine, which in turn produced huge evaporative rates that led to parched and cracked soils, plunging river and reservoir levels, and depleted water wells. Crops with no access to irrigation water wilted in the unrelenting heat, with many becoming total losses. Cotton production dropped 25 percent, as did grain sorghum yields—the largest decline in a quarter of a century in South Texas. Estimated losses to crops and livestock varied between $250 million and $500 million. In heavily populated Harris County, streets cracked and buckled, some 100,000 acres (40,470 hectares) of corn and soybeans were either lost or badly damaged, and power consumption soared to record levels as residents fought to stay somewhat comfortable.

With few exceptions, the hottest temperatures in any year occur in one, or several, locations in the arid basins and valleys of the Trans Pecos. To many, the names Presidio, Lajitas, and Terlingua are synonymous with hot weather, for those small communities in the Big Bend of Texas experience 100°F heat on scores of occasions every year. Presidio does collect, on average, eighty-one 100° days every year (table 4.2), beginning in April and sometimes lasting well into October. Occasionally, triple-digit heat is observed west of the Pecos River earlier in spring—or later in autumn (table 4.3). In some years, though, midafternoon temperatures in parts of the Low Rolling Plains or North Central Texas exceed those of the Trans Pecos, especially in the latter half of summer.

In two of every three years, some location in the Trans Pecos, with a temperature in excess of 110°F (43°C), garners the distinction of being the hot spot in Texas (appendix 6). These inflated extremes in the Trans Pecos most often occur sometime in June; by contrast, when the hottest point is elsewhere in Texas, the temperature, usually between 110°F (43°C) and 115°F (46°C), normally takes place in July or early August.

TABLE 4.2

Cities with, on Average, the Most 100° Days Annually[1]

LOCATION	DAYS
Boquillas[2]	100
Castolon	97
Lajitas	97
Presidio	81
Laredo	71
Zapata	55

[1] Based on the period 1981-2010.

[2] Also known as Rio Grande Village, Brewster County.

TABLE 4.3

Earliest and Latest 100° Days on Record

LOCATION	EARLIEST	LATEST
Amarillo	May 15, 1996	Sep 10, 2000
Austin	May 25, 1925	Oct 3, 1923
Big Bend NP	Mar 7, 1991	Oct 23, 2001
Corpus Christi	Mar 27, 1984	Oct 17, 2012
Dallas	Apr 17, 2006	Oct 1, 1979
El Paso	May 8, 1989	Sep 16, 1956
Houston	May 31, 1998	Sep 21, 2005
Laredo	Feb 18, 1986	Oct 24, 2001
Midland	Apr 21, 1989	Oct 8, 1979
San Antonio	Feb 21, 1996	Sep 28, 2005
Texarkana	May 11, 1922	Oct 1, 1938

The summer, taken as a whole, can be just as hot, if not hotter, in the southern quarter of Texas as in the Trans Pecos. In most years, the cities in the south will endure the highest average monthly temperatures of any region. Almost invariably, July or August will be the warmest month, with mean daily temperatures often in the mid or upper 80s. Daytime temperatures almost always reach well into the 90s or low 100s throughout the whole summer, while nighttime lows rarely dip below the mid or upper 70s.

Safety Precautions

The human body is assaulted in a number of ways by prolonged, excessive heat like that of the killer heat waves of recent years. More than any other organ in the body, the heart is subjected to a great amount of stress during heat waves. When the weather is hot, the heart must work harder, pumping more than the usual amount of blood to tiny capillaries in the outermost layer of skin, through which the blood sheds some of its heat to the atmosphere. Usually, in this way, the temperature of the body can be maintained in the neighborhood of 98.6°F (37°C). However, if the air temperature climbs beyond that level, the blood—and hence the body—cannot give off some of its heat. One of the most basic laws of thermodynamics states that heat energy flows from a body having a higher temperature to one with a lower temperature; the reverse cannot happen. Since the atmosphere is warmer than the blood of the human body during a heat wave, the atmosphere is prone not to accept the heat of which the blood strives to rid itself. The only other means by which the body can control its temperature is to lose some of its heat through perspiration.

Human sweat plays a critical role in cooling the skin and, subsequently, the body's blood. When the air is relatively dry (say, when the relative humidity is less than 30 or 40 percent), the atmosphere accepts a great deal of moisture from the skin; as a result, a person feels tolerably well even though the temperature may be as high as 100°F (38°C). But if the humidity is high (say, more than 60 percent), the moisture-rich atmosphere will extract much less water from the skin. Thus, cooling of the skin and blood is greatly diminished, and an individual feels quite uncomfortable. To compensate for excessive heat, the body's respiration rate may increase to the extent that an abnormal amount of carbon dioxide is lost from the blood and hyperventilation ensues. There are limits of temperature and humidity that the human body can tolerate. When these limits are exceeded for a lengthy period or to a great degree, unconsciousness and even death may become real threats.

Problems from extreme heat are often compounded in large, heavily industrialized metropolitan areas. In these regions, air pollution becomes a key factor when the atmosphere does a poor job of ventilating itself. Staying comfortable and healthy is often a challenge during summer in the Upper Coast, where air pollution advisories issued by the National Weather Service frequently warn residents with respiratory problems who live in Houston and other nearby locales to confine themselves indoors. The large dome of high pressure that often settles over Texas at this time of the year entraps hot and humid air near the ground, so that abnormally heavy concentrations of carbon monoxide, ozone, sulfur dioxide, and other particulate matter accumulate. Those folks most affected by the deadened and polluted air are the elderly, especially those with troubling heart conditions. The poor, unable to afford air conditioning, also suffer to an alarming degree. Even the ability to afford air conditioning may mean little in those situations in which severely hot weather strains the abilities of electric utilities to generate enough energy to keep cooling systems in operation. In recent years, some urbanites in Texas have come to know firsthand what life is like during a brownout or a blackout.

BEATING THE HEAT

Given the human body's vulnerability when the weather becomes unduly hot and sultry for long periods, emphasis has to be placed on finding ways to provide shade from the sun and to encourage evaporation of excessive moisture. Combatting the debilitating effects of the summer heat is partially accomplished by locating homes in the shade of trees to lessen the effect of solar insolation. In recent years we have gone one step further by using air conditioners, evaporative coolers, and dehumidifiers to create an artificial climate that satisfies our need for comfort. Yet, there are numerous other considerations that can have a pronounced effect on our ability to stay cool and comfortable in the midst of the stifling heat outdoors. The need for shade suggests the elimination of radiation on the east and west walls of the home, for example, and this can be attained in part by constructing houses with marked east-west elongation and small east and west walls. The use of attic and ceiling fans facilitates airflow within a dwelling and promotes cooling by evaporation as well as a feeling of comfort associated with air movement. In addition to the shade they provide, trees—along with shrubs, walls, and fences—can create pressure and suction zones in the wind flow and thereby influence the movement of air over and around low structures, such as houses and small office buildings. Heat-absorbing glass and double panes of glass in windows are effective in soaking up over 40 percent of the impinging radiant energy, although in winter such energy-conservation fixtures might work against the homeowner who desires to have the increased transmission of insolation. Consequently, shading devices—especially those that are movable—might be preferable. Given light colors reflect more sunlight than dark colors, white window blinds or shades would provide more protection than dark ones. Of more crucial significance, however, is the location of such shading devices; experiments have demonstrated that an average of about 35 percent in increased protection is afforded when outside, rather than inside, shading devices are used.

Precautionary measures like the following can be taken during a wave of torrid temperatures to help ensure that human health is not jeopardized:

- Pay attention to your body's early signals that heat syndrome is imminent; then slow down and get to a cooler environment. Drink an ample amount of fluids, especially water. Wear lightweight, light-colored clothing to reflect much of the sun's rays. This includes a covering for the top of the head.
- Consume only a modest amount of the foods (like proteins) that accelerate your metabolic heat production and enhance the loss of water from the body.
- Avoid sunburn, since ultraviolet radiation burns significantly retard the ability of the skin to shed excess heat.
- If you must be out in the heat, limit your exposure time. Try to get inside a cool house, store, restaurant, or theater for short spells several times during the day.
- If you discover one or more symptoms of heat syndrome, administer appropriate first aid immediately. Also recognize that the least threatening symptom is *heat asthenia*, a condition characterized by easy fatigue, headaches, a poor appetite, insomnia, profuse sweating, and shallow breathing. Heat cramps are nearly as common as heat asthenia in those individuals who physically exert themselves outdoors in the heat. Ironically, while it is prudent to drink lots of water when the weather is hot and sticky, it may be the intake of large quantities of water without salt that brings on heat cramps.

A prime heat-related risk during the hotter months of the year is exposure of children left, even for a brief time, in an enclosed vehicle. The temperature inside a vehicle with its windows rolled up can soar 20°F in 10 minutes or less—and as much as 50°F in less than an hour—which means someone left inside can experience a temperature of 130°–150°F (54°–66°C) in a mere moment! Children are especially vulnerable to such rapid temperature increases because their body temperature rises at a rate three to five times faster than that of an adult. Some five children, on average, die in Texas each year from vehicle hyperthermia.

To remind motorists of this danger, the National Weather Service regularly uses the slogan, "Beat the Heat, Check the Backseat." Children should never be left unattended in a vehicle, even for a minute. If a child is seen confined to a vehicle in hot weather, one should call 911 immediately. When leaving a vehicle, don't overlook sleeping babies. A good habit to cultivate: keep a stuffed animal in the car seat, then place it in the front next to the driver's seat when an infant or child is put in the car seat. A purse, or brief case, can be left in the back seat as a reminder that you have a child confined there. Ensure your children do not have access to keys or remote-entry devices and instill in them that an auto is never to be used as a play area.

Remember to treat pets in the same way as small children. For many folks, a pet is a family member too.

COMING TO THE RESCUE

Despite going to great lengths to protect one's body from excessive heat and humidity, providing first aid in varying degrees may still be necessary. When a person's skin becomes cool, pale, and clammy with perspiration and the body becomes weak and sustains heat cramps, very likely heat exhaustion has occurred. Other symptoms include nausea and vomiting or merely dizziness and a headache. While such symptoms may not seem so serious, suspected heat exhaustion should be dealt with immediately. Failure to provide treatment quickly could lead to heat stroke, a life-threatening condition. A key first step is to ensure the victim has ceased activity and is moved to a cooler place. Have the person lie down, with the legs raised as much as 12 inches. Spray water or apply a cool, wet cloth to the head and torso. If available, a fan can be used to speed evaporation from the victim's skin. Though the person may be nauseated at first, he or she usually can—and should—take fluids after a period of rest. A sports drink rich in carbohydrates and electrolytes is preferable. Certainly, if the heat exhaustion is severe, medical help should be sought as quickly as possible.

Similar steps can be taken to treat heat cramps, which are uncontrollable muscle spasms that can occur suddenly and be very painful to someone overexposed to heat.

A more serious medical condition, a heat stroke, occurs when intense heat and high humidity lead to the failure of the body's thermoregulatory and cardiovascular systems. In fact, if the temperature of one's body rises significantly, to as much as 106°F (41°C) or higher, permanent damage can occur to sensitive organs, including the brain and spinal cord. Other indications that a full-blown heat stroke has happened include: the pulse is pounding and full, and blood pressure is elevated; weakness, vertigo, nausea, headache, muscle cramps, and profuse sweating (although the sweating stops just prior to the onset of the heat stroke) are felt; and the skin, flushed and pink at first, becomes ashen and purplish. Someone suffering in these ways can be helped by spraying or pouring water on the person; applying ice packs to the person's neck, groin, and armpits; covering the body with a wet sheet while running a fan; and even immersing the person in cool water up to his or her neck. The heat stroke victim should not be made to drink fluids. If the person is unresponsive, the body should be placed on a side in the recovery position to protect the airway.

Delirium, seizure, and even coma are common during heat stroke as well. It is emphasized that if some or all of these symptoms are discerned, the victim has incurred a severe medical disorder and immediate emergency care by a physician is essential. Emergency medical service personnel should be summoned immediately. With early recognition and prompt cooling, the survival rate for a heat stroke victim approaches 90 percent.

The Scourge of Drought

It takes only a few weeks of rainless weather during Texas's hottest months to open the door for drought to return for yet another sequel. Unlike most other weather phenomena, drought is distinctly insidious. It slinks into position slowly and subtly, leaving us one day to realize it has become an intrusive and unwelcome visitor whom we are helpless to dislodge. Day upon endless day, with the last dash of rain a faint memory, the sky is filled with sun while clouds struggle to stay alive. Pastureland is so badly scorched as to be no longer edible for livestock; stock-tank and reservoir levels sag lower with each sun-splashed day; and crops visible as far as the human eye can see wither and wilt into oblivion.

Another reason drought is an enigma is its onset is difficult to recognize. Its effect can be anticipated: crops fail, the price of food skyrockets, water rationing is invoked. Much of the time, it is much easier to identify its effects long after it has become established than to discern its presence while it gradually grows more and more severe. Moreover, because it is commonly used to describe a wide range of different dry-weather conditions, it is difficult to categorize. Depending upon the context in which the word is sometimes used, drought can assume some entirely different meanings. For instance, permanent drought refers to a condition in which precipitation is never sufficient to meet needs, whereas invisible drought suggests a borderline inadequacy of rainfall—not quite enough to satisfy the needs of crops each month—the result being reduced yields at the end of the growing season.

Drought means different things to different people. What defines and quantifies drought depends upon someone's geographical location and vital interests—and the effect that a lack of rain has on those interests. For example, farmers discern the presence of drought when they notice its effects on their crops that can be traced to a lack of moisture during critical periods of the growing season. To them, agricultural drought, or that condition when rainfall and soil moisture are insufficient to support the healthy growth of crops and to prevent extreme crop stress, is the most relevant classification of drought. By contrast, water engineers get concerned about drought when lake levels or stream flows fall to threateningly low levels. Their primary interest is in hydrologic drought, which is a long-term condition of abnormally dry weather that ultimately leads to the depletion of surface and groundwater supplies, the drying up of rivers and streams, and the cessation of spring flows. Suburbanites might not notice the prevalence of drought until water shortages in their community necessitate a cutting back of lawn watering.

If the evidence exists to indicate drought has occurred, how then may it be quantified? Devising an appropriate measure has been a challenge for many years, and solutions offered have been the source of vigorous debate in scholarly circles. Numerous climatic classification schemes and indexes have been formulated to categorize the intensity of drought. One criterion with a lot of utility among analysts for comparing historical droughts is the Palmer Index. With this indicator, the duration and severity of Texas droughts widely separated in both time and space can be evaluated. By taking into account the amount of moisture required to have normal weather for a specific area, the Palmer Index describes departures from this normal condition in terms of a numerical index. Positive values indicate wetter than normal conditions, whereas negative values represent varying intensities of drought. The Palmer Index is the basis in this chapter for categorizing those droughts that have had a major effect on the Texas economy in the past 50 years (table 4.4).

No part of Texas is immune to drought. Texas's proximity to the Great American Desert of the southwestern United States means the state is vulnerable every time the desert expands—and it spreads with some semblance of regularity every few years. Indeed, the western extremity of Texas—where rainfall averages less than 10 inches annually—can be regarded as being on the periphery of this vast desert. All desert regions expand and contract intermittently, so an area on the fringe will be embraced from time to time. The more distant an area is from the edge of a drought region, the less accustomed it is to the long and hurtful dry spell that results when the desert expands to include it. In these unprepared areas—one of which includes most of the western half of Texas—a severe or extreme drought can be nothing short of calamitous. The amount of water extracted from Earth through evaporation and transpiration exceeds by far the meager amounts of rainfall that may accompany a lengthy period of severe or extreme drought. On the other hand, the great desert rarely, if ever, spreads far enough to the east to encompass all of Texas. Even in those years when drought is detected in the eastern sector of the state, rainfall usually is ample enough to negate the amount of moisture yielded through evapotranspiration.

While rainfall deficits are a principal influence on the intensification and spread of a drought, other terrestrial, even extraterrestrial, factors are often involved as well. Since the sun must ultimately be recognized as the sole source of energy that drives our atmospheric machine, it follows that quirks or anomalies in the sun's behavior doubtlessly affect our planet's climate in some fashion. One theory that has gained increasing attention—if not altogether acceptance—is that one solar phenomenon, known as the sunspot, can be linked directly to those prolonged periods of little or no rain on Earth. Sunspots are enormous magnetic storms that erupt within the torrid, gaseous atmosphere of the sun, and they appear to the protected eye on Earth as relatively small, dark areas on the sun's surface. Sunspot activity runs through an irregular cycle, usually lasting around 11 years but sometimes varying in duration between 10 and 15 years. During a cycle, the number of sunspots changes from a minimum to a maximum and then back to a minimum. On an average yearly basis, that number may range from near 0 to as many as 200. Some weather analysts, by matching the sunspot cycles with occurrences of drought on Earth, allege that a definite positive correlation exists between the two phenomena. However, evidence suggesting a definite cause-and-effect relationship between the two is not overwhelming.

A key terrestrial influence on drought in Texas is the vast subtropical high-pressure cell that drifts from the tropics to the midlatitudes

TABLE 4.4
Worst Midsummer Droughts in Texas

Shown is the average statewide Palmer Index for July. The index ends with "exceptional" drought between −4.0 and −5.0.

YEAR	INDEX
2011	−7.32
1956	−7.03
2006	−5.60
1955	−4.94
1971	−4.84

with the transition from spring to summer. As explained earlier, it is this large-scale weather system that, when it becomes entrenched in summer over the southern United States, may produce many days of rainless and searing hot weather. The position and strength of this ridge of dry air are undoubtedly linked to variations in the amount of insolation received from the sun. Another suspected conspirator is El Niño, the uncommonly warm ocean current in the equatorial Pacific that appears around Christmas every four or five years. The influence of the phenomenon may be subtle, but its effect is invariably felt worldwide. Not long after El Niño surfaced in 1982, a horrific drought seized West Texas and inexorably ravaged the area for nearly three years—or until El Niño vanished. Whatever the stimuli, the huge ridge foments drought by settling intransigently over the southern United States and shunting potential rain-producing systems out of the Pacific to the north and east.

Another terrestrial influence on drought occurrences is the eruption of volcanoes, and not necessarily those elsewhere in the United States and in Central America. Nearly invisible clouds of sulfur dioxide gas are injected high into Earth's atmosphere by active volcanoes and become entrapped within the stratosphere, where they encircle the globe and limit the amount of solar insolation reaching Earth's surface. A good example of the potential of volcanic activity to influence the climate is the eruption of the El Chichón volcano in the southern Mexican state of Chiapas in March and April 1982. Within four months of the initial series of volcanic blasts, satellite measurements indicated the massive cloud of sulfuric acid particles had spread over a broad area of at least 20°latitude stretching from Panama into the central Atlantic. While this was happening high in the atmosphere, Texas was enduring one of the driest and hottest summers of the century. Numerous localities in the Texas coastal plain suffered through the driest summer since 1917, and drought rapidly worsened from moderate to severe intensity. At Brownsville—or only about 700 miles (1,125 kilometers) from the El Chichón volcano—temperatures climbed to 90°F (38°C) or above on 118 straight days, the lengthiest string of such torrid weather in the 105-year history of that far southern city. We have yet to find indisputable evidence that the volcanic eruption caused or exacerbated the uncommon warmth that typified the Texas summer of 1982, but the idea that the two phenomena may be related seems too plausible to be dismissed.

Still another contributor to the unfolding and magnification of drought is the insertion into the atmosphere of smoke from various kinds of fires. Each spring farmers in southern Mexico and Central America prepare their fields for another growing season by burning off residue from a prior season. When the subtropical ridge of high pressure aloft edges northward and settles over Texas and the Gulf of Mexico for a week or longer, wind flow around this ridge pulls smoke-filled air from the burning fields into the Texas atmosphere. For days visibilities can be lowered significantly in much of Southern Texas, and the smoke may even be detected farther north. A relative scarcity of rain-producing thunderstorms during the usual peak period for them in late spring has led some researchers to infer that the smoke particles inhibit the coalescence of raindrops in those storms. On many occasions in recent years, towering cumuliform clouds have been observed on spring days with otherwise murky skies, but the only things generated by them have been lightning and gusty winds.

More study is needed on these circumstances to establish a strong correlation between the lack of plentiful thunderstorm rains and the prevalence of smoke.

Harsh droughts are certainly not confined to the hotter half of the year in Texas. In the absence of sumptuous autumn rains (often due to a lack of moisture normally supplied by dying hurricanes that hit the Mexican coastline and move inland over the Chihuahuan plateau), drought can get underway late in the year and flourish over the winter and following spring. Particularly during the cooler half of the year, drought may become established as the result of too frequent intrusions of polar air. Where rain occurs in Texas in autumn, winter, and spring is often governed by where invading cold air from the north or northwest encounters warm, moist air from the Gulf of Mexico. If the air enveloping Texas is not moist enough when a cold front arrives, the front passes without setting off precipitation. If the air covering Texas is only marginally moist, an incursion of cold air will trigger only scattered and mostly light precipitation—not the variety to arrest the formation or spread of a drought. The circulation pattern in the upper atmosphere may be structured such that it does not elicit much of an inflow of low-level air from the Gulf. It matters not that the number of triggering mechanisms (cold fronts) is ample; rather, it is the absence of enough moisture that inhibits the development of rainstorms. Most often in winter, the infusion of cold polar or Arctic air is so frequent that little opportunity is afforded for southerly winds to transport sufficient amounts of moisture back into Texas before the arrival of the next front. The wide variations in typical seasonal precipitation in all regions of Texas, and extremes in rainfall deficits and surpluses sustained in those regions, are evident from data given in appendixes 10–16.

Even that part of Texas closest to the Gulf of Mexico experiences drought, and, according to a growing body of evidence from recent research, the effect of prolonged dry weather can be disastrous to the coastal ecosystem. Drought slows the flow of freshwater into estuaries, for instance, causing the salinity of the estuary to spike from the usual 3–5 parts per thousand to as much as 30 parts, making the water almost as salty as that in the Gulf. Consequently, much of the plant and marine life in these areas where currents from rivers and streams mix with Gulf water can be wiped out if not severely stunted. In larger bodies of water along the Texas coast, such as Galveston Bay, the increase in the brackishness of water can dent the supply of oysters. In one respect, however, the drought can be a blessing in disguise to the coastal ecosystem. In some areas, particularly estuaries, a nonnative plant species that people grow for aquariums, Eurasian watermilfoil, becomes dominant in nondrought years. Because the plant is not tolerant of seawater, it diminishes during times of drought, and native sea grasses return to replace it.

The Worst of the Bad Droughts

Since Texas gained statehood in 1845, no decade has been bereft of at least one serious drought, and several of those droughts are distinguished by a year that numbers among the driest in state history (table 4.5). While rainfall records are scanty for much of the period before and during Reconstruction, anecdotal evidence helps shed light on the occurrence, and recurrence, of several extreme dry spells, nearly all of which were felt most acutely during a torrid summer (table 4.6). Unquestionably, the most calamitous drought to strike Texas during its recorded weather history was the severe-to-extreme drought that afflicted every region of the state from the late 1940s through the mid-1950s. That "super drought" was the most notorious of all not only for its intensity and vast coverage but for its endurance as well. The incipient stage of the drought first developed in late spring of 1949 in the Lower Valley, while in western portions of Texas the drought materialized a few months later in autumn. Several months of deficit rainfall in most of the state promoted the gradual development of a severe drought that was manifested fully in nearly all of Texas by midyear 1951. By the end of the following year, water shortages in many areas had become alarming: Lake Dallas, a critical source of water for many in the Dallas–Fort Worth metropolitan area, stood at only 11 percent of capacity. Generous spring rains in 1953 brought a brief respite from the drought to the northeastern quarter of Texas, but elsewhere the drought relaxed very little. The drought deteriorated to become extreme in the Trans Pecos that year, where rainfall for the whole year amounted to less than 8 inches in many areas. In fact, rainfall was so scanty that Imperial, Texas, measured a paltry 1.95 inches for the whole 12-month period, putting the location among the top ten driest communities in Texas in recorded history (appendix 13).

The 1950s drought, which became the benchmark for assessing all other droughts, grew worse again in 1954 and ultimately peaked in 1956 as the most intense ever. Cattle and sheep raisers battled desperately to survive. Ranges went bare and stock water became critically short or nonexistent on many farms. The flow of many rivers and streams dipped to near or even below record levels. The flow of the Guadalupe River near New Braunfels was deficient in 35 out of 36 months during 1954–1956. Some streams slowed to a trickle, while others ceased to flow or dried up completely. Many wells declined to record levels. Farmers sharply increased the amount of acreage of crops grown under irrigation in an effort to avoid being wiped out altogether. The

TABLE 4.5

Texas's Driest Years

Shown is the statewide average total rainfall (inches) and its percent of normal based on the twentieth-century average of 27.92 inches.

RANK	YEAR	TOTAL INCHES	PERCENT OF NORMAL
1st	1917	14.99	54
2nd	2011	15.18	54
3rd	1956	15.52	56
4th	1954	18.01	65
5th	1910	19.61	70
6th	1963	19.75	71
7th	1901	20.30	73
8th	1948	20.70	74
9th	1951	20.74	74
10th	1988	21.25	76

TABLE 4.6

Texas's Driest Summer Seasons

Shown is the statewide average summer rainfall (inches) and its percent of normal based on the twentieth-century average of 7.59 inches.

RANK	YEAR	TOTAL INCHES	PERCENT OF NORMAL
1st	2011	2.48	33
2nd	1956	3.48	46
3rd	1934	3.73	49
4th	1952	3.84	51
5th	1954	3.95	52
6th	1910	4.29	57

drought reached its utmost worst in the late summer of 1956, when it was gauged on the Palmer Index scale at −6.53 in North Central Texas. Rainfall was especially paltry west of the Pecos, where Presidio registered the least amount—a stunning sum of 1.61 inches—over any year in Texas history (fig. 4.5). Finally, in late winter and spring of 1957, the most devastating drought ever ended abruptly throughout Texas. Rains ranging from "slow soakers" to "gully washers" began falling in February, and within two months all regions in Texas had seen the last vestige of drought erased.

From a national perspective, the so-called Dust Bowl drought heads the list of the worst droughts in American history—but its effect was felt more acutely farther north in the Great Plains. That is not to say it spared the Lone Star State. Farmers who moved to the prairies and plains of Texas in the last few decades of the nineteenth century had plowed under the natural, deep-rooted grasses that they had found there upon their arrival. The grasses, which were capable of surviving prolonged droughts, were replaced by wheat, corn, and cotton, thus baring the topsoil to the mercy of the relentless winds that buffeted Texas and stirred up tons of dust. The first fingers of the Dust Bowl drought crept eastward out of the nation's southwestern desert into the Texas High Plains early in 1933. With the region collecting only about half of the normal rainfall, the drought steadily worsened until it reached extreme magnitude in July 1934. The Dust Bowl drought in the High Plains and the Trans Pecos, both of which were the regions of Texas most adversely affected by the drought, did not ease up perceptibly until appreciable rains came during the summer of 1935. Before the drought finally ended in the High Plains in late summer 1936, thousands of head of livestock had been lost to starvation and suffocation (from the dust). Crops that somehow survived the onslaught were withered and stunted.

One drought that tends to be overlooked, likely because of its separation in time from the present, was the pernicious drought preceding and during World War I. In several respects, it mirrored the landmark drought that would ravage Texas four decades later. It spanned nearly an entire decade (1909–1918) and featured a year (1917) that still stands as the driest year on record in Texas (table 4.5). Though drier than 2011 by a fraction of an inch, the year 1917 was no match to 2011 in terms of being hot. Its summer ranks only 28th on the list of hottest summer seasons, with 2011 topping that list. Like the 1950s drought, the drought of the "teens" ebbed and flowed, easing off for a year or so (1914–1915) when substantial rains gave promise of entirely ending the drought before it had a resurgence in 1916. These two worst statewide droughts also met the same fate: in the wake of bitterly dry years, in 1918 and 1956, both were abruptly quashed by rains that made the following years (1919 and 1957) among the wettest on record!

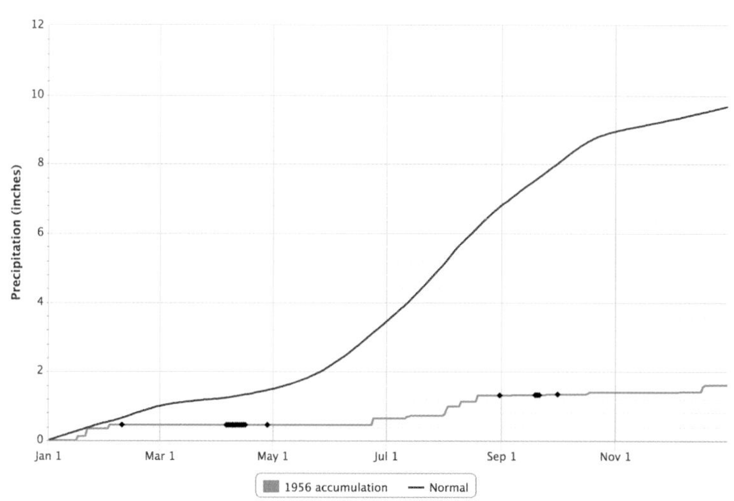

FIG. 4.5 Presidio's meager total of 1.61 inches was the least ever in a single year in Texas. Source: National Climatic Data Center

The exceptional drought in the early years of the current century, fed by the enervating heat described earlier in this chapter, deserves inclusion in the worst droughts to afflict Texas in the modern era. Like its predecessors mentioned earlier, the drought spanned virtually an entire decade and reached its apex during the hottest summer (2011) in history (fig. 4.6). It is distinguished for contributing to 3 of the 10 worst drought years (2011, 2012, 2013) on record in Texas. It followed the pattern of prior bad droughts by easing off after several years of severe drought, thanks to an extraordinarily wet year (2010), but then resumed with unparalleled intensity until it was vanquished by torrential rains that made 2015 one of the three wettest years in state history.

Other very potent, but comparatively short in duration, droughts have left Texas with scars since the granddaddy of them all was erased in 1957. A drought of the magnitude of the horrible 1950s drought—but one not nearly so protracted—gripped West Texas in 1982–1984. Little or no measurable rainfall for many weeks during the spring and summer of 1983 led to the deaths of multitudes of hardy mesquite trees in the Pecos River valley. Cumulative rainfall of only 2 or 3 inches over periods of nine months turned pastures into loathsome dust bowls, and scores of livestock producers were forced to cull their herds dramatically or confront financial ruin. Sometimes droughts have ended when tropical cyclones brought cloudbursts at the end of summer. For instance, Tropical Storm Amelia in 1978 spawned enough heavy rain to quash a severe-to-extreme drought that had tormented the central third of Texas for nearly a year. Unfortunately, Amelia went to alarming excess, dumping too much rain too quickly on the Texas Hill Country, causing devastating flash floods that claimed 33 lives and $50 million in damages.

Drought Forecasting

Those Texans who have wrestled with nasty droughts in semi-arid West Texas for decades are fond of saying, "We are either coming out of a drought—or we're about to go back into one." Its stubborn persistence does give the impression

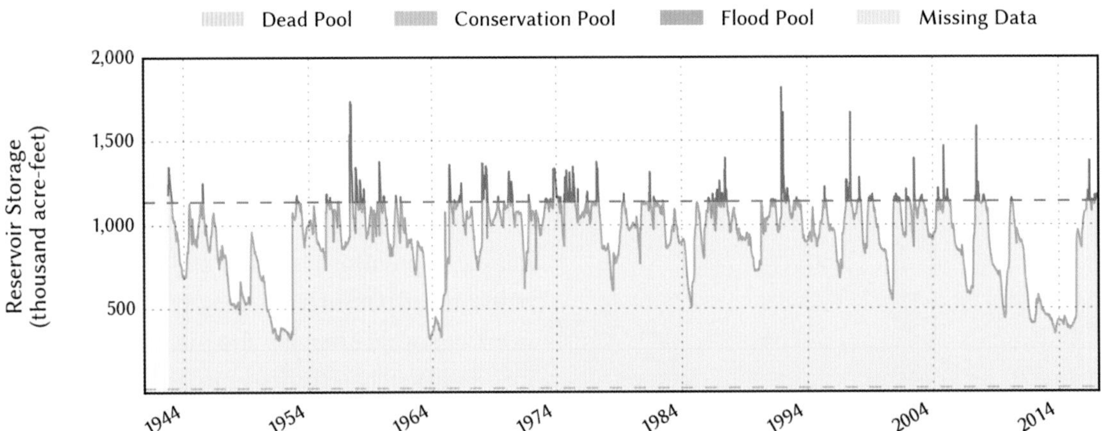

FIG. 4.6 Lake Travis, a key element of the Highland Lakes chain that provides millions with water in central Texas, plunged during the exceptional drought of 2011 to its lowest level (nearly one-third of its capacity) in nearly 50 years. Source: Texas Water Development Board

that the drought will never be gone for long. Regrettably, weather experts are hardly more in harmony about the predictability of drought than they are about its definition. Therein lies a formidable obstacle to forecasting the long-range likelihood that a drought will strike. Weather observers are reluctant to predict the onset, continuation, or cessation of a drought partly because drought is so difficult to define in the first place. What might constitute a drought in one area may not even be a climatological anomaly in another. Disagreement on what constitutes a drought, though, is not the primary reason for our inability to predict accurately droughts well in advance of their occurrence. Rather, our lack of confidence in long-range weather predictions is a reflection of two critical deficiencies. One is deficient information about the behavior of the atmosphere over the oceans and of the upper atmosphere over continents. This inadequacy persists because of the sparseness of upper-air continental stations that monitor conditions in the higher levels of the atmosphere and a paucity of sea-surface weather-sensing platforms.

Second, raising the confidence level of long-range drought forecasts is a daunting challenge because of the complexity of Earth's atmosphere and oceans and scientists' struggles to understand them satisfactorily. Much is yet to be learned about the effect of the sun's rays on the development and movement of the subtropical high-pressure system that dominates Texas's weather for much of every summer and sometimes produces virtually cloudless skies for days if not weeks on end. What is understood even less clearly is the impetus for the strengthening and positioning of this "blocking" ridge of high pressure. Why is the ridge stronger and more assertive in some summers than in others? Once the ridge takes hold, how long will it maintain its grip? What will be required to weaken the system or to get it to shift its position to allow a rain-producing, inclement spell of weather to enter Texas? Adequate answers to these queries continue to be elusive. Obtaining a better grasp of how the sun's volatility influences our weather will surely advance our capacity to foresee and predict accurately the onset and cessation of droughts as well as their intensity. While ample room remains for improving drought forecasts, the modest skill now demonstrated by prognosticators suggests headway is being made in understanding the long-range behavior of Earth's atmosphere. Still, this skill is not so substantial that planners give attention to them with the same confidence as they might with shorter-range outlooks.

5.

Winter's One-Two Punch

Arctic air gushed into the heart of Texas as residents wrapped up their holiday shopping on the eve of Christmas Day 2004, giving them a genuine sense that it really did look a lot like Christmas. As temperatures dipped toward the freezing level, an unusually potent upper-air storm center came spinning out of the Mexican desert toward South Texas, pulling in copious amounts of low- and mid-level moisture from both the Pacific and the Gulf of Mexico. At first, the precipitation at midday was a cold rain, some of which froze on its way to the surface. As more of the rain turned into sleet, roadways slickened from the Rio Grande across the Winter Garden area to the coastal bend. The pile of Arctic air intensified with nightfall, and so did the incoming moisture from lower latitudes. The result was several bands of thunderstorms, many of which pumped out snow, introducing coastal bend residents to an exceedingly rare showing of thunder-snow showers. By nightfall on Christmas Eve, all the precipitation, shaped by an Arctic air mass so intense that dew points stood in the teens, was descending as a monumentally wet snow. When the sun rose on Christmas morning, the scene was mind-blowing to those living on the coastal plain, from Goliad and Aransas Pass to Kingsville and Cotulla. Significant snow accumulations in these parts of Texas are quite rare, and to have enough snow to qualify the event as a "White Christmas" was a new experience for most. The sun shone on a snow cover so thick that volunteer observers needed a yardstick to gauge the depth of it. It was the most snow cover in at least an entire century. Victoria's storm total of 12.5 inches earned the city the unique distinction of having the most substantive White Christmas of any location in the Lone Star State—and Victoria has no other record of snowfall on that day in its history! Corpus Christi's snowfall total of 4.4 inches easily bested the coastal city's five other snow episodes in history, none of which came close to occurring in December. The phenomenal snowstorm's reach even extended to the Lower Valley, where Brownsville's snow cover of 1.5 inches on Christmas morning was only the second time snow has been seen on the ground there in over a century. At least 10 inches was measured in Alice, Beeville, and Goliad, and snow stacked up to over a half foot right up to the coastline, where Port Lavaca and Seadrift recorded 8 inches of snow and Port O'Connor registered 4 inches.

Nature's Immaculate Conception

Like the human fingerprint, the unique signature of a snowflake has confounded observers for centuries. The evolution of a snow crystal most often gets its start from a solid particle (known as a freezing nucleus) serving as a platform to which water vapor is attracted. These particles can vary from a tiny pollen or minute speck of dust from a cornfield to a salt particle from the sea, particulate matter from the exhaust of an automobile, or even a fragment spun off from another snow crystal. If the cloud environment is right—that is, if the temperature is ideal and if enough vapor is present—then a snow crystal likely will grow from the sublimation of tiny cloud water droplets onto the nucleus. The process of sublimation is one in which the water vapor condenses into ice on the surface of the host particle without first passing through the liquid phase. Regardless of the form a snow crystal initially assumes, its ultimate shape will be determined by such factors as changes in the pressure, temperature, and humidity of the air in which it moves. In fact, so many variables are involved that it is very likely that no two snowflakes in a yard or field are identical. Yet all snowflakes have the same origin, consisting of six-sided (or six-pointed) crystals of ice that grow by consuming water vapor through the sublimation process.

The stunning nature of the Christmas snowstorm of 2004 accentuates that almost invariably the heaviest snowfalls featuring huge, sticky snowflakes occur when the air temperature is near or only a few degrees below the freezing level. In fact, quite often in Texas, snow occurs at the surface even before the air temperature measured at human-eye level dips to 32°F, principally because the stratus deck producing the flakes is hundreds of feet above the land surface and has a temperature much colder. Plentiful snows happen, obviously, when moisture is abundant, and relatively warmer air (28°–32°F [−2°–0°C]) holds more moisture than colder air (24°F [−4°C]). At −10°F (−23°C) saturated air contains only a small fraction of the water vapor contained by saturated air with a temperature of 24°F. As the air temperature falls far below freezing, ice crystals are drier and do not bond well with neighbors, settling out as tiny single crystals rather than aggregating as large snowflakes. That explains why some generations of Texans have held to the theory that it can—and does—get too cold to snow. Fact is, the colder the temperature becomes, the lesser is the amount of snow produced.

An awareness of how a snow crystal forms and later becomes a segment of a larger snowflake has spawned efforts to alter these processes through cloud seeding to benefit humanity. The aim of this form of weather modification is to furnish additional snow and, hence, augment the amount of water reaching the surface of water-deficient areas of the country. No cloud seeding for snowfall augmentation has yet been attempted in Texas, but the seeding of stratiform clouds over mountain ranges is now a routine operation in a number of Rocky Mountain states. While the magnitude of results varies, in nearly every state where seeding has been practiced over several winters increases in snowpack have been documented in those regions where seeding was concentrated.

Recipe for a Texas Snowstorm

How memorable or unexceptional a snowstorm in Texas becomes depends on a lot of influences. The most critical determinants are the strength, position, and rate of movement of a low-pressure cell (low) often found in the middle levels of the atmosphere. This upper-air storm, embedded in a strong circulation pattern of high-level westerly winds, propels cold polar or Arctic air into Texas while also importing mid- and high-level moisture into the state from the Pacific Ocean and Gulf of Mexico. As a general rule, if the upper-air low maintains its vigor, or intensifies, while sliding far enough south to take it across some portion of Texas, the snow that begins falling likely will last for some time, and chances are good that accumulations will be substantial. Heaviest snow depths will occur in a swath that approximates the track of the center of the "upper low." On the other hand, if the low "lifts" out of the southern Rockies and moves on a more northward track that misses Texas, then snow, if it materializes, probably will be inconsequential and short-lived.

More specifically, the brewing of a significant snow event is recognized this way: a thick cloud cover develops prior to the passage of a cold front, and drizzle or light rain may fall for several hours; with the wind gradually shifting from southerly to westerly, the temperature begins to plummet; once the wind veers more northerly and the temperature falls more rapidly, light rain or drizzle changes into either sleet or freezing rain (this spell of frozen precipitation may last from less than an hour to several hours, depending upon the nature and rate of movement of the invading air mass); thoroughfares become glazed with a thin sheet of ice, and travel becomes increasingly hazardous; finally, the intruding cold air chills the temperature aloft enough to allow freezing of the cloud water, at which time snow forms. When snow first begins to fall, it may be mixed with sleet, freezing rain, or just a cold, liquid rain. Most often, the other forms of precipitation do not persist if snow continues to fall for a period lasting one or a few hours.

An episode of snow is defined by varying intensities of the rate of snowfall. The National Weather Service (NWS) reports a very light snow when scattered flakes do not completely cover or at least wet an exposed surface. Snow is regarded as light when the visibility caused by the falling snow is equal to or greater than ⅝ of a mile; moderate when the visibility is between 5/16 and ⅝ of a mile; and heavy when the visibility is less than 5/16 of a mile. When snowfall sticks to the surface, the amount of accumulation is measured by many of the more than 600 cooperative observing stations maintained in Texas by the NWS (table 5.1). These snowfall measurements customarily are made once daily, most often around dawn, and the data are published in the US Department of Commerce's *Climatological Data: Texas*. The NWS defines a heavy snow as either (a) an accumulation of 4 inches or more within 12 hours or (b) an accumulation of 6 inches or more in 24 hours.

In many winters, a snowstorm roaring from the lee side of the Rockies goes berserk. The storm need not generate prodigious amounts of snow; rather, it is the strong winds blowing the

TABLE 5.1
Snowiest Texas Cities

Average annual snowfall (inches) based on the 1981–2010 record.

CITY	INCHES
Stratford	20.6
Borger	20.3
Dalhart	18.9
Follett	18.6
Miami	17.9
Amarillo	17.8
Umbarger	17.1
Canadian	16.5
Hereford	16.0
Panhandle	16.0

snow that reduce visibilities and create hazards for travelers. A blizzard can strike more than once in some winters, but most are confined to the Panhandle and High Plains of Texas. A full-blown blizzard is rare elsewhere in Texas. Specifically, a blizzard is a severe wintry weather condition in which strong winds (with speeds of at least 35 miles per hour [mph]) bear enough snow in the air to limit the visibility to less than ¼ mile for a period lasting at least three hours. Often in a blizzard, the "blinding" snowstorm limits visibilities to less than a small fraction of a mile, creating "white-out" conditions. One example of how near-zero visibilities can be treacherous is the pileup of over 200 vehicles on Interstate Highway 40 near Amarillo during a blizzard on November 24, 1992. Amazingly, there were no fatalities or injuries from the accident.

A severe blizzard, while less common than its lesser brethren, is even more abrasive, as the term suggests. For a blizzard to qualify as such, winds must be or exceed 45 mph, the air temperature equal to or less than a bone-chilling 10°F (−12°C), and visibilities lowered to near zero by a heavy snow. Severe blizzards are not uncommon in the Panhandle, the number averaging no more than one or two in some winters and none in others. Almost always, blizzard conditions persist for less than a day—and frequently only for a few hours. Nonetheless, near-zero visibility can wreak havoc on motorists navigating highways. While ground blizzards are more common north of Texas, they can happen in the Panhandle. In this circumstance, blowing snow can hug the ground, covering the surface in an undulating layer of snow and causing motorists to become stranded off the road with no notion of where the road went! Areas from Colorado to Nebraska and the Dakotas install snow fences that run for many miles to protect motorists from drifting snow over roadways. Using snow plows to clear roads and highways can be far more expensive than erecting fences to intercept the snow. Yet these events are so uncommon in Texas that such fences are not widespread. Sometimes, the topography influences where heaviest snow covers occur—as the post-Christmas blizzard of 2015 illustrates (fig. 5.1).

On a perpetual basis, the NWS monitors closely the development of winter storms and issues statements and advisories to forewarn the public of impending and potentially hazardous weather. A winter storm watch covers the possible occurrence of the following weather elements, either separately or in combination: blizzard conditions, heavy snow (or just light snow in areas where snow is rare), the accumulation of freezing rain or freezing drizzle, and heavy sleet. A watch gives a longer advance notice of the potential for the occurrence of a winter storm event than does a warning; for this reason, a watch has somewhat less chance of verification.

FIG. 5.1 Visible satellite imagery reveals the extent of a snow cover in the state's northern sector from the post-Christmas blizzard of 2015—with heaviest snowfall above the Caprock. (Elsewhere in Texas is enshrouded in clouds.) Source: National Weather Service

A *winter storm warning* notifies the public of a high probability that severe winter weather will occur. This severe winter weather entails the same elements mentioned in conjunction with a winter storm watch. Whereas a watch is intended to alert the public of the possibility of bad wintry weather, a warning is notice that snowy or icy weather has actually materialized or is in the process of evolving and that the public should take necessary precautions. The NWS even may issue specialized advisories intended to forewarn particular segments of the economy. One such statement is a stock raisers' advisory, which usually describes inclement weather that does not constitute a serious enough threat to warrant the issuance of a winter storm warning. The stock raisers' advisory typically contains information for ranchers or livestock owners that helps them protect their stock.

Air Too Cold to Snow

A winter without measurable snowfall in the Texas High Plains is a rarity, since this is the region where snow events are almost always longer and accumulations heavier than anywhere else in Texas (tables 5.1, 5.2, 5.3, 5.4, 5.5). Other parts of Texas are spared significant snowfall in most winters, although virtually every region of the state has had a few episodes of stunningly great accumulations (figs. 5.2, 5.3, 5.4). The snowfall history for Amarillo spans over 125 years, and in no year have Amarillo residents been spared at least one measurable snow. In fact, the least amount of snowfall in any cold season for the central Panhandle city is 0.5 inch (1950). The Panhandle experiences at least 5 inches of snow every winter and early spring over 90 percent of the time. The region is also the first to record a snow accumulation in the autumn—and the last in the spring. In fact, snow on the ground there has been documented as early as the end of September and as late as the first week in May (tables 5.6, 5.7)! For folks living in the southern half of Texas, a cold rain is far more common than frozen precipitation. That is because the pile of cold air, by the time it spreads out all the way to the coastal plain of Texas, is too shallow to foster frozen precipitation. Cold air plunging southward into Texas behaves much like a large mound of sand when dumped on a flat surface. The sand spreads out in all directions, but the farther the spread of the sand, the more shallow is the depth of it on the periphery of the pile.

TABLE 5.2
Most One-Day Snow Accumulations on Record

LOCATION	INCHES	DATE
Plainview	24.0	Feb 4, 1956
Pampa	20.0	Mar 24, 1987
Amarillo	19.0	Feb 25, 2013
El Paso	14.5	Dec 18, 1987
Perryton	14.0	Dec 19, 1911
Dalhart	12.5	Jan 21, 1983
Lubbock	12.1	Feb 20, 1961
Childress	11.0	Dec 2, 1971
Midland	10.6	Jan 9, 2012
Wichita Falls	9.8	Jan 18, 1925

TABLE 5.3
Greatest Snowfall from a Single Snowstorm

LOCATION	INCHES	DATE
Plainview	30.0	Feb 1956
El Paso	22.4	Dec 1987
Pampa	22.0	Feb 1971
Amarillo	20.9	Feb 2013
Perryton	18.0	Feb 1964
Childress	16.9	Jan 1987
Lubbock	16.9	Jan 1983
Dalhart	16.1	Dec 1997
Texarkana	12.0	Feb 1982
Wichita Falls	9.9	Mar 1989

When mounds of very cold air from Canada spill across the Great Plains into Texas, points farther north in the state usually are covered by a much greater "thickness" of cold air than are locales in the south. The thickness of cold air over a given locality determines whether the precipitation that falls to the surface is snow, sleet, freezing rain, or just cold rain. To get snowflakes to the surface, the source of the precipitation—the overshadowing deck of clouds—must lie within the newly arrived mass of cold air (assuming the temperature of the air at that level is at or below freezing). Otherwise, if the dome of cold air is too shallow, the clouds bearing the moisture lie above it, where temperatures are above freezing. Then, the water droplets in the clouds obviously do not freeze into snowflakes. If the cold air is thick enough, precipitation falling as rain from

TABLE 5.4
Maximum Snow Depth Ever Observed

LOCATION	INCHES	DATE
Plainview	30.0	Feb 5, 1956
Borger	24.0	Feb 4, 1964
Miami	21.0	Feb 22, 1971
Lipscomb	20.0	Feb 22, 1971
Silverton	19.0	Feb 5, 1956
Canadian	19.0	Feb 21, 1971
Dumas	18.0	Feb 7, 1964
Sanford	18.0	Feb 26, 2013
Amarillo	17.0	Feb 26, 2013
Lubbock	17.0	Jan 21, 1983

TABLE 5.5
Most Consecutive Days with Measurable Snowfall

NUMBER	LOCATION	DATES
6	Vega	Feb 4-10, 1956
6	Amarillo	Feb 10-15, 1895
		Jan 24-29, 1948
6	Borger	Jan 31-Feb 5, 1983
5	Dalhart	Dec 6-10, 1960
5	Dumas	Jan 16-20, 1987
5	Borger	Jan 24-28, 1949
5	Pampa	Jan 25-29, 1949

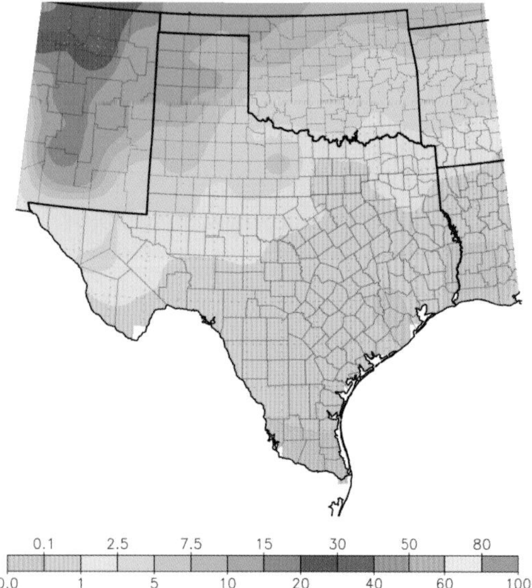

FIG. 5.2 Average winter snowfall. Source: Midwestern Regional Climate Center

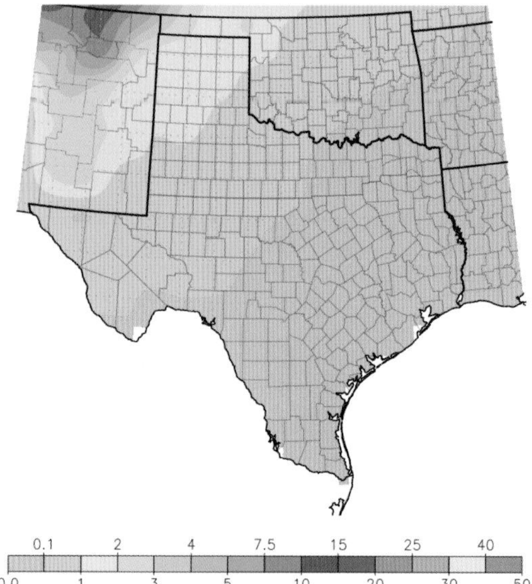

FIG. 5.3 Average autumn snowfall. Source: Midwestern Regional Climate Center

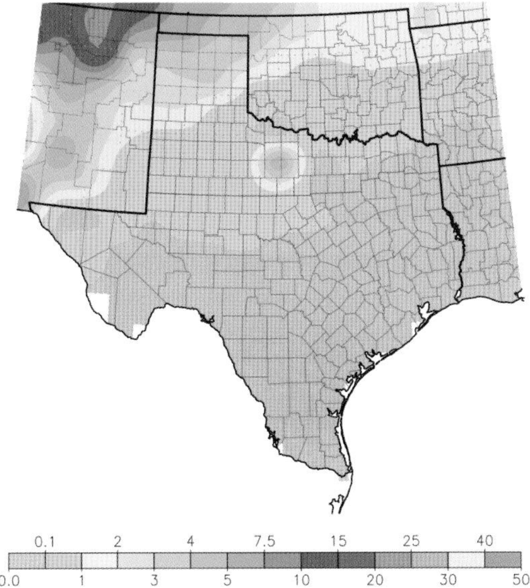

FIG. 5.4 Average spring snowfall. Source: Midwestern Regional Climate Center

TABLE 5.6
Earliest Dates for Measurable Snow Accumulation

LOCATION	DATE	INCHES	NORMAL[1]
Amarillo	Sep 29, 1984	0.3	Nov 23
Dalhart	Oct 8, 1970	5.0	Nov 28
Lubbock	Oct 17, 1999	0.6	Dec 11
El Paso	Oct 28, 1980	1.0	Dec 20
Abilene	Oct 29, 1993	0.3	Dec 25
Midland	Oct 30, 1993	0.6	Dec 20
Wichita Falls	Oct 30, 1993	1.0	Dec 31
San Angelo	Nov 8, 1955	1.5	Jan 3
Waco	Nov 12, 1976	0.7	Jan 25
Dallas	Nov 13, 1976	3.1	Jan 10
Texarkana	Nov 25, 2013	0.1	Jan 11

[1] Normal is a 30-year average date for the period 1981-2010.

TABLE 5.7
Latest Dates for Measurable Snow Accumulation

LOCATION	DATE	INCHES	NORMAL[1]
Dalhart	May 6, 1999	0.1	Mar 17
Amarillo	May 3, 1978	0.5	Mar 18
Lubbock	Apr 12, 1980	1.4	Mar 2
El Paso	Apr 12, 1980	2.0	Jan 25
Wichita Falls	Apr 8, 1973	0.8	Feb 6
Waco	Apr 8, 2007	0.1	Feb 9
San Angelo	Apr 7, 2007	0.9	Feb 3
Midland	Apr 7, 2007	1.5	Feb 7
Abilene	Apr 5, 1996	9.3	Feb 14
Dallas	Mar 21, 2010	1.4	Feb 4
Texarkana	Mar 21, 1968	0.1	Feb 6

[1] Normal is a 30-year average date for the period 1981-2010.

the cloud layer will freeze on the way down, and the result is sleet at the surface. Or, if the precipitation does not freeze during its descent, perhaps the cold air has been around long enough to freeze the ground so that the rain, upon impact, turns into ice. In that instance, a potentially hazardous condition of freezing rain (or drizzle) is set in motion. Even if initially the layer of cold air is not thick enough to support the formation of snow, snow may materialize later on if a reinforcement of Arctic air enters the state from the north.

Snow's Contribution to the Environment

The moisture and valuable nitrates that a bountiful snowfall supplies can be of immeasurable value to the prairie or High Plains farmer. Other nutritious elements such as potassium and sulphates, whose sources are atmospheric gases, dust, and ocean spray, as well as industrial

FIG. 5.5 Snow plows largely are confined to the Texas Panhandle, where the snow cover in most winters yields melt water that is substantive enough to replenish soil moisture. Source: Texas Department of Transportation

pollution, are delivered to the ground by the falling snow. Moreover, a blanket of snow also provides a degree of warmth to the soil, holding in the heat emanating from Earth's crust and warding off the chill of a frosty air mass. During much of winter in the High Plains of Texas, when the region is without a snow cover, the soil may be frozen to a depth of several inches. This bare soil sustains large fluctuations in temperature during the course of a day and a night, for it may be heated by direct sunlight for a short while in daytime, then sheltered by an intermittent cloud cover, and ultimately allowed to cool steadily with the setting of the sun. A layer of snow, however, brings moderation to these changes in temperature and also keeps the minimum soil temperature higher than it otherwise would be. At least one study has revealed that a snow cover of 6 inches ensures that frost penetrates less than an inch into the soil, while a field without the protection afforded by a snow blanket may be frozen to a depth of 6–12 inches. Snow can be advantageous to the grower in that, depending upon the hardiness of the plants or crops, it may limit winterkill or stunted growth.

While most snowstorms affecting the Texas Plains yield only modest amounts of snowfall, the quantity of water supplied to the soil often can be appreciable. Snow is especially welcome in this sector of the state, for it is in winter that the High Plains sustains its seasonal precipitation minimum. Much of the water equivalent gauged during winter at various weather stations in the region stems from snowfall. For instance, it is common for snow to constitute at least half of the total water equivalent of about 0.5 inch of precipitation that is normal in January for cities like Dumas, Miami, and Spearman. The adage that 10 inches of snow are needed to supply the equivalent of 1 inch of liquid water usually—but not always—applies to the semi-arid High Plains. Since some of the snow that occurs in this northernmost sector is of the "dry" variety, some 6 inches of the crystalline substance often are required to give 0.5 inch of water to the soil.

A key consideration in how beneficial a snow cover may be is the rate at which snow melts. If the snow falls on soil and a plant cover that have relatively warm temperatures (i.e., readings at least several degrees above freezing), melting of the snow begins immediately. However, if the ground and the layer of air next to it have temperatures at or below freezing, the delay in snow melting may last several hours or even a number of days in places such as the Texas Panhandle (fig. 5.5). How much of the snow cover contributes to runoff depends upon the terrain and soil characteristics as well as the rate at which snow melts. Another critical factor is the rate of sublimation. In the semi-arid Texas High Plains, where the relative humidity of the lower atmosphere is often quite low in the wake of a snowstorm, a substantial amount of the snow cover is lost to the air through this process.

A blanket of snow is erased much more readily by a warm, dry wind than by sunshine. If the wind happens to be quite arid, then much of the water content of the snow cover is carried away into the atmosphere and very little enters the soil. Sunlight is not a major factor in melting snow because of the high albedo, or reflective power, of a snow cover; in other words, snow tends to reflect nearly all the incoming solar rays so that sunshine contributes very little to melting the snow. Yet another factor in snowmelt runoff is the temperature of the soil underneath the snow cover. If the soil is frozen, there is very little melting and runoff of water under the layer of snow. In Texas, subsurface soil temperatures usually do not remain at or below freezing but for a few days at a time. Consequently, the melting process is active most of the time. Since the process is a slow one, most of the melted snow enters the ground to become groundwater rather than runoff.

For all the positives that a snow cover can mean to farmers, it also can be a nemesis to them. Snow made into tall drifts by strong winds can inhibit livestock owners from reaching their herds to feed and care for them. The blizzard that struck the western third of Texas on Christmas weekend 2015 exposed dairy cattle and their offspring to extreme cold, resulting in the loss of hundreds and the concomitant scarcity of milk and other dairy products. Snow mold is a plague loathed by cereal growers. More than occasionally, when a snow comes early to soil that is not frozen, various types of fungus become active and threaten young crops. These fungi thrive from the ample moisture supplied by the snow and from temperatures that are maintained near—but above—the freezing level. Most of the time, plants are affected only modestly; even still, they may later respond only feebly to the warmth of spring because their leaves have been blighted by a deficiency of nitrogen. As a result, harvesting is delayed and the containment of weeds becomes more of a formidable challenge.

Epic Snowstorms of Yesteryear

Winters have buffeted parts of Texas with especially ferocious snowstorms on numerous occasions (tables 5.5, 5.6). The most prolific snowstorm in Texas history smothered the High Plains for a week in February 1956, snuffing out the lives of 20 persons and snarling all forms of transportation with snow drifts many feet high. Snow fell in some areas for as many as 92 consecutive hours. Hundreds of motorists had to be extricated from stranded autos by the National Guard and train crews, and snow-removal operations continued for nine days after the snowy siege ended. The severe cold wave deposited a record 61 inches of snow at Vega over a six-day period and—in a single day—a record 24 inches at Plainview. Amazingly, farther north in the Panhandle, where snowfalls are usually heaviest, a scanty 3 inches fell at Dalhart. Another blizzard a year later—in March 1957—had similarly devastating repercussions on Panhandle residents. The blizzard raged for three days, ranking as the third most significant weather event affecting the Texas Panhandle in the twentieth century. Heavy snow of nearly 1 foot, when whipped by 80-mph winds, caused drifts as high as 30 feet, paralyzing the whole region, in which 10 deaths resulted and 4,000 people were marooned. Many communities were isolated without power or means of communication for days. Ironically, both the

1956 and 1957 blizzards came near the end of the worst drought to plague Texas in modern times.

Other notably nasty blizzards have occurred smack in the middle of similarly bone-dry periods. The blizzard of 1934, during the infamous Dust Bowl drought, was noteworthy on two accounts: it came well beyond the typical time frame for such events—in the last week of March—and it was particularly intense, unloading nearly 2 feet of snow on Amarillo (or much more than the city normally collects in an entire winter) in only 23 hours! One of the longest-lasting blizzards, of some 84 hours in duration, pounded the eastern portion of the Panhandle even later in the spring (April 6–8) in 1938, when hurricane-force winds were logged at Pampa and 20-foot snowdrifts were observed.

Whereas the February 1956 snowstorm was extraordinarily prolific, the whole winter of 1982–1983 distinguished itself as one of the most protracted snow seasons of all time (table 5.7). A trio of cold waves in December 1982 produced a record amount of 18.2 inches of snow (and an all-time-high melted-precipitation total of 2.61 inches) at moisture-starved El Paso, while the following month bestowed a mammoth 25.3 inches of snow at Lubbock—16 inches of which fell in one 24-hour period. Then a near-record sum of 13–18 inches blanketed the Panhandle in February, thereby closing out a winter that, surprisingly, was not an uncommonly chilly season in most of Texas.

An intense blizzard that cost livestock owners dearly blasted the Panhandle in February 1971. Fierce 60-mph winds whipped up snowdrifts as high as 12 feet. Two young men died from asphyxiation while huddled in their automobile a mere 400 feet from shelter at a campground, and the body of an older man was found buried in a snowbank in Amarillo. A 6-engine, 90-car freight train balled up in a massive snowdrift and derailed near Borger the day after the great blizzard ended. Thirteen thousand cattle died during the ordeal, with most of them either smothering or being trampled to death as a result of their bunching together to stay warm. Three thousand hogs also perished, and overall livestock losses totaled $3 million.

While the lion's share of historic snowstorms belongs to the High Plains of Texas, other sectors of the state can point to extraordinary snow events, with the Christmas Day snowstorm of 2004 in the state's coastal plain heading the list. Few winter storms in this century have had as much effect on the farming economy of central and eastern Texas as the far-flung, severe snow-and-ice storm of January 8–11, 1973. A frigid blast of bitterly cold Arctic air knifed through Texas and far into the Gulf of Mexico, leaving a blanket of snow as deep as 6 inches in the piney woods of East Texas and 3 to 4 inches on Galveston Island. The numbing cold cost cattle owners $25 million from the loss of 150,000 head of cattle and another $25 million because of the surviving cattle losing weight. In the Texas Hill Country, the combination of an icy wind, sleet, and snow destroyed 25,000 turkeys, many of which were fully grown. Fruit and ornamental trees in the Upper Coast were damaged heavily, and cotton losses were substantial. Oddly, even though temperatures in the Lower Valley plunged far into the 20s, damage to the citrus crop was minimal, in no small way resulting from the hardiness acquired by the trees from previous cold spells that winter and from an abundance of moisture in the soil.

The plateaus of West Texas and the Hill Country bear scars from occasional, memorable snowstorms. The winter of 1984–1985 will long be remembered as the time not one but three snowstorms blitzed across the Edwards Plateau and deposited record-shattering snow cover at the foot of the escarpment. The most notable of the three dumped more than 1 foot of snow in and around San Antonio and along the Rio Grande at Eagle Pass. The snow was so substantial that its weight caused numerous carport roofs, storefront canopies, and the rooftops of several older buildings to collapse. The storm was far reaching, blanketing the scenic Big Bend with at least 0.5 foot of snow and the Davis Mountains with almost 1 foot, while merely dusting the northern half of the state.

A few major snowstorms have struck parts of Texas long before, or after, the traditional run of the winter season. Of note, not because of inordinately large snowfall accumulations but rather their untimeliness, are several autumn and spring snowstorms that smote the Panhandle of Texas as early as October and as late as May. An extraordinarily early and intense winter-like storm surged out of the Rockies on October 30, 1979, and supplied the northern extremity of Texas with 50-mph winds and snow depths of 3–6 inches. More than 9,000 cattle perished from exposure, costing livestock owners at least $3.5 million; about $1 million worth of grain sorghum was destroyed. Weather annals reveal that a snowstorm struck the Panhandle as early as October 8, 1970, although stock and crop losses from that modest blizzard were not of the magnitude of the mid-autumn storm of 1979. By contrast, the most memorable late-spring snowstorm left snowflakes as big as half-dollars and in depths of as much as 0.5 foot in the northern periphery of the Panhandle on May 2–3, 1978. Twelve inches of snow at Stratford nearly doubled the amount ever observed previously in May in that city. The heavy snowfall that struck Stratford was just one of a bizarre series of events illustrating the vagaries of Texas Panhandle weather. Just one day after the 12-inch snow coated the city, with temperatures only in the 40s a massive thunderstorm pushed through, generating a tornado and pummeling the town with 3-inch hail and a slashing rain.

TABLE 5.8
El Niño and Snowy Winters

Average snow accumulation (inches) during El Niño years compared with normal (1981-2010).

CITY	EL NIÑO	AVERAGE
Amarillo	22.3	16.2
Lubbock	10.6	8.4
El Paso	7.1	5.1
Wichita Falls	5.2	4.0
Midland	5.0	4.5
Dallas-Fort Worth	3.1	2.6

The Chance of Snow

With any snowfall dependent upon the depth of polar or Arctic air invading Texas, the closer a locale is to the source regions of these air masses (i.e., the Rocky Mountains and the central Great Plains states), the better the chance of a meaningful snow accumulation. Furthermore, the availability of moisture from the eastern Pacific and Gulf of Mexico are key determinants of snowstorm possibilities, as is the presence—or absence—of an El Niño in the tropical Pacific (table 5.8). Longtime snowfall statistics indicate that inhabitants of the Panhandle and adjacent Red River valley can expect at least one appreciable snow accumulation every winter. In fact, the issue is not whether but how often and how much. Farther south, in the state's midsection, the likelihood of snow is markedly reduced.

Average annual snowfall totals for various cities tell only part of the story (see appendix 17). With just over 20 inches of snow on average each cold season, locales closest to the Oklahoma border garner the most snow. Caution is due, however, in using snowfall averages. These averages are strictly arithmetic sums of observed snow accumulations for a given period divided by the length of that period—they are nothing more than mathematical means. To say the average amount of snow in January in Dallas is 1 inch is not to suggest that in any year in January there is a strong likelihood that Dallas will collect about an inch of snow. That average value of 1 inch is the mathematical mean of snowfall totals registered over a 30-year period; in many months of January no snowfall was observed, whereas in others totals of 3–4 inches or more were measured. What is true of Dallas's snowfall history is also valid for many other areas of Texas: some years afford one or several snowfall accumulations that are highly appreciable, while numerous other years elapse without even a trace of snow (tables 5.9, 5.10). Only in the northwestern quarter of Texas, where snowfall accumulations occur every year, can some importance be placed in the average snowfall value for a particular locale. Even in those instances, the variance about the mean is sizable.

Winters in which some sector of Texas other than the Panhandle receives the most substantial amount of snow are exceedingly few. In the Panhandle since 1900, only a few winter seasons have featured only a few snow events with the cumulative snowfall amounting to a few inches. The winter of 1950 was the leanest bearer of snow of the twentieth century, for it yielded, in total, 1 inch or less in most of the Panhandle. Ordinarily, snowfall in this northern extremity of the state is not confined to the winter season. More often than not, at least one storm will deposit one or several inches of snow in November, and seldom does March pass without at least one snowy spell. Snow also can be seen on the ground as late as April, particularly in the northern reaches of the Panhandle, in one out of every three years. About an equal amount of snow can be expected, on average, in each of

TABLE 5.9
Most Snow Accumulation in One Season[1]

LOCATION	AMOUNT	YEARS
Amarillo	47.9	1982-1983
Dalhart	47.1	1982-1983
Lubbock	41.2	1982-1983
Guadalupe Mtns NP	37.3	2009-2010
El Paso	35.0	1982-1983
Wichita Falls	20.0	1904-1905
Midland	19.5	2011-2012
Abilene	18.4	1918-1919
San Antonio	15.9	1984-1985
Dallas	14.1	1977-1978

1 A season extends from October to the following April.

TABLE 5.10
Most Snowfall in Any Winter[1]

LOCATION	AMOUNT	YEAR
Amarillo	19.0	2012-2013
El Paso	14.5	1987-1988
Pine Springs	14.0	1987-1988
San Antonio	13.2	1984-1985
Lubbock	12.1	1960-1961
Big Bend NP	12.0	1985-1986
Fort Worth	11.3	2009-2010
Midland	10.6	2011-2012
San Angelo	10.0	1918-1919

1 Winter includes the months of December through February.

the three months of winter (December, January, and February). In this region where, characteristically, at least a half-dozen significant snowfalls occur every winter, accumulations of snow are more common than ice.

To the south, in the South Plains, and to the east, in the Low Rolling Plains, annual snowfall totals are appreciably less than in the Panhandle. However, rare is the winter that does not yield at least one snowfall of several inches. Snow accumulations average from 5 to 9 inches from November through March in the Low Rolling Plains, while in the southern High Plains, in the vicinities of Plainview and Lubbock, average seasonal amounts are a little more than that. Snow is likely to be the heaviest in late January and early February, and the number of days with snow is approximately the same for both months.

Owing in part to insufficient moisture in the atmosphere and to the high elevation of the terrain, snowfall is significantly more sporadic in the area west of the Pecos River. Dense Arctic air, like water, flows with much greater ease downslope than upslope. Consequently, the bulk of an invading mass of very cold Arctic air flows south and eastward into the central and eastern sectors of the state, while the higher elevations in the west receive only a relatively thin layer. On those few occasions, accumulations typically amount to 2–5 inches in the northern and central sections of the Trans Pecos. Once in a decade, the snow blanket in the Guadalupe and Davis Mountains will be as much as 6–12 inches. One portion of the Trans Pecos almost always untouched by snowstorms is the Presidio area, where measurable snow cover can be anticipated only once or twice in every other decade.

Most of the Edwards Plateau and North Central and East Texas receives one or several spells of snowfall every winter, and these last only a day or so with amounts almost always a few inches at most. These regions usually serve as the boundary between snow to the north and ice or cold rain to the south. Ice is more common than snow for residents of South Central Texas and the Upper Coast. Any snowfall accumulation of 1 inch or more is no more common than once every three to five years. Snow is even more scarce farther south in Southern Texas.

Snow cover in the Lower Valley is, at best, a once or twice in a lifetime experience. Flurries may be seen once—or possibly twice—in every decade, but if any of the snow sticks to the ground, the accumulation is almost invariably too thin to be measured. Nonetheless, this tip of Texas closest to the Equator has had a couple of noteworthy snowfalls since weather records were begun more than 100 years ago. The most recent appreciable snowfall at Brownsville, however, came before the turn of the twentieth century. Newspaper accounts reveal that a 6-inch snow smothered Texas's southernmost metropolis in mid-February 1895. Those same records show that 4 inches of snow fell in the city in 1866. Sleet or freezing rain is more common than snowfall in the Lower Valley, but even those varieties of frozen precipitation are rare. The heaviest glaze on record in the Lower Valley accompanied a bitter cold wave in late winter of 1951; ice accumulated to as much as 1.5 inches in many places during a six-day period ending on February 3.

Ice Storms—Always a Thumb Down

If given a choice, most Texans would prefer a sumptuous snowstorm instead of a crackling ice storm. Freezing rain and sleet are more slippery than snow and have a propensity to cling to every object they touch. Yet, in much of the state, icy weather is as common as snow. The dreaded sleet, also called ice pellets, occurs when rain from a layer of relatively warm (above freezing) air aloft falls through a layer of cold air (subfreezing) near the ground. The falling raindrops do not turn into snow but rather into grains or pellets of ice. Closely akin to sleet is freezing rain, which is rain that falls through the lower atmosphere in liquid form but freezes upon impact to form a coating of glaze upon the ground and on exposed objects. To have freezing rain, the surface struck by the falling drops initially must be at or below freezing and, furthermore, the drops themselves must be supercooled. It is common, particularly in the northern third of Texas, for freezing rain to be a transient condition between the occurrence of rain and sleet or snow.

FIG. 5.6 In much of Texas, ice is dreaded more than snow because of the damage caused to trees and power lines. Source: Texas Department of Transportation

On many of those infrequent occasions when snow falls outside the High Plains and Trans Pecos areas, it is accompanied by sleet or freezing rain or a combination of the two. That combination is especially pernicious, as the late-arriving snow blankets the initial layer of ice on roadways and bridges, concealing the fact that the passageway is extremely treacherous. Very little snow fell on New Year's Eve 1978, when the worst ice storm in at least three decades struck North Central Texas. Layers of ice up to 2 inches thick produced heavy damage in a 100-mile-wide (160 kilometers) swath from Gatesville to Paris, including damage to trees that was the most extensive in 30 years. Some 2,000 residents were treated at area hospitals for injuries sustained in auto accidents, falls on the ice, and frostbite. Heavy accumulations of ice and a brisk wind, which maintained a chill temperature of 10°F (−12°C) or less, snapped power lines, leaving nearly 300,000 residents of Dallas County without electricity for two days. It took the power company ten days to restore service completely, at a cost of $3 million. A young lad in Dallas was killed when he contacted a downed electrical wire, and at least five other persons died in ice-related auto accidents. The Great Ice Storm of New Year's Eve 1978 was responsible for $14 million worth in damage in Dallas County alone (fig. 5.6).

When ice storms happen belatedly during the cold season, the accompanying cold-air outbreak wreaks exceptional hardship on fragile animal and plant life. A strong cold front brought bitterly cold air deep into South Texas on the last three days of March 1987, decimating virtually all of the Hill Country peach crop and laying waste to thousands of gardens. Some schools had to be closed as their heat sources had already been turned off for the season. Somehow the citrus crop in the lower Rio Grande valley survived, though temperatures plunged into the mid-20s as far south as Rio Grande City.

The Alberta Clipper

With a wind that blows unimpeded and with the state situated on the southern fringe of territory claimed by the polar jet stream, it is inevitable that cold-air outbreaks chill Texas with some degree of regularity during the three coldest months of the year. With few mountain ranges to obstruct it and little tall vegetation to arrest its acceleration, the bitterly cold air rarely stops until it encases the entire state. These "northers" consist of potent blasts of cold wind that accompanies the massive doses of polar air shoved Equator-ward by an invigorated polar jet. The term "clipper" has been coined to connote the speed of these biting winds: the frozen, snow-covered landscape originating north of the border in Canada that chills the air to astounding depths before the "dam" holding the pile of air bursts, allowing it to pour in at speeds 40–50 mph. Every once in a while, the rush of cold air can surge with such intensity that thick, ominous, bluish-gray layered clouds form along its leading edge, giving rise to the phrase "blue norther." The mound of Arctic air typically plunges air temperatures from balmy readings in the 70s and 80s to below freezing in a matter of only a few hours. The pile is so vast that, once it has settled in over the state, subfreezing spells can linger for days, if not weeks.

If the Christmas blitz of 2004 vied for the honor of the most stunning snowstorm to ever hit Texas (table 5.11), it was a momentary trauma compared with the seemingly interminable "Big Chill" that encased the entire state in the weeks leading up to Christmas 1983 (fig. 5.7). For 17 days that month, an immense pile of unimaginably frigid air kept nearly all of Texas in a hammerlock. The initial surge of Arctic air on December 14–15 was reinforced four times by fresh waves of even colder Arctic air, thereby giving Texans an unsavory taste of what Siberians have to tolerate every winter. The most massive of the mounds of Arctic air gripped the state on Christmas Eve, forcing the barometric pressure at Wichita Falls to an astonishing peak of 31.13 inches—the second-highest known pressure reading in Texas weather history. Like dozens of communities, Dallas–Fort Worth was subjected to temperatures below freezing for a record 296 hours, or more than 12 days. Such a protracted chill explained why stock tanks froze over so solidly that automobiles could be driven on their surfaces. Ranchers in deep South Texas repeatedly had to brave the deadly chill every few hours to break the ice in cisterns so their herds could have water to drink. Hordes of sport fish lined the beaches along the Texas coast as scores of hardy anglers and tourists picked them up by the ice-chest loads. Citrus growers farther south in the Lower Valley fought valiantly to save the bulk of the year's fruit by wrapping trees and burning smudge pots night after night, only to see the temperature dip even lower and decimate not only the fruit but the producing trees as well. Fractures in hundreds of water mains plunged water pressure to dangerously low levels, forcing communities like Fort Worth to declare city water emergencies. Frozen fire hydrants prevented fire fighters from battling myriads of fires, many of which were ignited by space heaters used carelessly by residents desperate to stay warm. Unparalleled consumption of electrical power forced scores of cities to the brink of brownouts. Thousands of holiday travelers were stranded for long hours in terminals when icy runways and roads canceled dozens of flights and rides at the height of the hectic Christmas travel season. Most tragically of all, people of all ages—even whole families—died when left overexposed to the awesome chill or trapped by fire racing through their homes. Some perished when the ice on frozen-over lakes and ponds gave way as they walked across them.

Few cold-air outbreaks have made as great an imprint on Texas as the two-week deep freeze that Christmas season. At least 13 people succumbed to the bitter cold. Agricultural losses amounted to tens of millions of dollars, and property damage sustained by residences and businesses exceeded $50 million. The loss of the citrus crop in the Lower Valley cost growers over $30 million and threw thousands of laborers out of work. To make matters even worse, many of the citrus trees were irreparably damaged by the hard freeze, thereby forcing growers to replant whole groves of trees. The worst fish kill in several decades hurt severely the state's multimillion dollar commercial fishing industry. Most livestock somehow survived the deep freeze, although ranchers had to shell out exorbitant amounts of extra food to keep their herds alive. As with many cold waves that encase Texas during winter, snow and ice coated vast expanses of the state and severely handicapped would-be travelers. The initial wave of Arctic air on December 14–15 precipitated the most snowfall, 4 to 6 inches in much of the northern half of Texas. More remarkably, the coating of snow and ice remained on the ground for more than two weeks—or until a welcome thaw got underway on New Year's Day 1984. Another Arctic blast encased northeast Texas on January 6, 1988, killing 1.75 million chickens exposed to the severe cold.

TABLE 5.11

Most Snow Occurring on Christmas Day[1]

LOCATION	INCHES	YEAR
Victoria	12.5	2004
Amarillo	4.6	1939
El Paso	4.1	1974
Lubbock	3.1	1997
Wichita Falls	2.5	2012
Corpus Christi	2.1	2004
San Angelo	2.0	1926
Texarkana	2.0	2012
Abilene	1.5	1987
Brownsville	1.5	2004
Midland	1.3	2011

[1] Deepest snow accumulation on Christmas morning includes Dalhart (10 inches, 1997), Wichita Falls (8 inches, 2009), Pampa (7 inches, 2002), and Amarillo (5 inches, 1997).

Other exceptional northers are blameworthy for some of Texas's most notorious dislocations—as well as seemingly unbreakable records. One of the longest-lasting Arctic deep freezes ever to paralyze the Texas Panhandle held the region in extreme cold for half of February in 1895, during which the temperature remained below 20°F for a solid week (fig. 5.8). Just four years later, a surge of Arctic air in February 1899 shoved the temperature to an all-time state low of −23°F (−31°C) at Tulia in the southern Panhandle and left a sheet of ice in Galveston Bay! (That state record was matched 34 years later when a similarly intense Arctic wave sent the temperature skidding to −23°F in Seminole.) Citrus groves in far Southern Texas were bitten by nighttime readings as cold as 12°F (−11°C), and people as far removed as El Salvador felt the nip of a freeze. The 1899 Arctic siege was so severe that it made the entire winter season the coldest ever documented in the state's history (tables 5.12, 5.13).

To be of near-record severity, the Arctic air need not be laden with snow. The most notable dry blue norther of a lifetime smote Texas with

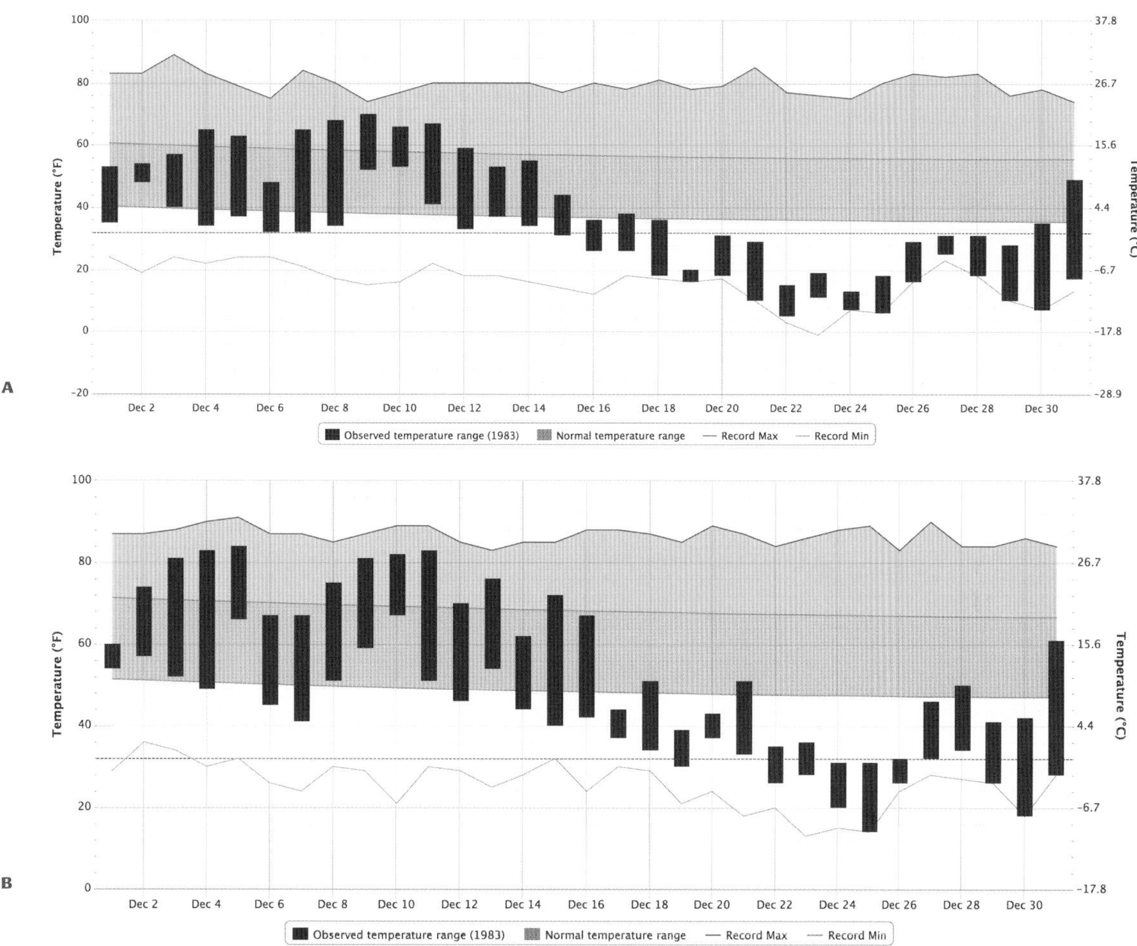

FIG. 5.7A & 5.7B During the rare deep freeze that engulfed Texas in 1983, (a) Dallas-Fort Worth went below freezing and remained there for a record 12 days, while (b) on the coast Corpus Christi endured subfreezing temperatures for 3 whole days. Source: National Climatic Data Center

a devastating lick on the eve of Christmas 1989. The bitter cold wave was short-lived but of epic dimensions, causing extensive damage to business and residential property as many holiday celebrants were neither at home nor open for business to take needed precautions. Temperatures dropped to an astounding 15°F (−9°C) in the Lower Valley, causing citrus fruit to freeze solid on trees, while subzero readings were common in the Hill Country. Cattle froze to death inland from the coastal bend, and vegetable crops and plant nurseries sustained huge losses. A massive fish kill occurred in coastal waters, where the seawater temperature in the surf at Matagorda Bay was 34°F (1°C). The small amount of frozen precipitation that accompanied the historic cold wave included a snow cover of 2 inches on Galveston Island.

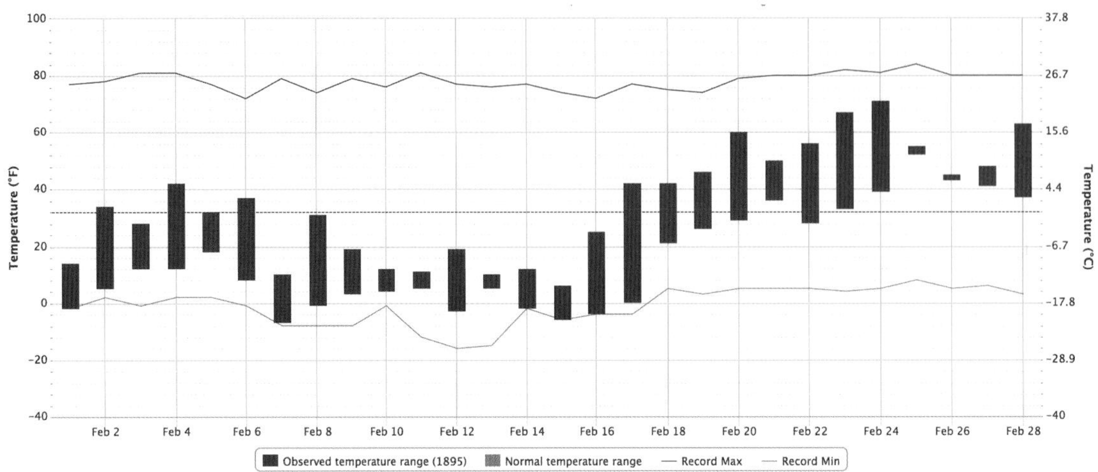

FIG. 5.8 The Texas Panhandle was gripped by a severe cold snap that spanned the first half of February 1895—and Amarillo stayed below 20°F for seven straight days, with four of those days having nighttime lows below 0°F. Source: National Oceanic and Atmospheric Administration

TABLE 5.12

Texas's Coldest Winters

RANK	YEAR	DEPARTURE[1]
1st	1899	−5.5°
2nd	1905	−5.1°
3rd	1978	−4.8°
4th	2010	−4.7°
5th	1979	−4.5°
6th	1964	−4.3°
7th	1984	−3.8°
8th	1973	−3.6°
9th	1912	−3.5°
10th	1977	−3.1°

[1] Twentieth-century average is 65.0° F (18° C); winter consists of December, January, and February. Source: www.ncdc.noaa.gov.

TABLE 5.13

Texas's Warmest Winters

RANK	YEAR	DEPARTURE[1]
1st	1907	5.1°
2nd	1952	4.6°
3rd	1911	4.4°
4th	2000	4.1°
5th	1923	4.0°
6th	1950	3.9°
7th	1999	3.7°
	1957	3.7°
9th	1909	3.5°
10th	1921	3.3°

[1] Twentieth-century average is 65.0° F (18° C); winter consists of December, January, and February.

It is in the "dead" of winter that the polar jet is most energetic, and it is in January and early February that coldest temperatures are usually observed in Texas. In the "typical" year, morning low temperatures steadily decline during October, November, and December, eventually bottoming out in mid-January in all sections of Texas (table 5.14). Morning minimum temperatures average in the low 20s in the Texas Panhandle (at Amarillo, for instance), whereas in the Lower Valley average low readings are no cooler than 50°F (10°C). Once every three or four years, however, winter is atypical in that coldest readings occur in December or February, and occasionally as late in the season as early March.

Almost always, the coldest temperatures of any winter are felt in the Texas Panhandle, where the names of Dalhart and Lipscomb are as synonymous with cold weather as Presidio is with excessive and prolonged heat in summer. As shown in appendix 6, during the period 1975–2016, either Dalhart or Lipscomb garnered the distinction as Texas's coldest spot about half of the time. At other times the state's lowest temperature is gauged elsewhere in the Panhandle, either in the northernmost tier of counties or in one of the counties that form the border with New Mexico. This sector also experiences the earliest of the inaugural autumn freezes to occur in Texas (fig. 5.9). Very occasionally, some locale in the northernmost Trans Pecos near the Texas–New Mexico border will register the lowest temperature statewide for the year. Rarely are these statewide extremes above 0°F (−18°C); in half of the years, the minimum is −10°F (−23°C) or colder. The High Plains region, week in and

TABLE 5.14
Earliest Freezes on Record

DATE	LOCATION
Sep 15, 1993	Lipscomb
Sep 21, 1983	Amarillo, Dalhart, Gruver, Hereford, Miami, Shamrock, Stratford
Sep 21, 1995	Panhandle
Sep 24, 1989	Clarendon, Perryton

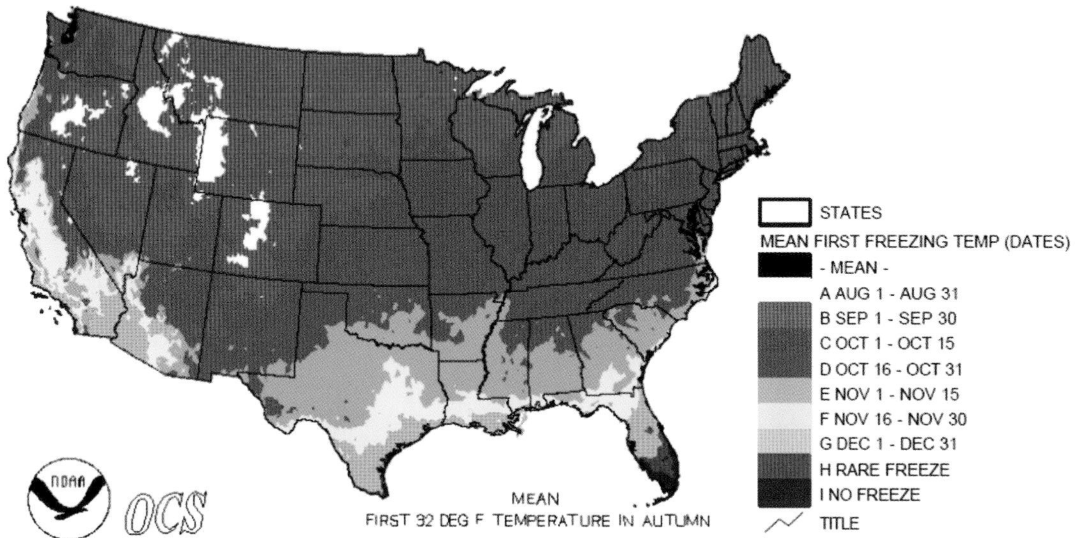

FIG. 5.9 Dates of the earliest autumn freeze during the 1981–2010 period. Source: National Climatic Data Center

week out, is also the most persistently cold of any sector of Texas. Invariably Texas's most poleward region registers the coldest average monthly temperature of any of the state's ten climatic regions.

The Texas Panhandle, not coincidentally, also features more freeze occurrences than any other region—as well as most of the earliest, and latest, freezes on record (tables 5.14, 5.15). Moreover, the freeze-free season is shorter there than elsewhere, with the latest spring freeze on average detected in late April or early May in most years (fig. 5.10; table 5.15). Nighttime temperatures dip to 32°F (0°C) or below on more than 130 days during the seven-month period ending in April in a normal year in the northern fringe of the Panhandle. January traditionally qualifies as the year's coldest month, not only because winter's lowest temperatures usually are recorded at that time but also because the month is marked by the greatest number of freeze days of any month of the year (appendix 3). Indeed, in much of Texas, the frequency of occurrence of a freezing (or subfreezing) temperature is at least twice as great in January as for any other month.

TABLE 5.15
Latest Freezes on Record

DATE	LOCATION
May 25, 2001	Wellington
May 19, 1971	Stratford, Vega
May 16, 1967	Hereford
May 16, 1983	Dumas
May 15, 1967	Dalhart
May 15, 1983	Bravo

Safety Precautions

The scarcity of long winters and substantive snowfall leaves many Texans longing for at least one or two glimpses of a winter wonderland. However, a sudden—if short-lived—outbreak of wet snowfall and bitter cold can immobilize an entire region, isolating communities by cutting off power and making roadways unsafe to navigate, if not altogether impassable. Almost invariably, major winter storms in Texas involve human suffering.

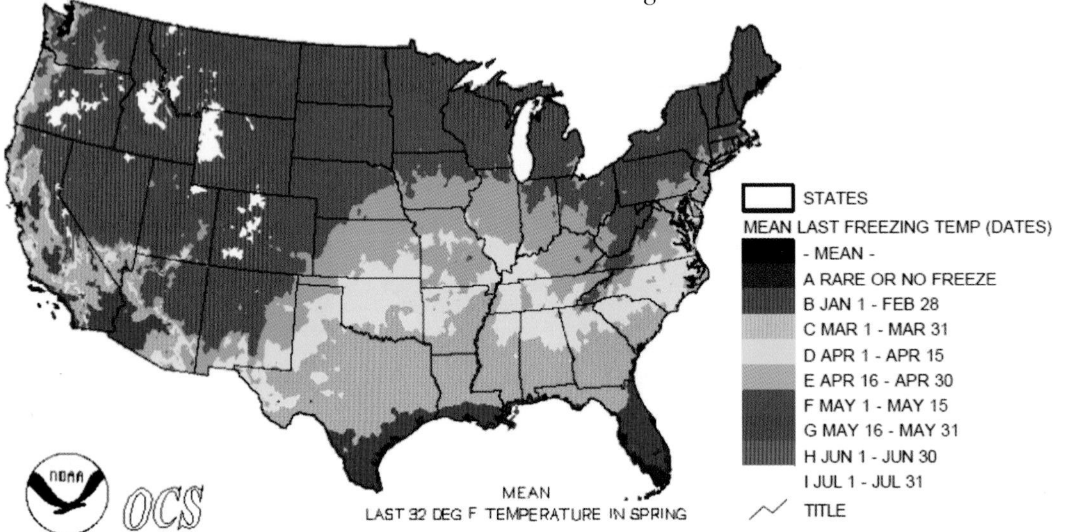

FIG. 5.10 Dates of the latest spring freeze during the 1981-2010 period. Source: National Climatic Data Center

PREPARING YOUR HOME

It pays to prepare for an icy onslaught. At home, a prime danger is loss of power and therefore heat. Be sure, well before the first cold snap hits, to have emergency heat sources, such as a fireplace or electric heaters, in working order. Do not depend on your stove or oven as it is not advisable to use them for warmth. If you rely on space heaters, make certain that you use them as prescribed by the manufacturer. Refrain from using a space heater to dry any wet clothing. Don't limit your readiness to the home's interior either. Identify all exterior water pipes and outlets and adequately wrap them. When cold air is forecast, conserve power by closing off all unused rooms in the house. Leave cabinet doors open where water pipes can feel the warmth within the house. Run the tap in the kitchen and bathroom—only a trickle of warm water is needed to prevent pipes from freezing and ultimately bursting. Place towels in cracks under doors and cover windows at night (to lessen the escape of warmth within the house through panes of glass).

NAVIGATING THE ROADWAYS

While driving in icy weather should be avoided, it is not always possible to stay off roadways when surfaces are slickened by snow or ice. A driver can never be sure that he or she will not get stuck, so one's cell phone should be charged and the car's fuel tank adequately filled. Prepare your auto beforehand by checking fluid levels, wiper blades, tires, and other features. Something most drivers who leave their cars unprotected during adverse weather seldom remember to do is to check the car's tailpipe to be certain it is not full of snow before driving off.

If you must travel during a severe frigid spell, take public transportation whenever possible. If you must use your own vehicle, take winter driving seriously. Travel by daylight and keep others informed of your travel schedule. Drive with extreme caution; never try to save time by driving fast or using back-road shortcuts. Keep your car winterized with sufficient antifreeze. It is prudent to carry a winter car kit that contains a windshield scraper, flashlight, tow chain or rope, shovel, tire chains, blanket, bag of sand or salt, a fluorescent distress flag, and emergency flare. Keep extra mittens, hats, and outerwear in the car.

It is enough of a challenge for a driver to navigate snow on roadways. When ice has fallen, the risks soar exponentially, especially at night. Perhaps the greatest threat comes in the form of "black ice," where a thin sheen of frozen moisture on roadways appears as rain—when in fact it is ice. Bridges and overpasses tend to ice up more quickly than the rest of the roadway, so motorists approaching these elevated, and less insulated, passageways should slow down and watch very carefully for ice. A moistened roadway, especially in freezing weather conditions, warrants putting greater distance between your and other vehicles. In mere snow, a very light touch on the brakes is the prudent choice; in ice, however, a driver has virtually no control, particularly if your speed is not extremely slow. While it seems counterintuitive, if you go into a spin, or skid, on a slickened roadway you should turn the steering wheel *into* the direction of the spin. No matter what is responsible for a slick roadway, remaining composed allows a driver to have a wider vision and better balance. The best drivers stay calm.

If you become stranded on a roadway by a snow or ice storm, do the following:

- Pull off the highway and remain in your vehicle to enable rescuers to find you.
- Set your turn signals to simultaneous flashing and hang a cloth or distress flag from the radio aerial or a closed window.
- Do not set out on foot unless you can see a building close by where you know you can take shelter. Be careful: distances are distorted by blowing snow, and you may discover that a building is too distant for you to walk to in deep snow.
- If you run the engine to keep warm, open a window slightly for ventilation. This will protect you from possible carbon monoxide poisoning. Periodically, clear away snow from the exhaust pipe.
- Find ways to exercise to maintain body heat but avoid overexertion. In extreme cold, use road maps, seat covers, and floor mats for insulation. Huddle with passengers and use your coat as a blanket.
- Never allow everyone in the car to sleep at the same time. One person should look out for rescue crews.
- Watch the use of battery power. Balance electrical energy needs–the use of lights, heat, and radio–with available supply. At night, turn on the inside dome light so rescue crews can spot you.

If you are stranded in a remote rural or wilderness area, spread a large cloth over the snow to attract the attention of rescue personnel who may be surveying the area by airplane. Once the blizzard passes, you may need to leave your car and proceed on foot.

AVOIDING BODILY HARM

You can cope with a bad winter storm by remembering that overexertion can bring on a heart attack, a major cause of death during and after winter storms. If shoveling snow is not critically important, do not do it. If you must remove snow by hand, do not overdo it. Conserve fuel by keeping your house cooler than usual and by temporarily closing off heat to some rooms. If kerosene heaters are used, maintain ventilation to avoid build-up of toxic fumes. Be sure to use only the fuel recommended by the manufacturer, and follow the operating instructions.

The key to withstanding a bitter wintry wind is in wearing the proper clothing. In fact, one's ability to withstand cold temperatures depends more upon the maintenance of an adequate amount of air space between skin and clothing than upon the thickness and weight of the clothing. The capacity of clothing to protect the body has been found to be proportional to the amount of "dead air" that exists between the outer layer of clothing and the surface of one's skin. A vigorous wind diminishes this insulating capacity of the dead air by penetrating the clothing and pressing it against the body. A string vest or some other soft, but heavy, garment can be worn to prevent the wind from plastering the inner clothing against the body. Care should be taken, however, when wearing clothing that is impenetrable by the wind; garments so impermeable as to impede the evaporation of perspiration from the body should be avoided.

By any means, protect the extremities of the body–the hands, ears, face, and feet–to prevent chapped skin, chilblains, and frostbite. The greater the surface area of the skin exposed to the air, the more rapidly that part of the body loses heat. Possibly the greatest loss of body heat is through the head area. Studies have indicated that, with an air temperature of 5°F (-15°C), about three-fourths of the body's heat is lost from the head. Insulated hats with earmuffs, even a covering over the face, are essential at very cold temperatures to stem undue heat loss from the body. Without adequate covering, extremities of the body may quickly turn numb and pale, and in extreme cases, with the body's blood supply cut off, the danger of gangrene becomes a real threat.

Here are some simple axioms to learn to help you dress for bitterly cold weather:

- Many layers of thin clothing are warmer than single layers of thick clothing.
- Mittens are warmer than gloves.
- Wearing a hat prevents a substantial loss of body heat.
- Covering your mouth with scarves protects the lungs from directly inhaling the extremely cold air.

An increase in wind speed also means that additional energy is needed to maintain a level of warmth in the home in winter or sufficient cooling in summer. The degree of heat loss in a home during a cold spell is approximately proportional to the square root of the wind speed. This means, for instance, that a poorly insulated home stands to lose up to five times as much heat when winds of 20–30 mph are blowing than if the air outside is still. As with clothing, the key to proper insulation is the amount of "dead air" between the inner wall of the house and the building's exterior. Even the type of material used on the exterior of the home contributes significantly to heating efficiency (e.g., a substance like sandstone, with high porosity, would be preferable to cement or wood).

In the event of a severe wintry outbreak, you can be prepared for the possibility of isolation in your home:

- Be sure you have sufficient heating fuel—regular fuel sources (e.g., electricity, natural gas) may be cut off. Have available some kind of emergency heating equipment and fuel (e.g., a kerosene heater, a gas fireplace, or a wood-burning stove or fireplace) to enable you to keep at least one room of your house warm enough to be livable. If you have a wood-burning fireplace, store a good supply of dry, seasoned wood.
- Keep fire extinguishers on hand and make sure your family knows how to use them and knows fire-prevention rules.
- Stock emergency water and cooking supplies and store food that can be prepared without an electric or gas stove.
- Keep a battery-powered radio and flashlight in working order, stock extra batteries, and have candles and matches available in case of a power outage.

Excessive exposure to the cold can result in a lowering of the internal body temperature, also known as hypothermia. This condition, when the body temperature drops to 95°F (35°C) or less, can be life threatening. It is evidenced by a pale, cold skin with uncontrollable shivering, as well as a loss of coordination, difficulty speaking, and often an altered mental state. A victim of hypothermia should be carefully, and gently, relocated to a warmer place. If one's clothing is wet, it should be removed, and the person should be covered with something dry and warm, with special attention given to protecting the head and neck. It is wise to recognize and treat hypothermia early, as the chance for survival decreases as the condition worsens.

Frostbite, where a portion of human skin freezes from too much exposure to extreme cold, is a serious matter as well. A tip that frostbite is imminent consists of a pins-and-needles sensation and throbbing of a body part, a condition when left untreated that can lead to a loss of feeling. The earliest stage of frostbite can be dealt with by rewarming the skin. A more serious stage of frostbite requires the victim be removed to a warmer place quickly. Jewelry should be taken off the affected area, which should be wrapped with a clean towel or pad. If fingers or toes are frostbitten, clean pads should be placed between them. The frostbitten part of the body should be immersed in warm—but not hot—water for up to 30 minutes. A victim of frostbite should not be served alcoholic beverages, and chemical warmers should not be placed directly on frostbitten tissue as that can cause burns. A victim should not use the affected body part after it is thawed. Rather, the person should get professional medical care as soon as possible.

REMEMBERING THE PETS

Contrary to popular belief, pets are not fine outside in a bitter cold spell because they have fur. In fact, they are at risk as much as humans. Small dogs are more vulnerable to the cold than larger ones, and more are lost in winter than any other time of year because their sense of smell is impaired. Make sure your pet has an identification tag on at all times, and when you walk your pet, always carry your cell phone. Keep your dog's hair brushed regularly, as knotted or matted hair does not insulate properly. Never leave your pet outside in the cold—even a doghouse—and report a pet locked outside to local animal-control authorities. Just as you would in the heat of summer, do not leave your pet in a car in cold weather—an auto can get as cold as an icebox. Store liquids like antifreeze and solids like rock salt where your pets cannot get to them. If you observe your pet lifting his feet a lot or walking oddly, check them for ice balls or forming ice. Finally, keep an eye on the water dish to make sure the water does not freeze.

6. Cascading Rains

Without access to weather radar information, folks living in and near Wimberley, Texas, would not have known on Memorial Day weekend in May 2015 that repeated cloudbursts miles upstream from the notoriously rambunctious Blanco River were feeding the waterway that cuts through the Hill Country community an hour's drive southwest of Austin. As the river began rising after nightfall, the area's reverse-911 alerting system began notifying residents of the threat of a major flood event. Yet valuable communication between local officials and residents was interrupted when cell phone service crashed. Folks familiar with the river's reputation to burst out of its banks on very short notice wisely grabbed their belongings and fled toward higher ground. But it was a holiday weekend, and the area known for its gift and souvenir shops swelled with visitors, some of whom camped out in cabins and houses nestled among the massive live oaks that shaded the river bank.

One house serving as a temporary vacation home for out-of-town visitors was abruptly lifted off its concrete foundation and sent floating rapidly downstream, eventually crashing into a bridge smack in the middle of town—and likely disgorging the more than a dozen guests, including several school-age children. One inhabitant, the mother of two, phoned her sister to say that the structure was loose on the river—and to call her parents, giving them her love. It was the final conversation between the two women. Authorities searching along the river found the body of the woman, along with 10 others who had been in the house when the rising waters swept it away.

The Blanco River is a strikingly sedate waterway at least 99 percent of the time. On most days of the year, a person can wade across the riverbed in a minute or less at many points. Yet it rests in the middle of one of the nation's three most flash-flood-prone regions. Occasionally, it teams with nearby streams, such as the equally volatile

Pedernales River farther north, to make the most dreadful of headlines (fig. 6.1). On May 23, 2015, a wall of water over 40 feet high gushed through narrow canyons, obliterating practically everything in its path. The flood happened so quickly that folks caught by the overwhelming surge had little or no time to react. Some residents were alarmed, if not awakened, in Wimberley's Cedar Oak Mesa subdivision when items, such as dinnerware and mattresses, began floating through rooms of their homes. Fighting for their lives, they quickly exited the structures, only to discover they were surrounded by a swift-moving current that forced them to climb up on roof tops. One man, 75, perished when the satellite dish he was clinging to collapsed as his wife watched in horror; she was rescued six hours later.

Types of Floods

The torrential rains that sent the Blanco River into apoplexy is a prime example of one of the two types of storm events that initiate ruinous flooding in Texas. Common in the warmer half of the year, and the precursor to the flooding that devastated Wimberley, is the concentration of very intense thunderstorms that erupt in minutes and unleash massive amounts of rain—to be followed by subsequent storm cells, equally water rich, that course downwind, following essentially the same path taken by their predecessors. At times the "training" effect of these huge thunderstorm complexes generates rains well beyond an inch in a matter of minutes, and this enormous amount of water is deposited on such a small area of land surface in so short a period that most of the water cannot be absorbed by the ground. Consequently, a flood erupts in a flash, hence a flash flood, when this large volume of rainwater quickly leaves the watershed, bloating streams and rivers with runoff and leaving unspeakable wreckage in its wake (fig. 6.2). If that same load of rainfall had been distributed rather uniformly over the whole watershed, some runoff might have occurred—but not of the magnitude to burst rivers out of their banks. Yet, the concentration of such a heavy downpour in so small an area ensures a rapid peaking of stream flow, which inundates usually dry terrain and, all too often tragically, the people that inhabit the territory. The abrupt swelling of the waterway is followed by a not-nearly-so rapid recession of the flow—and unforgettable impressions of how forceful the raging water can be (fig. 6.3). The other type of flood event is the widespread, prolonged rain event that, through sheer quantity of water,

FIG. 6.1 The Blanco River near Austin has a reputation for bursting out of its banks after heavy rainstorms hit Central Texas—as it did in May 2015, causing catastrophic flooding downstream in Wimberley. Source: George W. Bomar

FIG. 6.2 Flood waters congregate in low-lying areas, snarling traffic and posing a threat to drivers, who should remember to "turn around, don't drown." Source: Texas Department of Transportation

FIG. 6.3 Trees strong enough to stay rooted in the ground after a flood but leaving telltale signs of the awesome force of floodwaters. Source: George W. Bomar

induces widespread flooding in much if not all of a watershed—and possibly even beyond. Known as an area flood, it is observed to evolve over an extended stretch of time, so much so that ample warnings can be issued and elaborate precautions taken to limit, if not avoid, casualties—but not necessarily restrict the extent of damage to property.

Origins in the Ocean

Once in a while, these protracted flood events are spawned by slow-moving weather systems emanating out of the Gulf of Mexico, which include tropical storms, even hurricanes, before they make landfall. These systems spawn incredibly torrential rains, at times in only a few hours (table 6.1). There is no more classic an example of this phenomenon than the fallout from an exceptionally minor tropical disturbance that, once it migrated inland from the Gulf, appeared to get lost in the coastal prairie of South Texas in the summer of 1978. Prior to the arrival of that season's inaugural tropical storm, the center of Texas was languishing in the throes of a severe drought. With the passing of each rainless day, cracks in the ground yawned a bit wider, while reservoir levels sank lower. Hopes were raised that relief from the crippling drought was imminent when the storm, to be given the name Amelia, spun up just off the lower Texas coastline one sizzling Saturday afternoon in late July. With so little opportunity to intensify, Amelia moved ashore bearing a near minimum of ferocity: She almost lost her designation as a tropical storm. She spilled only modest amounts of rainfall inland along the lower third of the Texas coastline, giving hopeful residents farther north no reason to hold out hope for thirst-slaking rains.

Shocking anyone still paying attention to what seemed a disintegrating disturbance, Amelia somehow reinvigorated, unleashing torrents of rain that spurred record flash floods in the Texas Hill Country in the predawn darkness of August 2. Within minutes tranquil rivers were transformed into veritable tidal waves as huge walls of water, moving at incredible speeds, tore through numerous communities situated within or near the rivers' flood plains. The flash floods were nothing short of calamitous, resulting in tens of millions of dollars in property damages and the loss of 27 lives. Downpours of more than 20 inches cascaded onto the headwaters of the Medina, Sabinal, and Guadalupe Rivers, creating record flood crests and discharge rates that led to the engulfment of resort camps and picnic areas. Campers at Camp Bandina were alarmed to find their site inundated in a matter of seconds; eight of them drowned, while others, eventually rescued by helicopters, clung tenaciously to trees. Massive cypress trees lining the low-water banks of the rivers and ranging in size up to 6 feet in diameter were either yanked from the ground or snapped in two by the raging flood. Four unsuspecting persons spending the night in a cabin near the edge of the Medina River at Peaceful Valley Ranch were carried to their deaths. The Guadalupe River, rising at a rate of 1 foot per minute at Kerrville, reached the bridge on US Highway 281, which stands 59 feet above the normally serene river near the community of Spring Branch. The river flowed at a rate of 149 *billion* gallons per day (230,537 cubic feet per second [cfs]), or more than twice the previous record flow established in 1959. (The normal flow rate is 104 *million* gallons per day, or 161 cfs.)

TABLE 6.1
Most Extreme Rain Events

INCHES	DURATION	LOCATION (COUNTY)	DATE
24.8	3.5 hours	San Patricio	Oct 19, 1984
26.9	10 hours	Harris	Jun 4-10, 2001
42.9	1 day	Brazoria	Jul 24, 1979
23.6	1 day	Val Verde	Jun 23-24, 1948
20.7	1 day	Blanco	Sep 9-11, 1952

Amelia, displaying a demeanor very uncharacteristic of nearly all tropical storms that move ashore out of the Gulf, drifted northward into western North Central Texas on the following day, dumping more than 30 inches of rain on parts of Shackelford County—located nearly 400 miles (620 kilometers) from the Texas coast. A wall of water 20 feet high formed on Little Hubbard Creek and crashed through Albany, covering more than three-fourths of the city and drowning six of its residents. Many inhabitants of the city spent the night on roofs of houses, on top of oil derricks, and in trees before they were rescued the next day by helicopters and boats. A nearby earthen dam developed a fault 50 feet deep and 25 feet wide, and water pouring out of the dam rushed into Stephens County, destroying 12 homes and damaging 300 others. The Clear Fork of the Brazos River swelled to a width of 2 miles (3.2 kilometers) near Graham, and a 17-foot crest on the river washed ranchlands and submerged the US Highway 183 bridge.

Perhaps no other event testifies so persuasively to nature's proclivity for carrying a blessing to excess than Amelia's killer floods. Of all Earth's vast resources, none is more vital to the survival of its inhabitants than water. A perpetual lack of sufficient water has led to the extinction of some civilizations, while a dependable abundance of water has contributed to the prosperity of many others. In an ideal world, the blessing of rainfall would come in modest to generous amounts in most weeks uniformly spread over an entire region. Nature, too often it seems, allows one's thirst to mount intolerably, then supplies a drink through the proverbial fire hose. Not a year passes without some sector of the state being doused with far more water than nature's infrastructure can handle, and the results too often are the loss of human lives and damage to property that runs into many millions of dollars. Sizable floods have occurred in every month, but as a general rule spring and early autumn are the worst seasons for floods. In a typical year, runoff into rivers and streams in most of Texas reaches a peak in spring then declines during summer only to ascend again with the onset of autumn. More frequent, heavy thunderstorm rains—a common trait of a Texas spring—quickly can soak the ground, so if any storm episode unfolds in phases (because of an increasingly sluggish jet stream), subsequent waves of thunderstorms supply surplus rainfall that becomes runoff—swelling rivers and streams out of their banks. Often, a secondary maximum of runoff in late summer and early autumn stems from heavy rains from one, or more, tropical weather disturbances, from the Gulf of Mexico and the eastern North Pacific. In spring, flash floods are virtually a guarantee, if rainfall during the preceding autumn and winter has been appreciable. Moisture from the soil is removed at greatly reduced rates during these seasons, so when the usual barrage of heavy thunderstorms arrives in April, and particularly May, much of the rainwater produced is shed by the moist landscape. The resulting flash floods are common in the High and Low Rolling Plains and the Edwards Plateau from late spring to early summer because ground and tree cover is sparse in much of these regions and the slopes of streams and creeks are fairly steep. Flash floods are common later in the summer in the mountainous Trans Pecos, when a sudden deluge transforms a normally quiet stream or dry gulch into a torrent of water potent enough to displace boulders. However, no portion of Texas—or, for that matter, the entire United States—is as prone to be afflicted by flash floods as the segment of central Texas in the vicinity of the Balcones Escarpment (fig. 6.4). This topographic anomaly at the juncture of the Edwards Plateau with the coastal plain is cut in hundreds of places by rivers, streams, creeks, and arroyos that fill rapidly when appreciable rains fall upstream on their watersheds. These waterways are narrow, so they overflow in a matter of minutes, and the water that rages along carries a deadly cargo of smashed structures, uprooted trees, boulders, mud, and other debris. Tropical Storm Amelia's unleashing of Niagara-like rains on scores of communities in the Texas Hill Country in August 1978 is a vivid reminder of how vulnerable the region is to the sudden eruption of flash floods.

FIG. 6.4 Floods are particularly lethal along the Balcones Escarpment on the southern edge of the Hill Country, where usually narrow rivers and streams fill quickly from excessive rains nearby. Source: Texas Department of Public Safety

The late-summer flood that had much to do with the founding of the city of San Angelo is also a reminder of that region's vulnerability. With a wet summer having left the Concho valley primed for the bursting of creeks and streams feeding the Concho River, night-long rains on August 24, 1882 created a wave of high water that roared down on the community of Ben Ficklin at midmorning, washing away the entire town except for the courthouse, jail, and two residences and drowning 65 people. Fifteen other homes and a schoolhouse were spared, only because they sat on a hill overlooking the rest of the town. County offices and the post office were resituated in nearby San Angela, which nearly a decade earlier had vied with Ben Ficklin for the distinction of being the Tom Green County seat. When San Angela was awarded the seat of government in 1883, it was renamed San Angelo.

Much of the flooding in the eastern half of Texas is more extensive, slower to materialize, and much longer lasting than the flash floods that are almost routine farther west. From the Red River valley across the Blackland Belt to the coastal plain, the terrain is characterized in many places by broad, flat valleys with considerable timber and brush land. The natural drainage channels in these areas have gentle slopes and limited capacity, and they follow meandering courses from headwater areas all the way to the Gulf of Mexico. Runoff is usually slow, but a broad, flat-crested, slow-moving flood is set in motion when substantial amounts of rain occur over periods lasting several, if not many, days. Occasionally, bands of scattered convective storms or a line of frontal thunderstorms contribute enough rainfall to burst a river or stream out of its banks, but most often floods in eastern Texas stem from long, continued, warm, rainy weather. These persistently appreciable rains last a few or several days and are associated with a slow-moving upper-atmospheric storm system or a surface front that has stalled. In autumn, they can be the product of the dying residue of a hurricane or a tropical storm. As long as relatively warm, very moist Gulf air is fed into the large-scale weather system responsible for the inclement weather, the rain will continue and waterways will expand further. In some years in the coastal plain, the lower basin regions of some of Texas's largest rivers will remain inundated for many days and, sometimes, even several weeks.

Water in a Circle

The ample water in the multitude of reservoirs and rivers that pockmark and dissect the state is in continual transition. Large quantities of freshwater are lost every day when some of the water stored in lakes and reservoirs is removed into the atmosphere by evaporation, when some of the water load in rivers and streams pours into the Gulf of Mexico and mixes with salt water to become unfit for human consumption, and when an unsaturated atmosphere extracts moisture from the ground and adjacent plant life through the process of evapotranspiration. That loss is compensated for by the withdrawing of water from the Gulf of Mexico and the Pacific Ocean and its eventual placement on land as rain. This intricate exchange of water among the land surface, atmosphere, and the adjacent ocean is called the hydrologic, or water, cycle. Some of the water vapor supplied to the atmosphere by the ocean is carried inland where it combines with smaller quantities of land-evaporated water vapor to form precipitation. Some of the precipitation that reaches the ground soaks into it and replenishes the supply of groundwater, while some is returned to the ocean by runoff into rivers and streams. The remainder of the precipitation is given back to the atmosphere by evaporation. The hydrologic cycle is seldom ever completed locally; rather, moisture evaporated from coastal waters usually is precipitated many miles away and far inland. The continual migration of air masses across Texas in much of the year facilitates the operation of the hydrologic cycle. Humid air from the Gulf of Mexico and from the eastern Pacific Ocean near Mexico is channeled into Texas, where it condenses to form clouds and rain droplets, some of which ultimately fall to the surface as rain. Much drier continental air masses that envelop the state then absorb much of the moisture evaporated from the land.

The ongoing displacement of atmospheric moisture is of fundamental importance to weather for a variety of reasons: (a) it often condenses to form clouds and precipitation and, occasionally, fog, dew, and frost; (b) its concentration in the air influences the rate of evaporation, a process of monumental significance to animal and plant behavior; (c) it absorbs radiation from both the sun and the land surface; and (d) its transformation from one state to another (vapor to liquid, for example) releases heat energy that contributes to the vertical motion of air in the lower atmosphere. All of these attributes or tendencies are of equal importance. In terms of supplying vital amounts of water to Earth's surface, however, the process of condensation is most crucial to the formation of precipitation. Water vapor will not condense into droplets until it is cooled to its dew-point temperature or unless more water vapor is added. Of all the potential rain-producing clouds that form above us each month or season, only a very small percentage shed any part of their load of moisture. This may result from the overabundance of condensation nuclei, so that too many particles compete for the available supply of cloud moisture. The result is too many water droplets too small in size (and weight) to fall out of the cloud as rain. As discussed in chapter 11, this tendency of nature toward excess has led to numerous efforts to increase rain through cloud seeding.

TABLE 6.2
Texas's Wettest Years

RANK	YEAR	Total INCHES[1]	Percent OF NORMAL[2]
1st	2015	41.13	152
2nd	1941	40.22	149
3rd	1917	39.45	146
4th	2004	39.36	145
5th	1991	37.20	137
6th	2007	36.20	134
7th	1957	35.78	132
8th	1973	35.30	130

[1] Statewide average.
[2] Twentieth-century average is 27.92 inches.

The Distribution of Rainfall

Precipitation over the course of an entire year is distributed over Texas unevenly. Moreover, exceedingly wet—and dry—years occur seemingly at random (table 6.2), though some very wet years, notably 2015, are linked to the El Niño phenomenon (fig. 6.5). Totals vary somewhat, but not greatly so, from north to south across Texas, as indicated in fig. 6.6 by the lines connecting points having equal amounts of precipitation (isohyets)—lines that roughly approximate lines of longitude. A good rule of thumb is annual rainfall decreases by 1 inch with every 15-mile

(24 kilometer) displacement from east to west across Texas. More than half of Texas, in a "normal" year, collects less than 30 inches of precipitation, virtually all of which occurs as rainfall. Indeed, the mean annual rainfall for the entire state, based on rain-gauge data for the entire twentieth century, is 27.92 inches. In the western third of the state, the annual sum is considerably smaller than that—less than 20 inches in a year. By contrast, the eastern third of Texas is almost invariably endowed with at least 35 inches of rain over a 12-month period. So diverse are the climatic regimes that typify the western and eastern ends of the state that average annual precipitation varies from as little as 8.93 inches at Fort Hancock (near El Paso), in the extreme west, to 58.93 inches near Orange, in the lower Sabine River valley of extreme East Texas. Average annual precipitation in the northern edge of the Texas Panhandle amounts to about 20 inches, the same sum that characterizes the Lower Valley region of extreme Southern Texas. Accordingly, the Trans Pecos is the driest region of the state, with an average region-wide precipitation total for the year of only about 12 inches. On the other hand, the Upper Coast and East Texas are almost always the wettest, with average annual totals of 46 and 45 inches, respectively. While invariably uneven in the way it is distributed across Texas, annual rainfall in a typical year is enough to supply Texans with some 25 million acre-feet in their lakes and reservoirs (fig. 6.7).

One oddity in the annual distribution of rainfall is in the middle of the Trans Pecos region, which in many years collects 16–18 inches of rain, or 4 to 6 inches more than points 50 miles (80 kilometers) or more to the east and the west. This rainfall "oasis" is due to the influence of the mountainous topography, which forces

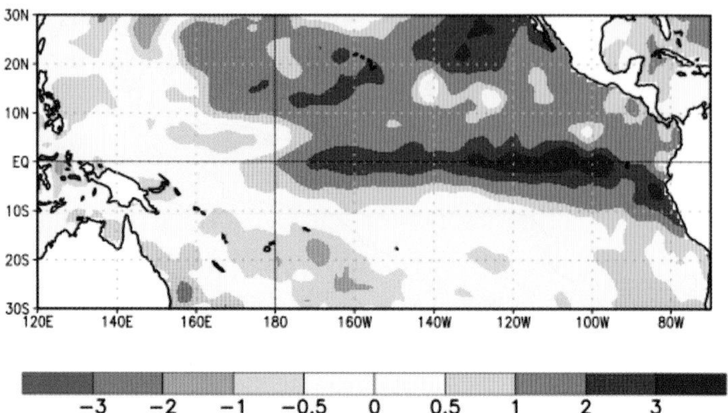

FIG. 6.5 The El Niño phenomenon of 2015-2016 was one of the strongest on record—and its presence coincided with historic rains that made 2015 the wettest year in Texas history. Source: National Oceanic and Atmospheric Administration

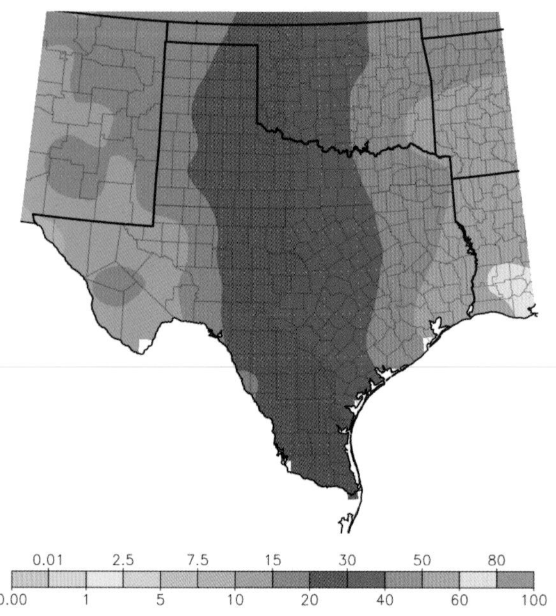

FIG. 6.6 Average annual precipitation (inches). Source: National Climatic Data Center

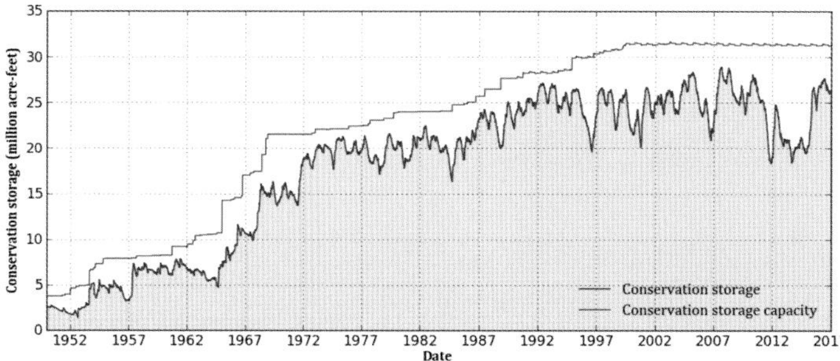

FIG. 6.7 Ample rains help maintain at least 25 million acre-feet of water in the state's lakes and reservoirs in most years—though droughts intermittently produce sharp declines. Source: Texas Water Development Board

moisture-laden winds from the Gulf of Mexico—and even the Pacific Ocean—to be lifted great distances. The lifting of relatively humid air to levels of lesser pressure results in cooling of the air to its saturation point, a process that is conducive to the formation of rain-bearing clouds.

A visitor to the Davis Mountains seeing the abundance of vegetation can appreciate the role of the terrain in "squeezing out" quantities of moisture from the atmosphere that lower elevations elsewhere in the Trans Pecos do not receive. The other region where rainfall does not decrease fairly uniformly in a longitudinal direction is along the Balcones Escarpment, which is the juncture of the Edwards Plateau with South Central Texas. Average annual rainfall at Boerne (in Kendall County) is several inches more than that in Austin, a city that is more than 60 miles (97 kilometers) to the east. This reversal in the rainfall pattern is a result of the influence of the Balcones Escarpment, characterized by sharp rises in elevation of 1,000 feet or more over distances of only a few miles. As in the Trans-Pecos, warm, moisture-laden air from the Gulf pumped inland through central Texas is forced vertically by this topographic feature. If the humid air is channeled into the region in sufficient quantities—such as when remnants of tropical storms or hurricanes drift inland—the additional rain extracted by sudden lifting can be sizable enough to cause flooding.

TABLE 6.3
Driest Texas Communities

Average annual precipitation (inches) based on record for 1981-2010.

LOCATION	INCHES
Fort Hancock	8.93
Salt Flat	9.15
Tornillo	9.16
La Tuna	9.52
Presidio	9.66
El Paso	9.71
Boquillas	9.91
Dell City	10.79
Castolon	10.85
Lajitas	10.86

It is rare for rainfall totals over any year to be least in a region other than the westernmost Trans Pecos (table 6.3). In most years some locales in this arid region receive less than 8 inches of rainfall—and every once in a while, less than half of that. Many of the scantiest annual rainfall totals measured in Texas since 1950 come from somewhere in the Trans Pecos, and all but a few occurred in one of the seven years of intense drought in Texas that marked the decade of the 1950s. However, the annual sums for several locations in the far west for calendar year 2011 are even more stunning: 1.30 inches at Terlingua, 1.55 inches at Terlingua Ranch, and 1.70 inches at McCamey. Rainfall in some localities in the same region collected little more than that at the peak of the horrific 1950s drought (appendix 13). By the same token, the most bountiful amounts of rainfall in any year almost invariably come from either East Texas or the Upper Coast (table 6.4). Yearly sums of 60 inches or more are not uncommon in at least one locale in either of these regions every year. In fact, rainfall totals for some months can exceed by a factor of 2 or 3 the total yearly rainfall observed in the western half of the state (fig. 6.8). Indeed, in five of the years between 1951 and 1980, one or more locales collected 80 inches of rain or more. Owing largely

TABLE 6.4
Wettest Texas Communities

Average annual precipitation (inches) based on record for 1981-2010.

LOCATION	INCHES
Liberty	61.25
Lumberton	61.06
Port Arthur	60.47
Beaumont	60.42
Baytown	59.92
Orange	59.13
Corrigan	57.98
Newton	57.45
Wildwood	57.31
Anahuac	57.11

to several weather disturbances of tropical origin, at least one Upper Coast city near the coastline received 100 inches or more of rain in the years 1973 and 1979. This includes the 1979 total of 106.44 inches of rain gauged at Freeport (fig. 6.9).

Just as rainfall, in spatial terms, over any year is not spread evenly, neither is it distributed evenly in temporal terms (figs. 6.10–6.13). Every region experiences wet seasons and dry seasons. Spring is the wettest season of the year in that part of Texas east of the 100th meridian, with May and June normally wetter by a good measure than April. At times the state's wettest season, the spring has delivered on numerous occasions enough rainfall to quash a serious drought in a matter of weeks (table 6.5). In the High Plains and Trans Pecos, rainfall is most plentiful in summer. Much of the rain received in those regions is generated by scattered and mostly semi-organized convective clouds (also regarded as thunderheads), which are numerous on many days from June through September. In fact, rainfall produced during the year's four warmest months in these two regions of highest elevation constitutes about two-thirds of the typical total for the entire year. Elsewhere in Texas, at such points as Dallas–Fort Worth, San Antonio, and Houston, rainfall reaches a secondary peak after the onset of autumn; October rainfall is almost as abundant as that in May, for instance. This pattern reflects the influence of tropical weather systems—most notably hurricanes and tropical storms—that migrate out of the Gulf of Mexico at that time of the year. In fact, in some years one or more major tropical disturbances may supply far more rainfall in August or September—or even October—than that collected in spring from nontropical weather events.

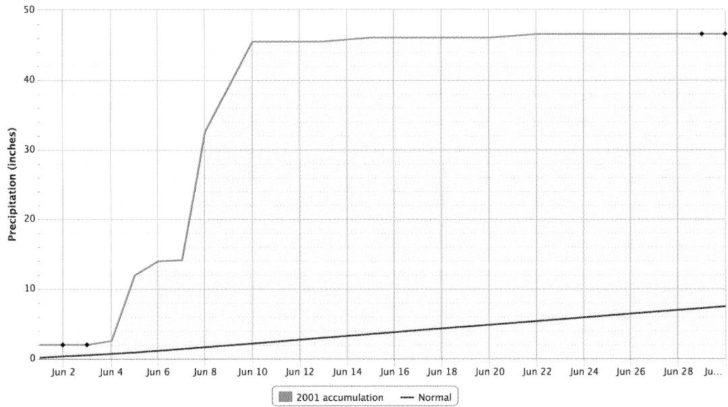

FIG. 6.8 The Port of Houston holds the state record for the wettest month in history; nearly all of the 46.55 inches that fell in June 2001 occurred in only a six-day period early in the month. Source: National Climatic Data Center

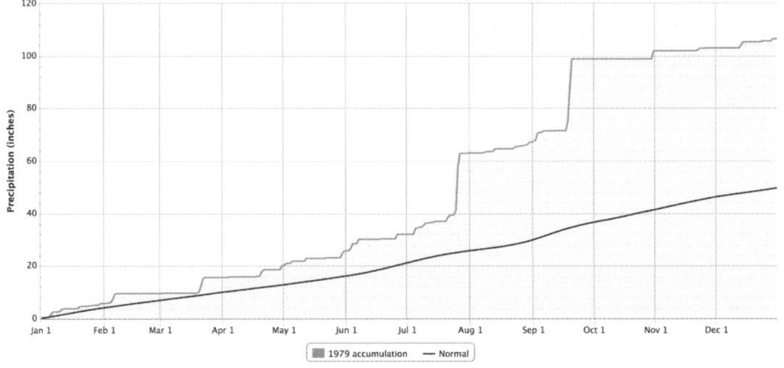

FIG. 6.9 Freeport collected the most-ever rainfall in a single year (106.44 inches) in 1979. Source: National Climatic Data Center

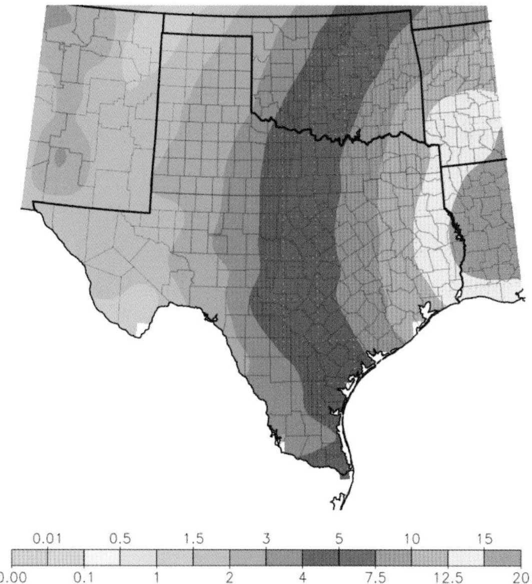

FIG. 6.10 Average annual precipitation (inches) in the Texas winter. Source: Illinois State Water Survey

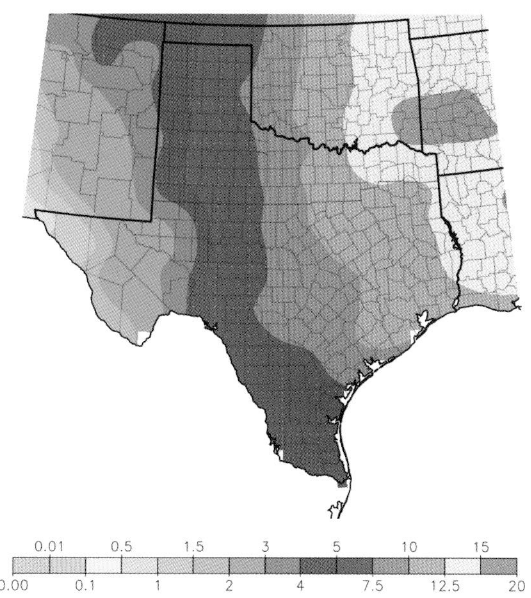

FIG. 6.11 Average annual precipitation (inches) in the Texas spring. Source: Illinois State Water Survey

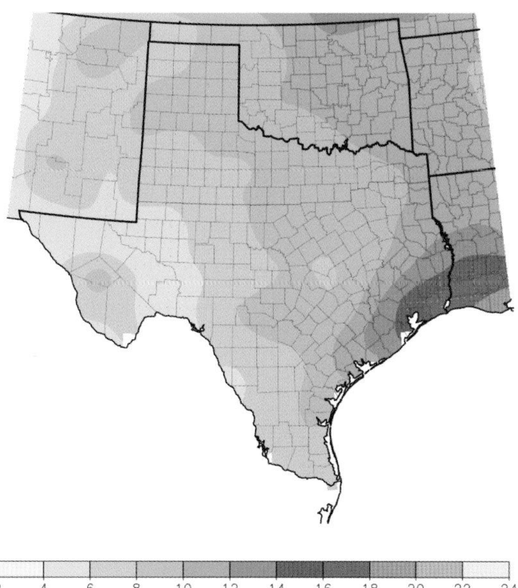

FIG. 6.12 Average annual precipitation (inches) in the Texas summer. Source: Illinois State Water Survey

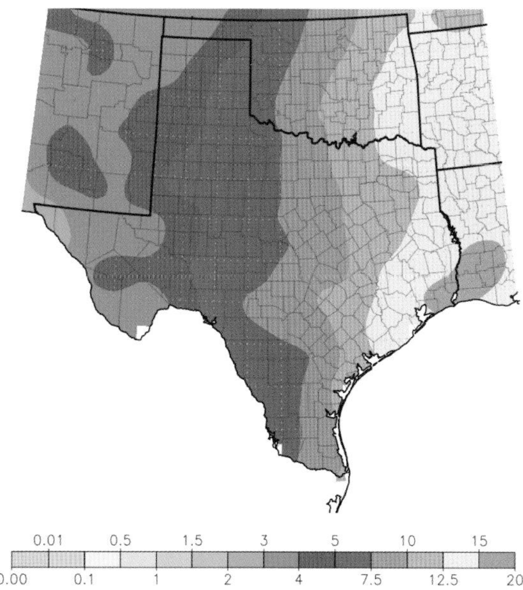

FIG. 6.13 Average annual precipitation (inches) in the Texas autumn. Source: Illinois State Water Survey

TABLE 6.5
Texas's Wettest Spring Seasons

RANK	YEAR	Total INCHES[1]	Percent OF NORMAL[2]
1st	2015	16.48	223
2nd	1957	14.75	200
3rd	1905	12.59	170
4th	1941	12.43	168
5th	1900	12.36	167
6th	2007	12.16	165
7th	1922	11.97	162
8th	1914	11.90	161

[1] Average statewide; spring consists of March-May.
[2] Twentieth-century average is 7.70 inches.

Summer rainfall is almost as lean as precipitation that comes in late winter—except in the High Plains and Trans-Pecos. Indeed, in East Texas, at such points as Lufkin, rainfall in July and August is less than that observed in February and March. Again, whether a summer in Texas is unusually wet or dry is often dictated by the degree of activity, or inactivity, of tropical weather systems in the Gulf of Mexico. Elsewhere, however, the three summer months ordinarily are a bit wetter than their winter counterparts. In Texas's southern quadrant, at such locales as Houston, San Antonio, and Corpus Christi, average monthly rainfall "bottoms out" in either late winter or early spring.

Where yearly rainfall is heaviest year in and year out, not surprisingly the same regions (East Texas, Upper Coast) also feature the largest number of rainy days. A "rain day" consists of any 24-hour period during which enough precipitation falls to be measured, with the minimum amount of measurable precipitation being 0.01 inch. About 150 days bring measurable precipitation in the Sabine River valley, while in the Trans Pecos the number of rain days is only 40–50 in a typical year. Since a rainfall amount of only one to a few hundredths of an inch is nearly always inconsequential, days with 0.1 inch of rain or more are more meaningful. Two to three times as many days with at least 0.1 inch occur in East Texas as in the western fringe of the state in every season of the year (appendix 16). Days that furnish 0.5 inch of rain are most numerous in the Upper Coast and East Texas, though the number of such days is appreciable in western sections during the summer month of July. Substantial rains of 1.00 inch or more are very occasional in the western half of Texas in midsummer, and they are infrequent even in eastern sections.

Rainfall Overloads

The part of the hydrologic cycle that garners the most attention of meteorologists is precipitation, in all its forms but especially rainfall. Because precipitation in Texas is almost always rainfall, the effect on the flow of water in rivers and streams is immediate. In the vast majority of years, only in the Panhandle in winter is the snowpack ever substantial enough to provide water in a delayed storage mode. Runoff, or that portion of precipitation that returns to the Gulf of Mexico or reservoirs within Texas either by flowing over the land surface or through the soil and water table, depends largely upon rainfall amount and intensity (i.e., the amount of rain that falls within a certain amount of time). Peak runoff on most rivers in Texas occurs in late spring or early summer, coincident with or just subsequent to the relatively heavy rains that usually take place in late April, May, and early June. Some rivers in the southern section of the state—such as the Nueces—sustain maximum runoff in autumn because of the influence of tropical cyclones. In the west—on the Pecos River, for example—peak runoff comes during or soon after relatively heavy summer rains and again in autumn from substantial rainfall induced by tropical cyclones. Most often, if rainfall is of low intensity, nearly all of it will seep into the soil and thus take a great deal of time in ultimately reaching a river or stream. On the other hand, a large amount of rain falling in a matter of minutes (or at most a few hours) may exceed the soil's infiltration capacity. That is to say the soil cannot absorb all the water it is receiving, so some portion of the rainfall becomes residual water that flows quickly to a nearby river or stream. If this excess water is of sufficiently large quantities, flooding results.

What determines the amount of rain that soaks in or runs off into a nearby channel also depends on the type of soil on which the rain falls and how much moisture that soil already contains. If the soil is largely or entirely sand, almost any reasonable amount of rain can be expected to be absorbed with little or no surface runoff. Clay soils, however, have very low infiltration capacities, and even rains of low intensity are likely to lead to some surface runoff. Soil that has a large humus content and is covered by a dense layer of grass enhances the absorption of rainwater by acting as a sponge. The presence of vegetation also will determine the amount of rain that runs off. Plants improve soil structure, and their roots provide a means of channeling excess soil water to greater depths within the ground. They also retard the horizontal movement of water and thus help hold down the rate of soil erosion. They have the ability to retain some rainfall on their external structures and to slow the rate of fall of raindrops. One other consideration in determining the likelihood of flooding is the duration of rainfall. The ability of the ground to absorb rainwater decreases as the duration of a rainy spell increases. Eventually, if the rain continues long enough, the ground's infiltration capacity becomes so small that even low-intensity rains lead to substantial runoff. This explains why, when a hurricane or other major tropical disturbance surges inland across the Texas coastline, rainfall that lasts for many hours may soak the ground to the extent that the soil's infiltration capacity reaches zero. At that instant, since the ground can take no more water, every drop of rain that falls becomes runoff—and potentially an element of a flood (fig. 6.14).

FIG. 6.14 Heavy rain events often last for days in eastern Texas, flooding vast stretches of roadway right of ways and interdicting traffic for many hours. Source: Texas Department of Transportation

The inability of soil types to hold much water can have a deleterious effect on the ecosystem as well. Major flooding in Texas's coastal plain often fuels the creation of a "dead zone" offshore in the Gulf of Mexico, causing significant problems for marine life and commercial fishing. These areas in the Gulf develop when too much freshwater is dumped into the salty waters near the coastline, resulting in plummeting oxygen levels, called hypoxia, that injure or destroy fish and other marine life. The less dense freshwater from the state's interior stays near the surface of the Gulf, putting a cap on saltier waters beneath it. Marine life that customarily lives at or near the ocean bottom is then unable to get enough oxygen. After torrential rains in the spring of 2015 swelled the Brazos, Trinity, Colorado, and other rivers out of their banks, a record amount of freshwater surged into the Gulf, and buoys in the Gulf used for oil-spill response registered very low salinity values. A similar circumstance in 2007 left dead fish on jetties near Freeport, where the Brazos empties into the Gulf. The phenomenon almost always happens during the warm season. In wintertime, massive flooding is more rare, and stronger surface winds help break down the capping of the freshwater.

Heavyweight Floods

Many of Texas's worst floods have come, ironically, smack in the middle of the state's worst droughts. When a conglomeration of intense thunderstorms begins dumping copious rainfall over a flash-flood-prone landscape hardened like rock from unrelenting heat and a dearth of antecedent rainfall, literally "walls" of water can form in a seeming nanosecond, then surge downstream to foment immense havoc on unsuspecting communities. Arguably the most exaggerated flash flood came in one of the harshest summers of the epic drought of the 1950s. Remnants of Hurricane Alice, moving inland parallel to the Rio Grande, spawned a nearly constant barrage of heavy rain storms, some of which yielded more than 2 feet of rainfall in a sector of the Pecos River watershed in late June 1954. Alice's swirling residue lingered in the area for 3 days, fostering one of the most astounding rises on any river in US history. A bridge on US Highway 290 west of Langtry that spanned the Pecos River—some 50 feet below in normal conditions—was no match for a wall of water that crested at 96.24 feet during the night of June 28. The bridge's center pier was washed out by the surge, which came some 18 hours after an earlier wave, estimated at 82 feet, wiped out the bridge's trusses. The discharge of floodwaters over the watershed between Comstock and Sheffield translated into a flow of 268.26 cfs, "probably the greatest rate of runoff for a watershed of this size in the United States," according to the International Boundary and Water Commission. Other nearby waterways also disgorged stupendous loads of rainwater, including Johnson Draw in Ozona, where residences and trailers were carried more than 1 mile downstream and 16 people died. The impact of the colossal bursting of the Pecos River and connected tributaries propagated downstream, wiping away the international bridge at Del Rio as if it were made of "kindling wood," then obliterating both railway and vehicular bridges spanning the Rio Grande at Eagle Pass. By the time the crest reached Laredo, debris from upstream—including railroad parts and autos—helped erase a trio of 150-foot sections of the international bridge. In Laredo, the Rio Grande peaked at 62.21 feet—five times higher than the previous record set in 1932! The Lower Valley was spared similar damage only because a dam had been completed a year earlier—and Falcon Reservoir behind it absorbed the 2.1 million acre-feet that accompanied the mammoth surge.

Another horrific flash flood struck the same region barely a decade later, in the middle of another severe drought. A barrage of very heavy thunderstorms unleashed night-long rains, including up to 8 inches in two hours, and filled two creeks that converge on the western edge of Sanderson, a community of 2,300. One of the two—Three-Mile Draw—dumped such a torrent of water into the other—Sanderson Creek—that a wall of water as high as 15 feet was sent crashing through part of the town about daybreak on June 11, 1965 (fig. 6.15). Houses, automobiles, and business structures were sent tumbling along like toys in a drainage canal. Twenty-six persons were drowned by the sudden, awesome gush of water. Another 450 people were left homeless. Damage worth $2.5 million was done to homes, businesses, and automobiles. The ravaging flood uncovered graves and washed away many headstones and markers, some of which were found as far as 4 miles away from their original location. The flow of water at the time of the flood peak on Sanderson Creek, which traditionally is dry on all but a few days each year, was measured as 76,400 cfs.

FIG. 6.15 The unique topography of West Texas occasionally gives rise to devastating flash floods, as the sudden cloudburst that flooded Sanderson in June 1965 illustrates. Source: Texas Department of Public Safety

A modest tropical storm that refused to die delivered a "world-class" flood on the Mexican border on August 1, 1978. The cyclone named Amelia lived only momentarily before hitting the lower Texas coast—and then appeared to perish just as abruptly. In fact, forming in the Gulf and moving ashore in the middle of the night, it caught most folks by surprise. Amelia was hardly finished with pulling off the unexpected, however. The leftovers of the cyclone unleashed torrential rains amounting to as much as 48 inches in only a 72-hour period at the Manatt Ranch near the Medina River. Floodwaters encircled the town of Medina and trapped campers at Peaceful Valley Ranch nearby, including Miss USA 1977, who, like dozens of other vacationers, narrowly escaped death by clinging to the last available tree. The Medina River burst forth from a tranquil stream to a churning cataract, rising from 4 feet (and 57 cfs) to almost 50 feet (and 281,000 cfs) in only eight hours. Amelia was hardly finished, however. Her residue drifted into drought-stricken North Central Texas. Incessant rainstorms pounded the dry, hard ground, creating a runoff so abrupt and violent that creeks and streams almost seemed to detonate. Albany captured more rain in one day than the town normally collects in an entire year; just west of the community, an observer measured 23 inches in only an eight-hour period. Most residents fled as floodwaters inundated some 80 percent of the town, with water up to rooftops in the neighborhoods. Four workers were stranded for 24 hours on an oil-rig in a field before being rescued. Crews had to repair a 14-mile (23-kilometer) stretch of US Highway 283 near Throckmorton that was damaged by the floodwaters. As a testament to the lingering effect of a flood event, an explosion that rocked Albany two weeks later was blamed on either a butane tank or a case of dynamite carried away and buried by the high waters.

Other parts of Texas, from the canyons of the Big Bend to the foothills of the Caprock and the Edwards Plateau, have been victimized repeatedly by raging floods in recent decades. Fierce thunderstorms that spawned a legion of twisters on May 26, 1978 also engendered torrents of rain that turned creeks and arroyos around Canyon into raging waterways that merged ahead of Palo Duro Canyon, where campers were awakened in the middle of the night by the roar of rising water that forced them to flee, some climbing atop their vehicles and others seeking refuge in trees while awaiting rescue. Well before daybreak, in only minutes, the often dry creek bed in the state park was overloaded with rushing water 20–25 feet deep and 8–10 feet above the campsite. Amazingly, loss of life was averted, in part because someone fired a gun in the middle of the night to awaken sleeping campers to the flood threat.

The area of Texas that is most notorious for catastrophic flash floods is along and above the Balcones Escarpment, the sharp gradation in terrain that marks the eastern limit of the Edwards Plateau. In fact, the region is recognized as one of the three most flash-flood-prone areas in the United States (fig. 6.16). In April 1900, just seven years after finishing touches were made to the first dam on the Colorado River near Austin, cloudbursts upstream sent floodwaters pouring 10 feet over the dam, which ripped out a pair of 250-foot sections and directed an ensuing 40-foot wave into the city. Eight workers in a lower section of the powerhouse were drowned, and another eight were carried a quarter mile before they were rescued. In Paul Revere-like fashion, a resident rode his horse through the streets downtown to warn of the impending flood. That heroic effort, along with other timely alerts, saved innumerable lives, even as residents on high ground watched as "everything imaginable" floated by, including at least 30 structures.

FIG. 6.16 The Hill Country is one of the three most flash-flood-prone regions of the United States. Source: Texas Department of Public Safety

Other waterways that course through Austin besides the Colorado River also have erupted from time to time with catastrophic repercussions. Likely the most infamous flash flood to decimate the capital city occurred on Memorial Day weekend in 1981, when a torrential downpour amounting to about 10 inches over a four-hour period fell on ground already saturated from previous heavy rains and instigated a severe flash flood that roared along Shoal Creek and several other neighboring streams. Many of the 13 drowning victims were at low-water crossings or were trying to drive through rapidly flowing water at the time. Creeks rose so quickly that many residents of west Austin had to seek refuge in second-story attics. Residential and commercial property damage amounted to about $40 million.

A cloudburst dumped almost 5 inches of rain on the capital city during a four-hour period early one night in October 1960; a resulting flash flood caused damages worth $2.5 million. On the same night, rains of as much as 10 inches elsewhere in central Texas sent rivers and streams raging out of their banks, and 11 persons were swept away. Similar flash floods erupted in central Texas a few days before Thanksgiving in 1974, claiming the lives of 13 people, 10 of whom resided in Travis County. Six months later, in May 1975, a barrage of vicious thunderstorms that battered Austin with hail and high winds also produced slashing rains that rapidly filled creeks and ravines in the area, drowning four people.

Some of the most volatile and potentially deadly waterways in the United States traverse the Balcones Escarpment west of Austin. The Blanco River, which exploded on Memorial Day weekend of 2015 to an unprecedented 41 feet at Wimberley and swept away unsuspecting vacationers, is one of the preeminently lethal ones. The Pedernales River, which courses through the bucolic meadows of Lyndon Johnson National Park, is another. An easterly wave drifting west out of the Gulf of Mexico triggered rains of 2 feet or more over the watershed of the Pedernales on September 8–10, 1952. To punctuate the fact that fast-flowing water has mind-bending potential, the river's current washed a tractor-trailer carrying 19 tons of structural steel off US Highway 290. The rig, with a gross load of 26 tons, was carried 400 yards downstream and then was wrapped around a tree 100 feet from the roadway. Just a day after the riverbed had had no flow whatsoever, the Pedernales's flow rate went from 9,230 cfs near dusk on September 10 to a stupefying 390,000 cfs only four hours later. By the next afternoon, the river swelled to an all-time high of 42.5 feet, obliterating the previous high-stage record by 10 feet. An even higher flow rate of 441,000 cfs had much to do with toppling cypress trees 5 feet in diameter! The flood on the river, and others elsewhere in the Hill Country that week, cost five lives, destroyed 17 homes, and damaged 454 others, with the total property loss amounting to many millions of dollars. An adjacent flood on the nearby Llano River combined with the eruption of the Pedernales to foment a stunning rise on Lake Travis, Austin's principal water supply. Days before, the lake was at an all-time low (372,700 acre-feet), just one-third of its capacity. In a single 24-hour period, the lake's volume almost tripled in capacity, taking in a mind-boggling 701,000 acre-feet! After rising 57 feet in that time frame, the lake was filled for the first time in seven years. Engineers calculated the inflow into Lake Travis averaged some 600,000 cfs for a 10-hour period on September 11.

It often takes a truly sultry atmosphere to muster the volume of moisture needed to trigger a torrential rain. One July night in 1987 was stifling enough to foster a spate of thunderstorms in the Hill Country that caused one of the most tragic life-taking events in Texas's history. Nearly 1 foot of rain fell over the watershed of the Guadalupe River, prompting a surge on the river near Comfort that swept away a bus and van containing youth-camp participants who were attempting to flee the area. Ten of the occupants were drowned, and another 33 had to be rescued, many clinging to trees as helicopters dropped lines to them. This happened less than two months after another historic flood event occurred, affecting numerous Hill Country rivers and streams. On May 29,

1987, rains of nearly 1 foot fed Medina Lake to an all-time record high (6 feet over its spillway) and ultimately filled up Choke Canyon Lake for the first time, three years earlier than had been anticipated. Still more rain cascaded down on South Texas in June of that year, producing the largest volume of water (an estimated 8.8 million acre-feet) to pass along South Texas rivers and streams in a century. The more-than-ample rainfall, including a record 18 inches at San Antonio in one 30-day period, fed the Edwards Aquifer to a record-high level of 699.2 feet on June 17.

While the typical flash flood affects drought in a marginal, highly localized way, some flash flood events punctuate an unfolding trend leading to the erasure of drought. The historic drought of the 1950s ended quite abruptly in the early spring of 1957 with widespread heavy rains drenching practically all of Texas, and some of that thirst-slaking water came in the form of flash floods. Rivers and streams from the Red River to the Rio Grande were at flood stage or above for much of the three-month period ending in July. Excluding those two great waterways and factoring in only the interior streams in the state, an astounding 38 million acre-feet of runoff was generated during the three months. Lake Texoma rose from a record low level to an historic high during that time. One of the most spectacular flash floods struck Lampasas on Mother's Day (May 12), with water rampaging through 68 blocks and destroying 38 residences and 5 businesses. With floodwaters 4 feet deep in the county courthouse, 90 percent of the city's business district was affected when Sulphur Creek overflowed.

Any flood episodes along and above the Balcones Escarpment are going to have an adverse effect on the "lee" side of the escarpment as well, since all rivers flow south and east into the Gulf of Mexico. Few floods were as pernicious or as costly as the ravaging floodwaters that struck San Marcos and New Braunfels on May 11–12, 1972. Rainfall of 1 foot or more in barely more than a two-hour period produced floods that killed 17 people in New Braunfels and exacted a toll in property damage of $17.5 million. The torrential rains fell below Canyon Dam—constructed in 1972 to handle floodwaters on the Guadalupe River like those that ravaged New Braunfels three times between 1921 and 1952—but above the city of New Braunfels. A peak discharge of 2,510 cfs—a Texas record for so small a watershed—was measured on Trough Creek near New Braunfels, or the equivalent of a torrent of water produced by a rainfall rate of 8.5 inches per hour. An official rain gauge on the creek captured 2.3 inches of rain in only 10 minutes! Several residents registered 12 inches of rain in only one hour, and the 16-inch storm total over four hours amounted to two and one-half times the 100-year rainfall frequency for the region. Water from the shortest river in Texas, the Comal River, fed into the Guadalupe River, raising its level 12.5 feet in a half hour—and 28 feet in only two hours!

Even in Texas's southern extremity, floods are hardly uncommon. Much of the Lower Valley was inundated on September 16–19, 1984, when an offshore weather disturbance dished out rains of over 2 feet. Forty-four straight hours of rain amounted to over 26 inches at Port Isabel—or more than that resort town normally collects in an entire year. Seagulls were seen floating on floodwaters in cotton fields west of Brownsville—or more than 20 miles (32 kilometers) inland—and portable office buildings bobbed atop floodwaters in the middle of a nearby five-lane thoroughfare.

The rain-rich northeastern quadrant of the state has had its share of heartbreak from ruinous floods. Among the most protracted spells of flood-producing rains since the Great Depression of the early 1930s ravaged the Blackland Belt during the last week in April 1966. Day upon day of torrential downpours caused rivers and streams to rampage in the area between Fort Worth and Texarkana, and the tempestuous waters swept away bridges, washed out dams, and caused damage worth $27 million to dwellings, businesses, farms, and roadways. Rains of 12–20 inches, including nearly 23 inches at Gladewater in only two and one-half days, were responsible for 33 drownings, including 14 in Dallas and Tarrant counties. Dams in the vicinity of Longview that had withstood floods for 40 years broke under the force of rapidly rising water. The Dallas–Fort Worth area, which had dealt with a pair of flash flood episodes that reached 50-year recurrence levels in 1962 and 1964, experienced some of the wildest flash floods imaginable on April 28–30, 1966. Rainfall with an intensity as high as 11 inches per hour filled creeks and streams to overflowing almost instantaneously in the densely populated metropolis. On Bachman Branch in north Dallas, water rose 18 feet in only two hours, and the peak discharge at the dam forming Bachman Lake, or 3,160 cfs per square mile over a 1.5-mile area, was the second-highest discharge rate in Texas history. Most of the area's 14 drownings occurred on April 28 when the victims were trapped in automobiles that were carried away by floodwaters swirling across streets and roads.

Whole river basins occasionally are affected by area floods, the Brazos River basin being perhaps the most notable for a pair of high-water episodes more than a century ago. An early summer outbreak of very heavy rains, as much as 33 inches spread over three days from a tropical disturbance in 1899 caused the river to overflow within the basin from near Waco to the coast at Freeport. Swelling to a width of 12 feet at one point, the river killed 35 people and caused more than $8.5 million in damage—no small sum in the late-nineteenth century. Folks rebuilt in the basin and constructed levees along the river in the years that followed. However, an extended heavy rain in December 1913 caused another flood, and because the levees were in place, the Brazos rose higher before it breached the barriers, creating a rush of water that caught many residents unaware. The death toll from that calamity was 177. But a lesson was learned: Do not rebuild in a flood-prone river basin. Fewer folks now live in the Brazos floodplain where reservoirs do not afford protection. In April 1900, swollen creeks and streams fed the Colorado River to the extent that McDonald Dam at Austin gave way suddenly, and the wall of water that ensued downstream took 23 persons to their deaths. A four-day rain that measured more than 25 inches at San Angelo in September 1936 forced the Concho River to flood the city's business district and about 500 homes.

Floods of a protracted nature are too commonplace in Texas's Upper Coast region, where many millions are put on alert for high water more than a few times in some years. Perhaps the most deleterious onslaught of heavy rains not attributable to a tropical weather disturbance occurred on June 12–13, 1973, when a massive rainstorm dumped 10–15 inches of rain centered in the vicinities of Houston, Liberty, and Conroe. Ten persons were drowned, and an astounding $50 million in crop and property damage was incurred. Almost a repeat performance took place three years later, when more than 13 inches of rain struck Houston, causing eight deaths and property losses of $25 million.

Though hundreds of miles from the coastline, Texas's second-largest metropolitan area has not been immune to the impetuosity of flash floods. Aside from the calamitous flood of April 1966 mentioned earlier, likely the most ruinous flood in modern history to afflict the Dallas–Fort Worth area occurred on May 16–17, 1949, when a 12-inch rain forced the Clear Fork of the Trinity River out of its banks. Ten square miles of the city of Fort Worth were flooded when levees constructed to contain the floodwaters broke. The flood's toll consisted of 10 deaths, 13,200 persons left homeless, and 3,000 residences and 250 businesses damaged or destroyed, with damages amounting to about $6 million. About half as much damage was wrought by another flood that occurred on the Trinity River, its tributaries, and other nearby creeks and streams on September 21–23, 1964. Considerable residential damage was inflicted on the Richland Hills suburb of Fort Worth along the Big Fossil Creek, and expensive homes in North Dallas were heavily damaged by the flooding of White Rock Creek. Late-spring rains of 1 foot or more created widespread flooding from the Red River to the coast in May 1989, forcing the floodgates at Toledo Bend Dam to be opened for the first time ever. The floods, which claimed 12 lives, made "disaster areas" out of 50 Texas counties. Still more widespread and severe flooding ensued the following winter, encompassing the Texas Hill Country and causing water to rise to record levels on the Highland Lakes chain. Most of the major rivers and streams in central and eastern Texas swelled to unparalleled levels as the entire region experienced more torrential rainfall in the spring of 1990.

Plenty of other floods have left indelible scars on the fabric of Texas history, but they happened so long ago that only the record books inform us about them. The most calamitous flood originated from a mammoth rainstorm that dumped more than 20 inches of rain on a large portion of central Texas on September 9–10, 1921. That weather event probably is best remembered for the record amount of rainfall that cascaded down on the community of Thrall: an incredible 36.4 inches in one 18-hour period, a record that still stands as the greatest high-intensity rainfall in US weather history. Central Texas had languished through two solid months without rain, and the ground had been baked as if it were concrete. Then, the skies opened up, unloading a record 24-hour rainfall total in Austin of 18.23 inches. So much rain fell north of Austin that farmers resorted to using water barrels to document the extent of the deluges. An official gauge at Taylor showed 23.11 inches in a 24-hour period, the greatest total for one day in US history up to that time. The leaden skies that emptied were attributed to a hurricane that struck south of Texas, near Tampico, then drifted northward into the heart of Texas. A total of 215 people perished in the 1921 flood—a stunning number given the fact that most people in that day did not have a vehicle with which to drive into high water or, if they did, knew not to do so. The storm also claimed $19 million worth of damage to property and crops.

Overshadowed, perhaps, by the epic rainstorm that immersed Thrall and nearby locales, a storm induced by the dissolving hurricane pounded San Antonio, causing Olmos Creek to burst open and devastate some of the city's most picturesque and popular parkland. Brackenridge Park was inundated, disrupting animal life at the zoo, where a sea lion floated away only to be seen later 75 miles (121 kilometers) down the San Antonio River. Soldiers from Fort Sam Houston wading through shoulder-deep floodwaters helped rescue some 500 trapped residents. A vivid description of the chaos was given by the *Austin American* newspaper: "By midnight, 40 or 50 houses that a few minutes before vomited men, women, and children in all stages of dress and undress, were being churned into a shapeless mass of debris where they lodged against the railroad bridge." When the San Antonio River peaked at 20.14 feet in the early morning of September 10, water was surging down Houston Street at 21,000 cfs. A 5-year-old boy sat on the shoulders of his 12-year-old brother for five hours while the older boy held on to a tree on South Flores Street awaiting rescue.

Public Alert System

Of all types of floods, the flash-flood variety is the most to be feared, if only because they are the most difficult to predict. Pinpointing the occurrence of thunderstorms, particularly their location and duration, remains a formidable task. By contrast, floods that result from widespread rains over several days usually are easier to anticipate. Still, the slowly-occurring flood also presents a substantial hazard because of the considerably large volume of water involved. To alert the public of any excessive accumulation of water that poses a hazard, the National Oceanic and Atmospheric Administration (NOAA) of the US Department of Commerce maintains a careful, endless watch on the nation's rivers, streams, and other waterways. By collecting and constantly analyzing a horde of river and rainfall data, NOAA's river forecast centers are equipped to provide river forecasts and flood advisories. Like the other warning services offered by the National Weather Service—those pertaining to tornadoes, severe thunderstorms, hurricanes, and strong winds—flood warnings provide the public with time to evacuate flood-prone areas, to move property and livestock to higher ground, and to take what other necessary emergency procedures are warranted. The river forecast and flood-warning service saves millions of dollars in flood losses annually and, most significant of all, countless lives as well.

As specialists at the River Forecast Center in Fort Worth ascertain the possibility of flash-flooding rains, advisories are issued to the public through radio, television, NOAA Weather Radio, social media outlets, and local emergency organizations. A flash flood watch, usually issued many hours in advance, means that the populace should remain informed of ongoing weather events (by staying tuned to the news media) and should be ready for immediate action if a flash flood warning is released. The flash flood watch does not mean that a flood is in progress; rather, it suggests that weather conditions exist, or are expected to develop, that have the potential for fomenting floods. When the trained weather observer detects, by radar, satellite, river-gauge monitoring, or field-observer reports, that a flood has materialized, then a flash flood warning is given out. The warning advises those persons living in an area subject to flooding to take prompt action. It cannot be overstated that when you realize a flood is imminent you should act quickly to save yourself. Time to take the necessary precautions may consist of only a few minutes, if not seconds.

Flood-alert systems are valuable tools for prompting the public to take action, but their value in saving lives is defined by the extent of the response from threatened communities. All residents of a community close enough to be affected by a nearby river or stream should know what a forecasted height of a river means in terms of their proximity to that water body. They ought to know where their property is situated with reference to the flood level of a nearby river. Equally important is the need for them to know where they can go to be safe from rising water. Most communities can either provide flood-mapping information or steer you to its source.

Safety Precautions

Few have not heard the prompting, "Turn around, don't drown." The slogan spread all over the state is a reminder of how treacherous rising water can be. In fact, over half of all deaths resulting from floods and flash floods occur in vehicles. It is not hyperbole to say the most deadly spot to be caught when water is rising is in your automobile. Even very small streams, gullies, creeks, culverts, dry streambeds, or low-lying ground that may appear harmless in dry weather can quickly become filled to overflowing with floodwater. No matter where you live, be aware of potential flooding hazards; be especially apprised of the threat if you live in a low-lying area, near water, or downstream from a dam.

BEFORE THE SKY DARKENS

There are measures you can take to be prepared in the event of a flood:

- Find out, from your insurance agent, community planner, or local emergency manager, whether you live in a flood-prone area and what the average flood depths in your community are.
- Know the elevation of your property in relation to nearby streams and dams so that you will know if the flood elevations forecasted will affect your home and property. (Your local emergency management office can help you with this.)
- Identify dams in your area and be aware of what could happen if they should fail.
- Be aware that flood losses are not covered under normal homeowners' insurance policies. Flood insurance is available in some communities through the National Flood Insurance Program. It is wise to secure flood coverage early, because there is usually a waiting period before the policy takes effect.

Of course, it is important to know the terms used to describe flooding conditions, which will be broadcast on television and radio. A flood forecast indicates rainfall has become or is likely to be substantial enough to cause rivers and streams to overflow their banks. A flood *warning* describes the affected river, lake, or tidewater; the severity of flooding (minor, moderate, or major); and when and where the flooding will begin. A flash flood watch means heavy rains are likely to cause sudden flooding in a specified area. Remember that a flash flood may occur without any visible sign of rainfall in your area. A flash flood warning speaks of flash flooding that is occurring or imminent along certain streams and in designated areas.

Upon receiving a flood warning, and even when you receive no warning but suspect that weather conditions have deteriorated to the extent that you are threatened, move to a safe area immediately. Scout your neighborhood and vicinity well enough to know where you should go when the need to flee arises. Do not procrastinate in getting away from a flood-threatened area; to delay may mean you are denied access to safety because roads have been cut off by rising water.

TRAPPED IN YOUR CAR

We tend to underestimate the force of moving water. We also should be aware that it doesn't take much water over a roadway to move a car. As little as 6 inches of water is enough to cause a motorist to lose control of his or her auto—or to cause the engine to stall. Water only 1 foot deep is plenty to float an auto, leaving the driver utterly helpless to do anything but try to escape. The best precaution is to avoid crossing a passageway covered with water. Water over a roadway is especially hard to assess at night. Don't be encouraged by seeing the vehicle in front of you make it through to the other side! If you find yourself in a car stalled on a flooded road put the windows down as quickly as you can—before the car's electrical system shorts out. (You may need a window as your escape hatch, if the door for some reason cannot be opened.) Abandon the vehicle, leaving behind any belongings in it. If you see that you are trapped inside, use a narrow but sharp object to break a window so you can climb out. If you do not have a clear path to higher ground, climb on top of the car and hold on. Use your smartphone, and its GPS feature, to notify rescuers where you are.

CAUGHT ON FOOT

If you are out in the middle of a flash-flooding rainstorm, remember the following:

- Do not attempt to cross on foot a flowing stream where water is above your knees. In fact, be aware that rolling water only 6 inches deep can knock you off your feet.
- If you are caught in water, choose where it is moving less forcefully, and use a stick to determine its depth in front of you.
- If rushing water has taken you off your feet, get in a "recovery position," on your back where you can see your toes and float. Point your toes downstream to reduce the likelihood of your head striking an object, such as a rock or tree limb. Look for something to grab and hold onto. If you can swim, move diagonally upstream to negate as much as possible the force of water being exerted on you. Get as much of yourself, as quickly as you can, out of the water, especially in colder weather, as hypothermia may set in quickly.
- At night, be especially circumspect when you are near high water, when it is more difficult to recognize flood dangers. Once you reach a place of safety, stay there. Do not venture out to areas that may be subject to sudden flooding.

CONFINED AT HOME

If rising water nearby affords you the time to vacate, then evacuate your dwelling, especially if you are asked or ordered to leave. Remember that floodwaters usually rise rapidly. A flash flood may give you minimal advance notice, so that you are forced to stay put. In that event, go to the highest point available in your dwelling, avoiding a basement or bottom level. If you come into contact with floodwater, use soap and disinfected water to wash yourself, since floodwater can become toxic and spread disease. In the event you are alerted and have opportunity to get out of your property before rising water threatens you, do the following only if you have time:

- Shut off all your utilities—electricity, gas, and water—by turning off all of the main switches. Avoid contacting any electrical equipment unless you and the device are in a dry area. It is wise to wear rubber boots and gloves when you are dealing with an electrical circuit switch.
- Transport valuable belongings—such as jewelry, clothing, papers, and firearms—to upper portions of your house or business or higher elevations of your property.
- If your property has a basement with windows, open them to allow equalization of water pressure on the walls and foundations of the structure.
- Remove from your home, or seal, all hazardous products.
- Unplug all electrical appliances and take them, with all your valuables, to the upstairs level of your house.
- Roll up all rugs and curtains from the floor and move furniture away from the walls.
- Secure any yard furniture, as these objects can pose a danger to anyone caught in floodwaters.

There are other measures you can take well before the skies grow dark and heavy rains threaten. Long before you find yourself in a flood situation, take time to make an itemized list of your personal property. Include on the list all your clothing, furnishings, and valuables. It helps the insurance adjuster to settle claims expeditiously if you are thoughtful enough to take photographs of your belongings and of the interior and exterior of your home. This precaution also is worth taking because you are better equipped in proving uninsured losses, which are tax deductible. Of course, do not leave this itemized list, with photographs, lying around the house somewhere. Put it, along with your insurance policy, in a place of safe keeping, such as a safe-deposit box.

After floodwaters subside, once you have the opportunity to ascertain damages done to your home or business, follow certain steps to aid in recovery efforts. If you sustain losses that are covered by a flood-insurance policy, you should immediately notify the insurance agent who sold the coverage. Before entering your property, you should look for structural damage and, even if you do not suspect the presence of gas, you should avoid using an open flame as a source of light; a battery-operated flashlight will suffice. Avoid turning on any lights or electrical appliances. Be sure not to touch any electrical wires that are loose or dangling in water. Opening windows and doors will facilitate the drying-out process. If perishable items are to be discarded, you should make a note of them and, if possible, get photographs before throwing the items away. If water is to be pumped out of a basement, the job should be done in stages to lessen likelihood of structural damage caused by rapid changes in water pressure.

SURPRISED WHILE CAMPING

Even before you set up a camping site, follow some tips that could save your life and that of fellow campers. Check the weather report before you head out for the wilderness (and be aware of any potential storms beyond your immediate area). Pick a spot that is at least 0.25 mile away from a river or stream and also look for evidence of previous flooding (such as high-water marks on creek banks, logs, or other debris littering the area around a creek bed, even a slow-moving bend in a river next to a low, flat area primed to collect water). Always camp or hike with others, freeing up someone to go for help. Do not rely on your cell phone. Once you realize the flash flood has arrived, do not try to outrun it. Always seek higher terrain and remain there until conditions improve. In most instances, water levels recede in a matter of hours.

7.

Nature's Rain Engines

Some 10,000 people had clustered at Trinity Park near downtown Fort Worth on the evening of May 5, 1995, for live music, festival food, and carnival rides when the sky darkened and thunder rumbled. The gathering storm blew in so quickly that not all the guests could get to their automobiles or other forms of shelter. Those exposed to the elements huddled together, hoping the wicked episode would be short lived. The fist-size hail propelled by 80 miles per hour (mph) winds pelted everything in sight, leaving many folks with 3-inch welts. Even those who sought refuge in their vehicles were not spared; the hail was so ferocious that windscreens and windows were shattered, showering the occupants with glass as well as ice. No one was killed by the bombardment, but 90 people were taken to Harris Methodist hospital in Fort Worth to be treated for injuries. Once the hail onslaught ended, heavy rain intensified. As the rainwater hit the accumulated hail on the ground, a dense fog set in. The city streets of Fort Worth, barely visible, had swirling water waist deep coursing through them. In all, 12 people died, including an area resident struck by lightning. Five more drowned in southwest Dallas when fierce rainwater runoff swept their vehicle into a swollen creek; three more vanished when a strong water current sucked them into a storm drain exposed by a missing manhole cover.

The devastating supercell thunderstorm that raked the area produced measured winds of near-hurricane force along with softball-size hail and flash flooding. It was a principal partner in a complex of storms that erupted when two outflow boundaries, spawned hours earlier from more distant thunderstorms, collided and sent highly unstable air soaring to great heights. The concoction of heavy rains, wind, and hail severely damaged many buildings, houses, and vehicles, including two bank buildings made of tiles (fig. 7.1). As with so many severe-thunderstorm incidents, structures lost their roofs, others collapsed, and countless trees were uprooted and blown over throughout the Dallas-Fort Worth metroplex; even a large communications tower was toppled. In all, property damage totaled $1 billion, making the episode one of the insurance industry's ten costliest disasters. The May 5 assault came barely a week after another savage superstorm pounded the area, with historic damage from 4-inch diameter hail at the Dallas-Fort Worth International Airport.

FIG. 7.1 Severe thunderstorms that target metropolitan areas often unleash destructively large hail and strong winds that can ravage commercial property. Source: Texas Department of Transportation

Few constituents of the ecosphere have as much a paradoxical nature as the thunderhead. Its worst form is that of a towering cumulus cloud gone berserk. In an earlier stage of maturation, the supercell's foamy, puffy exterior belies accelerating turmoil within its core. This behemoth of all clouds is known to be a generator of terrifying tornadoes and horrendous hailstones, destructive winds, and fearsome flash-flooding rains, as well as the killer lightning bolt. Yet for the hundreds of thousands of residents of the semi-arid plains and plateaus of West Texas, the thunderstorm, but only in more benign forms, is a cordially greeted guest in a water-deficient region. So dependent is West Texas on thunderstorms that without the short-lived torrents of water that gush from the warm-season varieties, the vast region would be a desert wasteland.

Moisture on the Rise

A thunderstorm can form under a variety of atmospheric conditions, but most often in Texas it is birthed by warm, moist unstable air interacting with some mechanism (such as an upper-level low-pressure cell, a frontal boundary, or a mountain range) that gives the air needed lift. Particularly in the hottest half of the year, a thunderstorm can arise from nothing other than moist air that is highly unstable (i.e., able to rise or sink more easily than usual): the heating by the sun's rays are sufficient to get the moist air rising (convection) to greater heights. All thunderstorms develop in a series of stages. The first sign of a possible thunderstorm is a cumulus cloud that has very little depth but is typified by strong vertical currents of warm, moist air feeding into the growing cloud from near the surface. This characteristic updraft resembles hot air ascending in spiral fashion through a tall chimney. The column of warm, moisture-laden air, with a typical diameter of less than 1 mile and a rate of ascent of 15–30 mph, is in part the result of differential heating of Earth's surface. Where cumulus clouds form is dictated, in part, by the landscape and its distinctive variations in composition, color, shape, and texture: some parts of the terrain absorb more sunlight and, hence, warm more rapidly and to a greater extent than others. A field of freshly plowed, rich, loamy soil, for example, captures more heat from the sun than a nearby acre of ripe wheat; a pond or reservoir of water collects even less solar energy than the wheat field. Air above these good absorbers of sunlight is, in turn, heated by them and made to expand. The warmed air is less dense and hence lighter than surrounding air, so that it rises away from near the surface while cooler and more dense neighboring air rushes in to fill the void. Thus, a convective current is set in motion.

Seeing a cumulus cloud on a warm day means some of the moisture in the rising column of air has condensed into droplets or ice crystals at an altitude of several thousand feet above the terrain. This conversion from the vapor state to the liquid state takes place when the parcel of air, while rising and expanding, is cooled to its dew-point temperature. In other words, the temperature of that parcel of air falls to the point that the air can no longer hold all its moisture. Further cooling leads to some of the moisture being "squeezed out" as droplets of water. The conversion of water vapor to liquid water, or the process called condensation, depends on the presence of tiny particles, such as dust or salt. These minuscule bits of matter, called condensation nuclei, serve as collection points for the formation of small cloud water droplets or ice crystals.

Many days from midspring to early autumn feature a preponderance of these small cumulus clouds, commonly referred to as "fair weather" cumulus. Because their existence is primarily dependent on heating of Earth's skin, these billowy clouds do not appear until late in the morning, when the surface has been heated sufficiently by the rising sun to generate the convective currents needed to grow them. A setting sun, and hence a cooling surface, cuts off the cloud's source of energy, so most cumuliform clouds perish not long before dark. That is true unless some other mechanism—such as a frontal boundary or pooling of cold air aloft (an upper low)—is at play to force the moist air near the surface aloft at other times of the day or night. The vast majority of cumuliform clouds do not grow very large and never attain the status of thunderstorm. They perish only a short time after they form because either the updraft feeding the infant cloud diminishes or the cloud grows into a layer of the atmosphere where air is so dry that the moisture in the cloud is eroded to the extent that the cloud dies.

A small percentage of these tiny cumulus grows much bigger, for reasons not fully understood (fig. 7.2). For growth to happen, the updraft feeding the cloud has to be sustained, even invigorated. Again, intense solar heating can be sufficient for this to happen, or some trigger (such as a wedge of cooler, drier air advancing as a front) can prompt expansion of the cloud, both vertically and horizontally. The taller these clouds grow, the speedier the updraft becomes, and more and more water is processed within the cloud; the cloud prospers, growing to heights of 20,000–25,000 feet (6–7.5 kilometers) above sea level. What gives the budding storm cloud a boost is the release of heat energy when water in the vapor state condenses into cloud droplets. Once the top of the blossoming cloud pushes through the freezing level, some of the incoming moisture is changed directly from vapor to tiny ice crystals. A large portion of the cloud moisture above the freezing level remains in liquid form, however, as "supercooled water." If the cloud builds further, say to an altitude of 30,000–40,000 feet (9–12 kilometers), more and more of the cloud water at this higher level becomes ice. In thunderstorms whose tops climb beyond 40,000 feet, practically all the moisture in the top portion of the cloud exists as ice.

FIG. 7.2 The towering cumulus grows above the atmosphere's freezing level and becomes a fairly efficient producer of hard—but usually short-lived—rains. Source: Texas Department of Transportation

Growth of a Load of Rainwater

With the maturing cumulus cloud growing taller, water droplets making up the bottom portion of the cloud collide and join themselves together to form raindrops, which in turn are enlarged by additional contact with other cloud droplets. Ultimately, when a raindrop enlarges to the point that its weight becomes too heavy to be supported by the incoming air current from below, it gathers with other similar drops to fall through the cloud and out the bottom as rainfall. With the onset of rain formation in a thunderstorm, marked changes occur in the cloud's internal circulation pattern. Up to this point, only an updraft has been at work, feeding the cloud with low-level moisture as fuel to energize the cloud further. Now, with the fallout of the first batch of raindrops, a downdraft is set in motion. This cascading pool of cold, damp air plunges to the ground, which then deflects that air over an even greater area of Earth's surface than that dampened by the falling rain. It is this downward-moving wedge of cold downdraft, known as a gust front, that produces an abrupt wind shift and a short period of rapidly falling temperatures at the surface. Someone in the path of this gust front will feel a chill from the air pulled from the interior of a cloud many thousands of feet above the surface, where the temperature may be 30°–50°F (17°–28°C) cooler than at ground level. In summer, the sudden cooling is often dramatic. An extreme case is the 45°F (25°C) fall in temperature that occurred at Midland on July 9, 1979, when the cold air outpouring from a hail-producing thunderstorm sent the temperature plunging from 101°F (38°C) to 56°F (13°C) in only 15 minutes.

The outflow of cold air often does more than afford folks a welcome chill. Particularly in West Texas, where much of the terrain is covered by dry, exposed soil, the potent outflow will pick up large quantities of dust particles and move them along as a dust cloud. Quite often, when the air near the surface is moist, the onrushing downdraft acts as a cold front, wedging underneath this near-surface layer of moist air and lifting it until condensation of some of the moisture occurs. This leads to the formation of an arcus, or roll cloud, which then precedes the advancing thunderstorm. Though its appearance can be threatening, the roll cloud, while suggesting extreme turbulence nearby, furnishes little if any rain.

In the absence of a "lid" or "cap" that inhibits further growth, the thunderstorm in its mature stage ascends to altitudes of 5 miles (8 kilometers) or greater, as both updrafts and downdrafts are moving vast quantities of moist air within the cloud body. The part of the cloud reaching well above the freezing level (usually between 15,000 and 20,000 feet [4.5–6 kilometers]) becomes a complex mixture of ice crystals, frozen rain (hail or even soft hail known as graupel), snowflakes, and supercooled rain droplets. This intricate movement of both updrafts and downdrafts sometimes gives rise to the formation of small flanking clouds, or turrets, that skirt the base of the parent cloud as appendages. Some of these offspring may grow to become sizable thunderstorms themselves, though the common fate of most of them is a short life without ever attaining the height of the parent cell. Close observation of some multicellular thunderstorms reveals that turrets form and dissipate in cyclic fashion, with each "pulsation" lasting 10–20 minutes. Still another distinguishing attribute of a mature thunderstorm is the spreading out of the top of the cloud as it approaches the tropopause. This feature, which resembles the top portion of an anvil, consists of ice crystals sheared off the top portion of the cumulonimbus by high-speed winds in the upper atmosphere.

Though subjects of an especially rancorous thunderstorm might think otherwise, no thunderstorm lives indefinitely. Once the downdraft becomes the predominant mechanism within the thunderstorm, the massive system begins to decay. The falling rain and companion downdraft usually restrict, if not inhibit altogether, any additional growth of the thunderstorm cell by reducing the updraft that feeds the system. With much, if not all, of the updraft shut off, the amount of incoming moisture is lessened and condensation of water vapor decreases. With less rain falling out of the cloud, even the downdraft wanes. Gradually, the temperature of the thundercloud tends toward that of the ambient air. Sadly—particularly in the semi-arid regions of West Texas—only a small fraction (say 20 or 30 percent) of the water vapor condensed in the updraft is left behind as rain on the ground; the remainder becomes cloud debris that ultimately vanishes in thin air. The perishing thunderstorm may not be finished, however, for during its life it may have so disturbed the atmosphere around it that other thunderheads are born several miles away.

Two brands of cumulonimbus clouds grow to become thunderstorms and assume importance as major producers of rainfall. The air-mass thunderstorm is most common in Texas during summer, and it tends to happen in an unorganized fashion. Known as "popcorn convection," it seems to form at random and shows little relationship with neighboring storm clouds. It is unlike the more organized and complex thunderstorms that occur in association with weather systems such as cold fronts. The air-mass variety is also known as a "heat thunderstorm," for it forms away from fronts and is caused largely by differential heating of the land surface, which sets an updraft in motion. Consequently, it is a largely daytime phenomenon, flourishing while the sun is high but then dissipating rapidly as the sun approaches the horizon. Because this variety is typically scattered or even widely scattered, predicting precisely where it will form is a challenge. Probably at least half—and possibly as many as three out of every four—thunderstorms that develop and supply showers of rain on the Texas coastal plain during the three warmest months of the year are of the air-mass variety. The mountain thunderstorm, also known as the orographic thunderstorm, is a variant of the air-mass thunderstorm. This variety of rainmaker is confined to the mountain ranges of the Trans Pecos region, where on most summer days one or several large thunderstorms will boom to lofty heights and send a torrent of rain cascading down onto a tree-decked hillside or a parched, dusty valley. When the moisture-laden Gulf air reaches the higher elevations, it is primarily the slopes of the mountains, which absorb more solar energy than the atmosphere, that initiate the thunderstorm updraft. A very large percentage—about three out of four—of the thunderstorms in summer that give the Trans Pecos much of its annual rainfall are due to heating and orographic lifting of warm and highly moist Gulf air.

Compared with the short-lived and usually harmless air-mass thunderstorm, the severe localized storm cell develops rapidly, persists for comparatively long periods, and often supplies flash-flooding rains and damaging hail. One element of a severe thunderstorm is the squall line, an arrangement of towering thunderheads in long lines so close together that it is sometimes regarded as a "line thunderstorm." Sometimes a squall line will develop well in advance of the leading edge of an advancing cold air mass; hence, it earns the moniker "prefrontal" squall line. On other occasions, the squall line marks the boundary of cold polar air as it wedges underneath warm, moist air from the Gulf of Mexico. With the warm air lifted by the intruding cold air beyond its lifting condensation level, a dark, sharply defined cloud base appears at the leading edge of the approaching line of storms. This lifting of moist air causes massive amounts of moisture to be condensed out, giving the dark, foreboding appearance that typifies squall lines. Squall lines almost always bring strong, chilling winds along with a slashing rain. Once they pass, the atmosphere becomes tranquil again. In fact, squall lines sometimes "use up" all the latent instability in the atmosphere to the extent that, if a cold front follows a few hours later, it is unable to generate a subsequent round of turbulence.

The multicell storm, which is made up of several individual cells, is another thunderstorm element having its own distinctive pattern of updrafts and downdrafts. The majority of severe thunderstorms that produce hail, high winds, and tornadoes in Texas each summer are multicell systems. They frequently display a peculiar kind of behavior in that they move systematically toward the right of (or not entirely parallel with) the prevailing environmental airflow in the middle of Earth's troposphere. During the lifetime of most multicell thunderstorms, the continuous generation of new cells on the right flank of the system, in concert with the dissipation of old cells on the opposite flank, is responsible for this drift toward the right of the prevailing wind.

The supercell, fortunately, is not nearly so prevalent as the other varieties of thunderstorms. While large and complex in organization, the elements of the supercell behave as a single entity—and the supercell usually is loaded with nasty elements that can do damage. One distinguishing feature of a tornado-producing supercell is the hook-shaped radar echo that usually forms on the right flank. It is the recognition of this peculiar characteristic by National Weather Service (NWS) forecasters that often leads to the issuance of a tornado warning. The Doppler radar allows the weather watcher to find areas of diverging and converging air, and where these areas co-locate is also a telltale indicator of a tornado. Another unique trait of a supercell is the presence of an echo-weak region, or vault, that corresponds to the area of maximum updraft. In this so-called vault, updrafts with speeds of more than 50 mph propel water droplets far into the cloud with such haste that they do not have time to grow large enough to reflect radar waves. Consequently, to the radar observer, the vault is that inner portion of a very intense thunderstorm marked by the conspicuous minimum level of radar echo. The image on the radar screen projects the appearance of an intense thunderstorm with a gaping hole in it. Much of the largest hail produced by a supercell occurs in a narrow band around the periphery of this vault.

TABLE 7.1

Where and When Thunderstorms Erupt

Average annual number of days (total days) with thunderstorms and busiest months (average number of days in parentheses). Based on data for the period 1948-2012.

LOCATION	TOTAL DAYS	BUSIEST MONTH(S)
Beaumont	66	Jul (13), Aug (12)
Houston	63	Jul (11), Aug (10)
Victoria	56	Aug (10), Jul & Sep (8 each)
Wichita Falls	49	May (9), Jun (7)
Amarillo	48	June (10), Jul & Aug (9 each)
Lubbock	47	June (9), May (8)
Dallas-Fort Worth	46	May (8), Apr & Jun (6 each)
Austin	43	May (7)
Waco	43	May (7), Jun (6)
Abilene	40	May (7), Jun (6)

A Warm-Season Sally

The thunderstorm is primarily a warm-season outburst, though in practically every year there will be at least a few outbreaks in the colder seasons. The May–July window is when days with thunderstorms are most numerous, though some coastal areas see a maximum even later—in August of all times—no doubt resulting from the prevalence of tropical disturbances that affect the coastline at irregular intervals (table 7.1). Most regions hear thunder at least once even in the winter months.

The Texas Panhandle joins its neighbors to the north across the US Great Plains as a prime area for some of the world's most boisterous storm episodes. Booming thunderheads that grow to heights of 50,000 feet (15 kilometers) or more and that unleash a menacing barrage of hail, gusty winds, and slashing rains are frequent intruders (once every three days, on average) from the Panhandle across the South Plains to the Permian Basin in summer. This inflated frequency of so many thunderstorms, especially in the Panhandle, is attributable to cool fronts that dip southward out of the central Great Plains, then stall across a heated Panhandle for several days at a time. In fact, these slow-moving summer frontal intrusions account for more than half of all the thunderstorms that erupt in Texas's far northern sector in most any year. By contrast, the cooler half of the year (November–April) is relatively sedate, with thunderstorms occurring an average of once or twice each month. The supply of moisture usually is too scanty to support the development of but a few thunderstorms, though the frequency of frontal passage is high.

Storm Alerts

Better modeling of the atmosphere has enabled forecasters to improve significantly their performance in predicting thunderstorm development, but the eruption of severe varieties continues to challenge. A thunderstorm is categorized by the NWS as "severe" when it is recognized as having either or both of the following characteristics: (a) winds with speeds of more than 58 mph or (b) large hail with a diameter of at least ¾ inch. An arm of the NWS, the Storm Prediction Center in Norman, Oklahoma continuously monitors weather conditions throughout the nation by means of a wide variety of weather data collected by radars, satellites, balloons, pilots, and ground stations. Meteorologists at the Storm Prediction Center use sophisticated computing systems to piece all this information together and formulate watches with which to alert the public (warnings emanate from local forecast offices). The forecasters use an array of public and social media to issue these alerts in the timeliest way possible.

A severe thunderstorm watch states where and for how long the severe storm threat will exist. A watch outlines an area where an organized episode of hail at least 1 inch in diameter or larger, damaging winds, or both are anticipated during a period from two to eight hours long. A typical watch area covers as much as 25,000 square miles (or 65,000 square kilometers, about half the size of Iowa). The watch is only an estimate of where and when the probabilities for severe thunderstorms are highest. Today, watches contain outlook probabilities: "low" (20 percent or less), "moderate" (up to 60 percent), and "high" (as high as 95 percent or even higher). It should not be construed as meaning that severe thunderstorms will not occur outside the area or time frame specified in the watch statement. Persons living near or on the fringe of the watch area are wise to be on the lookout for threatening weather conditions. When a watch is in effect, persons should be on guard for threatening weather and should be attuned to further information about the developing event. Keep in mind that a watch may not be issued for a severe storm affecting only a small area for a brief period.

A warning, on the other hand, warrants increased attention, and likely action, by the public. Simply stated, a watch means that severe thunderstorms are possible or even likely. A severe thunderstorm warning is issued by the NWS whenever a severe thunderstorm has been recognized or is believed to be imminent. The warning describes the area encompassing the severe thunderstorm, with special attention given to the downstream sector that stands to be affected by the thunderstorm given its location, size, and direction and speed of movement. Sometimes a warning will include wording to the effect that "this is a particularly dangerous situation."

Bolts Out of the Blue

Thunderstorms, by definition, bring about lightning, which to many is symbolic of terror and mystery—and rightfully so. After all, lightning is lethal and unpredictable. Potent enough to split huge trees and discard large chunks of wood many yards away, lightning warrants utmost respect as a display of nature's awesome power. Many strange, even bizarre, happenings are associated with the freakish and unpredictable behavior of so concentrated a charge of atmospheric electricity. Lightning, however, is one of several, and often savage, products of the tempestuous thunderstorm, that atmospheric behemoth responsible for causing extensive death and damage in Texas every year. Every now and then, the loss of death from lightning reminds us that the lightning bolt is an exceedingly potent and capricious force of nature. Its erratic and deadly character explains why it ranks near the top of the list of those natural phenomena responsible for human fatalities. On average, six people die from lightning every year in Texas, and nearly twice that many sustain serious injury. Nearly all lightning casualties occur during the months of April–September, when thunderstorms are most numerous. Most of the lightning tragedies that have occurred in recent years could have been avoided had the victims been better informed of when and where lightning was apt to strike. Too, the number of fatalities could have been reduced had the victims received more immediate and proper medical treatment.

Guilty of Charging

It seldom grabs headlines (as hurricanes and tornadoes do), and it appears in rather small numbers and stays for a mere instant. Yet, as a gigantic electrical spark whose path can never be anticipated, the lightning bolt is nothing to ignore. Many bolts go unseen by humans. Some lightning never leaves the confines of a thundercloud, whereas other strokes jump from one cloud to another. Though present for only a fraction of a second, the lightning bolt is anything but simple; and though unpredictable and destructive, lightning is also necessary, for it plays a vital role in maintaining electrical harmony between Earth and its atmosphere.

While our environment is rich with ions, or free-moving electrical charges that are either positive or negative, thunderstorms add to the congestion. A thunderstorm's ingredients (ice, water droplets, graupel, snow), when rubbing against one another, lose electrons to the adjacent air. Potent wind flow within a thundercloud redistributes these charges, with positive charges tending to congregate in the upper regions of the cloud and negative charges consolidating near the cloud base. Thus, a more extreme charge differential is established, one much more pronounced than in the atmosphere in general. Since opposite charges attract one another, positive charges cluster beneath the cloud in response to the high concentrations of negative charges at the cloud base. The same happens near the top of the cloud, where many positive charges induce a region of negative charges above the cloud. For a time, the atmosphere beneath the cloud acts as a huge insulator, inhibiting the flow of one charge to another, and the result is an immense buildup of charge centers.

Lightning strikes when a charge travels toward Earth from the base of the thundercloud in a succession of steps. Just as this initial surge of current, which is established in a tiny fraction of a second and is commonly known as the initial "stepped leader," nears Earth's surface, other discharge "streamers" leap from the surface of Earth to intercept this down-rushing streamer. The upwardly mobile streamer can emanate from a tall object, such as a telephone transmission tower, a tree, or pole—but also a human being as well, if he or she is among the taller objects in the area! When the two invisible streams of current meet each other, a charged path, or conductive channel, is completed that allows the leader from the base of the cloud to reach Earth. Instantaneously, a large flow of electrical charge travels back up this freshly carved-out channel, illuminating the branches of the leader track. This surge creates the brilliant flash that we see, though the impression it leaves with us is entirely erroneous. Whereas the lightning bolt appears to the naked eye to emanate from the storm cloud, it actually travels to the cloud from Earth's surface. This whole, elaborate series of processes consumes less than a second of time. No two flashes are identical, probably because the sponsoring cloud is constantly changing, as are the temperature, pressure, and electrical makeup of the subcloud layer of air. That is not to say that lightning never strikes twice in the same place. Tall objects protruding from the ground, such as church steeples, transmission towers, and trees, become inviting candidates as the conduit for the flow of electrical charge between the cloud and Earth. These vulnerable objects may be hit several times during a single thunderstorm event.

A Family of Bolts

Not all lightning forms in the lower portion of a thundercloud where negative charges proliferate. Some lightning occurs at or near the top of a cloud, where positive charges are concentrated. This area, including the anvil (if there is one), interacts with the negative charges above, producing positive lightning. This type of lightning is especially dangerous because it tends to strike away from the rain shaft, either ahead or behind the main thundercloud. Moreover, its continuing current lasts longer, so it is more capable of starting fires, and its peak electrical current makes it deadlier to human beings. Though the varieties of lightning are numerous, the most common kind in Texas is streak lightning, a cloud-to-ground discharge that appears to be concentrated in one channel (fig. 7.3). Most strokes of this type of lightning have branches, appearing as a photo rendition of a river with many tributaries appended to it. Often two or more of these branches hit the ground concurrently, causing what is popularly called forked lightning (fig. 7.4). Whenever a strong wind blows at right angles to the observer's line of sight, a bolt of streak lightning may appear to be spread horizontally as a ribbon of parallel luminous streaks. Each successive stroke is displaced by small angular amounts and may appear as distinct paths to the human eye or the camera. This variety is referred to as ribbon lightning or band lightning. Bead lightning (also known as pearl or chain lightning) is seen only occasionally when an observer is positioned relative to the lightning bolt so that his or her end-on view of a number of segments of the zigzag pattern gives an impression of unusually bright pockets of light at various points along the lightning channel.

FIG. 7.3 Streak lightning is the most common, and destructive, form of cloud-to-ground lightning. Source: National Oceanic and Atmospheric Administration

FIG. 7.4 Forked lightning teams with streak lightning to create an awesome display of natural fireworks—and remind us that lightning can, and does, strike twice in the same place. Source: National Oceanic and Atmospheric Administration

Often in areas of the state where the far-distant horizon can be easily viewed, light is seen to be emanating from a great distance although the observer cannot actually see a lightning stroke or hear the clap of thunder. This luminosity is known as heat lightning and can be reflected or diffused by clouds, leaving a person with a sensation of a broad area of flashing light. Another fairly bright illumination, which is blown by the wind and whose flash cannot be seen because it is obscured by clouds, is sheet lightning. It is so labeled because it seems to light up a large portion of the cloud in which it occurs, giving the impression of a "sheet" of diffuse but bright light. It really is not a distinct type of lightning but rather is a manifestation of an ordinary variety of lightning that is hidden by clouds. The one form of lightning that stirs the most conversation, and controversy, is ball lightning. It is uncommon, so much so that some suggest it is a figment of human imagination. People who have seen it say that it consists of a reddish, luminous ball that usually is about 1–2 feet in diameter that may zip across a floor, roll out of a tree, or float in midair. Hissing is sometimes heard, followed by a noisy explosion; but at other times, the phenomenon has been seen to disappear quietly after entering a home and moving around inside!

Lethal Fallout

Certain notions about lightning have long lives—even though they have no basis in fact. For instance, you may have heard it said that lightning never strikes twice in the same place. Truth is, lightning can—and often does—strike the same spot over and over again. Tall buildings in major cities are known to be hit dozens of times every year. Another myth is an automobile protects one from injury from lightning because of its rubber tires. The fact is it isn't the rubber meeting the surface that provides a measure of safety to a driver or occupant of a vehicle; rather, it is the steel frame of a hard-topped auto that affords protection (as long as one is not touching the metal shell of the vehicle). Are victims of lightning strikes not to be touched because they carry an electrical charge? No, such persons carry no electrical charge and should be tended to immediately.

Lightning poses a threat to a driver of an automobile, not so much a danger from electrocution as being blinded by the brilliant flash of a lightning bolt that hits nearby. Momentary blindness can lead to the loss of control of the automobile (especially at night) and the subsequent striking of an oncoming auto or a fixed object off the roadway. To be sure, it is possible to be hit by lightning while getting into or out of your automobile, as happened to a minister and his son near Murchison in Henderson County one afternoon in May 1979. Although the boy was only slightly injured, the father was killed while getting into their car when a lightning bolt hit a nearby tree and jumped to the automobile. A vehicle is a safe place to be during an electrical storm if it is fully enclosed—like a hard-topped car, minivan, bus, or truck. If you encounter a lightning storm, slow down, use extra caution, and consider pulling off the roadway into a safe area. By no means should you leave the vehicle. While inside the vehicle, avoid using any electronic equipment plugged into an electrical outlet because lightning striking the vehicle could cause serious injury. Vehicles not safe when lightning is near include convertibles, golf carts, riding lawn mowers, boats without cabins, and open-cab construction equipment.

Swimming is one of the most dangerous activities during a thunderstorm. Because water is a good conductor of electricity, you can still be injured even if you are in the end of a pool opposite the one receiving a lightning strike. Swimming pools are usually connected to a much larger vulnerable area by way of underground water pipes, electric and gas lines, and telephone cables. A strike anywhere on this metallic network can induce a shock nearby. Likewise, golfers are particularly exposed to danger, not only from golf clubs that are high conductors of electricity but from other metal objects like fences, power lines, and maintenance machinery.

Many of the fatalities that occur each year from lightning strikes take place in wide-open spaces and involve athletes and other recreational participants. A tally of athletes who died from lightning in Texas is instructive to all who dare to be exposed when thunder is rumbling nearby: a young man in San Angelo killed by lightning while holding an aluminum bat during a baseball game at a family reunion on an afternoon in late May; a Terrell high school lad felled by a lightning stroke from a leaden sky in the middle of an afternoon football practice in early September; a jogger in north Houston who, when suddenly stunned by a bolt of lightning, crumpled to the pavement and died on a hot, sticky day in July; and an aspiring golfer felled by lightning on a municipal golf course in Harlingen on a sultry evening in August. Spectators of outdoor athletic events are vulnerable too.

The best advice for anyone working outdoors when thunder and lightning are discerned: get inside! Those who choose not to go inside, and those unable to secure sanctuary inside a structure, are vulnerable. More than a few people have been struck and killed by lightning while seeking shelter under a tree. An 11-year-old Keller girl died in a Dallas hospital 10 days after being struck by lightning while sitting in a swing under a tree during an electrical storm. On a late summer afternoon in 1977, a man seeking refuge under a tree in a pecan orchard was hit by a lightning flash; the bolt first hit the tree, then traveled to the back of the neck of the victim and down his body, burning holes in his clothing and knocking the soles of his shoes off. Others have died while exposed in wide-open areas. Two men—and the horses they were riding—were slain by lightning while herding cattle across an open meadow in Montgomery County near Dobbin during a late-morning April thunderstorm. In another similar instance, a youth died from being hit by lightning near Dubina in Fayette County while hauling hay one August evening in 1978.

When caught in an electrical storm and shelter is not readily available, a good rule to follow is "If you can see it (lightning), flee it. If you can hear it (thunder), clear it." If you perceive that lightning is within 6 miles (10 kilometers) of your location, suspend whatever activity you may be engaged in, avoiding trees, poles, and other tall objects that attract lightning. Avoid wet areas, refrain from touching any metal objects, and seek out large, permanent structures or get into a fully enclosed metal vehicle. If the storm catches you by surprise and you cannot evacuate to a safer place, spread out from others, squat, tuck your head, and cover your ears. Head for the safest place available as soon as the immediate threat passes.

While structures like houses and commercial buildings are places to be during thunderstorms, there are some things to avoid doing while you are inside. Homeowners using an antenna for television should know that not only do most residential antennas provide no protection, they may in fact invite lightning into the home because their ground connections are usually inadequate. When lightning strikes, current can pile up and jump to a better-grounded conductor, such as a water pipe; a house fire then can break out when the current passes through a wall in the house. For homeowners who maintain residential phone lines, lightning arresters can be deployed where the phone line enters the house. Still, it is not altogether safe to use a residential telephone when lightning is around. A greater threat than being burned while on the phone is the potential of acoustic shock. A person's hearing may be affected by the loud click made in the telephone receiver when lightning strikes the circuit. To play it safe, delay making a phone call until the storm has passed.

There is a degree of vulnerability being in an airplane navigating near electrically charged clouds. It is not uncommon for airplanes, while airborne, to be struck frequently by lightning. The small burns, pits, or holes on such inviting targets as wing tips, rudders, and the nose of the fuselage attest to hits by lightning. Aerials that protrude into the air are especially vulnerable. However, pilots worry much more about turbulence than lightning. The stresses exerted on the structure of an aircraft by violent updrafts and downdrafts have been known to tear off wings. The battering of hail can also be a serious problem. On the other hand, lightning most often merely disrupts communications with the ground, although it can cause some structural damage and can be an irritant to the pilots. The encouraging word is airplane crashes directly attributable to lightning are extremely rare.

Safety Precautions

That 9 of every 10 people struck by lightning live to relate their experience is only marginally reassuring. Since few people care to take their chances with the lightning bolt, it pays to keep an eye to the sky when billowy cumulus clouds hint at becoming power generators. The more intense a thunderstorm, the more frequent are the lightning strokes generated by it. Thus, to apply a rule of thumb from the Lightning Safety Institute, Again: "If you can see it (lightning), flee it; if you can hear it (thunder), clear it."

When a thunderstorm approaches, seek shelter inside a home or a large building or, if neither of those is available, get into a fully enclosed, all-metal vehicle (such as an automobile). Suspend any outdoor activities when lightning is observed as much as 6 miles (10 kilometers) away. Once inside a structure, use the telephone land line and television sparingly, if at all. Of course, not everyone can reach a safe haven when lightning is detected or suspected. For the person caught in the open when lightning has begun, remember and abide by the following safety rules:

- Avoid getting underneath a tall object, such as a tree, that stands alone in an open area; it is a natural lightning rod. If you are in a forest, find cover in a low area under a thick growth of smaller trees.
- In wide-open areas, seek out a low place, such as a ravine or valley. However, avoid any low-lying wet area because surface water or saturated soil is likely to be a better conductor of electricity than the surrounding landscape. If you find yourself hopelessly stranded in a level field and you sense that lightning is about to strike (an event often presaged by hair standing on end), squat on the balls of your feet with your arms wrapped around under your knees (fig. 7.5). The important thing to remember is to keep as small an area of the body as possible from making contact with the ground. Do not lie flat on the ground.
- Try not to project yourself above the surrounding landscape, as you would if you stood on the top of a hill, in an open field, on a beach, or in a boat.
- Get out of, and as far away from, water as possible. Swimmers should keep in mind that pools are connected to a much larger surface area through water pipes and electric and telephone wiring. A lightning strike nearby could induce a shock traveling to a pool of water with virtually no advance notice. Pool activities should be suspended as long as 30 minutes after the last peal of thunder is heard.
- Stay away from objects like tractors and other farm equipment, motorcycles, golf carts, and bicycles.
- Get away from metallic objects (such as wire fences, rails, clotheslines, metal pipes, steel towers, even golf clubs) that could carry lightning to you from some distance away.
- Spread out from others if you are in a group (such as a party of hikers or mountain climbers) so that, if lightning should hit, a fewer number of people will be affected.

Many of us often encounter lightning while driving. In general, it may not be imperative that you get off the road—as long as your vehicle has a fully enclosed metal shell, such as a sedan,

FIG. 7.5 With no place to hide during an electrical storm, squat on the balls of your feet to minimize your exposure. Source: George W. Bomar

minivan, bus, or pickup truck. In fact, do not leave such a vehicle during a thunderstorm. Slow down, of course, and use extra caution. Refrain from using any electronic devices such as radio communication equipment. A lightning strike to the vehicle could cause serious injury if you happen to be talking on the device. Be aware that a lightning flash could disrupt your vision, putting you at peril especially if you are moving at a high rate of speed.

Being on open water is to be avoided when an electrical storm is approaching. The vast majority of lightning injuries and deaths on boats occur on small vessels having no cabins. So, if the forecast calls for thunderstorms, stay onshore. If you are out on the open water when a storm develops, head for land and find sanctuary. If you get caught in an electrical storm on a boat, drop anchor and get as low as possible. Although larger boats with cabins often have lightning protection systems installed, stay inside the cabin and avoid contact with anything capable of conducting an electrical current. Damage to pleasure craft is not uncommon and often is expensive. The masts of sailboats are highly susceptible, even when taller boats or other objects are nearby. One incident illustrative of the severe beating that lightning can administer to pleasure craft on water occurred on Eagle Mountain Lake in 1954. A blaze of lightning hit the mast of a small sailboat and surged down the head stay, putting the stem out of commission. It continued on down the shrouds, putting a large hole in the starboard side of the craft and numerous other holes the size of a fist in the port side. Even the sail, which was stowed below deck, sustained five burn holes. Fortunately, since all the holes in the hull were above the waterline, the boat did not sink. The little craft was not grounded; that is, none of the metal rigging was in contact with the water. Though the percentage of boat fires attributed to lightning is quite small, it still behooves a boat owner to take precautionary measures to limit the damage that might be done by a chance lightning hit.

The Lucky Survivors

Some stories about people being struck by lightning and surviving are true. There have been some rather bizarre instances in which people were struck by lightning but somehow survived the experience. In fact, available statistics suggest that more people struck by lightning live to tell about it than die from being hit. Most likely, however, survivors are never "hit" directly by lightning, for a direct strike leaves severe burns. Most persons injured by lightning—and even many who die—have few, if any, marks on their bodies; the current that passed through them was relatively small. The ability of the human body to accommodate an electrical current is very small; merely a small fraction of an ampere of current lasting only a fractional second can so affect one's central nervous system as to kill. Most lightning injuries result from the victim's being stunned or knocked unconscious. Those persons hit while standing under a tree, for instance, do not receive the brunt of the lightning bolt. The amount of electricity that passes through their bodies is but a small portion of the total amount of current that emanates outward along the ground from the tree. They are more likely to be harmed by the concussive effect of an exploding tree or by flying chunks of tree trunk the instant a lightning bolt registers a hit.

Damage wrought by lightning to timber resources and structures can be enormous. Every year hundreds, perhaps even thousands, of lightning-caused fires bring destruction of a hardly estimable dimension to timber, other vegetation, and wildlife. Without fail every year, homes, farm buildings, power facilities, fuel storage installations, and even aircraft become frequent targets of the lightning bolt. Property damage to homes and business establishments alone perennially runs into millions of dollars. Few structures are immune to the stroke of lightning. Objects susceptible to this type of natural violence range from roving livestock to underground circuitry and ships at sea. Grass fires triggered by lightning—like those that razed thousands of grazing acres one evening in August 1980 in Clay and Jack Counties—are common throughout much of the year. Explosions induced by lightning are not infrequent, either. One of the most notorious incidents of an oil storage facility being struck by lightning occurred at a dock in Nederland on April 19, 1979. A flash of lightning struck a Liberian oil tanker, igniting fumes from a recently emptied oil tank onboard the ship. One man died in the ensuing fire, another drowned when he was blown into the water, and 16 others aboard the ship at the time of the explosion were injured; the ship subsequently burned and sank. A thunderstorm on a cold January night in 1974 produced a lightning bolt that struck a large oil storage tank at Port Neches. The resulting fire, fed by strong winter winds, persisted for 24 hours and consumed 150,000 barrels of crude oil. Even subterranean objects are susceptible to lightning: about 5,000 feet of telephone cable were burned near Mount Pleasant one afternoon in March 1976, disrupting telephone service for two days and costing $275,000 worth of repairs. An untold number of livestock are also taken every year by lightning. The repercussions of a flash of lightning can be preposterous; for example, a bolt struck and shattered a tree in Kilgore before dawn one day in November 1977, and fragments of that tree blew across the street, smashing windows and damaging the roof of a church building.

Now, lightning is not all bad. Although the extent of the contribution is not quantifiable, and though lightning as a blessing seems counter-intuitive, it is a boon to farming. Crops need nitrogen to grow, and lightning supplies some of that natural fertilizer. Though nitrogen makes up about 79 percent of all the gases in Earth's atmosphere, it is of no use to plants unless and until it is joined with other chemicals. The lightning bolt is the catalyst for bringing some of the nitrogen in the air together with oxygen to form a nitric oxide gas, which is then dissolved and transported as nitrate to Earth's surface by precipitation. The soil absorbs the nitrate and then furnishes it to plants.

Thunder

When the electrical current that begins to flow in a new channel suddenly heats up the air, it causes a sonic boom called thunder. This very intense and rapid heating explodes the air out from the lightning channel, thereby compressing adjacent air, which in turn instigates sound waves. When the lightning channel is close to the observer, the sound made is more like a crack or a boom. If the lightning is more distant, the sound reaching the observer comes over a number of seconds, so the noise made is more of a rumbling or rolling. The loudness of thunder depends upon the magnitude of the electrical current as well as the rate at which the current builds up in the lightning channel. Louder thunder occurs when the current builds up more rapidly to a larger magnitude. Thunder most often can be heard for distances up to 10 miles (16 kilometers) away, although sometimes it can be heard at twice that distance. There are circumstances when it cannot be heard even at fairly close distances. The distance between the lightning and the observer determines the amount of time that elapses between seeing the lightning and hearing the thunder. This leads to a rule of thumb by which you can gauge your distance from lightning: since sound travels at a speed of 1,090 feet per second, or about 1 mile every 5 seconds, count the number of seconds between these two events, then divide by five to get the distance in miles. For example, if the sound of thunder follows the flash of lightning by 10 seconds, it may be assumed that the lightning flash is about 2 (10 ÷ 5) miles (3 kilometers) away. Similarly, the duration of thunder produced by a particular lightning bolt depends upon the distance from the observer to the closest and the farthest parts of the lightning flash.

Hail as Oddball

Of all the forms of precipitation engendered by the thunderstorm, hail is by far the most peculiar—and the most despised. Only those raising livestock in the wide-open spaces of West Texas—and nearly always in need of moisture, no matter the form it takes—welcome hail. Stated simply, hail forms when either (or both) large raindrops or snow pellets (also known as graupel) are repeatedly propelled up and down in a cloud, thereby allowing them to grow at the expense of millions of tiny cloud droplets. It is believed that graupel serves more often as a hail embryo than do frozen raindrops. While being carried within the thundercloud by its forceful updrafts and downdrafts, these embryos grow larger with each successive layering of opaque ice (rime), a result of the impact of supercooled cloud droplets onto the embryos. Each time additional water freezes onto the hailstone, a bit of heat energy is released. Consequently, the temperature of a growing hailstone may be several degrees warmer than its cloud environment. This is an important characteristic of the hailstone, for the temperature of the hailstone's surface in turn has a lot to do with its rate of growth. If the hailstone's surface has a temperature below freezing, the collected cloud droplets readily freeze and the surface of the stone remains relatively dry. However, if the temperature is right at the freezing level (32°F, 0°C), the collected water will not freeze immediately. The surface of the stone stays wet, and some of the water may be shed as the stone moves around inside the cloud, thereby limiting its growth. During its lifetime, a hailstone may sustain several "wet" and "dry" growths as it passes around within a large thunderstorm having a varying temperature and liquid water content. In this way, a hailstone develops the layered structure that is often observed when it is sliced into pieces.

Hailstones come to us in a myriad of shapes and sizes, though spheroidal stones are by far the most common (and it is this type that often exhibits the layered interior structure resembling an onion). It is not out of the ordinary, however, for hail to be either conical or otherwise generally irregular in shape. Some of the irregularly shaped hail consists of chunks or clusters of smaller hail elements frozen together. By the standard established by the World Meteorological Organization, for an ice particle to be classified as hail, it must have a diameter of at least 0.2 inch (5 millimeters)—anything smaller than that is classified as an ice pellet. Small hail or ice pellets may be found in almost any thunderstorm and, for that matter, in many towering cumulus clouds. The hail of most concern to us, known as large hail, by definition has a diameter of more than 0.8 inch (2 centimeters). It is usually found within, alongside, and underneath large convective clouds (cumulonimbus) whose tops may extend to 50,000 feet (15 kilometers) or more above sea level. In fact, some of the very prolific "hailers" that blossom in the High and Low Rolling Plains of Texas soar to levels of 60,000 feet (18 kilometers) or even higher. These hail-producing thunderheads typically have diameters ranging from 5 to 10 miles (8–16 kilometers), while the diameter of the area of hail deposits at any one instant is usually on the order of 1 to 3 miles (1.5–5 kilometers). Generally, for much of Texas, most of the hail, thankfully, is no larger than marbles, ranging in size from a small fraction of an inch to about 1 inch. However, hail the size of golf balls or even tennis balls is not uncommon, especially out west and in spring and early summer. Indeed, seldom a year passes without at least a dozen or two occurrences of hail as large as baseballs. Some of the largest hailstones observed in Texas weather history fell in San Antonio in May 1946; these stones, even larger than Texas grapefruit, struck the ground with such momentum that they bounced upward and broke second-story windows in some buildings.

On most any day with hail, the intensity with which hail is unleashed varies considerably among regions of Texas. One disastrous hailer can wipe out a dozen farms while leaving hundreds more between them unharmed. One measure of a hailstorm's intensity, other than the appearance of crops shredded or beaten into the ground, is the depth of hail accumulation on the ground. The majority of Texas hailstorms fail to deliver enough hailstones to cover the ground completely. Some hail is plentiful enough to do that, however, and in a few instances the hail may accumulate to astounding depths. Likely the record for most hail accumulation in state history is owned by the town of Ballinger, where hail covered the ground as much as 3 feet deep on May 16, 1917. It reportedly took the citizens of Ballinger seven days to clear the hail from streets and walkways. Another notable incident occurred in the far northern portion of the state on May 28, 1970, when hail up to the size of baseballs severely damaged wheat and other crops in a 450-square-mile area of eastern Carson County. That aspect of the storm is not so uncommon for the Texas High Plains, however; what is striking is that the hail piled up to 18 inches on Texas Farm-to-Market Road 294 so that only one lane could be used for several hours. Phenomenal hailfall accumulations are not confined to the "hail alley" of West Texas. Motorists on Texas Highway 323 near Henderson had to contend with small hail that was bumper deep after a severe thunderstorm pummeled Rusk County in May 1976. Yet, hail depths of more than an inch or two are rare in central and eastern sections of Texas on most hail days during spring.

Hail's Legacy

The far-ranging, fertile cropland of the Texas High Plains bears the brunt of most large hail onslaughts in most years—punctuating the reality that the sector of the Texas economy that stands to lose the most from hail is agriculture. Hail damage to crops in some parts of the Panhandle and plains of West Texas is a virtual certainty every year, with losses running into the tens—and sometimes hundreds—of millions of dollars annually. The hail event of August 1979 stands out as one of the most cataclysmic storms to hurt the agricultural sector. The remarkable hailstorm left some 150,000 acres of cotton, corn, and other High Plains crops "looking like fields in the dead of winter." Another 550,000 acres were damaged by the hail, most of which was no larger than marbles. In all, farmers lost on that "Black Friday" crops valued at an astounding $200 million. To make matters even worse, most of the cotton crop that was destroyed or heavily damaged was judged by area farmers to be "the most promising cotton crop in many years." The incident highlighted the fact that hail not only restricts the quantity of crops produced every growing season but also affects the quality of crop yields. While food growers suffer the most from crushing hailstorms, not to be ignored is the great amount of loss and damage that occurs each year to livestock and personal property in all regions of Texas.

In nearly every year, most of the annual loss due to hail is concentrated in a few storm days. Indeed, a single massive hailstorm, like that which ravaged the southern High Plains in August 1979, may account for a very large percentage of any year's total statewide. Obviously, most—if not all—of the loss consists of damage to crops. But a hailstorm hitting in the more densely settled areas of eastern Texas likely will result in much greater cost to personal and business property and a lesser amount to crops. One such hailstorm whose legacy consisted almost solely of losses to residential and business property pounded the city of Texarkana on April 22, 1978. In a mere 20 minutes the ferocious storm caused damage totaling $10 million to residences and businesses and another $5.4 million to automobiles. Hailstones as large as 2.25 inches were measured in the northern sector of the border city. At the same time on this memorable hail day, numerous other hailstorms were ravaging scattered communities from the Low Rolling Plains to East Texas; one of the hail-producing thunderstorms, whose top was gauged by weather radar to have extended to 70,000 feet (21 kilometers), caused many millions of dollars in damage to property in Mansfield.

Few types of crop can withstand an assault by hail and suffer little damage. The crops most easily hurt by hail are fruits, for they lose their value from even slight bruising by hail of any size. Luckily for the Texas food economy, much of the fruit crop is grown in the state's southern quarter, where damaging hail seldom occurs. Tobacco is also highly susceptible, but very little is grown in Texas. Soybeans, barley, rye, sugar beets, sorghum, potatoes, and other vegetables are also vulnerable to hail to some extent. By and large, however, most of the hail-induced crop loss sustained by Texas growers each year is made up of wheat, cotton, or corn. In fact, Texas leads the nation in sustaining the greatest average annual loss to such crops as wheat and cotton because of hail.

Damage from hail to nonagricultural assets can dwarf the loss incurred by crops. Loss of or damage to property on account of hail consists primarily of disfiguration to fixed structures (such as homes, business establishments, and automobiles) and injury (or even death) to livestock and trees. Much of the loss incurred in residential areas during hailstorms is made up of damage to roofs of homes. Of course, windows may be broken, paint may be chipped off, and siding may be damaged, but these types of losses usually are small in comparison to the damage inflicted on roofs. Even human beings sometimes become casualties. Injuries to the head are common, especially when hailstones reach golf ball size or larger. Obviously, a safe place to be during a hailstorm is within a stout, fixed structure like a home; still, seclusion in one's home may not guarantee safety from the ravages of hail. Although she was not seriously injured, a woman living in Comfort was knocked unconscious one day in April 1970 by a hailstone as big as a baseball that came through the window of her home and struck her on the head. Moreover, an automobile is not necessarily a safe place to be during hail. One onslaught on May 10, 1996, bombarded Big Spring with hail as big as softballs, injuring 48 people, including a motorist whose arm was broken after a hailstone shattered a side window of her car and struck her with enough force to cause the fracture! A Boy Scout caravan of five automobiles on the interstate highway was pummeled by 5-inch diameter hail that knocked out every window in each vehicle. Some 2,000 residential roofs had to be replaced, with many of those less than a year old, because of another disastrous hailstorm barely a year earlier. The advice given to residents during a lightning storm also applies for hailstorms: confine yourself to places away from doors and windows.

Pilots know to avoid flying near hail-bearing thunderstorms. Some can even relate stories of encountering hail not only within a thundercloud but near one as well. It is not uncommon to discover while in the air that a thunderstorm can and often does eject hailstones of varying sizes into clear air as much as 5 miles (8 kilometers) away from the main storm cell. The amount of damage that hail can do to an aircraft—whether a light version or a larger and heavier model—is stunning. A classic case of hail causing an extensive amount of damage occurred near Carswell Air Force Base in Fort Worth in 1959. A B-52 jet bomber, part of the Strategic Air Command fleet, penetrated a severe thunderstorm while cruising along at 8,000 feet (2 kilometers) when suddenly it encountered hailstones the size of baseballs. The ten-person crew lost control of the huge aircraft momentarily, but before they could bail out, the jet passed just as abruptly out of the storm cell. It was not until the crew took the plane to 23,000 feet (7 kilometers) for an assessment of the damage that the full effect of the hail outburst was realized. The huge hailstones had shattered the windshield and had ripped off the radome, which sheltered the radar's antenna assembly. The leading edges of the wings had been hammered almost flat, while numerous holes were discovered in the wings and the engine nacelles (coverings). The plane's electrical system had momentarily failed during the encounter with the hail because pieces of metal from the body of the plane had been swallowed by the plane's engines. Although the 47-second confrontation with the hail failed to disable the giant bomber, it did batter the $8 million jet extensively, and it took several months to refurbish the B-52 for duty. Airports around Texas are particularly vulnerable to hailstorms, as many of the facilities' assets sit exposed on tarmacs. A lone supercell thunderstorm that formed at midafternoon on April 5, 2003 in Kent County carved out a path of destruction from Padgett to near Sulphur Springs, a distance of nearly 200 miles (322 kilometers), along which hail up to golf ball size exacted one of the costliest tolls on property from hail in state history. Among the property damage, which totaled $885 million, were 59 aircraft—along with 121 commercial flights canceled at Dallas-Fort Worth airport.

Hail's Favored Locations

While no region of Texas is safe from hail, some areas are particularly vulnerable. Many points in the state's northwest quarter are struck by hail, on average, three or four times a year. Hail is most common in the southern Panhandle, the southern High Plains, the northern Edwards Plateau, and parts of the Low Rolling Plains and North Central Texas. On the other hand, hail is comparatively scarce in the coastal plain and in the Big Bend area of far West Texas. A few or even several years may pass between the occurrence of hail in these latter areas.

Mercifully, most hail outbreaks at any given point last no more than a few minutes—but the hail event can endure for hours, as the episode of April 5, 2003, described above, illustrates. Though it is fairly uncommon, hail may occur more than once on the same day in the same locale—first with one or more prefrontal squall lines, then later from frontally induced thunderstorms accompanying the invasion of cold air. Since thunderstorms are scarce during winter, hailfall also is rare. The lowest monthly hail frequency is in January, when hail is likely to be seen at any one locale only once every 15–20 years. For winter as a whole, hail is most rare in the Panhandle and the Trans Pecos. Even though the frequency of cold fronts is usually at a peak during this season, the thermodynamic state of the West Texas atmosphere is not conducive to the type of intense convection needed for the production of hail.

The worst that the hail season has to offer in much of Texas has happened by the time spring gives way to summer. A measure of the likely incidence of hail, known as the "significant hail parameter" and derived daily from sounding data produced by weather balloons, indicates that, on average, hail has highest probability at Amarillo in the period from mid-April to mid-July; the hail season peaks, on average, in late May and early June. The hail season peaks earlier in northeast Texas, for the entire months of April and May as well as early June (fig. 7.6). During May, nearly every community from the High and Low Rolling Plains to North Central and East Texas will be pelted at least once by hail. Farther south between the Balcones Escarpment and the Gulf of Mexico, hailstorms are also most frequent at this time of the year, although the frequency is not as high as in the Panhandle and the Red River valley. Residents of cities like Amarillo, Lubbock, Midland, Abilene, and Wichita Falls can count on two or three hailstorms during the March–May interval. In these areas, it is not uncommon for hailstones to be as large as baseballs, even softballs. Along and east of the Interstate Highway 35 corridor, the typical size of hail is markedly reduced, with anything larger than golf ball size rather rare. However, even in the more humid climes of North Central Texas, hailstones occasionally can be enormous. The frequency of hail occurrence is about half that much in places like San Angelo, Austin, Waco, and San Antonio. The number of hail-bearing thunderstorms wanes markedly in all but the extreme northern sector of the state when summer becomes entrenched. For those living in the Panhandle, two or three hail outbreaks are the rule in the typical summer. One or two summers in every 10 years may provide a few incidences of hail in the Trans Pecos and North Central Texas. Hail incidence increases again with autumn's approach, although the likelihood of hail occurrence is not nearly as great as during the spring—but it is significant nonetheless. Only in the High Plains, where thunderstorms abruptly become rather scanty with the onset of autumn, is there an appreciable diminution of hail potential. Hail can occur as late as November, but when it does fall that late in the year, it is almost always extremely spotty.

Even though hail is rather uncommon in Southern Texas, it can leave an indelible imprint when it happens. One most notable incident took place on May 11, 1971, when hailstones 4 inches in diameter and chunks of ice, each weighing nearly 1 pound and some 5 to 7 inches in diameter, smashed automobile windshields, greenhouses, and roofs and windows of homes in Brownsville. Damage to property in a three-county area including the city of Brownsville amounted to $2.8 million, including the total destruction of 80 acres of honeydew melons in Starr County.

The Art of Hail Suppression

Can anything be done to prevent or inhibit the growth of hail in a storm cloud? Off and on since the drought of the 1950s, various groups in West Texas have used cloud seeding to lessen the likelihood of damaging hail, if not eliminating the incidence of hail altogether. This intervention in the cloud's natural processes is meant either to stop outright the cloud's production of hailstones or to make many smaller hailstones (instead of a relatively few large stones) that will eventually melt into large raindrops as they fall through the relatively warm layer of air between the cloud and Earth's surface. Silver iodide has been and continues to be the most commonly used nucleating agent because it has a crystalline structure that closely resembles that of natural ice. The silver iodide, when injected into a cloud believed to have the potential for producing hail,

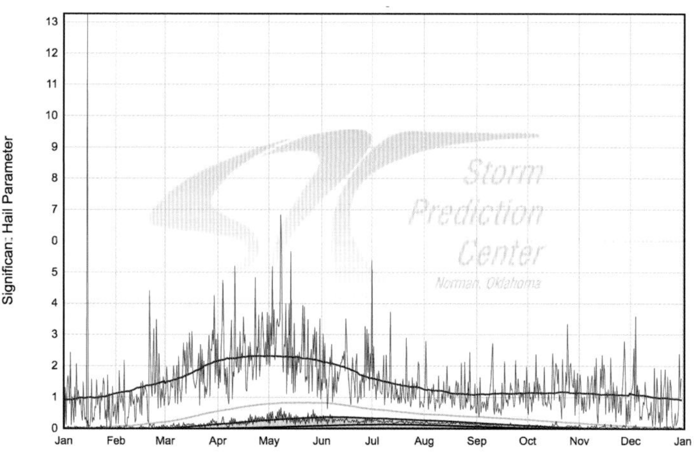

FIG. 7.6 Sounding data reveals hail with the highest probability of occurrence in northeast Texas is in spring. Source: National Oceanic and Atmospheric Administration

serves as surrogate ice crystals by attracting a large portion of the multitudes of droplets within the cloud. These droplets freeze into ice when they make contact with the silver iodide crystals. Theoretically, if the number of these hailstone embryos having silver iodide as their nuclei can be increased to a point that they compete for the available supply of supercooled water within the cloud, there is likely to be many more, but much smaller, hailstones. These would melt during their descent and ultimately reach the ground either as much smaller, and hence less damaging, hailstones or as nothing more harmful than large raindrops. A recent analysis by Texas Tech University of at least one hail-suppression project on the Edwards Plateau has produced evidence that the seeding is helpful in reducing hail occurrence in some thunderstorms. In semi-arid West Texas where hail suppression has been practiced in recent years, ample anecdotal evidence has been offered to encourage sponsors to continue the effort. Studies of crop-hail-loss statistics, furnished by insurance companies for areas targeted for seeding and areas adjacent to them, have shown the seeding activity coincided with reductions in crop losses. It remains the case that verifying the utility of hail-suppression programs requires that an initiative be designed and carried out in the form of careful, systematically controlled experiments. As discussed in chapter 11, that type of well-designed research, focused on augmenting rainfall from thunderstorms, showed seeding's potential to the extent that the state legislature invested, with water conservation districts, in seeding projects on a broader scale.

8. Cyclones from the Sea

Heed the warning to evacuate now or face "certain death" if you refuse to do so. Even storm-tracking enthusiasts living along the Texas coast could not recall the last time, if ever, when the government had been as candid in calling on the citizenry to evacuate in the face of an imminent cataclysm. With Hurricane Ike bearing down on Galveston Island, residents living in single-family homes were ordered to leave the island. That mandatory order to move out was merely the latest in a string of admonitions the National Weather Service (NWS) and other governmental agencies had issued in the days leading up to Ike's invasion of the island in the early morning of September 12, 2008. As a category 3 storm, Ike had hit the island of Cuba twice nearly a week earlier (forcing one million inhabitants to evacuate), and though such a lengthy interaction had nearly crippled the storm, Ike recouped once it got into the Gulf of Mexico and drew a bead on Texas (fig. 8.1). Many of the oil refineries and chemical plants on the Texas coast closed in advance of the storm, and President George W. Bush issued an emergency declaration to free up federal resources to aid with the evacuation. In spite of all the forewarnings of likely calamity, some 40 percent of Galveston Island residents spurned the order, digging in and riding out the storm.

FIG. 8.1 Outer bands of intense thunderstorms are visible in this view from space of Hurricane Ike prior to its landfall on Galveston Island on September 12, 2008. Source: National Aeronautics and Space Administration

The refusal to leave proved costly. Just before Ike landed, the NWS, in measuring maximum sustained winds from the storm of 110 miles per hour (mph), downgraded the system to a category 2 hurricane—which removed its "major" status. The tens of thousands remaining on the island chose to stay put, thinking the storm was losing its wallop. While winds near the eye of the storm had diminished somewhat, it was the 11-foot storm surge that posed the greatest risk to those hunkering down in their residences. (Warnings of a storm surge of as much as 25 feet proved overly ambitious.) Nonetheless, 6 to 7 feet of seawater covered the island as Ike eased inland. Seventeen buildings, including a pair of apartment complexes, collapsed from either the rising water or ensuing fires. The city's Moody Gardens was closed from flooding. While the height of the storm tide reached 10 to 13 feet along most of the island and Galveston Bay, an even higher surge (as much as 17 feet) did even more damage on the Bolivar Peninsula, where scores of homes were leveled. Countless residents of Orange and Bridge City were left trapped in attics and on roof tops, and some 100 caskets were unearthed from Hollywood Cemetery. While 12 people died (11 in Galveston County) from drowning, another 25 perished in ways indirectly related to the storm: carbon monoxide poisoning from generators, accidents while clearing debris, or house fires from candles.

Ike's fallout could have been worse. A slight shift in its path before landfall meant the storm's core missed the concentration of oil and petrochemical plants around Houston, and the storm surge over low-lying coastal islands and into the Port of Houston (the nation's second-largest seawater port) was weaker than forecasters had anticipated. Offshore, the Cypriot freighter *Antalina* and its 22-member crew became disabled, and an attempted airborne rescue had to be aborted because of excessively dangerous winds. The crew successfully rode out the storm. Ike assumed a path strikingly similar to the hurricane that inundated the island on September 8, 1900, which brought a storm surge that flooded the entire island, at that time Texas's largest city and a major US port. Galveston, which lost 6,000 of its citizens in only a few hours, was essentially destroyed by that colossal unnamed storm, the nation's worst natural disaster ever. Ike's impact likely was mitigated, in part, by a 17-foot seawall that was constructed in the wake of the 1900 hurricane to impede incoming waves.

Like so many cyclones that roar out of the Gulf of Mexico, Ike was hardly finished dealing out misery once the core of the storm went well inland. Downtown Houston was wrecked, with innumerable windows blown out of buildings, including the 75-story Chase Tower and the Reliant Stadium. Many of the city's millions lost electricity, and some outages continued for up to a month afterward. Mercifully, because Ike's core surged through the area at a rapid pace, the city—prone to flood because of its elevation and topography—was spared from much major flooding. Farther inland, Ike's remnants shed lots of rainwater, with Conroe and Evadale collecting over 1 foot of rain. When the final tally of human and property loss was calculated, Ike—which once had a diameter of 600 miles (966 kilometers) when it was out at sea—exacted a cost of some $14 billion in Texas alone, and nearly $38 billion overall in the United States and Cuba. (Ike's leftovers would spawn torrential rains in the Midwest, bursting a dam in Michigan, causing massive sewage overflows in Chicago, and closing parts of the Mississippi and Missouri Rivers to public access.)

If a category 2 hurricane (just barely under a 3) could earn the distinction of being the third costliest Atlantic hurricane of all time, what might a really major hurricane (a category 4 or 5 storm) do to the Texas coastline? Spanning several decades now, Texas has avoided interaction with a truly mammoth hurricane, like those (Katrina, Sandy) that have wrought unbelievable hardship elsewhere along the Gulf and Atlantic coasts of the United States The numbers, and dates, of past preeminent hurricanes hitting Texas, and nearby coasts in Mexico and Louisiana, imply it really is only a matter of time (fig. 8.2). When that time comes, how well will the event be anticipated, and how well will the public respond? Weather advisories will continue to improve in specificity and timeliness—but the desired precision and accuracy remains elusive. As the former lead hurricane forecaster, Max Mayfield, has observed, "Even public responsiveness, one would think, would respond to a demonstrated greater skill at forecasting hurricane growth and movement."

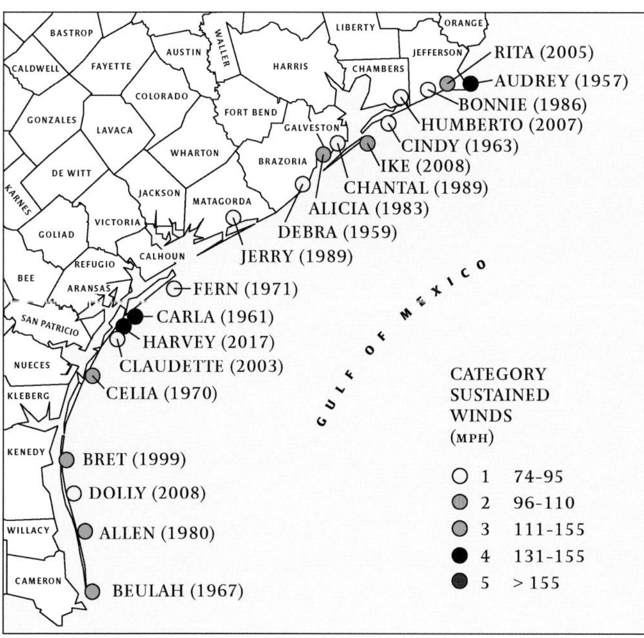

FIG. 8.2 Hurricanes striking the Texas coastline since 1950. Source: George W. Bomar

Greatest Storm on Earth

Unleashing incomprehensible amounts of energy over huge areas, the hurricane hovers over the sea as a gigantic whirlwind of awe-inspiring violence. Its inherent energy, that of several atomic bombs, qualifies it as the most destructive weather phenomenon known. The word "hurricane" likely stems from the Tainos word *huracán*, meaning evil spirit, a term appropriated by the native people of the Greater Antilles and Bahamas who undoubtedly experienced, in their lifetime, some of the worst tempests of the sea to come to America out of the Atlantic. (Texans use the term hurricane rather than typhoon; both words describe the same phenomenon, with typhoon reserved for the western Pacific Ocean.)

Hurricanes, and lesser cousins regarded as tropical storms, belong to the family of cyclones, an all-encompassing term used to describe all cyclonic (counter-clockwise) circulations originating over tropical waters. The progenitor to a named storm, known as a tropical or easterly wave, is sometimes birthed by the displacement of a vast high-pressure system centered near Bermuda. When in summer this "Bermuda high" relaxes its hold on the tropical Atlantic, a trough of low pressure may impinge upon it. When this low-pressure area gets drawn into the prevailing easterly winds (the easterlies) that flow continuously through the tropics, an "easterly wave" often is spawned. This wave then propagates westward and organizes the circulation pattern near the sea surface into areas of converging and diverging airflow. Where air converges, the depth of the moist layer of air near the ocean surface expands, and large cumulonimbus clouds (thunderheads), which may grow to heights of 40,000 feet (12 kilometers) or more above the ocean, sprout in the increasingly favorable environment. A spate of these clusters of thunderstorms often can be seen from satellite imagery made of the tropical Atlantic on a typical summer afternoon. Many of them travel westward without undergoing any intensification. Occasionally, an easterly wave can be organized further when forces high in the atmosphere intensify the circulation within the wave. In a matter of hours a vortex (much like a whirlpool) forms within the wave. Still, it may never develop into a storm of major significance.

To become a tropical storm, and potentially a hurricane, a weather disturbance above the sea surface has to be able to tap into warm seawater (in the low 80s to a significant depth of the ocean, as much as 150 feet). Conveniently, perhaps, the tropical Atlantic warms in early summer to that magnitude, allowing budding tropical "waves" to feed off the heat from this warming pool of water. But a wave, or disturbance, needs much more to become an organized cyclone worthy of a name. Air aloft in the middle atmosphere, from 3 miles (5 kilometers) up, needs to have moisture, and the atmosphere itself must be unstable, cooling with altitude and causing that moist air to rise and condense. Moreover, the embryo of a future tropical storm or hurricane needs to form within a few hundred miles of the Equator to allow the Coriolis force to be strong enough to sustain its rotation. All of these ingredients are frequently available, so numerous low-level low-pressure cells form just off the African coast (and sometimes even over the African mainland). They may blossom into full-fledged tropical waves as they drift westward from Africa to North America only to grow no more because they encounter a vertical shearing of the wind that disrupts their circulation. Other than a sea surface too cool to support cyclone evolution, the primary reason the hurricane season does not get underway until May or June is because strong wind shear is usually present in the upper atmosphere from winter deep into spring.

The precursor to a notable tropical cyclone also may originate within the ever-present equatorial trough, also known as the intertropical convergence zone (ITCZ). This band of towering convective clouds that encircles the Earth lies between the large high-pressure cell centered in the Atlantic near Bermuda and its counterpart in the Southern Hemisphere. Each year it follows the sun, migrating northward in spring, ultimately to a point about 12°N latitude in August. At times the ITCZ is observed to be 100 miles (161 kilometers) wide and is marked by huge clusters of thunderstorms that soar to heights of 35,000–50,000 feet (9–15 kilometers) over the open seas. During the North American summer, with the ITCZ well north of the Equator, an eddy within the ITCZ may be spun out northward into the prevailing easterlies, where it undergoes intensification and grows to become an easterly wave, possibly a depression. It too must find a lasting, favorable environment to survive and prosper. Its evolving circulation as a cyclone will be sustained, even enhanced, when more air is pumped out the top than is brought in at the bottom near the ocean surface. On the other hand, if more air converges on the storm than is discharged, the system fills up and the storm dissipates. Critical to its development is the flow of air from below whose heat and moisture is sufficient to keep the storm stoked.

Storm Categories

As elsewhere in the tropical Atlantic, and in the Pacific basin as well, tropical cyclones in the Gulf of Mexico evolve through stages, or categories, both descriptively and quantitatively. An easterly wave qualifies for the term tropical storm when it attains a closed-wind circulation with sustained winds of at least 39 mph. When it features sustained winds of 74 mph or greater, it becomes a hurricane. The intensity of hurricanes is measured by the Saffir-Simpson Scale, which varies between category 1 and category 5, the highest rating reserved for storms with sustained winds in excess of 155 mph (table 8.1). Any category 3 or higher storm is regarded as a "major" hurricane, capable of producing extensive damage. Theoretically, frictional force from the Earth's surface creates enough of a drag on a spinning phenomenon that a hurricane cannot muster winds much higher than 200 mph. Certainly lesser hurricanes, like Ike in 2008, can lead to immense damage, if not worse, and even some tropical storms are known for awe-inspiring damage and destruction. Both tropical storms and hurricanes are assigned names from lists maintained by the National Hurricane Center, based in Coral Gables, Florida. Each season, as tropical depressions advance into the higher categories, a name is given from the list of names, which are arranged in alphabetical order and alternate between male and female. A separate list is used for tropical storms and hurricanes that form in the eastern North Pacific, some of which make landfall in Mexico and funnel moisture into West and South Texas, occasionally creating bountiful rains, if not floods. Names on the list are rotated from year to year, and a name is re-used every sixth year unless it has been assigned to a well-known storm responsible for extensive damage and many deaths.

TABLE 8.1
Saffir-Simpson Hurricane Scale

Abbreviations are miles per hour (mph), kilometers per hour (kph), feet (ft.), and meters (m).

CATEGORY	WIND SPEED	STORM SURGE
1	74-95 mph	4-5 ft.
	119-153 kph	1.2-1.5 m
2	96-110 mph	6-8 ft.
	154-177 kph	1.8-2.4 m
3	111-130 mph	9-12 ft.
	178-209 kph	2.7-3.6 m
4	131-155 mph	13-18 ft.
	210-249 kph	3.9-5.4 m
5	155 mph or more	18 ft. or more
	250 kph or more	5.4 m or more

Most hurricanes emanating from the Gulf of Mexico and striking the Texas coastline are at least 100 miles (161 kilometers) in diameter. Gale-force winds (with speeds of more than 40 mph) typically extend 150–250 miles (240–400 kilometers) in all directions from the center. Seen from above with the aid of weather satellites, the cyclonic spiral of the storm mass is distinctive. Photos taken by the space station and orbiting satellites reveal the distinctive spiral of a hurricane as well as its eye. Ground-based weather radar highlights that a typical named storm consists of heavy rain bands encircling at least part of the eye, with areas of lighter rain—or none at all—sandwiched between the bands. Wispy cirrus clouds are invariably observed on the storm's periphery. The hurricane is distinctive among all other storm cells for the display of a calm center. More often than not, a hurricane that either forms in the Gulf of Mexico or migrates into the Gulf from the Caribbean Sea has an eye with a diameter of about 15 miles (24 kilometers) on average, although diameters of 25 to 30 miles (40–48 kilometers) are not rare. As the eye of the hurricane draws near, winds dramatically diminish to 15 mph or less, and the sun often appears as rainfall pauses. But then, as the opposite side of the wall approaches, winds accelerate just as dramatically but now from the opposite direction. This sequence of events can delude people into thinking the storm has passed once the eye moves overhead. After all, the change in weather mixed with a strange calm can be downright eerie. Folks unaware of this pattern of behavior may venture out from a safe sanctuary only to expose themselves, momentarily, to another round of battering. It is common to find flocks of birds flying within the eye of a hurricane—and those birds may have come great distances. Once entrapped in the center of the storm while it is still in its infancy, the fowl cannot escape until the storm runs aground or eventually blows itself out in colder waters thousands of miles from the birds' range.

With the air spinning around the center of a hurricane or tropical storm like water in a whirlpool, a concomitant tight pressure field is established from the storm's edge to its center. Normally, in the absence of storms, the barometric pressure at sea level in the tropics is close to 30 inches of mercury, or approximately the equivalent of 1,015 millibars (mb). As a hurricane core approaches, that pressure can drop as much as 1 inch of mercury per hour on occasion. (To see the needle on an aneroid barometer hanging on the wall in one's home actually move can be unsettling!) In some of the more intense hurricanes to affect Texas, the barometric pressure at or near the center of the storm can plunge to 28.00 inches or less. For instance, Hurricane Ike, in September 2008, had a central pressure of 28.10 inches of mercury (951.6 mb), as measured on a pier when its core made landfall.

The paths carved out by cyclones hitting the Texas coastline are as unique as the storms themselves. It is rather uncommon, for example, for a storm's movement offshore to suggest it will hit a certain point onshore—then hit the target. Predicting the movement of hurricanes is a challenge because the steering winds that control the rate and direction of movement of the storm mass can, and often do, change in the hours leading up to landfall. These changes in steering winds may be a reflection of movement of a nearby high-pressure cell, like the one that is usually resident over the northern Gulf coast in summer. Fewer data on the upper atmosphere out over the sea make the prediction challenge even more daunting. As a general rule, tropical storms and hurricanes that strike the Texas coastline move at speeds less than 30 mph at the time of landfall. These low-altitude steering currents are responsible for the storm's demise, either over land or out at sea.

As indicated earlier, a hurricane's longevity depends in part on the availability of energy from relatively warm water. To be sustained, or invigorated even further, an approaching hurricane must find surface-water temperatures of at least 78°–80°F (26°–27°C). Just off the Texas coast, that is usually not a problem from mid-June until September. In fact, temperatures on the sea surface for hundreds of miles distant from the coast can be as warm as 84°F (or 29°C) in midsummer. What contributes to this excessive warming near the coastline is a quite shallow continental shelf that allows the sun to warm the water at relatively great depths. Even though mixing of surface water and deeper, cooler water does occur, it is not enough to compensate for the inflated temperatures at the surface. Thus, it is more common for a cyclone moving west out of the central Gulf to be sustained, if not intensified, as it nears the Texas coast. In those instances when a cyclone does not thrive while in the western Gulf, it is often the case that sufficiently warm water was unavailable, a common development in the early autumn. It is rare, though, for a storm to meet water in the Gulf cold enough to cause it to die. Within a few hours after landfall in Texas, the typical hurricane is sapped of much of its vigor because, once over land, the storm's primary source of energy—the relatively warm waters of the western Gulf of Mexico—is obviously lost. Furthermore, the circulation of the hurricane is hampered by the additional deleterious effects of frictional drag. While winds inevitably diminish and storm surge is no longer a factor, torrential rains and undesirables like tornadoes and lightning may persist for many hours. Most often, once far inland, a Texas hurricane can act like a broad, deep low-pressure area, shedding lots of rainfall and posing a flood threat that can carry over to adjacent states and even regions of the country a thousand miles or more removed from Texas. Often that rainfall is needed badly, for the season, after all, is summer and any abatement of searing heat is most welcome.

Timing of Hurricanes

As the sun each day climbs a bit higher in the sky toward its apex on the summer solstice (on or about June 21), veteran coastal residents are already in a watchful mode for something from the sea. Officially, the "hurricane season" in the Gulf of Mexico extends from June 1 through November 30, though professional sky watchers are poised to "catch" a storm should it surface prematurely. Once in a great while, something of significance will crop up in the Gulf of Mexico as early as mid-May, while the warm waters off the western Mexican coastline likely will have started the parade with one, or several, tropical cyclones even earlier. If a noteworthy tropical weather disturbance materializes well before the solstice, it most likely will be found in either the Caribbean or the Gulf of Mexico. While once a quite uncommon occurrence, a tropical storm or hurricane in the Bay of Campeche or western Gulf of Mexico in June is not surprising at all any longer. As the summer progresses, the prime region for breeding tropical depressions shifts eastward in the Atlantic, and farther away from the Equator. Most hurricanes affecting Texas will form in these far more distant waters, giving Texans a longer time to prepare should any of the storms drift west into the Caribbean and then the Gulf of Mexico. By mid-September, the focal point for the generation of many tropical cyclones reverts back to the Gulf of Mexico and the Caribbean Sea. Then there is a rather brief window in which a major storm can develop not far from the Texas coast and strike quickly. By mid-October, cold fronts are arriving from Canada with some regularity, and frontal boundaries moving across Texas tend to shunt approaching Gulf storms away from Texas toward the central or eastern

Gulf coast. Since tropical weather records for the Texas coastline were begun in 1871, no cyclone has hit the coast of Texas any earlier than June 4 or any later than October 17. It is conceivable that a tropical cyclone could hit Texas outside the mid-May to mid-November time interval—though it is highly improbable. Named storms have occurred in December, and in January 2016 one was birthed, though it remained far at sea closer to Africa than North America.

TABLE 8.2

Major Hurricanes Hitting Texas

Category 3-5 storms making landfall.

DECADE	CATEGORY	NAME[1]	LOCATION	DATE
1900s	4		Galveston	Sep 8, 1900
	3		Freeport	Jul 21, 1909
1910s	4		Galveston	Aug 17, 1915
	3		Baffin Bay	Aug 18, 1916
1920s	-			
1930s	4		Freeport	Aug 13, 1932
	3		Brownsville	Sep 4, 1933
1940s	3		Matagorda Bay	Sep 23, 1941
1950s	4	Audrey	High Island	Jun 27, 1957
1960s	4	Carla	Port Lavaca	Sep 11, 1961
	3	Beulah	Brownsville	Sep 20, 1967
1970s	3	Celia	Corpus Christi	Aug 3, 1970
1980s	3	Allen	Port Mansfield	Aug 10, 1980
	3	Alicia	Houston	Aug 18, 1983
1990s	3	Bret	Padre Island	Aug 22, 1999
2000s	3	Rita	Sabine Pass	Sep 24, 2005
2010s	4	Harvey	Rockport	Aug 25, 2017

[1] Hurricanes were not assigned names until 1950.

The Unforgettable Ones

No one living today experienced the awful calamity that endures, more than 100 years later, as the nation's worst natural disaster. No other natural catastrophe can approach the "West India Hurricane" that slammed into Galveston Island on September 8, 1900, and claimed an estimated 5,000–8,000 lives (table 8.2). Secondarily, it also cost Texans a loss in property valued at \$30–\$40 million, an astounding price when thought of in terms of the value of a dollar five generations ago. While a wind velocity in excess of 100 mph was observed on Galveston Island as the eye of the storm came ashore, it is likely the speed was higher because the wind-measuring device in use was blown away. As if it were setting a benchmark for future hurricanes to aim for (and Ike in 2008 virtually matched it), the storm surge inundated much of the city of Galveston with water 8–15 feet deep. Much of the city, the state's largest at the time and a key US port, was swept clean from two to five blocks inland from the coastline—not one building was left standing. Most of those who died, including entire families, were drowned. Streets were filled with debris and, three weeks after the hurricane hit, bodies were still being removed from the debris at a rate of 20 to 30 per day. The stupendous loss of life was not due to inadequate warning of the impending disaster. Indeed, storm warnings had been hoisted one to two days in advance of the hurricane's onslaught. By heeding warnings as little as six hours prior to the onset of dangerous conditions, some 12,000 inhabitants of the island saved themselves. Of those who chose to stay, fewer than 100—or no more than 15 percent of the total remaining on the island—survived!

As a seemingly favorite target for tropical cyclones, the city—only recently recovered from the 1900 calamity—was lashed a second time by a vicious hurricane just 15 years after. Engineers had raised the island's elevation by 4 feet in the wake of the 1900 episode, and a seawall was constructed to blunt the impact of future storm surges. Sure enough, the added protection reduced the death toll from the hurricane that smashed into the island before dawn on August 17, 1915. However, that storm, whose death toll amounted to 275, was not the equal of the turn-of-the-century episode (table 8.3). The later cyclone, nonetheless, was nasty enough; its sustained winds, as high as 120 mph, an enormous storm surge, and heavy rains caused property losses of $56 million.

Many years passed before Galveston Island became another bull's-eye. Along with the Houston metropolitan area, the island (especially its western end) bore the brunt of Hurricane Alicia on August 18, 1983, which became the costliest storm in Texas history. From its point of landfall at San Luis Pass, the eye of Alicia trekked north-northwestward to skirt the western edge of Houston, thereby affecting a nine-county region with a population of 3.4 million people. Top winds of 115–130 mph and tides 12 feet higher than normal were primarily responsible for 21 deaths, 3,094 injuries, and damage and recovery costs of about $3 billion.

TABLE 8.3
Deadliest Tropical Cyclones

Storms resulting in 50 or more deaths in Texas.

LOCATION	DEATHS	DATE
Galveston	8,000+	Sep 8-9, 1900
Corpus Christi	284	Sep 14, 1919
Upper Texas coast	275	Aug 16-17, 1915
Indianola	176	Sep 16, 1875
Sabine	100+	Oct 12, 1886
Brownsville	70	Aug 5, 1844
San Antonio	51	Sep 23, 1921

Though far smaller than Galveston, the little community of Indianola, once situated on the coastline in Calhoun County, bore the brunt of more than one of Texas's all-time great hurricanes. Although details are sketchy on the hurricanes that hit the town of 6,000 residents in the latter portion of the nineteenth century, it is known that the storm surge associated with the hurricane on September 16, 1875, carried away three-fourths of the town and killed 176 of its inhabitants. Undaunted, survivors rebuilt the city, only to behold, 11 years later on August 20, 1886, another great cyclone whose storm surge carried away or left uninhabitable every building in the town! This time, those left to pick up the pieces abandoned hope of restoring trade and, because they feared yet another weather calamity, moved away to Port Lavaca, Victoria, and Cuero. Indianola was never rebuilt; today the site is marked by a park and an impressive statue of French explorer René Robert Cavelier, Sieur de la Salle.

For the oldest generation of Texans, when the subject of hurricanes is broached, one name readily comes to mind: Carla. With considerable advance warning, towns all along the coastline, from Port Arthur to Corpus Christi, evacuated—constituting the greatest mass movement of humanity in the United States during peacetime. Galveston, for the most part behind a 17-foot seawall, opted to stay put. During its slow, deliberate trek across the Gulf of Mexico for nearly a week, the colossal storm seldom deviated from a straight-line course, thus making it one of the most predictable hurricanes in Texas history. Hurricane Carla, with an eye measured at 30 miles (48 kilometers) in diameter and winds clocked at over an astonishing 150 mph, slammed ashore near Port Lavaca just after noon on September 11, 1961 (table 8.4).

Among those who stayed behind to brave Carla's rage, 34 of them did not survive. Unquestionably, the evacuation of more than a quarter-million Texas coastal residents helped ensure a rather modest death toll for such a violent storm. However, as one of the most intense hurricanes to strike Texas in recorded history, Carla wrought damage and destruction worth $408 million. She did not perish without a protracted struggle, meting out torrents of rain that flooded more than 1.5 million acres of land within Texas. In fact, Carla supplied heavy rains far inland in central Texas and could still be identified several days later while generating rain in North Dakota. In Carla's aftermath, residents of many communities in its path stepped out to behold the unmistakable signature of a hurricane: buckled utility poles hanging like corpses from taut power lines, twisted street signs pointing every direction but the correct one, mangled television antennae strewn on roofs and in yards, and boats of all sizes inverted in canals. Dead cattle were scattered about, leaving a sickening stench, and hundreds of rattlesnakes, forced out of their habitat by surging water, wriggled and hissed in yards and on streets. Some livestock, crazed by the ordeal, attacked people and had to be shot, and alligators were seen roaming about in neighborhoods. Shrimp boats and pleasure craft were carried far ashore by the storm surge, with even heavy steel boats as much as 70 feet in length displaced up to 500 feet from the shoreline.

The 1961 hurricane practically destroyed the fishing resort of Port O'Connor. Nothing but flattened debris was left of the downtown section, and nearly all the homes on the street fronting the bay were destroyed or so badly broken as to be irreparable. Port Lavaca also bore the brunt of Carla, but remarkably, because of a total evacuation hours before she struck, the city sustained no fatalities or serious injuries. Tides there were measured at 18.5 feet above normal, and winds estimated at 175 mph pummeled the city. The old causeway heading out of the city toward Point Comfort was demolished, while a second, modern causeway nearby was severely damaged with huge concrete slabs separated and lifted partially atop other broken pieces of the conduit. A heavy steel patrol boat some 70 feet in length was driven 50 yards onto land, and many huge planks and heavy chunks of driftwood littered the harbor. Meanwhile, at the height of the storm surge in Palacios, seawater covered nearly all the town at a depth estimated at 13 feet. Only the hospital, situated at the highest point in town and used as a haven for some 200 residents who chose to ride out the storm, avoided being flooded, although water crept to within a few feet of the front door.

In terms of fatalities, the great cyclone that slammed into Corpus Christi on September 14, 1919, was second only to the "West India Hurricane" that decimated Galveston in 1900. The

TABLE 8.4
Highest Hurricane Wind Speeds

Top wind gusts measured (miles per hour, mph) for the Atlantic Basin. The speeds are actual measurements made; three Atlantic storms made landfall on the US mainland with wind gust estimates in excess of 200 mph.

SPEED	NAME	DATE	LOCATION
186	None[1]	Sep 21, 1938	Blue Hill, Massachusetts
178	Betsy	Sep 6, 1965	Bahamas
175	Carla	Sep 11, 1961	Port Lavaca, Texas
175	Janet	Sep 27, 1955	Chetumal (Mexico)
174	Andrew	Aug 24, 1992	Coral Gables, Florida
172	Camille	Aug 17, 1969	Boothville, Louisiana

[1] No name was assigned at the time for the "Great New England" hurricane.

coastal bend city, which had been hit by another severe hurricane just three years earlier, caught the full force of the hurricane, whose eye crossed the coastline just south of town. A storm surge combined with winds measured as high as 110 mph erased 284 lives and caused damage and destruction amounting to more than $20 million. The memorable killer hurricane forced tides up to 16 feet above normal as far away as Galveston.

Hurricane Beulah rates among the most notable hurricanes in Texas history, in part because of the torrential rainfall and outrageous number of tornadoes it produced. As the third-largest hurricane in Texas weather history, Beulah dumped torrential rains of 10 inches or more on a vast area of Southern Texas from San Antonio southwestward to the Rio Grande and southeastward to the Gulf of Mexico. The mammoth flooding that resulted on many streams and rivers accounted for much of the astounding $150 million in damage to property and crops. To make matters worse, before and subsequent to Beulah's landfall around daybreak on September 20, 1967, more than 100 tornadoes were spawned by the sprawling storm. As a rule, hurricane-produced tornadoes are much smaller and remain on the ground for shorter periods than those that develop at other times of the year in interior portions of Texas. This may explain why, out of more than 100 tornadoes sighted during Beulah's lifetime, incredibly only a few caused significant damage and only 2 resulted in deaths. But more misfortune would follow.

Beulah was slow to disintegrate, and it traced out a remarkable path rather unique to most tropical cyclones entering Texas. After drifting northwestward during the first 24 hours of its existence over land, it inexplicably turned and moved southwestward toward the Rio Grande south of Laredo and into Mexico before vanishing on September 23. That course fostered rains of rare magnitude in South Central and Southern Texas, including, over five days, a total of 27.38 inches at Pettus in Bee County. Numerous locales between Corpus Christi and the Rio Grande collected more rainfall in less than four days than they normally receive in a whole year. No river or stream south of San Antonio was spared from major flooding; in fact, many of them sustained the highest flood levels in recorded history. The San Antonio River established an all-time high-water mark when it crested at 18.4 feet above its flood stage of 35.0 feet. Many locales in the area south of a line connecting Laredo, San Antonio, and Matagorda were isolated for more than a week because of flooded roads. The effects of raging floodwaters were especially hard to forget for residents of Ganado, where oily residues carried by the rising water from nearby oil fields were deposited on most buildings in that community.

Hurricane Celia earned distinction for its violent winds. Celia was not much of a rainmaker: heavy rains of up to 6–8 inches were confined to a three-county area encompassing Corpus Christi, and the band of moderately heavy rains (with storm totals of little more than 2 inches) was unusually narrow—merely 50 miles (80 kilometers) either side of the hurricane center. But the storm left nearly one-half billion dollars in damage to property and crops in the southern quarter of the state (table 8.5). Such heavy losses resulted from Celia unleashing her greatest fury on the major metropolitan area of Corpus Christi, where a peak wind gust of 161 mph was gauged at midafternoon on August 3, 1970, within one hour after the storm's eye crossed the coastline midway between Corpus Christi and

Aransas Pass. Towns like Pearsall and Jourdanton, located within 40 miles (64 kilometers) of the hurricane eye, received no rainfall at all. The highest storm surge, measured at Port Aransas, was only 9.2 feet. Another bizarre aspect of Celia was the location of the storm's strongest winds. Unlike most hurricanes, which feature highest winds in the right-front quadrant, Celia manifested greatest wind speeds in the left-rear quadrant. Furthermore, these strongest winds were observed in streaks spaced about 1.5 miles apart, with almost no damage resulting between them. Hurricane-force winds were felt as far inland as Del Rio, while wind gusts of more than 50 mph occurred in the Big Bend area.

Rainmakers

Some hurricanes are remembered for being largely one-dimensional in effects. Hurricane Cindy brought wind and storm surge, of course, but the storm distinguished itself for the torrents of rain it produced during the time that it moved onshore and drifted westward through Texas's Upper Coast in mid-September 1963. The flooding that ensued was on a scale similar to that instigated by Amelia. Surprisingly, however, a hurricane that cost Texas residents a loss in property of $12.1 million was not responsible for a single death or serious injury. After it made landfall at High Island on the morning of September 17, 1963, Cindy stalled for nearly 24 hours and sent incessant torrents of rainfall that totaled 15–20 inches over a 72-hour period in Texas's three easternmost counties.

People near the Rio Grande lived through the greatest floods in recorded history in the region downstream from the Big Bend, thanks to Hurricane Alice, an exceptionally early and prolific rainmaker that entered Texas by way of Mexico. After Alice made landfall in northeastern Mexico south of Brownsville on June 25, 1954, the slowly collapsing storm meted out driving rains over a 48-hour period that flooded much of the lower Pecos River valley. Flash floods in normally dry arroyos washed out railroad and highway bridges, including the one over the Pecos River upstream from Del Rio. A Southern Pacific train with about 265 passengers, along with about 200 automobiles, was stranded at Langtry; some of the travelers had to be evacuated by helicopter. More than 27 inches of rain fell in 48 hours at Pandale, while rains of 12 to 21 inches were common in lesser time in Comstock, Sonora, and Sheffield. Flood damage was particularly heavy at Laredo, although practically all deaths and extreme property damage attributed to Alice occurred on the Mexican side of the river.

Texas's history is replete with instances in which tropical storms, even the most minor variety among them, left a more indelible footprint on the state and its economy than the more potent and feared hurricanes. Tropical Storm Amelia is a foremost example, a benign system that cruised inland between Brownsville and Port Isabel on July 30, 1978, and gave only modest amounts of rain and minimal wind damage during landfall. It was a classic case of a weakening storm that waited to unleash its fury some time after it invaded the coast. No one

TABLE 8.5
Costliest Tropical Systems to Texans

Losses expressed in 2012 dollars (billions).

TROPICAL SYSTEM	DATE	LOCATION	LOSS
Hurricane Ike	Sep 2008	Galveston	12.8
T.S. Allison	Jun 2001	Houston	4.6
Hurricane Rita	Sep 2005	Sabine Pass	3.3
Hurricane Carla	Sep 1961	Port Lavaca	2.5
Hurricane Celia	Aug 1970	Corpus Christi	1.9

remembers Amelia for its modest storm surge, temperate rainfall, or fresh gales at the time it moved ashore. Rather, its persistence and its ferocity in triggering some of the worst flooding of the twentieth century in the Texas Hill Country and farther north in the Low Rolling Plains will forever be its distinguishing traits. Just hours after it seemed to perish some 200 miles (322 kilometers) from its primary source of energy—the Gulf of Mexico—the storm revived while nestled in the rolling hills of South Central Texas—spilling torrents of rain along the Balcones Escarpment; soaking the watersheds of the Guadalupe, Medina, and Sabinal Rivers almost instantaneously; and filling those rivers and numerous other streams and creeks in the area to overflowing. Before dawn broke on August 2, the raging floodwaters carried away 25 unsuspecting riverfront residents and campers. Even after exacting that death toll, as well as injuring 150 other people and causing $50 million in damages in flood-ravaged Bandera, Kerr, and Medina counties, Amelia was far from finished. Again the storm flirted with expiration as it drifted northward across the Edwards Plateau, only to be reinvigorated near Abilene. Copious rains—amounting to 20 inches in some locales—forced rivers and streams to burst out of their banks and reservoirs to fill quickly and overflow. At long last, the irrepressible storm waned and died over North Central Texas on August 12 but not before it had bestowed welcome rains of 5 inches on a drought-plagued stretch of terrain south of the Red River.

Another memorable tropical storm, named Allison, deluged the upper Texas coast with torrential rains in June 2001. It dumped some 3 feet of rain in locales between Houston and Beaumont, and the 43 inches measured at the Port of Houston over six days boosted the monthly aggregate to a stunning 46.55 inches—the heaviest 1-month rainfall total in Texas history! Interestingly, another tropical storm, also named Allison, struck the same region a dozen years earlier.

Hurricane Audrey stands out for its early season appearance and corroborating the notion that the storm tide may be the most destructive feature of some hurricanes. Despite warnings issued by the US Weather Bureau more than 12 hours in advance of the storm's landfall on June 27, 1957, few people evacuated the coastline from High Island, Texas, to Morgan City, Louisiana. The hurricane-induced sea surge sent floodwaters streaming inland, and 390 coastal residents (only 9 of whom lived in Texas) died from drowning at the outset or after falling from trees infested with snakes that also sought refuge from the rising water. Tens of thousands of other coastal inhabitants were saved, however, as a result of a carefully orchestrated mass evacuation from low-lying areas to higher ground in areas such as the Bolivar Peninsula and Sabine Pass.

At the other end of the hurricane calendar bearing the names of notable storms, Hurricane Jeanne, the next-to-last entry in the summer of 1980, almost earned the distinction of being the latest of late-arriving cyclones to hit Texas. It came within only a few hours of being the only hurricane to strike Texas during the month of November in at least the last 110 years. Undoubtedly, the modest hurricane's belatedness resulted from a continuation of uncommon warmth that bathed Texas and all of the Gulf of Mexico to an extreme, record-setting degree for practically all of summer 1980. Jeanne posed a serious threat to the lower Texas coast until it moved to within a few hundred miles of Brownsville, at which time it stalled and then retreated into the central Gulf in the face of a potent Arctic front that barreled through Texas and had earlier instigated a record snowstorm in the High Plains.

The Survivors Out West

Another family of cyclones that surfaces each year near Texas is largely ignored—except when one strays from home and brings heavy rains to semi-arid Texas. The warm waters of the eastern North Pacific that lap the western Mexican coastline foster as many—if not more—tropical cyclones in a typical year than the Atlantic and all its appendages. Most of the tropical storms and hurricanes spawned in the eastern Pacific during the period of June-November drift northwestward through open water without ever impinging on Central America. Occasionally, however, a major tropical system will deviate from this familiar path and hit the western coastline of Mexico. These exceptions may be intense enough or thrive long enough to whip high-level clouds across mainland Mexico into the western and southern extremities of Texas. In some years, a cyclone will subsist long enough during its trek across Mexico to provide parts of Texas with meaningful rain. One such hardy storm attacked Texas on its western flank with a vengeance in September 1978. The rare phenomenon—remnants of Tropical Storm Paul, which slammed into western Mexico on September 26—triggered historic flood crests on the Rio Grande above the Big Bend all the way to Falcon Reservoir. Rains totaling 5-15 inches—equal to what the region typically receives over a whole year—soaked the Trans Pecos region of Texas from the Guadalupe range to the Davis Mountains for one whole week late that month and combined with equally heavy rains in northern Mexico to swell the Rio Grande at Presidio to record-setting levels. The bloated Rio Grande rose to more than 25 feet (or 12 feet above flood stage) on three separate occasions in late September, inundating 7,000 acres of rich but unplanted farmland around Presidio and wiping out the railroad bridge connecting the United States and Mexico. Ordinarily no more than a trickle, the Rio Grande swelled to a width of 2 miles at the tiny community of Candelaria, which was isolated by road washouts for five days.

The most bounteous rainfall produced in the modern era in Texas by an eastern North Pacific hurricane occurred near the Red River in October 1981. Less than 24 hours after Hurricane Norma crashed into the western Mexican coastline near Mazatlán, a barrage of cloudbursts feeding off the copious moisture supplied by the dying hurricane dished out rains over the Chihuahuan Desert that, in some spots, were the equivalent of a whole year's worth of normal precipitation. Three-day rainfall amounts totaled more than 25 inches at Gainesville, Breckenridge, and Bridgeport, while much of the remainder of western North Central Texas collected 5-10 inches of rain in the same period. Tarrant County sustained more than $50 million in damage done to property, and a deluge of more than 21 inches in less than 24 hours led to property losses of over $20 million in nearby Stephens County. In Wise County, Lake Bridgeport had been 30 feet below normal before Norma made landfall, but in only a few days the torrential downpours generated by the dissipating cyclone raised the reservoir level to normal.

Some Pacific cyclones are especially remembered—and appreciated—for having brought relief from a disastrous drought. Remnants of Hurricane Odile spilled copious moisture into

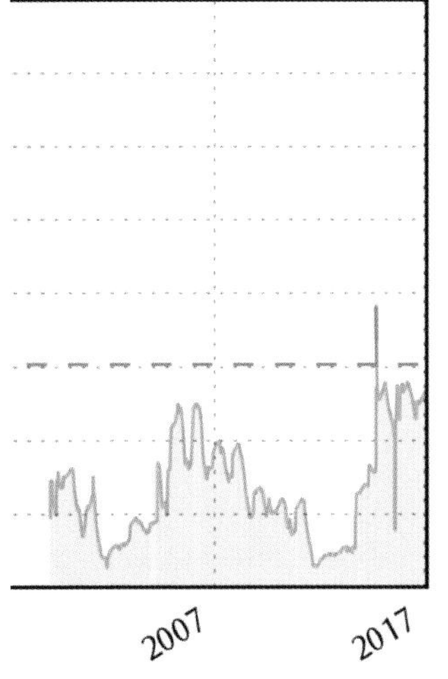

FIG. 8.3 Remnants of Hurricane Odile, from the eastern North Pacific, triggered torrential rains that swelled the Pecos River and nearly filled Red Bluff Reservoir on the Texas-New Mexico border in only a few days in October 2014. Source: Texas Water Development Board

southern New Mexico in October 2014, engendering thunderstorms whose torrential rains drenched the Pecos River watershed. The resultant runoff swelled the Pecos River and fed Red Bluff Reservoir, near Pecos, almost to overflowing. The lake, near the Texas-New Mexico border, had been woefully deficient from years of drought. More than 64,000 acre-feet of water from Odile's rainstorms brought the lake up to near capacity in just a matter of days (fig. 8.3). The residue of Hurricane Tico unleashed rains of 6–10 inches on the southern High and Low Rolling Plains in mid-October 1983, thereby easing dramatically a terrible drought that had tormented West Texas for over a year. Short-lived floodwaters on the flat plain in and around Lubbock, caused by 6 inches of rain in one day, enabled fun-loving residents to water-ski behind four-wheel-drive vehicles down city streets. The hefty and prolonged rains from Tico produced a record crest of 37 feet on the Red River near Gainesville.

In some years, the hemispheric circulation pattern assumes an orientation to allow not one, but several, wet Pacific cyclones to deliver rainfall into interior Texas. In 1986, Hurricane Newton careened into Mexico in mid-September and then launched waves of thunderstorms that deluged the southern High Plains of Texas with torrential rains and numerous funnel clouds. Within two weeks a second major Pacific storm, named Paine, replicated Newton's feat, producing up to 16 inches in one 24-hour period at McCamey and creating serious flooding along the Devils River.

Fallout from Storms

With the world's best radar and satellite coverage constantly monitoring conditions in the Gulf of Mexico, along with an extensive local storm-alerting system tied to television, radio, and social media, it is inconceivable these days that a hurricane or tropical storm could arrive unnoticed and, thus, unannounced. On the other hand, with the value of oceanfront property continually rising and the coastal population constantly increasing, the potential exists for the toll, in damage and destruction to property, to climb higher with each successive hurricane that spins out of the Gulf. More residents are at risk than ever before, so vigilance and prudence to take the right course when hurricanes threaten are preeminently important.

A Ruinous Wind

Most cyclones affecting the Texas coast feature winds within the system that are not distributed uniformly around the eye of the storm. Highest sustained wind speeds usually are observed in the area within 5–20 miles (8–32 kilometers) of the eye. Lesser, albeit damaging, winds may extend as far out from the eye as several hundred miles. A major determinant of wind damage is the angle at which the cyclone strikes the coastline. Building construction and the types of materials used in structures also factor into the damage done. Though such an occurrence is relatively infrequent, a northeastward-moving cyclone may pass along and parallel to the coastline, thereby exposing a greater land area of the coastal plain to hurricane winds than that affected by an approaching storm that traverses the coastline at an angle perpendicular to it.

Even today, most structures will sustain at least some damage from the strength of winds produced by hurricanes. With lesser cyclones, where winds are no higher than in the 40 mph range, slight structural damage, including the removal of shingles from the roofs of homes, is common. More appreciable damage to structures is a virtual certainty with winds in the 50–60 mph range. At this stage a hazard may develop when overhead power and telephone lines are broken. Equally serious may be debris blown from wrecked buildings, which can cause extensive damage to other structures and, especially, serious injuries to people in unsheltered areas. Moreover, vegetation damage is often significant. Trees with shallow roots, new trees inadequately supported or braced, and diseased trees are prone to removal from high winds. Matters are made worse when these trees take out power lines and aboveground phone and cable lines.

An Engulfing Storm Surge

It isn't so much a "wall" of water as it is a gradual building up of the ocean surface that constitutes a storm surge. It amplifies when each successive wave coming ashore cannot drain back to the ocean before the next wave comes ashore. The repeated crashing of waves can topple structures by undermining under-the-building supports (pilings). Indeed, since water is much heavier than air, the storm surge can dwarf winds in the capacity to damage and destroy. The size of the storm surge depends largely on offshore topography, with the highest surge associated with shallow continental shelf regions like that off the Texas coast. The persistent pounding of a storm surge that may reach heights of 20 feet or more, combined with waves superimposed on the elevated mound of water, can destroy almost any structure within its path. The majority of people who remained at home near the Texas coastline at the time of the 1900 Galveston hurricane and also during the two hurricanes that hit Indianola in 1875 and 1886 were buried by the storm surge, and many other residents who waited too long to abandon their homes were swept away by the storm surge and never found. The storm surge at Galveston in 1900 reached 14.5 feet, while the surge accompanying Hurricane Carla in 1961 reached 16.6 feet at Port Lavaca.

Key to the potential of the storm surge to damage and destroy is the state of astronomical tides that regularly occur along the coast. An approaching high tide can amplify the height of the storm surge by several feet. Just as the profile of the shoreline and the ocean bottom near the shore are of crucial importance, so too is the presence of estuaries, inlets, and offshore islands. Even the amount of vegetation and the extent of building construction can have an effect. Furthermore, the angle at which a cyclone hits the coastline also determines the height of a storm surge, with a higher storm surge associated with those cyclones that strike the coastline at right angles. The storm surge is most often highest where onshore winds are strongest: in the right-front quadrant of the hurricane mass. For example, a storm surge spawned by a hurricane moving northwestwardly and making landfall at Corpus Christi will be most intense along and up the coastline from (northeast of) Corpus Christi. It is not uncommon to observe a storm surge of 10 feet or more associated with a strong hurricane as far as 100–200 miles (160–320 kilometers) from the point of landfall. On beachfronts very distant from the point of landfall, the storm surge usually is evidenced by an increase in seaweed, Portuguese men-of-war, and debris washed up on the beaches. On the coastline nearer the eye of the storm, considerable erosion of some beaches and much deposition on others invariably occur.

While damage done by the storm surge to beaches can be substantial, the surge's effect on upper bays and estuaries often is more catastrophic. This is due to hurricane winds driving and channeling bay water to the extent that the water level is raised at the downwind (or landward) end of the bay while the level of the bay water is depressed at the upwind (or seaward) side of the bay. Water piles up more so, by several additional feet, in the upper reaches of bays and estuaries because the area over which the water spreads is small in relation to that along a smooth, clean, flat coastline. The magnitude of a storm surge entering from the Gulf increases if the estuary narrows inland from the mouth, while the height of the surge lessens if the estuary is over fairly flat land and expands out inland from the mouth. A storm surge may behave in completely different ways in many of the bays along the Texas coastline depending upon the angle of approach of a tropical cyclone. Moreover, the influx of saline water from the Gulf has a detrimental effect on the quality and productivity of fish and other marine organisms in the coastal bays and estuaries, although the extent of the harm done to bay and estuarine ecosystems is not yet fully known. On the other hand, not all the effects of the storm surge are always injurious. Bays are flushed of pollutants, and the surge may replenish sand on beaches. In addition, heavy rains from the tropical cyclone result in substantial freshwater inflow by way of rivers and streams that contributes to the vitality and productivity of the estuarine food chains.

Torrential Rains

How much rain is shed by a tropical cyclone depends on a number of factors, including the size of the rain area, the rate of movement of the storm mass, and the influence of upper-atmospheric weather conditions beyond the periphery of the storm. As a general rule, total storm rainfall, and hence the worst flooding, are greatest for broad hurricanes that drift slowly, both prior to and following landfall. Even tropical weather disturbances so minor as not to be assigned a name can drench the coastal plain with phenomenally heavy rains. The first tropical storm of the 1960 season provided the coastal bend section of Texas with good rains prior to its landfall near Corpus Christi around midnight on June 23, but then it dumped up to five times as much rainfall over three days as the remnants of the storm drifted through central Texas. Port Lavaca collected a bit more than 5 inches prior to storm landfall but later was inundated by 24 more inches, as serious local flooding from the torrential rains hit a five-county area extending from Aransas Pass to Freeport. That tropical cyclone, known otherwise only for its "modest" strength, caused flood damage in excess of $3.5 million and led to 15 drownings.

Hurricane Cindy is remembered for the disastrous flooding it triggered on September 16–20, 1963. Flood damage from Cindy's high tides was relatively light, but flooding from rains of 15–20 inches in a three-county region encompassing the Beaumont–Port Arthur–Orange metropolitan area sent water into 4,000 homes. At Deweyville more than 20 inches of a total storm rainfall of nearly 24 inches cascaded down on that Sabine River valley city in only 24 hours. Damage to both property and crops in the extreme eastern section of Texas amounted to over $12 million.

Most casualties connected to flooding caused by a cyclone stem from the flash flood variety. Residents living in areas where drainage is incapable of carrying away excess water without overflow are in greatest jeopardy. Short-term, heavy rains can fill a dry streambed in a matter of hours—if not minutes—and the resultant overflow inundates bridges, overpasses, and low-lying residential areas. On the other hand, river flooding usually is much slower to materialize. In fact, it may not begin until long after the hurricane or tropical storm has made landfall, and then it might persist for a week or longer. River flooding is frequently costlier in terms of property and crop losses than flash flooding because it covers a much more extensive area.

Deadly Tornadoes

The tornado is a common by-product of tropical disturbances. Most often they occur outside—from 50 up to 250 miles (80–400 kilometers)—the innermost portion of the cyclone where hurricane-force winds are present. Statistics gathered over the past several decades reveal that 9 out of every 10 tornadoes develop to the right of the direction of movement of the hurricane in an area bounded by radii with angles of 10°–120° from the direction of movement. Recent studies have concluded that tornadoes produced by hurricanes and tropical storms live for much shorter periods and are much smaller in size than those that dip out of murky skies on the Great Plains region. Usually these younger and leaner hurricane funnels cut a narrow swath or skip over the countryside, and damage done by them is mostly insignificant. However, if one of them sweeps through a heavily populated or industrialized area, the toll of casualties and the amount of property damage may skyrocket. Hurricane Beulah holds the record for most tornadoes generated by a tropical cyclone; that 1967 storm sent at least 115 tornadoes dancing across the southeastern half of Texas. Fortunately, they hit sparsely populated areas, so neither the death toll nor the total property damage was great. Hurricane Carla (1961) is the second-most prolific tornado producer (26) to plague Texas.

Depending upon the size and intensity of an incoming cyclone, the misery experienced by those living in its pathway can linger for days, weeks, and even months. Vehicular movement is inhibited because of washed out, clogged, or flooded bridges and roadways. Consequently, the movement of emergency equipment and personnel, as well as food, water, and medical supplies, is impeded. Drinking water is scarce—if not altogether unavailable—and sewage and other wastes cannot be disposed of as usual. Disease may spread from drowned animals, and numerous other problems stem from living in emergency shelter conditions. Electric power lines downed by high wind or water present a real hazard, while direct communication is severed because of disabled telephone and telegraph lines. Many citizens discover an abundance of

FIG. 8.4 Hurricane Allen, one of the strongest Atlantic storms in recorded history, filled much of the Gulf of Mexico prior to striking the lower Texas coast in August 1980. Source: National Aeronautics and Space Administration

snakes, some lethal, who have been driven from their natural habitat by high water. They take up sanctuary almost anywhere, especially along roads, in trees, within remnants of buildings, and, worst of all, in homes.

The Challenge of Prediction

Hurricanes and tropical storms develop and behave without regard to what their predecessors have done. Hurricanes obviously know nothing about historical averages. On average, the Texas coast experiences a hurricane every other year and a tropical storm every third year. We must use considerable caution, however, in applying these statistics because no regularity in hurricane or tropical storm occurrence exists; some years have furnished two or more tropical cyclones, while numerous other years have been marked by relative tranquility in the Gulf of Mexico. The twentieth century was characterized by many multiyear periods in which a hurricane, tropical storm, or both occurred and numerous periods without any significant cyclones. An unusually lengthy period of hurricane nonactivity ended when Hurricane Allen roared ashore near Port Mansfield on August 10, 1980 (fig. 8.4). Until then, no hurricanes had invaded Texas since Hurricane Fern on September 10, 1971 (Amelia, in 1978, was a tropical storm). Since Allen, however, an even longer void has resulted: after Hurricane Jerry struck the Texas coastline in 1989, 14 years elapsed before another hurricane, Claudette, struck in 2003.

The tracks of most of the major tropical cyclones that have affected Texas in recent decades reveal that most of them impinge on the coastline at, or very near at, right angles. In some unusual instances, cyclones approach the Texas coastline but then travel roughly parallel to the shoreline, causing damage along most, if not all, of the coast. In most instances, however, since the Texas coastline is lengthy, a hurricane or a tropical storm will not adversely affect all of it.

Based on nearly a century and a half of record keeping of cyclone occurrence, there is about a 1-in-8 chance that a particular sector of the Texas coast will be hit by the eye of either a hurricane or a tropical storm in any year. The odds of being hit by a hurricane are about 1 in 10 for most of the coastline. Texas weather annals also suggest that the likelihood of two or more tropical cyclones hitting the same sector (with a length of about 50 miles) of the Texas coast in any one year is no more than 1 in 25. On average, 15 to 20 years elapse between extreme hurricanes striking the same sector of the Texas coast; for any hurricane, the average number of years between any two occurrences is 4–5 years, and for any tropical cyclone (hurricanes and tropical storms) the average is 3–4 years. The earliest recorded disturbance to hit the Texas coastline was the tropical storm that made landfall near Galveston on June 4, 1871. A surprising number of cyclones have entered Texas in June. The likelihood of occurrence (about 1 of every 5) is about the same for July as for June and then peaks in

August and September; the latter two months are marked by an equal number of cyclones to hit the Texas coast. The frequency of occurrence drops off dramatically in October. In fact, the latest cyclone to strike the Texas coast was the tropical storm that hit near Matagorda on October 17, 1938.

Hurricane Prediction

Forecasters at the National Hurricane Center have an assortment of diagnostic tools with which to assess the state of convective complexes that may be organizing into a tropical wave or bigger. Still today, as for decades, the input furnished by reconnaissance aircraft that penetrate these disturbed areas one or several times a day is critical for predicting further storm development. Armed with direct measures of storm behavior from these hurricane hunter missions, forecasters issue consecutively numbered advisories online and through public and social media at regular intervals on a 24-hour basis. The advisories describe various features of the cyclone, such as size and strength, position relative to land, and maximum sustained winds near the center. They also invariably contain projections on what changes (if any) in strength and movement are anticipated in the short term. In particular, a watch informs about a possible, but as yet uncertain, threat to a particular coastal area, whereas a warning identifies a specific time frame and area along a coast where high winds, storm surge, and other aspects of a hurricane strike may be expected. The advisories also provide probabilities that the storm will strike certain areas along the coast, and forecasts of storm tides and the potential for flooding and tornadoes are also included.

With the help of computer modeling, forecasters today can digest an immense amount of data, then make projections of storm movement and strength with an accuracy unparalleled in history. This enhanced skill in forecasting storm movement comes in handy especially in instances in which tropical cyclones manifest highly erratic behavior and movement. Such late-course alteration in movement was observed with Hurricane Beulah, which recurved sharply to the southwest after striking the southern tip of the Texas coast on September 20, 1967. Some cyclones undergo rapid intensification or deterioration just before they push inland. Hurricane Celia sustained rapid growth just prior to its invasion of Corpus Christi on August 3, 1970, whereas Hurricane Allen—the second-strongest hurricane in history for much of its lengthy trek across the Caribbean and Gulf of Mexico—stalled and weakened just hours before it surged ashore near Port Mansfield on August 10, 1980. More has to be learned about these cyclones and the near environment with which they interact to make further advancements in forecasting skills.

Safety Precautions

Anyone enduring the fury of a hurricane never forgets the experience. Because of the great probability that these tempests will produce death and widespread destruction, it is imperative that residents in the Texas coastal plain—especially those who live within a few miles of the shoreline—take proper precautions. The key to hurricane protection is preparation. By taking adequate and sensible measures before, during, and after a hurricane strikes, many lives can be saved and considerable property damage averted. In the final analysis, the responsibility for hurricane preparedness rests with the individual. At the time a cyclone is churning in the open Gulf, local officials are usually implementing plans for the imminent emergency and are unable to assist individuals with planning or other background information.

To be adequately prepared for a tropical cyclone, people in coastal areas should be aware of the way hurricanes, tropical storms, and the potential damage they can cause are classified. The Saffir-Simpson Hurricane Scale (from 1 to 5), described earlier, evaluates winds generated by the storm and projects the extent of damage anticipated at specific times. Make sure your means of getting information (radio, cell phone, or other listening or viewing device) is powered up and that you have a fresh energy supply in reserve. Most weather radios have the capability to alert you when a storm advisory is issued, even waking you up at night when necessary.

FIG. 8.5 The hurricane's powerful storm surge can displace nonsecured objects as big as barges great distances inland from their normal location. Source: Texas Department of Transportation

LONG BEFORE THE STORM

Well in advance of a storm threat, learn about the degree to which your area is vulnerable to the forces of wind and water. Determine the elevation of your home (or business establishment) above sea level and its distance from open water. Also, find out if your neighborhood is susceptible to freshwater flooding. Learn what maximum storm-surge height you could expect in your locale. The NWS forecast office nearest you—in League City (for the Houston-Galveston area), Brownsville, Corpus Christi, and Lake Charles, Louisiana (for the Beaumont- Port Arthur Orange-area)—can supply estimates of the highest potential storm surge and the expected extent of inland flooding. Generally, if your home or business is less than 25 feet above sea level and no more than 20 miles (32 kilometers) from the shoreline, it could be highly vulnerable to storm-surge flooding (fig. 8.5).

Another early precaution is to secure adequate insurance for your home and other possessions from a reputable company. Be sure to determine whether your policies do or do not cover damage to your property caused by rising or wind-driven water. There are other measures to take as well. When—if not before—a hurricane watch is issued for your area, you may want to store drinking water in jugs, ensure that flashlights and other battery-operated equipment are adequately charged, obtain and store food that needs no refrigeration, and fill your car with gasoline. At the time a hurricane warning is issued—if not sooner—abandon low-lying beaches that may be swept by the storm surge; make sure young or helpless people and livestock are moved to higher, safer ground; secure all boats and other items on piers or boathouses. If you live in an area that is out of danger from high tides and is well built, plan to stay home. If you choose to leave, or if you live in an area for which a mass evacuation has been ordered, you may or may not have ample time in which to plan your escape. You will want to adhere to a predetermined evacuation plan to ensure the safety and well-being of your family.

- Review possible evacuation procedures with your family so that everyone understands what to do and where to meet if you are separated. Ask a friend or relative outside your area to be the checkpoint so that everyone in the family can call that person to say they are safe. Also, find out where children will be sent if they are in school when an evacuation is announced.
- Plan now where you would go if you had to evacuate. Consider the homes of relatives or friends. You may wish to contact the local emergency-management or civil defense office for community evacuation plans.
- Keep fuel in your car at all times. During emergencies, filling stations may not be open. Never store extra fuel in the garage.
- If you are without the use of a vehicle, make transportation arrangements with friends, neighbors, or your local emergency-management office.
- Know how to shut off electricity, gas, and water at main switches and valves. Be sure you have the tools (pipe, crescent, or adjustable wrenches) needed to do this.

Keep in mind that if you delay your departure, roads to safer areas may become flooded before the main portion of the storm arrives. Board up windows or otherwise protect them with shutters, sturdy tape, or both. Tie down any items (such as garbage cans, porch or patio furniture, and outdoor toys) that might be picked up by the strong winds and hurled through the air.

If you live in a mobile home, check tie-downs for rust and breakage. Keep in mind that mobile homes can be destroyed or seriously damaged even in a minimal hurricane (category 1 or 2). Evacuate your dwelling as soon as you are told by local authorities to do so.

If you are in a high-rise apartment or condominium, consider investing in shutters or impact-resistant glass for your doors and windows. Remember that wind forces are greater the higher you are above the ground. Be sure all exits are clearly marked in hallways and memorize where the stairs are located in case a power outage puts you in darkness. (Never take an elevator in an emergency situation. Use the stairs.) If your unit has a balcony or terrace, secure all items there so that nothing you own becomes airborne and causes damage or injury.

Don't forget your pets. If you must evacuate your neighborhood, do not leave your animal behind. You may not be able to check on a pet for days, even weeks, if the roads leading to your home cannot be readily cleared of debris. A devoted pet owner will make sure his emergency pet supply kit is stocked with essentials like food, water, litter and litter box, eyewash, cotton swabs, antibiotic ointment, tweezers, bandages, and more. Make sure your pet is wearing identification. In the absence of a microchip (the best insurance against getting a pet lost), keep a photo of yourself with your pet. Collaborate with a neighbor in sharing keys and instructions on caring for each other's pets. Keep a list handy of temporary shelter sites away from the affected area.

WHEN THE STORM IS RAGING

As the brunt of the storm begins bearing down, it is important that someone in your group stay awake at all times to keep track of the storm's progress through NWS advisories and bulletins and to guard against such hazards as fire and snakes. A weather radio is a handy source of information for you during a storm. Stay indoors during a hurricane, for it is treacherous to travel or move about when winds and tides are lashing your vicinity. Take cover within a small, interior room—even a closet or hallway on the lowest level—and lie on the floor under a table or other sturdy object. Refrain from looking out a window or walking outside to take note of what is happening. Flying debris can be unimaginably injurious. At some point during the storm, you will notice the wind dying down. That is an indication that the core (or "eye") of the storm is passing overhead. Do not be tricked into thinking that the storm has passed. Such a respite from the storm's fury usually lasts up to a half-hour or even longer, but the second half of the cyclone inevitably will come, with winds rising very rapidly to hurricane force or greater in a matter of minutes. To help eliminate the risk that windows or doors in your home will be blown out due to great pressure variations set up by the storm, keep a window partially open on the downwind side of your home (i.e., opposite the direction from which the storm is approaching). Be sure, though, not to situate yourself near that open window or door. By following these instructions and using common sense, most of those residents who experience a hurricane will remember it as little more than a dramatic event.

ONCE THE STORM HAS PASSED

If you are returning after an evacuation, make sure public officials have declared the storm event has ended. Visually survey the area, making note of any downed trees, power lines, and wires. Check for exterior structural damage to the building you are about to enter and be confident it is structurally safe before you go in. Do not enter if you smell gas, you can see floodwater around the building, or the structure has been damaged by fire and authorities have not yet declared it to be safe.

When you enter your home, do so carefully. Be aware of loose boards, dangling wires, and slippery floors. Do not check the home's electrical system if you are wet or standing in water. If you can, turn off the electricity at the main fuse box or circuit breaker. Even if power to your home has not been disrupted, do not turn on lights until you are certain it is safe to do so. If you smell gas or hear a hissing sound, open a window, then leave immediately. If possible, turn off the main gas valve from the outside and then contact the gas company. Avoid using lanterns, candles, or torches for lighting until you are sure there is no leaking gas or other flammable materials.

Anyone who is not an evacuee or a rescue worker should stay out of a storm disaster area. The presence of large numbers of unqualified people hampers rescue and first-aid operations. It is after such a storm that the extent of property damage, as well as injuries and deaths, can cause widespread shock.

Those persons having good reason to return to an evacuated area should seek medical care at a disaster station or nearby hospital for anyone they encounter who has been injured. Be constantly aware that health hazards are in abundance. Avoid loose or dangling wires and report them to a law-enforcement officer or power company. Also report to the proper authorities any broken sewer or water mains. Be careful what water you drink; private wells and municipal water supplies may be contaminated. Check for food that may have been spoiled due to lack of refrigeration. If you travel, drive carefully along those streets and roads that are strewn with debris and remember that some roads, undermined by floodwaters, may collapse under the weight of your car. Stay away from the banks of rivers and streams, for they often become unsafe after a deluge.

9.

Whirlwind at Its Worst

Residents of Williamson County attuned to a swirling sky had to know the afternoon of May 27, 1997 would be most unusual. After all, who in central Texas had ever seen rope-shaped funnel clouds dangling from the deep blue base of a towering thunderhead? A supercell thunderstorm was advancing toward the town of Jarrell, with one funnel that appeared for only a few moments to be replaced by a subsequent funnel that also dipped to the ground, then ascended quickly before being replaced by yet another. But the last snake-like tornado in the sequence went off script, expanding quickly into a rotating wall of cloud that blew up to a width of 0.5 mile as it plowed the ground near Jarrell. Some witnesses claimed to have seen several rotating funnels within the larger vortex. As the tornado crossed a network of paved county roads, more than 500 feet of asphalt was peeled like a potato from each of the roadways. By the time the storm cloud reached the edge of town, it had evolved into a rare EF5 tornado, with winds in excess of 200 miles per hour (mph) buffeting whatever lay in its path. Officially, the twister struck at 3:48 p.m., a time derived from a clock recovered from a residence in the extreme northwest corner of the community that was otherwise obliterated in only an instant. By this time, the tornado, on a rather uncommon north-to-south trajectory, took a sudden turn toward the southeast as it entered the Double Creek subdivision. Its path of destruction had expanded to an astounding 0.75 mile in diameter.

The distinctive roaring of the vortex, like that of a locomotive, revealed to residents that the tornado was upon them. There was too little time to flee, and even those who sought refuge within homes and businesses were left helpless when the violent winds swept those structures off their foundations. Twenty-seven residents were killed, from age 5 to 50, and another 12 were injured, while damage to property in the community of several hundred totaled $40 million and crop losses were valued at $100,000.

Some 300 cattle grazing nearby were slain, with many of the carcasses—their hides stripped from them—blown over 0.25 mile. Automobiles had been flattened as if they had been in a junkyard compactor, many of them encrusted with mud and grass. Trees in neighborhoods were denuded of their bark. Teams later assessing the damage found most of the debris left in the community was extremely small—a testament to the potency of the tornadic winds that displaced anything of size, much of it at great distances from where it belonged. The path of destruction extended 5.1 miles (8.2 kilometers) and ended in a heavily wooded area of cedar trees, whose damage pattern suggested the "mother" twister may have, at times, consisted of multiple, smaller vortices. Survivors told of a sequence of events unlike any usually associated with tornado incidence. In most cases, wind gusts with rain introduce a spell of hail, followed by relative calm before the blast of tornadic winds arrives. In Jarrell's experience, the exact opposite took place, which attests to the odd behavior of the supercell that "backed" into the area from the northeast.

A League of Their Own

Of all the intimidating—and treacherous—elements in Mother Nature's arsenal, the tornado rates as the one most feared. Its behavior is also the most bizarre of atmospheric convulsions, a fact that fosters its reputation as the most terrifying of all of weather's offerings. Spinning toward Earth in corkscrew fashion from the underside of a darkening thunderstorm, it can happen at any time of day or night, on prairies and plateaus as well as forests and swamps. It can dip down and dance near or on the surface of Earth for only an instant, or it can drop to the ground and wreak havoc like a giant weed eater for great distances. It can leave barely an imprint in a remote area seldom touched by humans, or it can carve out a swath of destruction smack in the middle of a heavily populated urban area (fig. 9.1). The word tornado originates from the Latin word *tornare*, which understatedly means to twist or to turn. The Italian *tornare*, the Spanish *tornear*, and the French *tornade* all mean the same thing. What these descriptors identify is a small yet violent body of winds packing a concentrated wallop more powerful than that of any windstorm on Earth. Though tornadoes usually affect relatively small areas, they strike faster and with more savagery than any other storm.

Tornadoes are the prodigy of thunderstorms—but very few thunderclouds, maybe 1 in 100, actually give birth to them. Many funnel clouds that are spawned never reach the ground and thus maintain the distinction of merely being a funnel cloud. When the violently rotating column of air makes contact with the ground, its identity then changes to a tornado. Tornadoes occur in every month, though in many years the lion's share of them occurs in spring or in a shorter window of time in late summer or early autumn. Most reported funnel clouds are spotted visually by trained weather watchers, and many of them are "sighted" by National Weather Service (NWS) personnel staffing weather radar facilities. Still, it is probable that the NWS weather-observing network fails to detect quite a few of the tornadoes that form, especially those that are short lived and occur in sparsely settled regions of the state.

The tornado is among the least of atmospheric phenomena to be well understood. It happens so quickly, and its potency makes it difficult, if not impossible, to get close enough to evaluate it fully. What is known is, like the

FIG. 9.1 A tornado that dipped out of the sky over Dallas killed 10 people and injured 200 on April 2, 1957—part of a wet spring that ended the notorious drought of the 1950s. Source: Texas Department of Public Safety

formation and growth of hurricanes, conservation of angular momentum is key to a tornado's existence. Tornadoes are the product of large, intense thunderstorms that grow in an excessively unstable atmosphere. They seem to evolve from very strong updrafts, or highly energetic flows of moist air from near the surface that feed into the base of a growing thunderhead. Apparently, buoyant forces that drive the thunderstorm enhance the convergence of this low-level moist air in toward the center, or core, of the updraft. In the same way that ice skaters quicken the rate at which they spin by drawing in their arms, air entering a column from different directions is made to accelerate rapidly. This means that as air near and beneath the thunderstorm is directed into the updraft, the speed of the air may easily be tripled or quadrupled. Recent research suggests that many tornado-producing thunderstorms have updrafts with a pronounced rotation within a deep layer of the atmosphere extending upward from the cloud base for several thousand feet, which undoubtedly contributes to the development of a twisting funnel that suspends itself beneath the base of a cloud near where the updraft enters the cloud.

With the Gulf of Mexico on its southeastern flank and the Rocky Mountains on its western periphery, Texas is well situated for spawning tornadoes, particularly in the spring, late summer, and autumn. Often during these seasons, three main flows of air converge on Texas to establish an environment that aids and abets the formation and development of tornadoes. As a cold front pushes into the state from the higher elevations to the northwest, the flow of near-surface, warm, and moisture-laden air from the Gulf of Mexico is accelerated. At the same time, high in the atmosphere (between 10,000 and 15,000 feet [3–4.5 kilometers]), very warm and much drier air pours northeastward out of Mexico. It is where the very dry air intrudes into or over the lower, moister air from the Gulf that a very sharp gradient of moisture is established, and it is in this mixing zone that very intense thunderstorms erupt with the potential of spawning tornadoes. The presence of a very strong jet-stream wind even higher in the atmosphere exacerbates this unsettled situation. Towering thunderheads that grow almost explosively upward are exposed to an intensifying and shifting wind as they reach levels of 30,000 feet (9 kilometers) and even higher. It is this shearing wind that enhances the likelihood that a thunderhead will produce one or more funnels.

The Worst of the Vortices

The majority of tornadoes hit in sparsely populated areas, so damage is relatively minor if not inconsequential. Those comparatively few that do strike urban areas are capable of doing immense damage, however, and weather analysts classify them, along with the mostly harmless ones, according to their wind speed and the damage they inflict (fig. 9.2). A system to categorize tornadoes by examining the damage to structures and debris fields in the wake of a tornado was devised by the late Dr. Ted Fujita at the University of Chicago and is now referred to as the Enhanced Fujita Scale (EF) (table 9.1). In the six and one-half decades since radar has been available to assist with documenting tornadic events, more than 8,200 individual tornadoes in Texas have been classified. The vast majority (81 percent) of all tornadoes in the state have been relatively weak (EF0–EF1), while nearly one-fifth (18 percent) are strong (EF2–EF3), doing significant, if not serious (even severe), damage. Fortuitously, the worst types (EF4–EF5) are quite uncommon (only 0.5 percent), but they are responsible for devastating damage as well as loss of life, accounting for well over half of all fatalities. Since 1950, Texas has experienced only seven of the worst variety (EF5), all of them occurring in the late spring (table 9.2). In fact, over half (54 percent) of all tornadoes known to have occurred in Texas since 1950 struck during the three months of spring (March, April, May), with May on average delivering more (30 percent of the total) than any other month. April, the second-most active month for tornado incidence (17 percent) is followed closely by June (16 percent).

FIG. 9.2 Though relatively few tornadoes in Texas hit populated areas, those that do leave very little property intact. Source: Texas Department of Public Safety

TABLE 9.1

Categorizing Tornadoes

Tornadoes are categorized by the Enhanced Fujita Scale (EF).

RANK	CATEGORY	MILES PER HOUR
EF5	Violent	261 or more
EF4	Violent	207-260
EF3	Strong	158-206
EF2	Strong	113-157
EF1	Weak	73-112
EF0	Weak	less than 73

TABLE 9.2

Texas's Most Powerful Twisters

History of EF5 tornadoes in Texas.

LOCATION	DATE
Waco	May 11, 1953
Wichita Falls	Apr 3, 1964
Lubbock	May 11, 1970
Waco (Valley Mills)	May 6, 1973
Brownwood	Apr 19, 1976
Wichita Falls/Vernon	Apr 10, 1979
Jarrell	May 27, 1997

Of the half-dozen recorded EF5 tornadoes ever to scar the surface of Texas, two inflicted immense havoc on a pair of population centers, one of them a commercial hub in central Texas. Of the hundreds of tornadoes that have ripped their way through rural hamlets, small towns, and bustling cities, these two stand alone because they were the deadliest of them all.

No one living today witnessed the black twister that smashed through the town of Goliad on May 18, 1902, extinguishing the lives of 114 of its citizens and injuring more than double that number. With damage amounting to $50,000—a vast sum of money to those living around the turn of the century—a large part of the town was decimated. Oddly, the other biggest killer tornado took exactly the same number of fatalities (114) as the Goliad event. The EF5 tornado that tore through the heart of Waco on the afternoon of May 11, 1953 carved out a path of destruction 23 miles (37 kilometers) long that knifed through the downtown section of a city that, at the time, contained about 85,000 residents. The twister finally ascended near the community of Axtell, leaving grim rescue workers to discover carnage unmatched anywhere else: in addition to the 114 who died, there were almost 1,100 injured, 196 buildings demolished or in need of removal for safety's sake, 850 homes wrecked or partially destroyed, 376 other buildings declared to be unsafe, and about 2,000 automobiles ruined or severely damaged. The total property loss to the McClennan County seat amounted to more than $51 million. Ninety-four of the dead were found within a two-block area that included the square around City Hall. Scores of people were buried under tons of rubble. Ambulance sirens wailed almost continuously far into the evening, ferrying to hospitals those who had been found alive and pried loose from the piles of debris that filled the streets of the roped-off downtown section. Broken power and telephone lines and ruptured gas mains made rescue attempts even more treacherous. The rain that fell throughout the evening would have been scorned as yet another handicap had it not been an aid in putting out numerous fires. For hours, rescuers brought out injured survivors, some of whom had endured only because workers piped oxygen down through cracks leading to would-be graves far below the tops of the heaps of debris. After many hours in which the air had been pierced repeatedly by screams and cries for help, those agonizing sounds ceased, and every body retrieved thereafter was lifeless. Area hospitals were filled to overflowing, and many of the injured had to sit or lie on floors in corridors. As if nature was not content to confine its fury to Waco on that day in May 1953, another intense thunderstorm spun out a second deadly tornado that rent asunder the Lakeview section of San Angelo, killing 11, injuring 159, and wiping out 320 homes.

Not all of the half-dozen recorded EF5's to hit Texas were calamitous, but only because they traced a path that bypassed big population centers. The monstrous tornado that dipped out of a murky sky near Brownwood one April evening in 1976 appeared as a massive column, at least 0.25 mile wide, surging northeastward toward the city and shredding mesquite trees along the way. Mercifully, it chose a path north of the city, leveling a farm and pecan orchard while picking up a pair of teen-age boys who had been fishing in Lake Brownwood and throwing them over a thousand yards. Miraculously, the boys survived. The owner of the farm and orchard had his house totally destroyed, but he too was spared: the awful tornado hit while he was listening to storm warnings on a radio. He had just enough time to grip the side of his bathtub, and when the storm pulled away, nothing was left on the foundation but the tub! Workers at the Brownwood airport sought refuge in a large hangar when the tornado bore down, decimating a set of T-hangars and a half-dozen private airplanes but leaving the biggest structure intact. The EF5 tornado that hit near Waco at dusk on May 6, 1973 was likewise gargantuan—but it remained in the country near Valley Mills, demolishing two barns and carrying a pair of pickups up to 0.5 mile before wrecking them. The tornado—one of the seven most prodigious tornadoes ever spotted in Texas—stayed on the ground for over 10 miles (16 kilometers), but it exacted no deaths or injuries! The only thing recovered from two barns was a small piece of tin found lying in a field.

Other major Texas cities have been targeted for direct hits by massive tornadoes. The tornado that gave Lubbock the darkest day in its history was like the one in 1953 that hit Waco in that it caused immense destruction by plowing through the very hub of the sprawling urban center on the Texas South Plains. In sculpting out a path about 8 miles (13 kilometers) long and as much as 1.5 miles wide that began near the Texas Tech University campus and ended minutes later at the Lubbock Municipal Airport, the broad tornado caused damage and destruction over 15 square miles—or about one-quarter of the whole city. The loss of property totaled an incredible $135 million. Twenty-six persons died when the tornado snaked through the downtown section of Lubbock not long after dark on May 11, 1970. As with most tornadoes, nearly all the deaths stemmed from either flying debris or the collapse of structures. The tornado exerted such force that numerous large and tall office buildings were damaged extensively. About 80 percent of all plate-glass windows were smashed in the downtown area. Some cars were flattened to within 2 or 3 feet of the ground. At least 500 persons were injured; likely the injury toll was much higher, for crowded hospitals were forced to turn away scores of people with cuts and bruises seeking admittance.

The Lubbock tornado of May 1970 earned the distinction of being one of two twisters regarded as the largest ever witnessed in Texas. The other, with a path of devastation measuring 1.5 miles wide, slashed through the town of Higgins in Lipscomb County in the far northeastern corner of the Texas Panhandle on April 9, 1947. The same tornado also struck and totally wiped out the little community of Glazier in Hemphill County. In fact, the tornado ripped out a path having a length of 221 miles (356 kilometers), shredding a part of Kansas and Oklahoma as well as the Texas Panhandle. The twister's death toll in Texas amounted to 68, with another 201 seriously harmed. Damage totaled $1.55 million. Few tornadoes ever live as long—more than six hours—as the one that demolished Glazier, Texas.

Smack in the middle of "tornado alley," Wichita Falls has borne an inordinately high number of weather calamities over the past several decades. The city near the Red River has been wracked several times by blockbuster tornadoes that roared through the gently rolling hills of an area esteemed for its endurance in dealing almost annually with scorching summer heat waves, bone-chilling winter winds, and vicious spring thunderstorms. None of the twisters, of course, had an effect comparable with the tornado that devastated the southern sector of the city on April 10, 1979. In only 30 minutes, the EF5 tornado, 1.5 miles wide, cut through 8 miles (13 kilometers) within the city, leaving 42 dead among the litter and debris. More than half of those killed were in their automobiles—some intentionally trying to flee the storm—when the twister lifted and spun the vehicles in the air as if they were bottle caps. Nearly 2,000 other people were left hurting, while thousands more agonized at the sight of 3,000 homes demolished and another 600 heavily damaged. Another very large tornado that razed neighborhoods on the opposite side of town in April 1964 left death, destruction, and misery on a scale almost as lamentable as that which superseded it 15 years later. It ripped up a 6-mile-long (10 kilometers) swath of northwestern Wichita Falls at midafternoon on April 3, 1964, killing 7 residents, injuring others, and costing the community $15 million worth in property damage (fig. 9.3).

FIG. 9.3 Despite its rope-like appearance, the elongated tornadic cloud can still exact substantial damage, as the tornado that razed Sheppard Air Force Base in April 1964 demonstrated. Source: Texas Department of Public Safety

While Waco, Lubbock, and Wichita Falls suffered severely from massive tornadoes yet recovered to grow and prosper, smaller communities have been demolished totally by twisters. When the path of a twister happened to trek through the little town of Bellevue, in Clay County, on April 26, 1906, practically everything was demolished, 17 people were killed, and 20 were injured; damage amounted to $300,000. Much the same thing happened to Melissa on April 13, 1921; the little town in northern Collin County was practically destroyed when a tornado tore through it one evening, killing about a dozen people and hurting several scores of other residents. Add Rocksprings to the list of locales virtually wiped out by tornadoes. The county seat of Edwards County was leveled by a twister that hit suddenly on April 12, 1927. Seventy-two persons died there, about 200 were harmed, and property damage exceeded $1 million.

If any area of Texas would seem to be insulated from tornado outbreaks, it would be the plateaus and canyons west of the Pecos River. Yet, where moist air needed to fuel large thunderstorms is largely lacking much of the time in the Trans Pecos, tornadoes in the modern era are no longer rarely seen intruders, as the town of Saragosa can attest. A supercell thunderstorm unleashed a violent multiple-vortex tornado 0.5 mile wide that decimated the community of 200 on May 22, 1987. Autos and trucks were hurled through adobe and wood-frame buildings, some ending up as much as 500 yards from their point of origin. Most of the 30 people killed were parents or grandparents attending a graduation ceremony in a schoolhouse; they grabbed their children to shield them from the debris. Another 121 residents were injured. The twister lifted from the ground just after it passed through the heart of town.

Tornadoes often populate a hurricane event, though for the most part they have lesser longevity than their more continental counterparts and tend not to be as potent. The greatest single outbreak of tornadoes in Texas weather history occurred in conjunction with Hurricane Beulah. For as much as 12 hours before and subsequent to Beulah's landfall near Brownsville on September 20, 1967, a multitude of at least 115 tornadoes roamed across most of the southern half of Texas. One of them hit near Palacios, killing four persons and injuring six others. Other Beulah-inspired twisters caused extensive damage in Burnet, Louise (in Wharton County), and New Braunfels. The more than 100 tornadoes engendered by Beulah easily erased the previous record total of 26 hurricane-related tornadoes established by Carla.

Sometimes, the ruinous tornado garnering headlines is but one of a rash of twisters that erupt at about the same time in a region. When nature succeeds in assembling the right atmospheric conditions for fomenting a tornado, the end result is sometimes not a single tornado but rather a whole horde of them. If several of the twisters hit populated areas, the cumulative effect can be enormous. On May 6, 1930, a twister tore through Ennis and several other small towns in Hill and Navarro Counties, killing 41 people, while a second tornado hit Kenedy and two other towns in Karnes and DeWitt Counties, taking another 36 lives. The sum total of deaths for the day—77—is second only to the 114 dead exacted by the tornadoes that struck Waco and Goliad. The death toll reached 76 when a wave of tornadoes roared through Sherman and two smaller communities on May 15, 1896, while other one-day fatality totals of at least two score included 74 at Rocksprings and surrounding locales in April 1927, 68 in several Panhandle communities in April 1947, and 42 in a five-county area of northeastern Texas on April 9, 1919.

The threat of tornadoes is today a year-round concern for Texans. Though the three winter months historically have seen tornadoes on a very infrequent basis, in years with an invigorated El Niño, even the dead of winter is not exempt from an occasional burst. That December is host to only about 3 percent of all twisters that are spawned in Texas over many years was no consolation to residents of North Texas who witnessed a spate of tornadoes, one of them an EF4, the day after Christmas in 2015. Of the 11 people who died near Dallas when the powerful funnel cloud roared out of a murky sky just after dusk on December 26, 2015, 8 were in automobiles driving on the President George Bush Turnpike in Rowlett when their vehicles were abruptly swept off the elevated freeway to an access road below, crushing the cars beyond recognition. The outbreak of seven tornadoes, the first to occur in December in nine years, happened just as a blizzard was coming together over much of West Texas; that blizzard would dump a foot of snow in parts of the South Plains near Lubbock.

While tornadoes do visit in winter, they are mostly a springtime phenomenon—though a secondary season for them is in autumn. From rawinsonde data obtained by weather balloons, a tornado parameter identifies the probability of occurrence of a tornado in each month of the year. Along the upper Texas coast, tornado incidence spikes in May, then tails off markedly as spring winds down and summer takes hold (fig. 9.4a). Chances for tornadoes rebound significantly in September, probably because of the frequency of occurrence of tropical cyclones, which are known for tornado genesis. The potential for tornadic activity deep into autumn remains high until winter sets in. Much farther north and west, a strong likelihood for tornado occurrence starts in April and persists until June (fig. 9.4b), then maintains a "modest" chance until autumn ends.

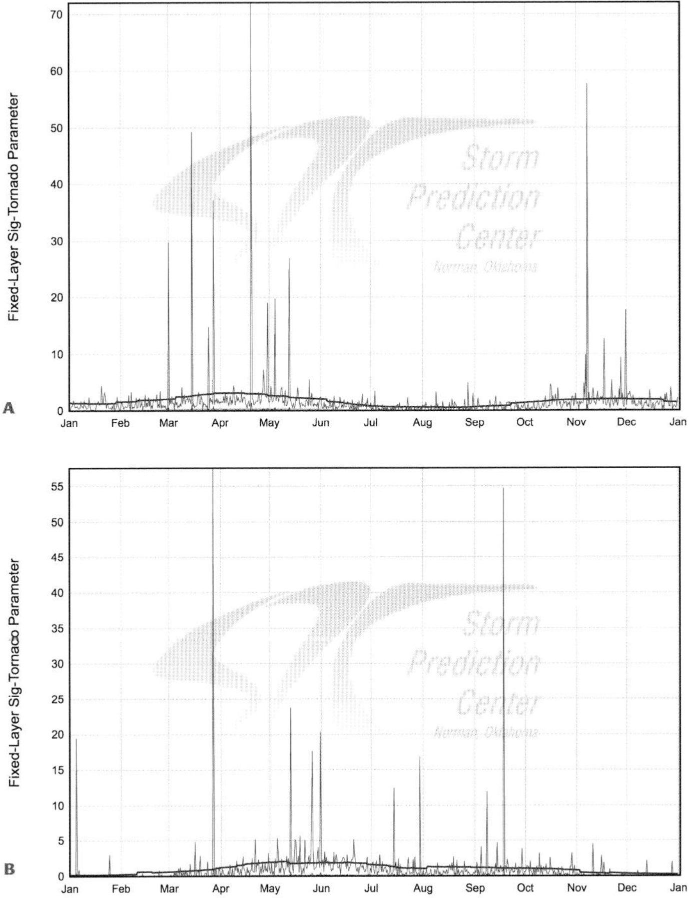

FIG. 9.4A & 9.4B A "tornado parameter" derived from weather balloon data reveals the likelihood of tornado occurrence (a) in southeast Texas, and (b) in the Texas Panhandle. Source: National Oceanic and Atmospheric Administration

Inscrutable at Night

It is often easy to confuse a funnel cloud with other low-hanging cloud forms, especially "scud" clouds that exhibit a wind-torn motion (not a rotating motion). The key to recognizing a tornado is finding an organized rotary motion. Spotting a tornado can be a challenge when it descends from the base of a thundercloud without developing a visible funnel of its own. In such instances, you can ascertain its existence by noticing debris or dirt being picked up in a spinning motion from the ground. Do not confuse these rotating whirlwinds with "dust devils," a phenomenon hardly ever associated with clouds. As a rule, if the tornado persists for any length of time, material from the ground will be lifted higher and higher toward the bottom of the thunderhead, thereby "filling in" the spinning funnel to the extent that it becomes readily recognizable.

Spotting a tornado at night can be extremely hard to do, and seeing one may be possible only when there are brilliant flashes of lightning. Even in daytime, a tornado may not be visible because of heavy rain or nearby tall buildings that obscure one's vision. Nonetheless a tornado can be detected, for its violently spinning column produces a distinctive roar that often can be heard for several miles. Some witnesses describe the sound of a twister as that of a loud freight train or a large jet aircraft. While the precise sound generated by a funnel cloud or tornado may be in the ear of the listener, it is known that the noise of a funnel cloud increases as the funnel approaches the ground and that it is loudest when the twister is moving along the ground.

Freak Incidents

No element of nature is more fickle than a tornado, and what it destroys and what it spares can be downright implausible. The EF5 tornado that struck Jarrell on May 27, 1997 tore one house apart, leaving unscathed a homeowner who sought refuge in her bathtub, which sat by itself amidst the wreckage where the house had been. She recovered a stack of photo albums, which had been stored in her linen closet, some 20 feet away—all perfectly intact and stacked exactly the way she had left them in the closet. A neighbor 1 mile away had everything "mulched" by the same tornado, with stacks of 2-by-4 lumber in their yard reduced to splinters, yet his reclining chair was found sitting in a nearby field, intact and upright. The same tornado had struck nearby Cedar Park earlier in the afternoon, destroying one house whose owner had a bible that was found a block away, with a marriage license still tucked inside. There are documented cases of chickens being plucked of their feathers by the strong, vacuum-cleaning effect of tornadic winds. Blades of grass and straw have been driven through telephone and fence posts. Motor vehicles have been lifted off highways and then dashed down in the middle of wheat fields. Heavy railroad cars have been hoisted from tracks and inverted hundreds of yards away in valleys and ravines. One of the most bizarre happenings in Texas's colorful weather history, an event verified by the US Weather Bureau, took place in the northeastern corner of the Texas Panhandle near the town of Higgins in April 1947. The owner of a home in rural Lipscomb County, upon hearing the loud train-like noise of an approaching twister, opened his front door and was lifted hundreds of feet into the air over the tops of nearby trees. A visitor in the man's home then went to the same front entrance to check on his friend and was also carried high into the air but on a slightly different course. After a few very anxious moments, both men were lowered to the ground several hundred feet away from where the house had originally stood. Unharmed but understandably shaken, the pair proceeded to try to walk back to the house but the persistent strong wind forced them to crawl. When they ultimately got back to the site of the house, they found nothing but the foundation. Sitting on the floor was a lamp and a couch, which contained the owner's terrified but unharmed wife and two children.

In far too many cases, however, what survivors discover is a scene resembling in many ways the devastation wrought by a heavy demolition squad. Fallen trees with their root systems displayed and virtually defrocked of their leaves lie across streets. Other trees nearby, still decked out in full foliage, stand erect as they were in the pre-storm period. Houses, furniture, and automobiles are left strewn along the storm's path, sometimes piled up as much as a dozen feet. Within sight nearby are other homes and vehicles standing as they were, not disturbed at all by the tornadic blitz. Vehicles of all types are rolled over and crushed as if they were nothing but small toys. Where office buildings once stood are piles of broken boards, shattered glass, chunks of concrete, and gnarled pipes. Telltale signs of a twister's strike in the country often consist of uprooted trees, some stripped of their foliage and limbs, and fields of crops looking as if they had been scathed by a bulldozer.

Tornadoes assume a variety of sizes and shapes, with the majority appearing as funnels—broad at the top where they are attached to the base of a thunderstorm but tapering to a small diameter at the end touching the ground. The funnel sometimes undergoes strange twists and stretches that make it appear as a swaying trunk of an elephant or a writhing snake. Some of the time, winds at cloud level are swifter than those at the surface of the ground, and the upper portion of the tornado moves along faster than the bottom; the pendant cloud is stretched to the extent that it resembles a slender string or rope. On other occasions, the tornado may hang straight down, and as the diameter of the base of the funnel expands and grows to become as broad as the top portion, the tornado takes on the appearance of a huge, thick pillar or column.

Tornadoes manifest different shades of black or gray in part because of the diffraction of light by the water droplets that make up the dangling, twisting cloud. A tornado will appear light or dark depending upon the amount of light available to the observer and the type of material picked up by the tornado as it cuts across the landscape. If you spot a tornado between yourself and the sun, for instance, it is apt to be darker than if sunlight were directly hitting the side of the tornado visible to you. If the soil or debris lifted by the tornado is dark colored, the funnel most probably will have a swarthy appearance, possibly even black.

Waterspouts

The waterspout, a tornado that occurs over water, is spawned when very cold air at high altitude moves over relatively warm water. In the same way that a tornado stirs up sand and soil as it rolls across the landscape, the waterspout draws up spray from the body of water over which it moves. The most common kind of waterspout observed in Texas's coastal waters builds downward from a towering cumuliform cloud. Initially, the base of the cloud lowers toward the surface of the water, which at the same time is disturbed by vigorous winds blowing across the water's surface. About the time the whirling cloud material forms a distinct funnel, spray is thrust upward out of the sea. When the dipping funnel reaches the sea surface, water droplets from the cloud are merged with the saltwater spray to form the waterspout. Ordinarily, waterspouts are not nearly as intense as their land-based cousins, though some have produced wind speeds in excess of 100 mph. With an average size of 100–150 feet in diameter, the waterspout is considerably smaller than the tornado. Boats have been known to pass through weak waterspouts and sustain little or no damage, although some of the larger, more intense waterspouts are capable of destroying small craft. One such notable incident occurred in San Antonio Bay around noon on May 8, 1980. A waterspout ripped off the cabin from a shrimp boat, then overturned and sank the craft. Two of the three crewmen aboard were injured but rescued, while the third person was never found. From almost any vantage point along the Texas coastline, at least a score of waterspouts can be seen in some summer months. Waterspouts are most apt to occur near the Texas coastline in summer, though sometimes a few form as early as midspring or as late as midautumn. Most of them live less than half an hour. Occasionally, a waterspout occurs in interior sections of Texas when a tornado moves over a body of water, such as a large lake. In such instances, waterspouts can be just as devastating as their counterparts on land.

Tornado Recognition

The certain recurrence of tornadic events, and the formulation of well-defined measures to deal with them, bear out the fact that a quick and credible alert, when responded to in the right ways, saves lives. With the advent of highly sensitive Doppler radar, the NWS has enhanced its capacity to recognize threatening conditions in the atmosphere that are associated with tornado generation. Today, it is a reasonable expectation that a timely alert will be issued by the NWS and that the whole citizenry will be awarded sufficient notice to get to safety. Until a totally leak-proof detection system has been devised, the NWS must rely upon the involvement of hundreds of trained storm reporters, or SKYWARN "spotters," for quick, accurate detection of tornadoes from their infancy to their expiration. These volunteers possess a thorough knowledge of local severe storm characteristics, and their observations of developing weather hazards have contributed immeasurably to the saving of lives.

While much of the burden of tornado detection rests with professional analysts using the tools that taxpayers have provided them, it remains incumbent upon citizens to take all alerts issued by the NWS seriously—and to be familiar with the "dos" and "don'ts" and resolve to see them through. Yet, an additional burden falls back on the people who issue the warnings: limit, if not eliminate, alerts that are followed by nonevents. The "cry wolf" syndrome is still in circulation. Warn excessively and be proven wrong, and people will increasingly tune out—and leave themselves exposed. So the experts feel the pressure to refine their skills, all the while training more spotters and pursuing new avenues of tornado detection. Even now, the limited amount of weather data, combined with limitations in our knowledge of what causes tornadoes, leads weather experts to struggle in predicting accurately the incidence of tornadoes. But these inadequacies do not thwart forecasters in giving best estimates of the likely time and place of tornado occurrence. Present-day capability enables forecasters to specify areas (often a rectangle at least 120 miles wide and 100 miles long [193 by 161 kilometers] or more) where most tornadoes can be anticipated to occur. Most tornado watches are issued with a "lead" time (i.e., the interval between time of issuance and the beginning of the valid watch period) of about one hour, and watches ordinarily cover time periods of five to six hours.

Better lead times appear inevitable as scientists scour storm systems for more reliable signals that hint at the formation of funnels within the tumult of a blossoming thunderstorm. Lightning may be one key to recognizing the earliest stages of an evolving tornado. By tracking static bursts of electrical energy by means of untapped television frequencies, researchers are finding a revealing pattern deep within cloud masses that engender tornadoes. New satellite technology due for implementation soon should allow scientists to map effectively the occurrence of lightning inside storm clouds. Another approach taps into the low-frequency rumbles from severe thunderstorms that precede the formation of a funnel. This ultrasound, well below the threshold of human hearing, may tip off meteorologists to the formation of a funnel which otherwise stays hidden deep within the cloud mass and beyond the reach of conventional weather radar.

It is essential to know that a watch is not the same as a warning. A tornado watch suggests that people go about their business as usual, but because weather conditions are expected to become unstable enough to have the potential for producing tornadoes, persons should check the skies periodically and stay within reach of special weather statements disseminated by the NWS through the news media and the National Oceanographic and Atmospheric Administration's own radio network. On the other hand, a tornado warning informs the populace that a tornado actually has been sighted, either by a public spotter or by weather radar. The tornado warning contains information on the location and movement of the tornado, the area through which it is expected to move, and the interval of time during which it will pass through the area that is being forewarned. It also urges people in the vicinity of the detected tornado to take immediate cover, and it advises other persons near the reported site of the tornado to be prepared to seek safety.

Safety Precautions

The risk of being killed by a tornado has been reduced dramatically in recent years. Today, the chance of dying, on a nationwide basis, is estimated at 1 in 5 million, according to the National Severe Storms Laboratory based in Norman, Oklahoma. Prior to 1925, the death rate was nine times as high as it is today. After a spate of tornadoes took 695 lives in the mid-Mississippi River valley that year, heightened public awareness, improved means of communicating with the public, and the practice of constructing more resistant houses in the decades that followed brought about a steady decline in fatality rates. By the 1990s, however, the decline in deaths slowed because more people began living in mobile homes, where an inhabitant is 15 times more likely to be killed than in permanent housing.

What, then, is the appropriate response when you realize the threat of a tornado is imminent? What you do is dictated, naturally, by the circumstances of the moment. There are different measures to take—and some actions to avoid—depending upon where you happen to be at the time you are made aware of a tornado threat. The following is a list of tornado safety rules intended to afford you the maximum amount of protection possible when a tornado threatens.

OUTDOORS

If you are outdoors in the open and shelter in a nearby sturdy building is not available, move away from the oncoming tornado at a right angle (e.g., if the tornado is moving west to east, move toward either north or south). If there is no time to escape, lie flat face down in the nearest low spot, such as a ditch or ravine, and protect the back of your head with your arms.

AT HOME

If you are in a home with a basement, seek refuge next to the wall in the most sheltered and deepest portion of the basement. For added protection, get under heavy furniture or a workbench. If you are in a home without a basement, go to the lowest floor and to the smallest room having stout walls, such as a bathroom, closet, or stairwell—or an interior hallway without windows. Get under some heavy furniture (e.g., a tipped-over couch or chair) or thick padding such as a mattress or blanket. Stay away from doors and windows, so that you are less apt to be struck by flying glass and other debris.

AT SCHOOL

Students, faculty members, and staff should follow the drill. All should be familiar with designated shelter areas and proper measures to be taken when a tornado threat is made known. School administrators ought to ensure that a special alarm system is available to indicate to school personnel that a tornado has been sighted and is approaching. School supervisors should be assigned to round up children who may be on playgrounds or in other outdoor areas. Students should be escorted from structures of weak fabrication (e.g., portable or temporary buildings) to sturdier ones. When the danger of a tornado is imminent, students should be assembled in school basements or interior hallways and instructed to crouch on elbows and knees facing the wall. Buses should not be operated, but if a bus is caught out in the open when a tornado is approaching, the occupants should leave the bus and go to a nearby ditch or ravine to lie down with their arms over their heads. It is wise for school administrators to drill their students periodically, so that they will know precisely what to do to ensure their safety.

IN A HIGH-RISE BUILDING

Go to the basement or an interior hallway on one of the lower floors. If you have no time to descend to a lower area, get in a closet or other small room having stout walls. Otherwise, crawl under heavy furniture. Be sure to stay away from windows. Avoid using an elevator.

IN A MOBILE HOME

Vacate the structure, even when it is tied down, and seek shelter in another, more fortified, preselected structure. If your only alternative is to get in a ditch out in the open, you will be safer than in a mobile home. Make sure the spot you pick to lie flat on the ground is away from the mobile home as well as trees and cars, as these can be blown onto you.

IN A MEDICAL FACILITY OR SHOPPING MALL

Go to predesignated shelter areas. Interior hallways on the lowest floor are usually safest. Stay away from open spaces and windows. Cooperate with the staff and authorities who have had training about how to deal with emergencies.

IN A VEHICLE

An automobile is not a safe haven from a tornado, unless of course the driver can be certain of getting out of the twister's path. Even then, it can be a tragic mistake to get into your auto and attempt to outrun a twister. One lesson gleaned from the investigation of the death and destruction wrought by the April 10, 1979 tornado in Wichita Falls was that an auto may become nothing other than a sealed tomb when a tornado strikes an area. About half of the 45 persons who died in the vicinity of the Wichita Falls tornado were occupants of autos; many of them had been trying to run away from the storm and were caught in massive traffic jams from which they could not extricate themselves. An automobile may be useful when a ravine or ditch is not available, in that you may obtain some shelter from flying debris by crawling under one. If, however, the funnel cloud is distant and traffic is light, you may consider driving out of its path by moving at a right angle to the path of the cloud. Any doubt that you can navigate away from the tornado's path should prompt you to abandon your vehicle and seek shelter in a sturdy structure. Make sure when you leave your vehicle that it is not blocking a traffic lane, especially under bridges and overpasses. If you must seek shelter under an overpass, get as far away from the traffic lanes as possible and do your utmost to protect yourself from flying debris.

More often than not, tornado victims never see the funnel before it strikes, especially when the event happens at night. So while staying alert to the skies as thunderstorms are approaching, know what to look and listen for: a spinning of the base of the storm cloud; whirling debris on the ground below the cloud base; an eerie calm, or an abrupt and intense wind shift, that follows a burst of hail or heavy rain; a loud, continuous roar (akin to a rumbling freight train so many witnesses have remembered) that does not dissipate in a few seconds, like thunder does; or flashes of light near ground level (caused by power lines being snapped by the potent, rotating winds).

Every homeowner should have a kit easily accessible in the house that contains, at a minimum, a flashlight (with spare batteries), first-aid supplies, a commercial radio (preferably a "weather radio"), and a whistle or some other device that emits a sound recognizable by rescuers. Keep in mind that cell phones can, and do, fail easily when nearby towers are damaged or networks get overloaded from usage.

There are other measures that residents and businesses can take long before the onset of tornado season to ensure the safety of family members and employees should a tornado threaten. More homeowners, particularly in that part of west and north Texas encompassing "tornado alley," are investing in steel storm shelters. These rather small structures (4 by 6 feet) are designed to hold up to six people and cost several thousand dollars. They frequently are situated in garages and are bolted to a concrete foundation. As new houses are built, some homeowners design a closet or utility room to serve also as a "safe room" into which family members can find refuge when a tornado threatens. These rooms, as big as 8 by 8 feet, have walls of brick or concrete and feature an air vent to allow air in and keep debris out. They are entered through a 2-inch-thick steel door, and the entire structure is bolted to a concrete foundation. Storm shelters certified by the National Storm Shelter Association are tested against 250-mph winds and debris traveling at that speed, thereby affording residents a safe haven that is not underground. Larger storm shelters are designed to accommodate dozens, if not hundreds, of people seeking safety from tornadoes. Round-topped versions are fastened aboveground to concrete foundations in schools, trailer parks, or workplaces, and at least one version can house up to 500 people.

If you have access to a storm shelter or safe room, it is a good idea to place a battery-operated radio in it, so that you and other occupants can remain apprised of weather developments even if the home's electrical power supply is severed. Also, a thoughtful step is to store other necessities—such as drinking water, supplemental clothing, even food—in these protected areas. This will ensure that the family members have sufficient provisions should they be confined for a lengthy period or if it should be their misfortune to have a tornado remove all their other, unpreserved belongings. If you do not have access to a basement or cellar, and if you think that other areas of your home are unsafe, you should preselect a nearby culvert or deep ditch to which you can flee should the need arise. An employer should see that shelter areas are selected and marked for use by all employees. Someone should be trained to direct the building's occupants to these shelters when the situation warrants it. Those who live in mobile home parks would do well to select a leader responsible for ensuring constant radio monitoring and storm spotting and for sounding an alarm if a storm cloud approaches.

In the wake of a tornado, heed any direction given by local law enforcement and emergency personnel. If they suggest you can stay and help, do so, but if your presence will complicate matters, leave as directed. Never drive to an area just to see how much damage has been incurred from a tornado. Gawkers hamper rescue efforts, making a terrible situation even worse. Use great caution when entering a house or building damaged by the storm. It bears repeating: if you detect leaking natural gas or other harmful agents, do not stay around. Be sure that walls, ceiling, and roof are in place and that the structure rests firmly on the foundation. Look out for broken glass and downed power lines. In checking for injuries, do not attempt to move seriously injured persons unless they are in imminent danger of further injury, but call for help immediately.

Some Reassurance

Given that sharper, and quicker, recognition of imminent tornadic activity is now attainable, with more effective ways of disseminating information in the form of alerts to the public, Texans in the twenty-first century are safer than ever before from these whirlwinds. Improvement in the way homes and other structures are being built is protecting more residents more effectively than at any time in history. It has been documented, by a *Popular Mechanics* study in 2007, that the death toll from tornadoes in the United States has been reduced by 90 percent over the past century. Whereas some 500 Americans perished from twisters on average each year in the early 1900s, the death toll has been shaved to an average today of 50. This undoubtedly helps explain the tendency for people to grow complacent about the threat of tornadoes, especially if their area has not been affected by one for several years. Though most Texas communities are included in at least several tornado watches and warnings every year, relatively few of them are ever affected appreciably by a twister. Consequently, some people deduce that because tornado advisories covering their area of concern seem to be followed repeatedly by an absence of tornadic activity, those alerts needlessly alarm the public and should be ignored. In reality, no weather alert is given without sufficient cause. The tornado advisory is not meant to guarantee that you will be affected but rather to signal the potential danger that actually exists. No preparedness program can be effective if the citizenry does not have a due regard for severe storm advisories and if people subject to them are reluctant, for whatever reason, to take immediate action to ensure their safety.

Regrettably, far too little attention has been devoted to the matter of how human beings might influence a tornado's behavior. It is no stretch to suggest that someday the capability will exist for modifying thunderclouds to alter, if not suppress, the development of tornadoes.

Since we know that seeding a thunderstorm alters its capacity to engender hail, might the same approach be effective in redistributing its water content and, thus, its energy in ways that inhibit the formation of funnels? Hypotheses have been offered by some in the scientific community as to how the behavior of a tornado might be controlled, in spite of the reality that the types of thunderstorms that produce tornadoes experience explosive growth in very concise time frames. Not all notions about taming a prospective tornadic cloud should be summarily dismissed. Rather, research vigorously pursued, even if confined for now to computer modeling, would inform us on whether it is practical to move ahead with tornado suppression. Such a concentration of our investigative resources seems justified by the continuing, serious threat to life and property posed by this most dangerous—and feared—weather phenomenon. Until that capability is identified and cultivated, we have to resolve to know and to follow tornado safety rules, realizing at the same time that we still are very much at the mercy of nature's whims.

10.

Airfield in Motion

As the most excruciating summer in Texas history wound to a conclusion, in the wake of wilting heat and debilitating humidity coupled with a dearth of meaningful rainfall, Texans peered longingly in the direction of the coastline, desperate for relief. A tropical weather system spawned in the Gulf of Mexico was pushing landward as Labor Day 2011 approached, seemingly bearing the promise of desperately needed rainfall and a momentary cessation of relentless sun. Tropical Storm Lee, however, as tropical cyclones are often prone to do, veered to the north, aiming its rain bands at the Louisiana coast, leaving Texas residents despondent over another missed opportunity to break a smothering drought.

But the potent tropical storm hardly ignored the Lone Star State, leaving it to deal with the cyclone's collateral damage. While drenching Cajun country with torrential rains, Lee's spinning mass yanked down into East Texas a desiccating north wind from the nation's midsection. It not only prolonged the stifling conditions that had tormented Texans for months—it fed something far worse than a heat wave. With much of Texas tinder dry, the stage was set for an outburst of raging wildfires fed by this moisture-deprived wind imported from a scorched Mississippi River valley. When power lines snapped near the community of Bastrop, a pair of wildfires erupted that soon merged into a colossal firestorm that swept through Bastrop State Park, decimating the famous Lost Pines cluster of coniferous trees. With firefighters battling the blazes fed by sustained winds of 30 miles per hour (mph), the fire swept beyond the park, eventually engulfing a massive chunk of Bastrop County, or some 34,068 acres. It was the most ruinous single fire in Texas history, consuming 1,669 houses and 40 commercial buildings while taking the lives of two people.

Lee's backdoor effect on Texas illustrates how, on occasion, what would be welcome as a break in the debilitating heat of summer can be a region's worst nightmare. In Lee's instance, the first infusion of normally milder Canadian air, usually in September, was anything but an invigorating tonic for Texans broiled for months by unrelenting heat. An uneventful—essentially rainless—summer had ensured that tinder dry conditions were ripe for a lone spark to progress quickly into a monumental fireball that defied firefighters' efforts to contain it for days on end.

As the Labor Day fire of 2011 attests, wind can be blessing or curse. The wind is air in horizontal—but not vertical—motion. It courses along at all levels of the atmosphere and at varying rates as invisible streams of energy possessing considerable power. It can suddenly obscure the sky with layers of clouds then just as rapidly clear it again. It is a key player in completing the hydrologic cycle, channeling vast quantities of water inland from the sea and then manipulating the cargo to shed rain on parched hillsides and dusty valleys. It pushes an enshrouding fog landward early at night, then whisks it away not long after the next day's sunrise. It brings masses of air of differing densities together, often fostering a conflagration consisting of raucous thunderstorms. It refreshes coastal residents beleaguered by an unrelenting summer sun and humidity that suffocates. It ventilates our smog-clogged cities, escorting away the poisonous exhalations of our machines, both sedentary and mobile. It deposits seeds and scatters pollen.

The wind blows because of differences in atmospheric pressure, which in turn stem from variations in temperature throughout Earth's atmosphere, a result of the change in the tilt of Earth's axis toward the sun with the changing of the seasons. Where differences in air temperature—and hence pressure—exist, there is a constant striving by the forces of nature to balance them. Wind, consequently, is a highly important regulator of the atmosphere in that, while the equalization of temperature, pressure, and humidity is never attained, wind does help to maintain an approximate average state for these differences.

Thankfully, the wind at Earth's surface most often is weaker than at any other altitude. That is because movement of the air is strongly influenced by the force of friction that is exerted when the air "rubs" against a surface such as the ground. While higher in the atmosphere the flow of air is predominantly smooth and continuous, in the lowest layer of the atmosphere adjacent to Earth's crust, air motion consists mostly of gusts and lulls because of this frictional influence. In daytime, intense heating of Earth's skin by the sun initiates thermal convection currents that further disturb the air near the surface. Winds are apt to be gustier in regions where the terrain is rougher and where temperature contrasts between a warm surface and cooler air aloft are common. This helps explain why, over large bodies of water, wind speed and wind direction are more uniform than over land areas, which are characterized by more roughness and greater temperature variations.

While it is spared some of the species of dangerous winds that plague other sections of the country, like Chinooks, Santa Ana, and Diablo winds, Texas remains one of the windiest places of the western hemisphere. The High Plains of Texas vie with points farther north on the Great Plains for the distinction of windiest cities in the United States. In fact, 3 of the 10 consistently windiest cities reside in the Lone Star State, with Amarillo second only to Dodge City, Kansas, in terms of average wind speed for the whole of a year (table 10.1). Corpus Christi also ranks among the breeziest places, owing to its proximity to the Gulf of Mexico.

The speed of the wind at the surface in all sectors of Texas is seldom constant, and if so, it is for very short periods, while its direction can be steady for days on end. When the wind shifts in clockwise fashion (i.e., from east through south to the west), such a change is called a veering wind. The opposite of this (i.e., a wind originally blowing from the west but changing into an east wind through the south direction) is known as a backing wind. On the average, however—for intervals of a few days if not a few hours—the primary flow of air, or the prevailing wind, is usually rather steady from one general direction. What is commonly referred to as "wind" is this average air motion over a short span of time (e.g., one or a few minutes) and does not include short-lived gusts and lulls. A National Weather Service (NWS) report that "the wind is from the south at 12 miles per hour" should be construed as the average wind speed and direction over a 1-minute interval at the time the observation was made (usually 5 or 10 minutes before the top of the hour). Even though during that period of 1 minute wind speed may have varied between 8 and 15 mph and wind direction may have modulated between the southwest and southeast, the average value of wind speed and wind direction is cited to describe the nature of the prevailing wind.

When wind is measured and reported, both direction and speed are given, with gusts reported when wind speeds exceed 18 mph. Wind direction is taken to be that sector of the compass *from* which the wind is blowing, and in common parlance the direction is referred to as a particular compass point. Wind speed most often is expressed in miles per hour (fig. 10.1), although for marine interests in coastal areas and out at sea it may be given in knots. On most weather maps, wind movement is depicted with vectors; the arrow points in the direction from which the wind is blowing, in the same way a wind vane points into the wind (fig. 10.2). The number and length of the tails (or barbs) denote the speed of the wind observed at the measuring point.

TABLE 10.1

Windiest Cities in the United States

Average daily wind speed (miles per hour, mph) based on data for the period 1981-2010.

CITY	MPH
Dodge City, Kansas	13.2
Amarillo, Texas	12.8
Rochester, Minnesota	12.2
Goodland, Kansas	12.1
Casper, Wyoming	12.0
Lubbock, Texas	12.0
Cheyenne, Wyoming	11.9
Corpus Christi, Texas	11.7
Boston, Massachusetts	11.6
Great Falls, Montana	11.5
Wichita, Kansas	11.5

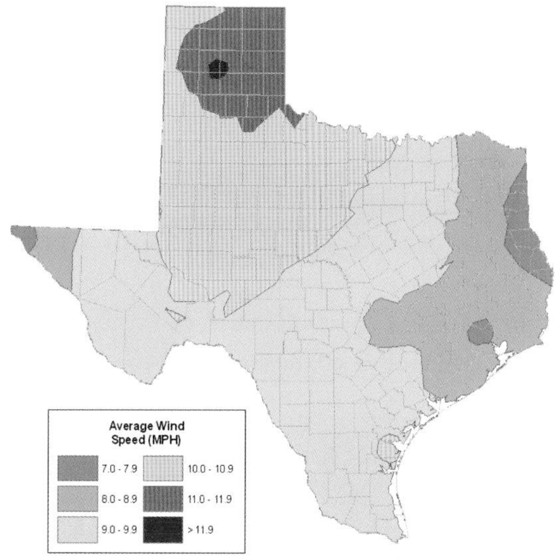

FIG. 10.1 Average annual wind speed in Texas. Source: Texas Water Development Board

FIG. 10.2 A Texas-size wind vane points into the direction of the wind atop a hotel in Kerrville. Source: George W. Bomar

To express the average wind condition at a given locality for a period of time (say, a month or a season), a wind rose is devised. Given in a circular format, the wind rose shows the frequency of winds blowing *from* a specific direction. The length of each "spoke" around the circle identifies the amount of time the wind blows from a particular direction. Each concentric circle represents a different frequency, from zero at the center to the maximum frequency at the outermost circle. For example, in Dallas, on average, at all hours of the day for all days in July the wind blows from the south (S), south-southeast, or southeast (SE) about 75 percent of the time. Moreover, winds blow from the south at speeds between 10 and 15 mph about 13 percent of the time in July (fig. 10.3). Since July is made up of 744 hours, about 96 hours (0.13 x 744) typically have winds from the south at those speeds.

The South Wind Reigns

South winds—or some component of them (such as a southeasterly wind)—dominate in Texas. This is especially true during summer, when wind shifts prompted by the invasion of cool fronts are uncommon. In fact, except for the Texas Panhandle, where weak cool fronts often ease southward before dissipating, Texas is under the influence of a southerly wind virtually exclusively during July and August. The wind rose for midsummer for Amarillo, for example, reveals that, on average, a wind from the south quadrant prevails more than 80 percent of the time (fig. 10.4). On the South Plains, where blowing dust is most likely to occur, especially in springtime, the wind blows out of the southwest and southeast quadrants about 75 percent of the time in Lubbock (fig. 10.5a). During the spring, the wind speed

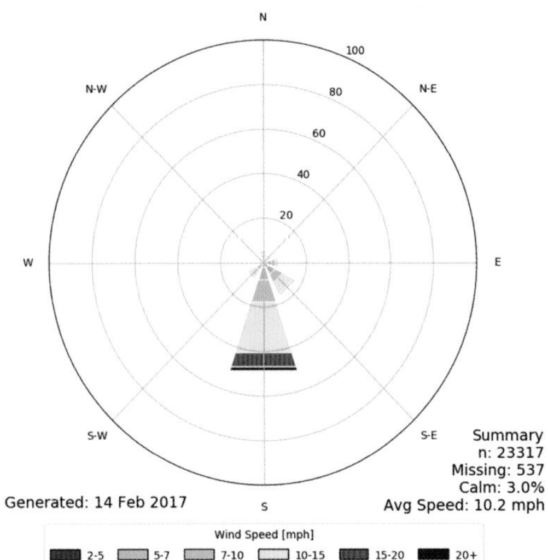

FIG. 10.3 Wind rose depicting average wind speed and direction in Dallas in a typical month of July. Source: Iowa State University

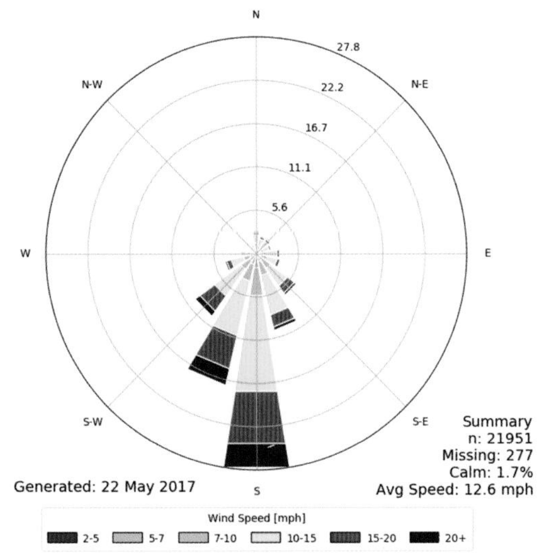

FIG. 10.4 Wind rose depicting average wind speed and direction in Amarillo in a typical month of July. Source: Iowa State University

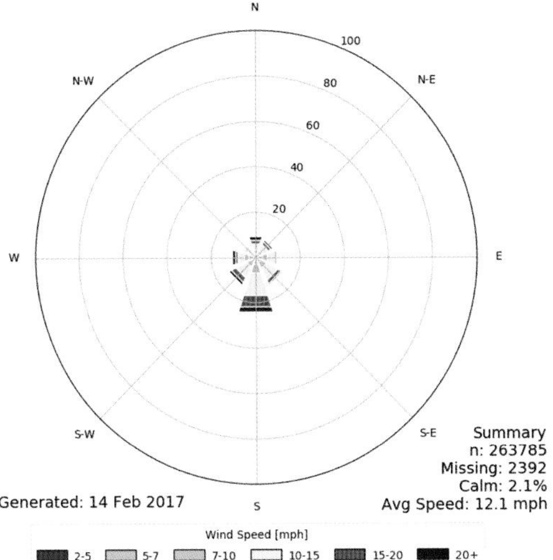

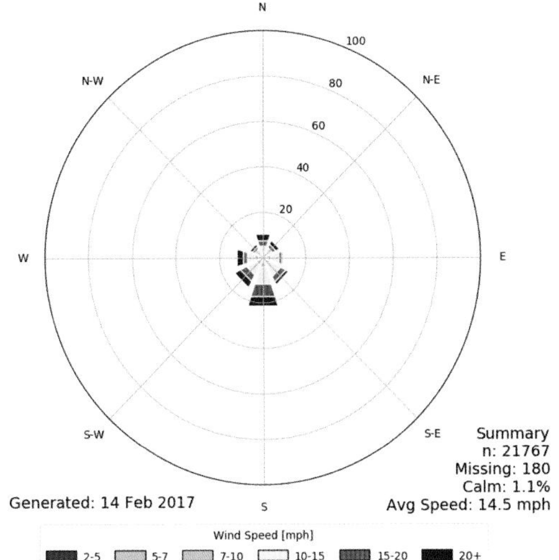

FIG. 10.5A & 10.5B Wind roses depicting average wind speed and direction in Lubbock (a) on a year-round basis and (b) for a typical April. Source: Iowa State University

from those quadrants is accelerated substantially, with 20 mph winds or stronger a frequent feature of the area's climatology (fig 10.5b).

The rejuvenation of the polar jet stream with the onset of autumn and its propensity to send Canadian air masses into Texas, usually beginning in September, lessens the dominance of the south wind. As winter approaches, more cold fronts intrude, allowing northerly winds to compete with the south wind. Cold polar or Arctic air is frequent enough (once every 4–5 days on average) to generate a northerly wind, or some variation of it, about half the time in January. In fact, the persistent influence of these cold-air incursions is such that the average wind direction for January in some locales in South Central Texas and the Upper Coast is northerly (fig. 10.6). In reality, even in these areas southerly and northerly winds are about equal in frequency of occurrence during the year's coldest month. The wind invariably veers into the north at the time of arrival of a cold air mass, and it usually remains northerly for one to three days afterward. The passage of a cold front—and its concomitant wind shift into the north—merely signals that the edge of the usually massive mound of cold air has penetrated the area; the bulk of the air mass has yet to arrive. Winds persist from the north for one or a few days as the cold air "builds" into the state. Wind speeds, while vigorous or even tempestuous at first, always wane with the passing of time. One almost sure sign of the proximity of the center of the dome of cold air is a very light, if not calm, wind. After the center of the mound of cold air, or the "ridge line," passes a locale, the wind gradually increases in speed, but from the opposite (southerly) direction. The return of the southerly wind one or more days after the arrival of a cold front signals a warming trend, because air is then

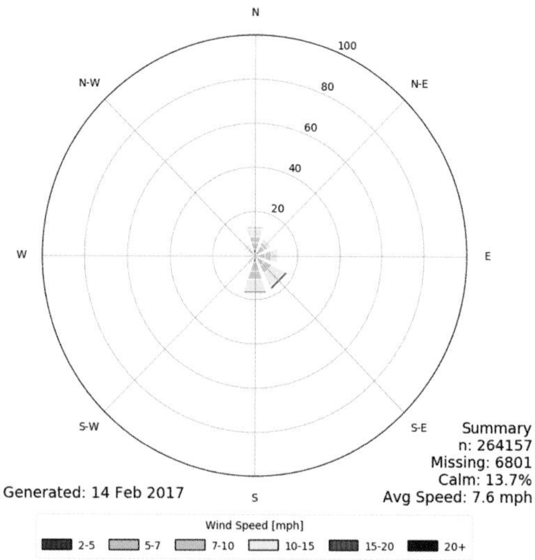

FIG. 10.6 Wind rose depicting average wind speed and direction in Houston on an annual basis. Source: Iowa State University

being channeled from the relatively warm waters of the Gulf of Mexico. Clearly, it also indicates an increase in moisture in the lower atmosphere.

The boisterous winds of spring nurture the reputation of the High Plains of Texas as one of the windiest regions in North America. On those not-so-infrequent occasions when stiff westerly winds whip tons of dust into the air, prior to and after the arrival of cold fronts, work out of doors becomes difficult if not impossible and walking into the wind requires superhuman exertion. While "average" wind speeds from the Permian Basin in the south to the Canadian River valley in the north vary between 13 and 17 mph during March, April, and May, sustained wind speeds that often amount to two or three times that modest magnitude may persist over periods of more than a few hours. Gusts of wind exceeding 60 mph are not infrequent. The strongest winds observed in the western third of Texas have occurred during either late winter or spring, with maximum 1-minute wind speeds of 70–80 mph egressing from the southwest-to-northwest quadrant. Guadalupe Pass in the northern Trans Pecos region is notorious for some of the worst windstorms. While peak wind gusts of 128 mph were ripping through the pass one day in January 1996, only slightly less potent straight-line winds were pounding Guadalupe Mountains National Park, ripping up over 100 feet of chain-link fence, tossing picnic tables across campgrounds, and sending rocks that broke the windows and chipped the paint off a score of automobiles.

Except for brief intervals in the late summer or early autumn, when disturbances migrate inland off the waters of the Gulf of Mexico, spring is the windiest season of the year for the entire state. Prevailing wind direction is southerly most of the time, especially in the latter half of the season when the number of cool fronts ushering in northerly winds drops off markedly. As in the High Plains, winds in other sections intensify in advance of the arrival of a cold front and often blow in gusts of as much as 30 or 40 mph. Though on an average basis the wind is most blustery along the Texas coast in spring, in some years the strongest winds occur in late summer or early autumn as a result of tropical weather disturbances. It is not uncommon for winds to be clocked in excess of 100 mph at points along the coast in proximity to the center of an approaching hurricane.

Measurement of Wind's Discomfort

The Texas winter is responsible for more human discomfort than any other season because of the combined role of air temperature and wind speed. This discomfort is measured in terms of wind chill, a recognized index of heat loss and cold injury. The human body can tolerate subfreezing, even subzero, temperatures for long periods of time—as long as there is little or no wind. But at extremely low temperatures, the speed of the wind becomes a far greater determinant of physical well-being than does an additional drop in temperature. During winter in Texas, when "blue northers" often shove the temperature well below the freezing level, it is not so much the cold temperature that makes outdoor activity torturous and numbing as it is the bone-chilling combination of the cold temperature and the strong winds. The cold wind removes the body-warmed air next to one's skin and clothing so that the body must heat more air. If it is unable to supply heat at the rate it is being lost to the wind, the body then has the sensation of being cool, cold, or even bitterly cold.

Air temperature customarily means the warmth, or chill, of air independent of the speed of the wind. We rely on a thermometer to quantify that degree of warmth without factoring in how that air "feels" to us because of air movement. To the human body, a temperature of 30°F (−1°C) with a calm wind is much more desirable than the same temperature combined with a 30-mph gale. Neither temperature nor wind alone gives a meaningful index to how cold a person feels under different conditions of wind and temperature. As a result, an empirical formula yielding the windchill index was developed after a number of experiments were performed in Antarctica in 1939–1940. The index indicates that a temperature of 35°F (2°C) accompanied by a wind of 10 mph will turn one's ears white and numb just as quickly as still air at a temperature of 21°F (−6°C); for a wind twice as strong, the effect is the same as that of a calm condition where the temperature is 12°F (−11°C). It is not uncommon for residents of the Texas Panhandle in winter to be subjected to temperatures near 0°F and wind gusts of 40 mph or more, which translates into a "sensed" temperature of −53°F (−47°C).

Anyone using the windchill index should remember it is only an approximation, since how one feels depends not only on temperature of the air and wind speed but also on other variables, such as the amount of exposed flesh, the type of clothing worn, the amount of radiation, the relative humidity, and even the physical condition of the person. Nonetheless, the index is a useful indicator for those planning outdoor activities where proper clothing and protection from the wind are important concerns.

Wind as a Renewable Resource

With the world's population increasing while the amount of nonrenewable resources like oil and natural gas remain finite, the wind has become an appealing source of power. Wind costs nothing and is available virtually all the time while being generously distributed over the entire land surface. Earlier generations recognized these realities about the wind when they erected windmills to produce power and retrieve groundwater. It would be difficult to find a cheaper, simpler device for pumping water. What is more, windmills can be equipped with a small generator to deliver relatively inexpensive electricity.

While windmills remain a fixture on many rural properties, it is the swarm of wind turbines that are tapping into the plentiful supply of wind energy. These towering power generators are especially cost efficient in the plains and prairies of West Texas, where winds of 10 mph or more blow almost incessantly on virtually every day of the year. For instance, a windmill in Midland would generate 80 percent more power in an average month of May than one in Austin because of that western city's characteristically higher wind speed; in a typical September, a windmill owner in Amarillo would garner nearly three times as much wind power as an operator of a similar device in Dallas. Still another advantage in wind power is the virtual absence of adverse environmental effects. While wind is not likely to replace most other sources of power in the near term, it will continue to contribute significantly toward meeting Texas's power needs for years to come. The fuel for these multiplying networks of wind turbines is ample, inexhaustible, and—most important—free.

The proliferation of "wind farms" in Texas, and elsewhere in the Great Plains, has not happened without controversy. The boom has evoked increasing resistance in recent times as these farms move ever closer to cities, blight scenic views, make noise, and emit flashing lights that dot the horizon at night. Moreover, there is lingering concern that wind turbines threaten the well-being of birds and bats. Some public officials want to pursue regulating the business, and at least one high official has suggested the state should consider ending tax credits to allow the industry "to stand on its own two feet." Still, Texas has led the way in recent years in adding more wind power than any other state. Its installed capacity in 2013 was more than double that of the closest competing state, California. A steady growth in wind farms and transmission lines have allowed wind generation to more than triple since 2009, and wind power's share of total energy supplied has increased from less than 1 percent at the turn of the twenty-first century to about 10 percent today.

The Wind's Grand Larceny

As costly as the removal of precious topsoil by a raging wind can be to landowners, it is of secondary concern to the role that wind plays in stealing water from the surfaces of exposed bodies of water such as the state's reservoirs. This natural and unavoidable extraction of water results from the process of evaporation and is an important factor in reducing the quantity of water available for domestic supply and irrigation. What is more, the movement of dry air over the landscape removes valuable moisture from fields, dictating the extent of crop production, especially in areas where groundwater is not available for irrigation. In fact, the evaporation of water from the soil can have almost as much influence upon crop production as does rainfall.

Of course, the toll exacted by evaporation is an integration of many components of the weather—not just the rate of movement of the air. Rates of evaporation depend on temperature, precipitation, and moisture content of the air (relative humidity) as well as wind speed. Consequently, it is more difficult to quantify evaporation from land surfaces because the rate of water loss from soil depends on the availability of water in the soil as well as on other factors, such as soil type and exposure to sun and wind. Nonetheless, for decades the NWS and the State of Texas have invested in instrumentation to measure water loss from exposed pans of water placed at strategic points around the state. By applying appropriate numerical coefficients to the data to relate them to the actual loss of water from a large water surface (such as a reservoir), it is possible to derive estimates of the actual amount of water lost through evaporation on large water bodies in Texas. The total amount of water lost through

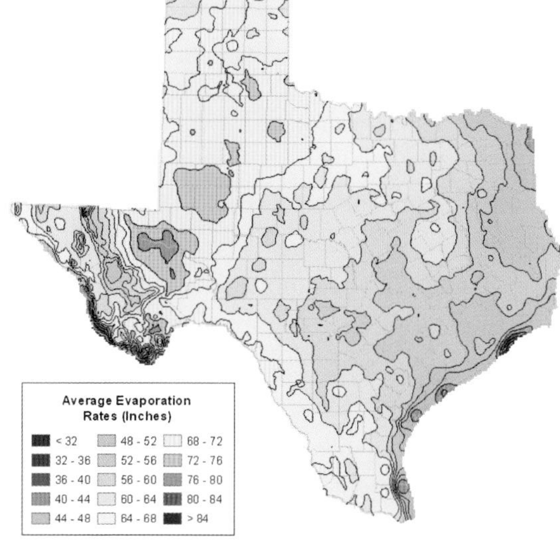

A

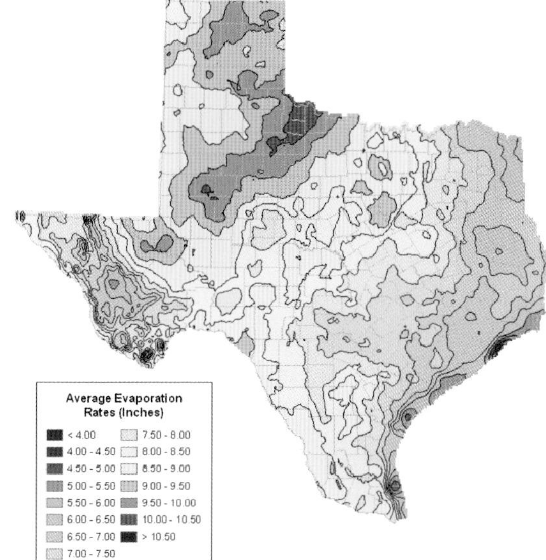

B

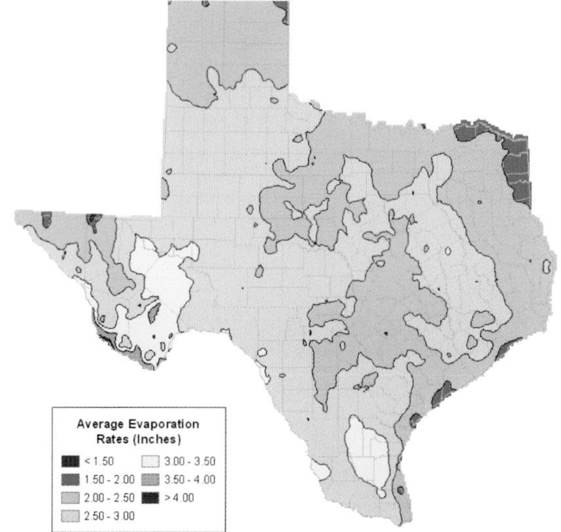

C

evaporation from a unit area of lake surface is commonly referred to as gross lake surface evaporation. The average annual rate of gross lake surface evaporation varies from less than 45 inches in the Sabine River valley in extreme eastern Texas to more than 80 inches in the Pecos River valley and in the Big Bend area of far West Texas (fig. 10.7a). One would expect such a wide range in gross evaporation rates, for the Trans Pecos area on average receives far more sunshine and experiences much lower relative humidities, higher daytime temperatures, and more vigorous winds than the wooded areas of East Texas (see appendix 18 for seasonal relative humidities around the state). Evaporation rates also vary greatly by season, with summer rates of 8 inches or more per month prevalent across most of the northwestern half of Texas (fig. 10.7b). By contrast, a typical winter month brings a loss of 3 inches or less in virtually all of the state (fig. 10.7c).

A more common, and meaningful, measure of the amount of water lost from water bodies resulting from evaporation is the net lake surface evaporation rate. It is referred to more often than gross lake surface evaporation because it reflects the contribution of rainfall to the maintenance of water in the reservoir. The net evaporation rate consists of the gross evaporation rate minus the amount of rainfall that fell over the reservoir watershed (excluding the portion lost as runoff). Because rainfall in the eastern extremity of Texas usually is ample (50 inches or more per year, or some 10 inches more than the average annual gross lake surface evaporation rate), the average annual net lake surface evaporation rate is 10 inches or less. By contrast, in the arid valleys and plateaus of the Big Bend, where yearly rainfall is

FIG. 10.7A, 10.7B & 10.7C Average monthly gross lake surface evaporation rates (a) on a year-round basis, (b) for the month of July, and (c) for January. Source: Texas Water Development Board

meager and gross evaporation rates are almost 100 inches per year, the average annual net rate of lake surface evaporation is 90 inches or more. In relatively wet years, evaporation rates characteristically are low, but in dry years, rates are high and the water supply is correspondingly low. These relationships are particularly meaningful to water engineers, who realize that in critical drought years evaporation losses not only contribute significantly to major water-supply problems but also influence decisions on reservoir design and operation.

The net evaporation rate is not evenly distributed throughout the year in Texas. In much of the state, maximum rates of water loss occur in August, and minimum rates are usually sustained in February. Of course, in years of subpar rainfall, net evaporation rates usually are higher in most months, but the monthly distribution of the evaporation tends to be more uniform than in wet years. The evaporation of water is a continuous process in both the desert climate of far West Texas and the humid subtropical climate of the extreme eastern sector of the state. While evaporation is taking place almost all the time, the net rates of evaporation demonstrate in some months that loss of water is partially or totally offset by appreciable rainfall.

An Unseemly Partner for Fire

The 2011 Bastrop fire attests to the volatility of wind when mixed with only a spark from something as natural as a lightning bolt or as careless as a smoker tossing a cigarette into a bar ditch. The trend toward larger and more destructive fires has accelerated in recent decades in Texas, in part resulting from a warming climate and a burgeoning population. Wildfires most often initiate as small blazes, but when fed by desiccating, blustery winds, they grow into gargantuan cauldrons that engulf thousands of acres of rangeland and have devastating effects on communities lying in their paths.

People who live in areas prone to wildfire can take measures to lessen the chance that their property is not consumed. Those vulnerable should cultivate a "defensible space" around their homes by making sure trees, shrubs, and grasses are well contained if not altogether removed. By eliminating or reducing potential fuel sources near the structure, you are working to impede the fire's ability to reach your home. Moreover, you are fostering a larger, workable area within which firefighters can function to contain the fire and save your home. In fact, firefighters typically make a quick assessment upon arriving at the site of a fire to determine if the property is "defendable." By nurturing a defensible space, you increase the likelihood that enough firefighting resources are applied to save your property.

Other steps to protect your property from fire include keeping your roof and gutters free of debris; ensuring chimney screens are intact and in good condition; maintaining functional fire extinguishers; clearing space around an outdoor water supply so that firefighters can get ready access; keeping lawn and farm equipment in good working order and less prone to produce sparks; and positioning a storage area containing firefighting gear like rakes, hoses, axes, and shovels so that it is readily accessible to anyone fighting the fire.

Marfa's Own Front

The desiccating effect of desert-like winds is felt most acutely in Texas's far western region, where maritime and continental air masses compete in the summer for territory almost on a daily basis.

A rising sun produces strong heating of the air near the surface in New Mexico, where vegetation is sparse, while at lower elevations in central Texas, an overcast that built during the night from moisture-laden air out of the Gulf keeps the air near the surface relatively cooler before midday. Then, by midday, that moist air drifts westward, pushing the "dry line" closer to El Paso and giving much of the Trans Pecos a sometimes vigorous east or southeasterly breeze along with increasing humidities (fig. 10.8a). This persists until nightfall, when the moist air retreats and is replaced once again by dry air from the higher elevations. Because the dry desert air is denser than the tropical air inland from the Texas coast, the air from New Mexico undercuts the moist, mild air, forcing it to rise and acting as a "dry line," known popularly in the region as the Marfa front. The front ushers in northerly breezes at night (fig. 10.8b), and by morning the temperature will have dipped delightfully into the 50s. This term, coined generations ago, derives from the community of Marfa, which often lies in the path of these competing air masses. For decades, weather analysts have monitored the phenomenon because Marfa's airport is the site of a remote weather station that measures and transmits hourly data that quantify the ebb and flow of these dissimilar air masses across the region.

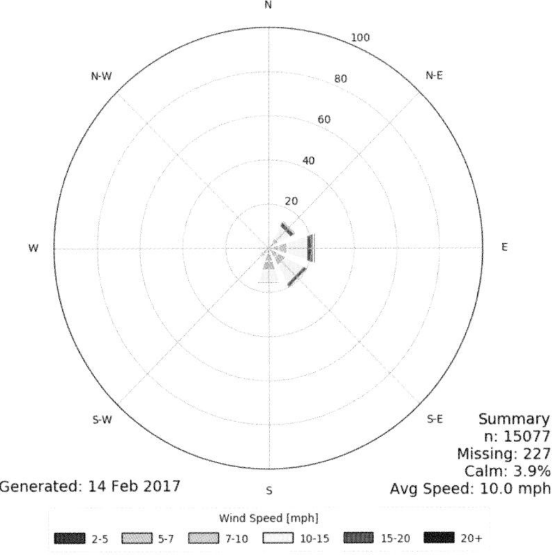

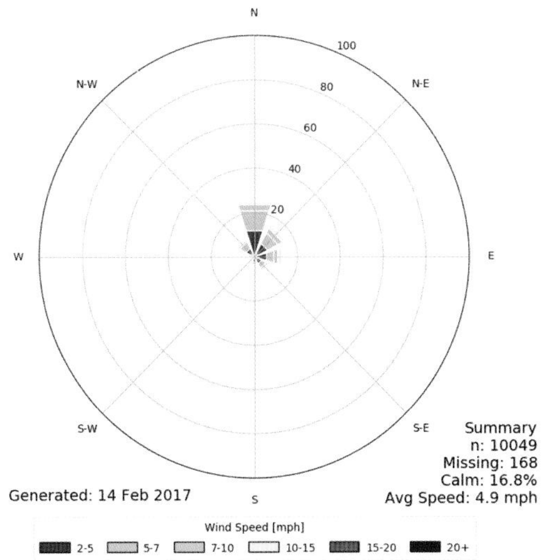

FIG. 10.8A & 10.8B Wind roses depicting average wind speed and direction at Marfa in a typical July (a) from noon until dusk and (b) from midnight to daybreak. Source: Iowa State University

The movement of the dry line can be equally pronounced farther north, up on the Texas High Plains above the Caprock, and resemble the surge of a cool front. Its passage brings a shift in wind direction, most often from southeasterly to westerly in a matter of minutes. In addition, with the influx of desert air from the west, the humidity plummets. On some days, especially in spring, a change in dew-point temperature of 40°–50°F (22°–28°C) can occur over a few dozen miles in the neighborhood of the Texas–New Mexico border—or from one end of the Pecos River valley to the other. On the windward side of the dry line, the moisture-deficient air can inflame temperatures to eye-catching levels beyond 100°F (38°C). Closer to the Mexican desert, the cascading dry air, plunging from a higher elevation to a lower one, overheats and inflates afternoon readings as high as 110°F (43°C) in isolated hamlets like Presidio and Lajitas upstream from Big Bend National Park. This exaggerated mini-heat wave in some years occurs as early as late winter.

The dry line, or Marfa front, is of crucial importance to far West Texas because of its role in fomenting thunderstorms. The customary cooling down that occurs after midafternoon fosters a dry wind that often knifes underneath less dense and more moist air to trigger towering thunderheads that can be seen for great distances. These immense heat towers supply a sizable fraction of the total yearly rainfall in the Trans Pecos and High Plains. It is common for a locale that happens to lie in the path of one of these gargantuan thunderstorms to collect an inch or more of rain in one hour or less on a late afternoon or early evening in summer.

The Breeze from the Sea

Given its proximity to the Gulf of Mexico, the Texas coastal plain is notorious for its stifling and insufferably sultry summer days. But the same body of water, the Gulf, that elevates humidities over land also bestows refreshment to the city dweller and the shoreline visitor in the form of an invigorating sea breeze. Of all the winds that blow across Texas, the sea breeze is arguably the most predictable—and the most desirable.

The sea breeze and its nocturnal opposite, the land breeze, are also consistent, each occurring with regularity along the Texas coast. Both types of breezes are prevalent in the coastal plain on most days from late spring to midautumn and are set in motion by differences in the temperature of the air between land and sea. Land areas are heated much more quickly by a rising sun than are adjacent bodies of water. As a result, this rapid warming of the ground by radiation heats the air above it, which then rises and is replaced by cooler, heavier air flowing in from the sea. This landward influx of not-so-warm air is the sea breeze.

The Texas summer is when the sea breeze is the strongest, since the intense heat of a sun almost directly overhead causes the air above the land to rise more rapidly than at any other time. The more intense the heat, the faster air currents rise, and the greater the pressure difference grows between land and sea. Since the atmosphere continually is striving to equalize the disparity in pressure from one locale to another (e.g., land to sea), the more the land air is heated, the lighter it becomes and the greater the contrast between air pressure over land versus that over water. The cooler and, hence, heavier air over the sea surges toward the land to restore the equilibrium, in the same way that water always flows from a higher point to a lower one. On most days, the sea breeze attains its maximum speed at midafternoon, or the time of highest land-surface temperature. In Texas the sea breeze customarily blows at speeds of 8–15 mph and reaches distances of 10 to 15 miles (16–24 kilometers) inland. Its ceiling usually is no more than 600–1,000 feet above the land surface. Occasionally, however, the breeze may be of greater depth and may extend up to 50 miles (80 kilometers) inland during the peak heating period. A wind rose for Corpus Christi for the mornings in August depicts the prevalence of a south wind, with wind speed gentle for the most part (fig. 10.9a). Once the sea breeze takes over, however, from early afternoon until dusk, more vigorous southeasterly winds dominate (fig. 10.9b). This means relief to many coastal cities, where the air tends to stagnate and become hot and stifling. It is no overstatement to assert that when the sea breeze surges into a coastal hamlet or inland metropolis, in a matter of a few minutes its soothing effect can adjust a person's attitude in remarkable ways.

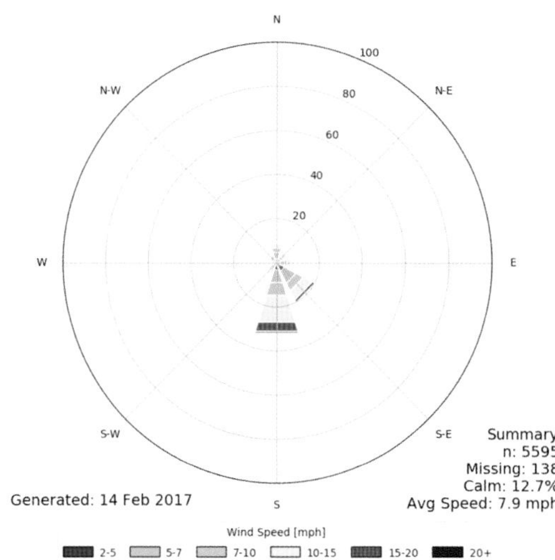

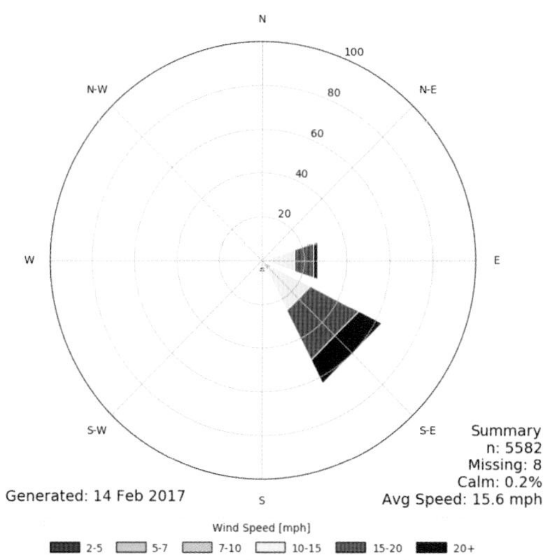

FIG. 10.9A & 10.9B Wind roses depicting average wind speed and direction at Corpus Christi in a typical August (a) from daybreak to noon and (b) from midafternoon to nightfall. Source: Iowa State University

With striking regularity on most summer days, another feature of an advancing sea breeze is the upcropping of many cumulus, or "fair weather," clouds inland of the coastline. These small convective clouds first sprout late in the morning near the shoreline and then migrate inland, where they grow to more appreciable heights. By noontime or early in the afternoon, most of the sky above the whole coastal plain of Texas is bespeckled by these growing cumuli. Whereas the first few batches of puffy white cumuli seen along the coast around midmorning result from rising land-air currents, later in the day the clouds grow taller and more numerous as some of the moisture-laden air from the Gulf surges inland and is also heated by the hot land surface. Unless the upper atmosphere is nearly void of moisture, quite a few of these sea-breeze-induced convective clouds may blossom into full-fledged thunderstorms capable of generating noteworthy rains onto the coastal plain.

The Straight-Line Downburst

The potent and massive gust of wind that often emanates from the base of a thunderstorm not only plunges the air temperature at the surface by as much as 20°–30°F in a matter of minutes—it can be grossly destructive as well, ripping trees out of the ground and shingles from roof tops and leaving some residents to deduce that they were hit by a tornado. The damage, though, is caused by a near hurricane-force wind (50–70 mph) that is linear, rather than circular, yielding a pattern of destruction in which vegetation and property are strewn in the same direction. One notable variety of a downburst wind is known as a *derecho*, whose derivative word in Spanish means "straight." This phenomenon is, by definition, a broad swath of damaging wind whose gusts can exceed 100 mph, and it has been known to cut a path of destruction for hundreds of square miles.

Because they are prevalent in the lowest 5,000-foot layer of the atmosphere, downbursts can wreak havoc on aircraft, abruptly converting a 35-mph headwind into a tailwind of equal potency in a matter of seconds. Aircraft are most vulnerable to this threat during takeoffs and landings, and airport runways can be momentarily closed when virga, a rain shaft out of the base of a thunderstorm, is spotted by air-traffic controllers. The state's major airports are now equipped with sophisticated sensing devices that alert pilots of a potential downburst as much as a minute before it threatens. Of the major aircraft mishaps attributable to downbursts, the most tragic one was the crash of a Delta 747 airliner at Dallas–Fort Worth International Airport on August 2, 1985. The commercial jet was thrust downward into the ground on its final approach, killing all 133 passengers and crew members onboard.

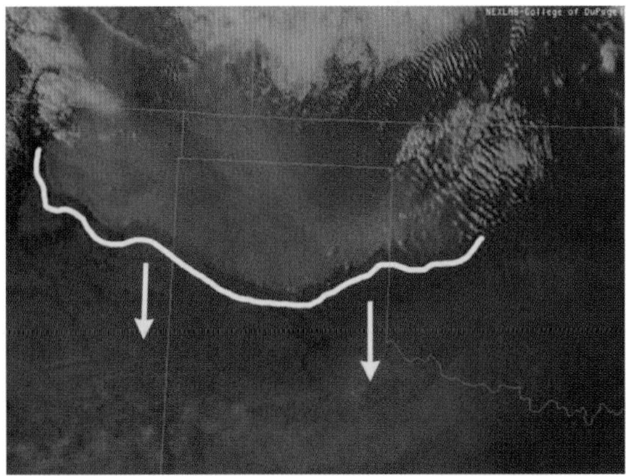

FIG. 10.10 The haboob, a vast and dense wall of dirt sometimes visible from space, stretched 350 miles across as it swept over the Panhandle on March 18, 2014. Source: National Oceanic and Atmospheric Administration

Another wind-related phenomenon that can spell trouble for aviation and other forms of transportation is the visually dramatic and violently whirling wall of dust known as a haboob (fig. 10.10). It stems from a strong outflow boundary emanating from a cluster of potent thunderstorms, most often occurring in semi-arid West Texas. While its winds are not particularly strong (less than 40–50 mph), the haboob can stir up massive quantities of topsoil that blind motorists and damage crops. By plunging visibilities to near zero, the haboob that hit the southern High Plains on June 22, 2006, caused 27 multivehicle accidents on a stretch of highway near Brownfield, killing a motorist who rammed his auto into a jackknifed tractor-trailer rig and injuring 15 other motorists in a series of chain collisions. It also destroyed some 10,000 acres of cotton, as wind-driven dust "burned" the young plants already stressed by drought.

The haboob also can pose a hazard to aircraft. A haboob borne out of a pool of cold air outflowing from a severe thunderstorm complex on June 18, 2009, near Lubbock in Floyd County roiled soil into the air over 6,500 feet (2 kilometers) above ground level, well above where a small single-engine aircraft was known to be operating before it plunged into a field near Floydada, killing a prominent business owner from the region and a passenger. Nearly $6 million in agricultural and property losses were attributed to the haboob, which was sustained for over two hours.

A Texas-Size Dustup

Despite improved methods of land cultivation now practiced in semi-arid West Texas, blowing dust remains a predictable menace in much of Texas, most especially in the late winter and spring when potent storms surge out of the Rockies and rake the usually bone-dry landscape along the Texas–New Mexico border with hurricane-like winds. Blowing dust is a particular menace in those spring seasons preceded by bone-dry autumns and winters. Still, dust storms now are less frequent and not quite so abrasive as during the scourges that earned the decade of the 1930s the moniker of the Dust Bowl era—and again afflicted Texans during the epic drought of the 1950s.

Dust, from the meteorologist's perspective, consists of solid materials suspended in the atmosphere in the form of small irregular particles, most of which are microscopic in size. Dust cannot be a stable component of the atmosphere because it must eventually fall back to Earth's surface when winds and turbulence become too weak to bear it aloft. While some dust found in the Texas atmosphere has as its source plant pollen and bacteria, salt spray from the Gulf of Mexico, and smoke and ashes from forest fires and industrial combustion processes, much of the material in a Texas dust storm consists of solid soil particles removed by winds raking the surface of Earth. For such a dislocation to occur, a period of drought over what is normally arable land is needed to loosen the material in the outermost layer of Earth's surface. Most often a dust storm arrives suddenly in the form of an advancing dust wall that may be many miles long and thousands of feet high.

A dust storm is defined as an episode of blowing dust that reduces visibility to between 5/8 and 5/16 of a mile; if the visibility plunges to or below 5/16 of a mile, the event is designated as a severe dust storm. By this definition, the Texas South Plains area is most often the source region for blowing dust that may affect the state, sometimes for hundreds of miles downwind. In a typical winter–spring, Lubbock experiences three times as many days as either Amarillo or Midland with reduced visibilities due to dust. In the shadow of a bad drought, the number of dusty days on the South Plains can be as high as 15–20 per season, while following a wet autumn the number can be as few as 3–5. Dust storms also are referred to as dusters and black blizzards. Dust storms in Texas are differentiated from "sandstorms" in several ways: Blowing sand particles are confined mostly to the lowest 10 feet of the atmosphere, rarely rising to much above 50 feet; dust storms invariably grow much, much larger. Sandstorms are confined to select areas of Texas where loose sand, often in sand dunes and without much admixture of dust, is prevalent. Sandstorms usually are restricted to parts of the Trans Pecos and select portions of the High and Low Rolling Plains. They are also known as haboobs and "desert winds."

Those who know best the uneasy coexistence with nettlesome dust are the inhabitants of the Llano Estacado. The flat plains from the Permian Basin to the Panhandle are the source for much of the dust that beleaguers Texans. One consolation to these hardy plains people is that dust usually is not a year-round misery. The ingredients for a typical blowout of dust usually mesh together early in the year, or at the end of the customary dry season in West

Texas and just when the racing winds that hint of spring become an almost everyday feature. The strong westerly winds that propel the dust rip across the High and Low Rolling Plains once a strong low-pressure center forms at the surface on the lee side of the Rockies. These very blustery winds, with gusts of 30–50 mph, strafe the surface, lifting tons of topsoil into the lower atmosphere as the humidity plunges to single digits. The needle on barometers approaches the 29-inch mark, and the temperature escalates for hours as a prelude to the invasion of colder Rocky Mountain air that signals the eventual end of the dust episode. As evening approaches, some dust begins to settle out and visibilities begin to improve—while much of the displaced topsoil surges east to obscure skies as far away as Dallas and San Antonio.

The Worst of the Worst

The enormous and inveterate spells of choking dust that highlighted the Dust Bowl era of the mid-1930s were known as "black snow." On many occasions during the severe drought that came in the years of the Great Depression, street lamps in many West Texas locales began glowing in the middle of the day, appearing as a faint green glow in the distance. Tumbling tumbleweeds by the dozens rolled for great distances as hollow, bounding boulders, while cattle in fields died of asphyxiation. Motorists pulled to the side of highways with their headlights on, waiting restlessly for the tirade to end. Housekeepers struggled to keep out the dust by shoving cloth of various sizes around the edges of windows and doors.

Much of the same still happens when nature goes on a rampage. Perhaps the most injurious dust storm in recent years came to West Texas in February 1977. A very intense surface low-pressure center that moved out of the Colorado Rockies early on February 22 sent extremely strong winds into the northwestern quarter of Texas, where tons of soil were whirled into the atmosphere, so beclouding the air at Lubbock that visibilities were restricted to 1 mile or less for 34 consecutive hours. Winds blasted through Guadalupe Pass at speeds clocked as high as 114 mph, blowing several tractor-trailer rigs off the highway. Winds of near-hurricane force in El Paso caused extensive damage to roofs of homes and businesses, while signs and utility poles were felled and 20 persons were injured; property damage amounted to $650,000. Just two weeks later, the awesome dust storm of March 11, 1977, struck the Panhandle, destroying one-fourth of the total winter wheat crop. Winds pounding the northern High Plains at speeds as high as 75–80 mph raked up enough dust to hold visibilities at Amarillo to a ½ mile for 10 hours. The very intense duster blasted to death a wheat crop valued in excess of $6 million. Still reeling from the destruction wrought by the late-February dust storm, El Paso at the same time sustained more sizable property damage ($250,000) from winds measured as high as 84 mph.

Not surprisingly, the worst episodes of blowing dust tend to occur during years when the lack of rainfall in the autumn and winter has fed a worsening drought. A couple of prodigious dust storms struck the western half of the state in the mid-1950s near the end of the twentieth century's worst drought in Texas. More than 250,000 acres of cropland suffered moderate to severe wind erosion from a highly perilous storm that struck the High Plains with winds of hurricane force on March 2–3, 1956. Dust so clogged the air in Odessa that street lights came on at midafternoon, and in

Lubbock visibilities were held to half a city block for hours. The blinding dust caused numerous traffic accidents, some of which led to the deaths of three motorists. Dust residue quickly spread over almost all the remainder of Texas. Later that same year in November—or just four months before that devastating mid-1950s drought was abruptly terminated—so much dust was blown across the southern High and Low Rolling Plains that unpicked cotton was buried in the dust. According to US Weather Bureau reports, homes and other buildings at Matador in Motley County were "filled with dirt." Winds with speeds of 70–75 mph yanked trees out of the ground and ripped shingles from the roofs of houses in the area.

Once or twice during the late winter or spring, blowing dust will migrate into nearly every corner of Texas. Very few dust episodes were as far reaching as the mammoth dust storm of January 25–26, 1965, which limited visibilities to 1–2 miles in such disparate locations as El Paso, San Angelo, Dallas, San Antonio, and Houston. Fourteen months later a dust storm emanating from West Texas had similar effect, substantially reducing visibilities from Austin to Brownsville and Port Arthur. Also ranked near the top was the colossal dust storm of March 14–15, 1971; after moving out of northWest Texas, it sent visibilities plunging to less than 1 mile at Dallas and just barely more than that as far south as Brownsville.

A few dust storms are remembered for either tragic, or bizarre, outcomes. Dust that billowed to more than 15,000 feet (4.5 kilometers) and held visibilities to zero was driven by winds gauged in excess of 100 mph at Guadalupe Pass in far West Texas in February 1960; those winds accounted for the death of a small child, who was blown under a bus and killed. Some years later, on January 25, 1965, aircraft pilots reported dust as high as 31,000 feet (9 kilometers) from the Texas–New Mexico border to as far east as Abilene, and motorists traveling on the open highway at maximum legal speeds saw tumbleweeds overtaking them. Dust was whipped along by winds that toppled three 160-foot light towers at Jones Stadium in Lubbock in January 1967; damage to the towers, which were designed to withstand winds of 100 mph, amounted to $100,000. On the same day, residents in the Panhandle were besieged by a combination of dust and snow being driven along by winds of near-hurricane force. Visibilities were reduced by blowing dust at Shamrock in Wheeler County to the extent that a car pileup involving as many as a score of automobiles resulted in 32 injured motorists.

Powerful dust storms affecting thousands of square miles have been known to happen in winter, often in conjunction with a major snowstorm. A massive outburst of dust hit the southern High Plains on February 24, 2007, blowing out windows and ripping up utility poles and roofs from houses in over two dozen counties. Snow flurries mixed with the dust to shorten visibilities at times to only a few feet.

The quantity of soil that can be displaced often is astounding. One dust storm that lasted half a day left drifts of topsoil as high as 10 feet in Lamb County near Littlefield on March 17, 1977. A weather observer at Reese Air Force Base near Lubbock found a layer of dust 3.5 inches thick in his rain gauge after a dust storm raged across the southern High Plains in January 1965. A study made of a series of ten dust storms that hit Lubbock during the severe drought of the mid-1930s revealed that an average of 122 tons of sediment was carried through that High Plains city each hour during those storms.

An Invasive and Pervasive Event

Annoying dust storms are as common to the southern High Plains as thunderheads, mesquite, and rattlesnakes. With much of the terrain of this sector of Texas marked by quarter-section subdivisions with the familiar inscribed circles denoting irrigated cropland, and given that brisk winds blow almost incessantly during spring, numerous dust storms are inevitable. Circumstances are aggravated all the more early in the year before irrigation water is applied and particularly when the preceding winter has been unusually dry. In these instances the fertile cropland is highly susceptible to wind erosion. Consequently, most spring seasons bring as few as a half-dozen and sometimes as many as a score of notable dust storms. The phenomena are especially prevalent in a 20-county area centered at Lubbock. Skies beclouded by dust are most frequent in March, with occurrences later in spring not uncommon. Most spells of dust prevail for only six hours or less, when visibilities are restricted to ½ mile or less. Summers, by contrast, are rather free of the large-scale, stifling dust storms common in spring. Much of the dust seen in summer in the southern High Plains is highly localized and the result of gusts of cold air plummeting down out of thunderstorms.

Blowing dust farther north in the Panhandle is most often not as long lasting or nettlesome as those dust events that visit the southern High Plains. Nevertheless, it is rare when a year does not provide at least a few dust storms that reduce visibilities to 3 miles (5 kilometers) or less in this northernmost sector of Texas. More than half of all dust storms in the Panhandle occur during March and April, and dusters are not uncommon in the late winter or autumn. While the event is rare, dust storms in this region have been known to coincide with snowstorms, as happened during the mammoth dust storm of March 11–12, 1977. The combination of blowing dust and blowing snow driven by high winds stifled visibilities to as little as ½ mile during that time.

In some years, the northern Trans Pecos rates as the dustiest strip anywhere in Texas. More than half of all dust storms come with the very brisk winds of spring, which is not only the most blustery time of the year but also the conclusion of the lengthy dry season. Farther east, it is a rare year that fails to furnish at least one or two dust storms in the Low Rolling Plains and Edwards Plateau. Nearly always the dust is not thick enough to drop and maintain visibilities as little as 1–2 miles for any appreciable length of time. Over half of all dust storms persist in any one locale no longer than six hours. The vigorous dusters that materialize over the Trans Pecos and High Plains sometimes remain intact as far east as the state's Blackland Belt. If a dust storm occurs early in the year, it is an even bet that a second or third will follow before spring has ended. Dust in the air sufficient to restrict visibilities substantially in autumn or early winter is seen only once every three to four years.

The southern quarter of Texas, while far removed from the breeding grounds of most dust storms, is touched every few years by a modest-size dust storm or sandstorm. Usually the dust is not so thick as to lessen visibilities to 1–2 miles or less, and dust most often limits visibilities for periods no longer than six to nine hours. With the lush cover of native grasslands interspersed with numerous thickets of piney woods and post oaks, East Texas and the Upper Coast regions are the least likely of all sectors of Texas to suffer from a dust storm or a sandstorm. It is an extreme rarity for dust to congest the atmosphere there such that visibilities dip to one or a few miles. Severely restricted visibilities due to dust are observed only once every three to five years, on average.

Despite the high number of dust storms in a typical spring in West Texas, the good news is the loss of valuable topsoil has been substantially reduced. Like their counterparts in other Great Plains states, West Texas farmers have embraced modern soil conservation measures to a significant degree—to the extent that the loss of topsoil, according to the Natural Resource Conservation Service, has been effectively cut in half in the last 40 years.

Dust Bedevilment on a Smaller Scale

West Texans can count on one hand the number of nasty dust storms they must endure in a typical year—but another manifestation of dust or sand is far more frequent, though thankfully its effect is brief and exceedingly localized. On many warm afternoons, a motorist navigating the myriad of county roads and highways that traverse West Texas need not look far, or for very long, to see a dust devil, a whirling column of air resembling a miniature tornado. Dust devils are particularly prominent on days with a blazing sun and hot, gusty winds. Unlike tornadoes, dust devils develop on Earth's surface and seldom, if ever, attain the violence of funnels that drop from clouds. Sometimes these rapidly spinning columns of dust mingled with small twigs, leaves, and other lightweight debris attain heights of several hundred feet. Most of them occur over dusty roads or plowed fields, extend only a few feet in diameter and less than 50 feet in height, and persist for no more than a few minutes. A flat, hot surface, such as a hardened, dusty road or a barren stretch of desert, and a burst of wind are the ingredients necessary for a dust devil. Air next to the bare, dusty surface is heated rapidly by the intense rays of the sun and, as this warmed air expands and rises, cooler air nearby swarms in to replace the rising hot air. As little as a gentle breeze, and more often a gust of wind, provides this rising air column with a twist, such that a spiraling eddy of air—a dust devil—is formed in only a matter of seconds.

The vast majority of dust devils go undetected, so a typical number of dust devils on a characteristically hot, windy summer day is not known. Likely, tens—if not hundreds—of the small spinning dust demons form every summer afternoon. What is more, dust devils may be seen on hot, breezy days in any region of the state, although, naturally, the frequency lessens greatly in heavily wooded areas of eastern Texas. Mercifully, the vast majority of dust devils in Texas advance at such slow speeds that people rarely are injured, and damage to property, if sustained at all, usually is insignificant. Being struck by a dust devil usually means no more severe damage to a person than an eye, or ear, full of dust and small debris. There are a few notable exceptions to this rule, however, for a few dust devils may grow large enough and persist long enough to cause meaningful damage to property unfortunately positioned in the devil's erratic path. For example, a dust devil slammed into a prison facility near Amarillo on April 3, 2008, blowing out windows in the facility as well as in autos parked in a lot nearby. On a hot, sultry afternoon in the middle of the summer heat wave of 1980, after a dust devil ripped off the roof of a ranch barn and downed power lines near Granite Mountain in Burnet County, the owner of the barn described the noise made by the strong whirlwind as similar to that made by a jet aircraft.

11. Harvesting the Skies

Among our most precious resources are the natural environment and the people who live and work in it. It is the right of human inhabitants of Earth to use those resources for the benefit of all, and it is our obligation to protect those resources for the benefit of future generations. A critically important element of our natural environment is the existence of freshwater, not only in surface and underground repositories such as lakes and aquifers but also aboveground in our troposphere. Much of that water in the air is often invisible, and inaccessible, but not infrequently it shows itself in the form of towering convective clouds, some of which blossom large enough to grow a rain shaft. For generations, our ancestors plumbed the depths of groundwater, using wells and pipelines, to ensure the growing need for freshwater was met. Now that groundwater in Texas is being depleted and not replenished, at alarming rates in some regions, those responsible for procuring enough water supplies have had to look elsewhere for the additional water sources needed to sustain a growing populace in the decades ahead. Some have lifted their gaze heavenward—observing clouds now known to need help in engendering a load of rain (fig. 11.1).

FIG. 11.1 Cloud seeding has potential to provide some relief during drought—whose end would be welcomed by worshippers in a church, reminded weekly by this banner to use every avenue available. Source: George W. Bomar

Finding ways to augment our water resources has become an imperative. A United Nations study projects that one-third of the world's population will live under severe water stress by the middle of the twenty-first century. Even in Texas, securing additional sources of freshwater is essential if the state is to sustain a level of growth similar to what it has experienced in recent decades. That is why Texas has a storied history of using cloud seeding to mitigate the adverse effects of periodic, severe droughts. During the epic drought of the 1950s, a rash of "rainmaking" initiatives sprouted, many of them of dubious quality and promoted by get-rich-quick charlatans who promised satiating deluges and seldom delivered anything remotely resembling them. Some initiatives, however, had scientific authenticity to them but failed to reveal much about cloud seeding's potential—other than the reality that making rain in a drought is a formidable challenge, given that clouds often do not proliferate when drought is dominant. Efforts, however legitimate, to dent the Great Plains drought during the 1950s gave rise to the adoption of laws in states to protect the citizenry from being taken for a ride by opportunistic charlatans. Texas was one of those states, enacting a law in 1967 requiring anyone attempting to modify the weather to be scrutinized by both government and the public.

Giving Nature a Nudge

Rainwater never materializes within any cloud formation without two available ingredients: a sufficient supply of molecules of water, known as vapor or droplets (moisture); and a focal point, a speck of something known as a condensation nucleus. In every season, especially in the warmer half of the year, as puffy, billowy clouds known as cumuli form in the sky, cloud vapor congregates on these specks, known as nature's "seeds," to make these clouds visible. The seeds on which this moisture aggregates can be as disparate as salt, sand, and smoke particles—even specks of ice. Not all cumuli become rain producers, however (fig. 11.2). Many live barely half an hour, not nearly enough time for these tiny cloud droplets to collide with neighbors to form increasingly larger water droplets that eventually get big and heavy enough to begin falling as part of a rain shaft. In some cases, nature solves the problem by using a supply of ice crystals. Since the vapor pressure gradient over ice is less than that over water, tiny water droplets more easily gravitate toward and merge with an ice crystal than with neighboring droplets. It is the ice crystal, when "fed" with many cloud droplets, that quickly grows into a sizeable raindrop. Cloud droplets lifted high in the sky, though in air colder than 32°F, do not freeze but remain in liquid form (supercooled), and these are particularly susceptible to joining an ice crystal, enabling it to grow quickly, and efficiently, into a raindrop.

The problem, however, is not enough growing cumuli have enough of these natural ice crystals to rapidly engender a load of rainwater. The key to rainfall production, then, is to furnish a moisture-rich cloud with lots more ice with which the cloud droplets can be captured quickly and transformed into raindrops. At one time in the distant past, cloud "seeding" was done with ice, some of it in the form of dry ice. But the effort of unloading vast quantities of ice into the air is, at best, logistically cumbersome. After World War II, scientists working in a lab in upstate New York discovered that crystals of silver iodide (AgI), when sprinkled into a cold chamber containing moisture-rich air, spawned a tangible, visible cloud that ultimately precipitated some of its moisture. Thus, the science of cloud seeding was born.

It would not be long before researchers would consolidate these crystals of silver iodide into pyrotechnics, or flares, that could be carried

FIG. 11.2 The towering cumulus cloud that blossoms on a warm spring, or summer, day is the target of cloud-seeding efforts to extract more rainwater. Source: Texas Department of Transportation

onboard aircraft and activated by pilots as the aircraft flew within the updrafts of growing cumulus clouds. Key to successful seeding is the proper placement of these artificial seeds so that the strong updraft within a growing thundercloud can carry them into the vast field of supercooled water often found above the freezing level within the cloud. An aircraft, even a small, single-engine variety, is capable of finding and staying mainly within these updrafts for appreciable periods of time, thereby allowing the burning flares to disseminate the ice crystals effectively (fig. 11.3). The flares, by the dozens, usually reside on specially designed racks that hang behind the wings of a seeding aircraft—and they can be configured to ignite when prompted by a pilot operating the aircraft (fig. 11.4). A typical flare contains 40 to 80 grams of silver iodide, and each gram of silver oxide provides 1 trillion to 100 trillion ice crystals. More recently, an ejectable flare was devised to allow seeding to occur from above a cloud top: a pilot of a multi-engine aircraft, with a rack of ejectable flares mounted on the underside of the fuselage, can fly over 20,000 feet (6 kilometers) and drop the flares into the growing cumulus before its top has reached flying altitude, thereby affording the pilot greater, and more rapid, access to an entire field of prospective rain-producing thunderheads in a reasonable amount of time (fig. 11.5).

Sowing Seeds of Success

Not long after the Texas Weather Modification Act in 1967 became law—and state government began regulating the use of weather modification through a process of licenses and permits—state officials at the Texas Water Development Board obtained federal funds to conduct cloud-seeding experiments in a part of West Texas's Permian Basin. The region encompassing Big Spring was chosen because the Colorado River Municipal Water District, led by the visionary O. H. Ivie, had begun seeding clouds by means of aircraft to induce convective towers (precursors of thunderstorms) to shed more rainwater over the watersheds of the district's two reservoirs, Lake J. B. Thomas and E. V. Spence Reservoir. A firm believer that seeding worked to invigorate these budding thunderclouds, Mr. Ivie allowed researchers to perform a series of randomized experiments, in which some promising clouds were treated with seeds while others were left unseeded. The experiment was randomized

FIG. 11.3 A twin-engine aircraft carries cloud-seeding materials in the form of pyrotechnics (flares) mounted on both wings. Source: George W. Bomar

FIG. 11.4 These burn-in-place flares are ignited by the pilot when the aircraft is beneath a growing thunderstorm that is deemed a candidate for successful rain enhancement. Source: George W. Bomar

FIG. 11.5 Occasionally the need to seed many growing cumulus clouds quickly is addressed by deploying an aircraft above the cloud tops, which are seeded by burning flares ejected by the pilot from beneath the belly of the aircraft. Source: George W. Bomar

based on the type of envelope drawn out of a box at random each time a researcher, using weather radar and working closely with a pilot, recognized a candidate. For a number of years, Mr. Ivie sacrificed his program to allow the randomization of seeding operations to proceed to fruition. On numerous occasions, clouds needing a nudge from seeding were left to their own devices, so that an adequate number of "control" cases could be accumulated to allow a meaningful—and scientifically significant—analysis of target-versus-control events to be done.

Mr. Ivie's beneficent gesture paid off. Over several seasons, scores of cases of seeded clouds were contrasted with highly similar cloud occurrences that were left alone, and the results argued for further exploration—and implementation of a systematic approach to treating all qualified storm clouds to give them a needed nudge. Under the capable tutelage of Dr. William L. Woodley, who had overseen research in Florida in the 1960s on the seeding of hurricane eye walls to diminish their intensities prior to landfall, the scientific team produced quantifiable measures of the differences seeding made in growing thunderstorms: seeded clouds tended to live as much as 40 percent longer than their untreated counterparts, and the extent of land area wetted by these storms was as much as 35 percent greater than that wetted by similar clouds nearby whose only seeds were supplied by Mother Nature.

For all the investment various government, and private, interests have put into cloud seeding in Texas, have the results of intentional modification been worth the effort? It is by no means a bottom-line question with an easy answer. That is because evaluating cloud seeding involves separating the effect of seeding (more rainfall) from the highly variable, natural occurrence of rain. Though daunting, the challenge of making sense of human intervention can be tackled by means of an array of analytical tools unavailable a generation ago when seeding first began to be performed in Texas. Each method of assessment has its own strengths and weaknesses, and each is only as good as the type, quality, and quantity of data available.

EVIDENCE OF EFFICACY

Among the direct evidence that there is efficacy to cloud seeding is the abundance of rain-gauge data for areas within which seeding has been practiced systematically over many years as well as areas adjacent to the targets. While few question the veracity of rainfall data obtained from standardized and properly exposed gauges, the ability of the data to suggest success is limited by the number of gauges involved in the data-collection effort. This limitation is especially acute in Texas, where almost all cloud seeding has focused on treating scattered and relatively small convective towers, whose rain shafts often miss gauges that are situated several miles apart over many tens, if not hundreds, of square miles. Even saturating a multicounty target with hundreds of reliable gauges may not be adequate to catch rainfall produced from every cloud tower, seeded or left untreated for various reasons.

In recent years, that deficiency in ground-based rain-gauge networks has been addressed by relying on estimated rainfall from sophisticated, high-resolution radar data yielded by the National Weather Service's Doppler network. While the accuracy of rainfall estimates has improved dramatically in the past two decades, even radar-derived measures of rainfall have their shortcomings. The sensitivity of Doppler radars diminishes with increasing distance from the radar site, resulting in degradations in the data with range. While not a formidable problem for quantifying rainfall in Texas, the radar beam can give misleading results because uneven terrain can disrupt it, yielding inaccurate estimates. Seeding projects in Texas have been analyzed using a combination of ground-based rain gauges and Doppler radar output.

In projects that seed to suppress hail as well as increase rain, hail pads are a necessary addition to the evaluation arsenal. Yet, because hail is a product of scattered, heavy convective complexes whose occurrence is usually spotty and localized, even a dense network of pads will miss a significant number of hail episodes. For example, a network covering a 30-by-30-mile area (the typical size of a West Texas county) with a pad every square mile requires 900 hail pads. Since each pad has to be checked manually by a trained observer after every storm event, the very high-labor-intensive effort can be unaffordably expensive to program sponsors.

Nonetheless, it was rain-gauge data showing average increases in growing-season rainfall in the watersheds of Thomas and Spence reservoirs of 20–30 percent that spurred the Colorado River Municipal Water District to maintain its cloud-seeding program for more than three decades. Other ground-truth rain-gauge data gathered on the Edwards Plateau during a five-year rain-enhancement initiative by the City of San Angelo showed increases in rainfall from midspring to midautumn averaged 25 to 42 percent above the long-term average for the region.

Where dense rain-gauge networks are impractical (as in sparsely populated areas where roadways are few and far between, thus making gauges hardly accessible), weather modification programs sometimes rely on crop and property insurance statistics. A history of drought is documented in advance, prior to the onset of any seeding, with crop output quantified for both seeding targets and adjacent areas where seeding is off-limits. Results can be quite persuasive, particularly when target and nearby control areas compare favorably before the seeding effort starts and then show remarkable dissimilarities during years of seeding. Crop-yield and insurance statistics also are relied on when assessing the effectiveness of hail suppression operations. Measurements of stream flow and runoff, both within and outside seeding targets, also may yield results that suggest a project's efficacy.

COSTS AND BENEFITS

No matter the approach used to quantify the effect of seeding, in the end a seeding initiative, to have lasting support, has to produce benefits that surpass the cost to conduct it. In areas of the American West, where cloud seeding has been ongoing in mountainous terrain to produce additional snow cover for decades, various studies show that increases in the water equivalent of snow have been as much as 20 percent over an entire winter storm season. Such increases translate into benefit-to-cost ratios as high as 60 to 1—meaning every dollar invested to achieve the seeding has led to a gain of $60—with increased water production costing as little as $1 per acre-foot. This is a very significant development when one considers that an acre-foot of water can cost consumers 50 to 100 times that amount. One project sponsor, the Panhandle Groundwater Conservation District, calculated that the cost of additional rain resulting from its cloud-seeding effort averaged less than $10 an acre-foot. Results like these have been the impetus for groundwater districts in many parts of Texas to continue for nearly two decades to seed convective towers, ever since state funding support first began during the drought-ravaged 1990s. These districts, and others involved in water-development strategies at the state and local levels, see even greater potential for what is still a relatively young science.

In Texas, where cloud seeding has been applied almost exclusively over the past two decades to yield increases in rainfall from summer thunderstorms, results have been just as impressive as those of the wintertime snowpack projects from California to Colorado. Since 2004, when access to newly implemented Doppler weather radar by the National Weather Service became available to weather modification projects in Texas, an independent annual assessment of each rain-enhancement effort by water conservation districts has supplied quantitative measures of success. The amount of rainwater believed to have been produced from seeding missions has varied from year to year because of the availability, or lack, of suitable clouds, but the increases have been consistently substantial. For the 11-year period ending in 2014, seeded convective towers, on average, lived 57 percent longer (than unseeded towers nearby), wetted 29 percent more ground area, and prompted a "precipitation mass" that was 88 percent greater. That translates into 167,700 acre-feet of rainwater per season.

The ultimate way to demonstrate and quantify the effect of seeding is through a procedure known as randomization. Using this approach entails selecting, at random, some storms to seed while leaving the rest of seeding opportunities unseeded. When done over an extended period, and for several years, seeding in such a selective way yields two sets of storm data that are ripe for conclusive study. The huge drawback to this approach, though, is that only half of all storms get treated, making sponsors of rain-enhancement efforts reluctant to "sacrifice" so many opportunities. That selective approach affects the benefit-to-cost ratio in ways that make the strategy hardly palatable to cost-conscious public officials. Without randomization, seeding projects are left to treat every storm that meets criteria within the target area and then to compare results with the behavior of untreated storms elsewhere in the region. While understandable as a balance between containing costs and striving for benefit, foregoing randomization means that securing the proof that seeding works to supply more rain will continue to be a daunting challenge.

Exercising Control

Because our natural environment is something we share with others, any effort to modify it to benefit some necessarily has ramifications for others who reside nearby. That is why the practice of weather modification is regulated in Texas, as it is in most regions of the United States, even where rainfall is traditionally plentiful. Even if it can be shown that any change in a region's weather resulting from human intervention is confined to that region only, governmental regulation still is needed to screen a prospective practitioner to protect the public from exploitation. History is replete with instances of supposed "rainmakers" who convinced desperate landowners and city dwellers to spend their hard-earned dollars on a cloud-seeding approach, only to be revealed later as charlatans. Furthermore, regulation is justified because, in many other instances, government regulates the allocation of water from waterways to users—and cloud seeding is commonly viewed as a means of augmenting water supplies.

Regulation of weather modification by the Texas Department of Licensing and Regulation (TDLR), headquartered in Austin, is aimed at ensuring that anyone using a weather modification approach is competent and that the individual, or business, has the resources to compensate anyone harmed by that practice. Before someone can conduct a weather modification operation, the individual or business must obtain from the state agency a license, a process by which that entity demonstrates that whoever is in control of the operation has the requisite training and work experience. In Texas, anyone in charge of an attempt to modify the weather must hold an academic degree in meteorology or atmospheric science and must have substantial experience using the technology. Once someone is licensed (a year at a time), the licensee then must obtain a permit for any specific program, or project, to modify the weather within Texas. A key component of getting a permit involves publishing a "Notice of Intention" to conduct weather modification operations. Such notices, usually in newspapers circulated in the area where the operation is to be conducted, informs the public when and how the modification is to be done—what regions constitute the "target area" and where the effect of the modification is aimed. The notice also gives information about the type of equipment, such as aircraft or ground-based generators, to be used and where it will be deployed (known as an "operational area"). Most importantly, the notice informs residents in both target and operational areas where to obtain additional information and how to express their views on what is being proposed. State law requires the TDLR to hold a public hearing in the area where weather modification is proposed if enough eligible residents request in writing such a forum.

Licensees who hold permits to do weather modification in Texas are required by law to collect and preserve relevant data that would allow investigators to "reconstruct" a particular operation, should it be questioned by affected residents. They must report their activities to the TDLR and the federal government on a periodic basis. In most cases, those modifying the weather display data about their operations on a website that is dedicated to keeping the sponsors and the public fully informed about their work. In instances in which aircraft are deployed for cloud seeding, a resident living in a weather modification target area can download a track depicting where the aircraft flew during an operation and when seeding materials were released—along with the amount of seeds used.

Relatively few lawsuits have been filed in US courts claiming the use of weather modification technologies was harmful. A suit filed by landowners in the region west of the Pecos River during the terrible drought of the 1950s is the only one of note to ever be adjudicated in Texas. Even that case, which landed in the Texas Supreme Court and led to a determination about the rights of landowners to claim water above them (as well as beneath them), did not lead to a cessation of efforts to seed thunderstorms to lessen the likelihood of damaging hail. Litigation can be filed prior to the onset of weather modification operations to prevent them—or after operations, when a weather event perceived to be related to attempts to modify the weather led to damage or other harm. Anyone trying to stop a weather modification project before it gets underway must show irreparable harm is in prospect—that something unique or irreplaceable is about to be lost or damaged. None of the dozen court cases filed nationwide since 1950 has resolved the most important issues pertaining to the practice of weather modification. Very few judicial opinions have addressed the property rights of landowners to the water above their property—or upwind of that property. One legal issue yet to be addressed in the US court system relates to the use of extra water that is produced by cloud seeding. Should the weather modifier be regarded like other professionals (such as surgeons, engineers, and investment counselors) who provide services for pay—but the benefits and risks stemming from those services belong to their clients?

Likely the most daunting issue relating to weather modification has to do with the not uncommon perception, still unsubstantiated, that increasing rainfall in one area must result in a corresponding diminution in adjacent areas, especially downwind of a target area. It is usually couched in terms of "robbing Peter to pay Paul." Assuming landowners are entitled to naturally occurring rainfall over their property, would a landowner have a legitimate case if it could be demonstrated that cloud seeding elsewhere was responsible for a rainfall reduction in his or her neighborhood? The vast majority of atmospheric physicists regard any deprivation of rain suffered by landowners downwind as *de minimis*, a harm too trifling to be compensated and arguably too much a scientific challenge to uphold in a satisfactory way. Experts maintain the amount of water in the atmosphere affected by cloud seeding is only a tiny fraction of the total water volume in the air on a given day in any particular region. Moreover, studies have shown that increases in rainfall in one area need not translate into decreases elsewhere. In fact, any "extra-area" effect is likely positive, as storms invigorated by seeding live longer and become more productive, even as they propagate out of the target and are no longer fed nucleating material. Crop yield data analyzed after each seeding season of the Colorado River Municipal Water District in the 1980s and 1990s suggested strongly that farmers living as much as 100 miles (161 kilometers) north and east of the District's long-term target benefited from seeding operations.

Countering Contamination—Natural and Otherwise

For years now, with increasing industrialization along and south of the Texas-Mexico border—and the polluted air that results—more and more unintentional seeding of clouds has occurred. But this kind of "seeding" is actually counterproductive to the manufacture of rainfall. In recent years, measurements of pollution aerosols and their interactions with potential rain clouds, particularly in California, have shown how these aerosols, when ingested by potential rain clouds, actually suppress the development of rainfall in those clouds. Mostly pristine air moving inland off the Gulf of Mexico becomes contaminated as it moves through major urban areas along the Texas coast. When air becomes polluted and then forms clouds, those clouds tend to have reduced drop sizes. These smaller cloud droplets are slower to freeze into ice crystals and are collected less efficiently by ice crystals that do form by other means. In recent years, advanced sensors aboard weather satellites circling Earth have provided a capability for understanding the composition of clouds—and have suggested ways that cloud seeding can "reverse" the negative effects that pollution has on clouds' ability to grow and produce rainfall.

Since much of the seeding material used in Texas rain-enhancement projects contains silver, sponsors have addressed the concern of some that seeding might contribute to contamination of drinking water. Sponsors have collected rainwater samples from storms known to have been seeded and had them analyzed for mineral content, only to discover that silver detected in those samples was of such minute quantities (less than 0.1 microgram per liter, or 1 part in 10 billion) that no threat to the environment was conceivable. These results were consistent with what other regions of the American West found when snowmelt was chemically analyzed for silver content in regions where wintertime seeding was practiced. In case after case, the concentration of silver was far below the acceptable concentration of 50 micrograms per liter established by the US Public Health Service. In fact, it is often found that the amount of silver in the soil is higher than that in rainwater from seeded storm clouds, and there is more iodine in iodized salt used on food than in rainwater.

Plodding toward Proof

There is now little doubt that the technology exists to bring about changes in cloud behavior to get a greater yield of rain from a thunderstorm or to inhibit it from producing ruinous hail. More effective strategies for altering cloud processes are indubitably in the offing. There is no question that our society would benefit immensely if damage from drought, floods, and severe storms could be mitigated, even eliminated. To get these practical benefits, though, a substantial and steady investment in basic scientific research on clouds and their response to seeding is a must. Nothing short of that kind of focus and commitment will move us to a point of demonstrating the efficacy of cloud seeding beyond a reasonable doubt.

Quantitative scientific proof that cloud seeding works much, if not all, of the time is hard to secure. That is because of uncertainties about what constitutes "normal" precipitation patterns as well as inadequate understanding about associated background aerosol and "micro" physical characteristics of the atmosphere. If our knowledge of what clouds consist of on a typical summer day is incomplete, then getting a fix on how seeding alters cloud behavior becomes an even greater challenge. The quest to produce proof is made even more daunting by those who sponsor cloud seeding who, in response to pressure to meet short-term objectives (e.g., substantial rain to quash a worsening drought), set aside the priority to achieve long-term scientific understanding of what happened and why. After all, funds most often are limited, so every available dollar is poured into flights and flares, and collecting relevant cloud data gets sacrificed. It is to be emphasized that the concept of seeding clouds to prolong their lives and generate additional rainfall is not in question. Rather, it is the absence of an adequate understanding of the behavior of clouds—and conditions in the neighborhood—that has impeded the production of predictable, repeatable, detectable, and verifiable results.

More substantive proof that cloud seeding works is coming. Access to continuous satellite imagery is allowing the concentrations of aerosols in, and near, clouds to be identified—and their role in influencing the growth of clouds, rainwater, and lightning can be measured quantitatively.

Appendixes

APPENDIX 1

Extremes in Texas Weather

CATEGORY	RECORD	LOCATION	DATE(S)
Temperature (°F)			
Coldest morning low	–23°	Tulia	Feb 12, 1899
		Seminole	Feb 8, 1933
Hottest daytime high	120°	Seymour	Aug 12, 1936
		Monahans	Jun 28, 1944
Coldest year statewide	62.3°		1895
Hottest year statewide	67.8°		2012
Coldest winter statewide	42.5°		Dec 1898-Feb 1899
Warmest winter statewide	52.6°		Dec 1906-Feb 1907
Coldest spring statewide	59.9°		Mar-May 1931
Warmest spring statewide	69.7°		Mar-May 2012
Coolest summer statewide	78.7°		Jun-Aug 1976
Hottest summer statewide	86.6°		Jun-Aug 2011
Coolest autumn statewide	60.0°		Sep-Nov 1976
Warmest autumn statewide	69.9°		Sep-Nov 1931

Rainfall (inches)			
Greatest in 24-hour period[1]	29.05	Albany	Aug 4, 1978
Greatest in one month[2]	54.74	Port Arthur	Aug 2017
Greatest single-storm rainfall	51.85	Cedar Bayou	Aug 2017
Greatest in one year	109.38	Clarksville	1873
Greatest surplus in one year[3]	57.30	Freeport	1979
Least in one year[4]	1.30	Terlingua	2011
Greatest deficit in one year	39.10	Orange	1896
Wettest year statewide	41.13		2015
Driest year statewide	14.30		1917
Wettest winter statewide	12.72		Dec 1991-Feb 1992
Driest winter statewide	1.54		Dec 2008-Feb 2009
Wettest spring statewide	16.48		Mar-May 2015
Driest spring statewide	2.53		Mar-May 2011
Wettest summer statewide	13.62		Jun-Aug 2007
Driest summer statewide	2.46		Jun-Aug 2011
Wettest autumn statewide	13.37		Sep-Nov 1919
Driest autumn statewide	2.95		Sep-Nov 1917
Snowfall (inches)			
Greatest in 24-hour period	25.0	Follett	Mar 28, 2009
Greatest maximum depth at time of observation	33.0	Hale Center	Feb 4, 1956
Greatest in a single storm	61.0	Vega	Feb 1-8, 1956
Greatest in one month	61.0	Vega	Feb 1956
Greatest in one season	65.0	Romero	1923-1924
Hail (depth on ground, inches)			
Greatest depth of hailstones	8.0	Winkler County	May 31, 1960
Wind (miles per hour)[5]			
Highest sustained speed	145 (SE)	Matagorda	Sep 11, 1961
	145 (NE)	Port Lavaca	Sep 11, 1961
Highest peak gust	180 (SW)	Aransas Pass	Aug 3, 1970
	180 (WSW)	Robstown	Aug 3, 1970

Source for apps. 1-17: Based upon data archived at the National Climatic Data Center for 1880-2015.

[1] An unofficial 24-hour total of 38.20 inches (and a 12-hour total of 32.0 inches) occurred 2 miles north of Thrall (Williamson County) on September 9-10, 1921.

[2] An amount of 45 inches, judged by National Weather Service (NWS) investigators to be of reasonable accuracy, was reported 3 miles northwest of Alvin (Brazoria County) in July 1979 as a result of Tropical Storm Claudette. However, the site was not an official observing station maintained by the NWS.

[3] Greatest departure from long-term normal (1941-1970) in use at that time.

[4] An estimated amount, since some daily data were missing.

[5] These extremes in wind speed were associated with hurricanes (Carla, 1961; Celia, 1970). Higher wind speeds have occurred in numerous tornadoes, but measurements have not been made by the conventional NWS network.

APPENDIX 2

Average Dates of First and Last Freezes

LOCATION[1]	LAST SPRING FREEZE	FIRST FALL FREEZE	LENGTH OF SEASON
Abilene (1,791)	Mar 22	Nov 12	234
Amarillo (3,602)	Apr 17	Oct 18	184
Austin (669)	Feb 15	Dec 6	293
Beeville (66)	Feb 15	Dec 5	288
Beaumont-Port Arthur (16)	Feb 9	Dec 8	302
Big Spring (2,510)	Apr 18	Nov 16	245
Brownsville (23)[2,3]	Jan 10	Dec 29	341
Brownwood (1,401)	Mar 25	Nov 5	225
Childress (1,952)	Mar 31	Nov 6	218
College Station (305)	Feb 27	Nov 29	275
Corpus Christi (43)	Jan 29	Dec 19	323
Dalhart (3,990)	Apr 23	Oct 13	172
Dallas-Fort Worth (561)	Mar 10	Nov 22	257
Del Rio (997)	Feb 20	Dec 1	284
El Paso (3,917)	Mar 15	Nov 11	241
Hereford (3,819)	Apr 14	Oct 20	188
Houston (44)	Feb 2	Dec 24	326
Kerrville (1,785)	Apr 1	Nov 6	217
Laredo (430)	Feb 5	Dec 11	309
Longview (364)	Mar 8	Nov 18	255
Lubbock (3,255)	Apr 2	Oct 31	211
Lufkin (289)	Mar 11	Nov 16	250
Marfa (4,790)	Apr 11	Oct 29	201
Midland-Odessa (2,861)	Mar 29	Nov 11	226
Mount Locke (6,790)	Apr 15	Oct 27	194
Palacios (12)	Feb 6	Dec 11	309
Palestine (465)	Mar 18	Nov 15	243
Pampa (3,150)	Apr 10	Oct 24	195
Paris (541)	Mar 19	Nov 15	240
San Angelo (1,916)	Mar 28	Nov 12	228

San Antonio (787)	Feb 28	Nov 27	272
Sanderson (2,789)	Mar 19	Nov 8	237
Sherman (761)	Mar 21	Nov 16	239
Texarkana (390)	Mar 17	Nov 15	241
Tyler (545)	Mar 8	Nov 19	256
Van Horn (4,065)	Mar 31	Nov 3	217
Victoria (105)	Feb 11	Dec 9	300
Waco (499)	Mar 14	Nov 19	249
Wichita Falls (1,017)	Mar 25	Nov 12	231

Note: Cities listed above were chosen because their weather records were complete, or nearly so, for the 30-year period ending in 2010. Average values are derived from the arithmetic means of data for the period 1981-2010.

[1] Feet above mean sea level given in parentheses.

[2] No freeze occurs on, or after, January 1 in 1 of every 2 years at Brownsville, 1 of every 3 years at McAllen, and 1 of every 4 years at Galveston.

[3] The season's initial freeze does not occur until January 1 or later, on average, in 2 of every 3 years at Brownsville, Galveston, and McAllen.

APPENDIX 3

Average and Extreme Number of Freeze Occurrences

									Most in any season	
LOCATION	OCT	NOV	DEC	JAN	FEB	MAR	APR	TOTAL	NUMBER	YEARS
Abilene	*	4	14	15	8	4	*	45	73	1976-1977
Alice	0	*	1	2	*	*	0	4	20	1979-1980
Alpine	1	8	17	18	13	8	2	66	97	1979-1980
Amarillo	2	15	27	27	21	13	4	107	139	1898-1899
Angleton	0	1	3	5	2	1	0	10	30	1939-1940
Austin	0	*	4	4	2	1	0	12	56	1898-1899
Beeville	0	*	3	1	1	0	0	5	31	1917-1918
Big Bend NP	*	3	8	8	5	3	1	27	52	1976-1977
Big Spring	0	5	15	17	10	4	*	52	88	1972-1973
Brownsville	0	0	1	*	0	0	0	1	11	1911-1912
Brownwood	*	6	17	19	11	5	1	60	84	2013-2014
Childress	*	7	19	22	13	6	1*	67	92	2013-2014
College Station	0	1	5	5	3	1	0	14	37	1977-1978[1]
Corpus Christi	0	0	2	2	1	*	0	4	15	1962-1963
Corsicana	0	2	9	9	5	2	*	26	66	2013-2014
Dalhart	4	21	29	30	25	19	7	134	153	1972-1973[1]
Dallas-Fort Worth	0	2	9	11	6	2	0	29	74	1911-1912
Del Rio	0	1	4	4	2	1	0	11	29	1963-1964
Eagle Pass	0	1*	3	4	2	*	0	10	42	1903-1904
El Paso	*	5	15	15	7	3	*	44	94	1880-1881
Fort Stockton	0	2	9	10	5	2	*	28	83	1918-1919
Galveston	0	0	0	1	0	0	0	1	15	1929-1930
Hereford	2	17	27	28	22	15	5	116	150	1908-1909
Houston[2]	0	*	3	4	2	1	0	10	42	1977-1978
Junction	1*	5	17	15	10	4	1	52	97	2009-2010
Kerrville	1*	5	13	15	9	4	1*	46	88	1929-1930
Killeen	0	3	10	11	6	2	0	32	60	1977-1978
Laredo	0	*	2	2	1	*	0	5	18	1984-1985
Longview	0	2	11	13	8	2	0	35	66	2013-2014
Lubbock	1	10	23	24	17	9	1	84	124	1950-1951[1]

Lufkin	0	3	9	10	5	2	0	27	63	1977-1978
Marfa	2	16	26	28	21	14	4	111	157	2009-2010
Midland	*	6	17	18	11	5	1	58	99	1895-1896
Pampa	2	14	26	27	21	14	4	107	138	1969-1970[1]
Paris	*	4	13	17	9	3	*	46	81	1995-1996
Perryton	4	20	29	30	25	19	7	135	158	1969-1970
Pine Springs	1	6	16	17	10	7	1	58	102	2000-2001
Plainview	1	11	24	25	18	9	2	90	133	2013-2014[1]
Port Arthur	0	*	3	4	1	1*	0	9	24	1976-1977[1]
Presidio	0	2	11	12	4	1	0	30	80	1938-1939
San Angelo	*	5	14	15	8	4	1	46	76	1911-1912
San Antonio	0	1	5	5	3	1	0	15	40	1966-1967
Sanderson	*	5	16	17	9	3	*	50	83	1963-1964
Sherman	0	3	12	15	9	3	*	42	83	1977-1978
Sonora	1	8	20	20	13	6	2	69	87	2013-2014
Temple	0	3	10	10	6	1	0	30	54	1898-1899
Texarkana	*	4	13	16	9	3	*	45	81	1976-1977
Tyler	0	2	8	11	6	2	*	29	59	1898-1899
Uvalde	0	2	8	7	3	1	0	20	56	1963-1964
Van Horn	1	8	20	22	13	6	1	70	107	1997-1998
Victoria	0	*	1	3	1	*	0	5	22	1917-1918
Waco	0	3	10	11	5	2	*	31	70	2013-2014
Wichita Falls	0*	6	17	19	11	5	1*	59	89	1970-1971
Wink	1	9	21	20	13	5	1	69	90	1972-1973[1]

Note: Seasonal totals, when added, may differ from the annual total because of rounding. Monthly averages, or means, are based on records for 1981-2010.

* Denotes one occurrence every other year or less often.

[1] Also on dates occurring earlier in the historical record for that station.

[2] Location in Houston is Bush International Airport.

APPENDIX 4

Greatest Number of Days of 32°F and below during Most Severe Cold Winters

LOCATION	SEASON	TOTAL DAYS	Consecutive days NUMBER	DATES
Abilene	1911-1912, 1972-1973, 1976-1977	73	27	Jan 8-Feb 3, 1978
	1977-1978, 1987-1988	69	20	Jan 5-24, 1962
	2013-2014	68	20	Dec 14, 1983-Jan 2, 1984
Amarillo	1976-1977, 1979-1980	130	68	Dec 5, 1960-Feb 10, 1961
	1993-1994	129	65	Nov 6, 2000-Jan 9, 2001
	1955-1956, 1963-1964	128	57	Nov 26, 1976-Jan 21, 1977
	1943-1944, 1982-1983, 1992-1993	127		
Austin	1898-1899	56	16	Jan 14-29, 1940
	1924-1925	51	15	Dec 11-25, 1989
	1925-1926	47	14	Dec 18-31, 1983
Brownsville	1901-1902	23	11	Dec 13-23, 1901
	1900-1901	13	6	Jan 29-Feb 3, 1951
Corpus Christi	1962-1963	15	10	Jan 18-27, 1940
	1898-1899, 1984-1985	14	5	Feb 10-14, 1899
			5	Jan 25-29, 1897
Dallas	1911-1912	74	22	Dec 25, 1987-Jan 15, 1988
	1903-1904	67	17	Dec 15-31, 1983
	1909-1910	66	17	Dec 30, 1978-Jan 15, 1979
El Paso	1880-1881	94	27	Dec 27, 1943-Jan 22, 1944
	1987-1988	87	25	Dec 5-29, 1960
	1976-1977, 1986-1987	84	23	Jan 1-23, 1925
	1960-1961	78		
	1966-1967	77		
Galveston	1962-1963	15	10	Jan 18-27, 1940
	1947-1948	10	7	Feb 12-18, 1895
			7	Jan 7-13, 1886

Houston[1]	1939-1940	28	12	Jan 18-29, 1940
	1878-1879	23	11	Dec 21-31, 1983
	1977-1978, 1983-1984	20	7	Jan 5-11, 2010
Laredo	1950-1951, 1962-1963	14	7	Jan 29-Feb 4, 1951
	1963-1964	10	6	Dec 31, 1946-Jan 5, 1947
Lubbock	1950-1951	114	69	Dec 5, 1960-Feb 11, 1961
	1947-1948	111	50	Nov 19, 1938-Jan 7, 1939
	1959-1960, 1963-1964	110	47	Jan 8-Feb 23, 1978
	1955-1956, 1958-1959	108		
	1957-1958, 1969-1970, 2013-2014	106		
Midland	1987-1988	91	29	Jan 24-Feb 21, 1936
	1932-1933	89	25	Jan 12-Feb 5, 2007
	1938-1939	82	25	Jan 13-Feb 6, 1966
	1936-1937	81	22	Dec 22, 1966-Jan 12, 1967
San Angelo	1911-1912	76	25	Dec 23, 1911-Jan 16, 1912
	2013-2014	75	22	Jan 3-24, 1944
	1914-1915	74	22	Jan 11-Feb 1, 1930
	1942-1943	72	22	Jan 6-27, 1915
San Antonio	1966-1967	40	15	Dec 17-31, 1983
	1977-1978	39	10	Jan 8-17, 1982
	1947-1948, 1976-1977	36		

[1] The location, near downtown at Hobby Airport, is used because it has a much longer weather history than Houston's Bush International Airport.

APPENDIX 5

Greatest Number of Consecutive Days with Maximum Daily Temperature at or below Freezing

LOCATION	NUMBER	DATES
Abilene	7	Dec 19-25, 1983; Dec 29, 1946-Jan 4, 1947; Feb 10-16, 1895
	6	Jan 6-11, 1973; Feb 2-7, 1905
Amarillo	12	Dec 30, 1978-Jan 10, 1979
	8	Dec 18-25, 1983; Jan 16-23, 1960; Jan 23-30, 1948
	7	Jan 19-25, 1966
Austin	5	Dec 22-26, 1983
	4	Jan 29-Feb 1, 1951; Jan 22-25, 1897
Brownsville	2	Jan 10-11, 1962; Jan 30-31, 1951
Corpus Christi	3	Dec 24-26, 1983; Jan 30-Feb 1, 1951
Dallas[1]	6	Dec 21-26, 1983; Jan 17-22, 1978; Jan 24-29, 1948
	5	Jan 31-Feb 4, 1996; Jan 31-Feb 4, 1985; Jan 4-8, 1942
El Paso	4	Jan 4-7, 1971; Dec 31, 1946-Jan 3, 1947
Fort Worth[2]	7	Dec 29, 1946-Jan 4, 1947
Galveston	3	Dec 23-25, 1983; Feb 14-16, 1895
Houston[3]	4	Feb 4-7, 1989; Dec 23-26, 1983; Jan 30-Feb 2, 1951
Laredo	2	Dec 24-25, 1983
Lubbock	8	Dec 18-25, 1983
	7	Dec 28, 1982-Jan 3, 1983
Lufkin	5	Dec 22-26, 1983
Midland	5	Jan 13-17, 2007; Jan 7-11, 1973
San Angelo	6	Dec 31, 1946-Jan 5, 1947

San Antonio	4	Jan 29-Feb 1, 1951
Texarkana	6	Dec 22-27, 1983
Waco	6	Jan 24-29, 1948
	5	Dec 22-26, 1983
Wichita Falls	11	Dec 19-29, 1983
	8	Dec 29, 1946-Jan 5, 1947; Jan 15-22, 1930

[1] The Dallas Love Field is used because its weather history is much longer than the Dallas-Fort Worth International Airport.

[2] The Fort Worth Meacham Airport location is used for its lengthy history.

[3] The Houston Hobby Airport is used because its weather history is much longer than Bush International Airport.

APPENDIX 6

Coldest and Hottest Temperatures Statewide, 1975-2016

YEAR	°F	COLDEST LOCATION	DATE	°F	HOTTEST LOCATION	DATE
1975	−7	Dalhart	Jan 12	111	Falcon Dam	Aug 1
	−7	Perryton	Jan 12			
1976	−11	Lipscomb	Jan 8	115	Pecos	Jun 23
1977	−8	Lipscomb	Jan 10, 12	114	Pecos	Jun 18
1978	−10	Bootleg Corn	Dec 9	116	Munday	Jul 15
				116	Olney	Jul 15
1979	−12	Bravo	Jan 2	112	El Paso	Jul 10
	−12	Lipscomb	Jan 2			
1980	−2	Boys Ranch	Nov 26	119	Weatherford	Jun 26
	−2	Lipscomb	Mar 2			
1981	−10	Gruver	Feb 11	114	Boquillas	Jun 10
	−10	Vega	Feb 11	114	Castolon	Jun 10
1982	−15	Perryton	Feb 6	114	Lajitas	Jun 28
1983	−16	Lipscomb	Dec 30	113	Boquillas	Jun 19
				113	Presidio	Jul 5
				113	Robstown	Aug 31
1984	−14	Dalhart	Jan 19	115	Glen Rose	Aug 19
	−14	Stratford	Jan 19			
1985	−13	Sterling City	Feb 2	112	Boquillas	May 30
1986	−12	Amarillo	Feb 11	113	Henrietta	Jul 31
	−12	Perryton	Feb 12			
1987	−9	Muleshoe	Dec 16	115	Boquillas	Jul 6
1988	−17	Perryton	Jan 7	114	Eagle Pass	Jun 10
1989	−15	Glen Rose	Dec 23	116	Boquillas	May 25
	−15	Lipscomb	Dec 23	116	Grandfalls	Jul 3
	−15	Quanah	Dec 23			
1990	−12	Bravo	Dec 23	114	Red Bluff Dam	Jun 25
				114	Ysleta	Jun 26
1991	−3	Stratford	Nov 4	112	Castolon	Jun 24
	−3	Tulia	Nov 3	112	Laredo	Jul 31
				112	Monahans	Jun 24
1992	1	Boys Ranch	Dec 15	117	Castolon	Jun 17
1993	−1	Stratford	Jan 10	113	Castolon	Jun 6
1994	−6	Follett	Jan 31	120	Monahans	Jun 28
	−6	Silverton	Feb 1			

1995	–1	Bravo	Dec 9	115	Heath Canyon	Jul 25
1996	–13	Perryton	Feb 3	115	Boquillas	May 23
				115	Heath Canyon	May 23
1997	–2	Follett	Jan 14	113	Castolon	Jun 4
1998	–6	Stratford	Dec 22	117	Boquillas	Jul 11
	–6	Dalhart	Dec 23	117	Red Bluff Dam	Jun 22
1999	3	Follett	Jan 3	115	Heath Canyon	Jul 1
2000	0	Lipscomb	Dec 15	116	Columbus	Sep 4
2001	1	Lipscomb	Feb 10	116	Heath Canyon	May 29
2002	–6	Dalhart	Dec 26	115	Heath Canyon	Aug 28
2003	–2	Lipscomb	Feb 25	116	Heath Canyon	May 19
2004	–11	Hart	Dec 25	114	Heath Canyon	Jun 3
2005	–8	Lipscomb	Dec 8	117	Heath Canyon	Jul 5
2006	0	Stratford	Feb 19	115	Greenville	Aug 20
2007	–4	Bushland	Feb 15	110	Presidio	Jun 27
		Vega	Feb 15	110	Wink	Jun 18
2008	0	Stratford	Jan 18	115	Castolon	Jun 16
				115	Wink	Jun 16
2009	–3	Bravo	Dec 10	118	Hebbronville	Jul 9
				118	Wash. St. Park	Aug 27
2010	–6	Lipscomb	Jan 5	115	Boquillas	Jun 7
		Perryton	Jan 10	115	Presidio	Jun 7
				115	Castolon	Jun 8
				115	Lajitas	Jun 8
2011	–17	Bravo	Feb 4	119	Shamrock	Sep 4
		Lipscomb	Feb 10			
2012	0	Bravo	Dec 25	115	Wellington	Aug 2
2013	–4	Paducah	Dec 21	114	Hebbronville	Jul 15
2014	–6	Lipscomb	Mar 3	120	Monahans	Jun 28
2015	–2	Boys Ranch	Jan 4	113	Ozona	Aug 3
2016	–12	Boys Ranch	Dec 18	116	Falfurrias	Jul 13

APPENDIX 7

Average Low and High Temperatures (°F) by Season and Annually in Selected Locations[1]

LOCATION	WINTER	SPRING	SUMMER	AUTUMN	ANNUAL
Abilene	34.4-58.0	52.5-76.8	70.7-92.9	53.8-76.8	52.9-76.2
Amarillo	24.5-51.4	42.2-71.0	63.5-89.5	44.5-71.5	43.8-71.0
Austin	42.8-63.1	58.8-79.5	73.8-94.9	60.2-81.2	59.0-79.8
Beeville	45.2-66.6	60.4-80.6	73.1-93.7	61.4-83.2	60.1-81.1
Big Bend NP	38.2-58.4	51.4-74.3	63.7-83.3	51.8-71.7	51.3-72.0
Big Spring	32.8-58.6	50.6-78.2	69.8-93.6	52.5-77.4	51.5-77.0
Brownsville	52.9-72.0	65.9-83.6	76.1-93.4	66.5-85.1	65.4-83.6
Brownwood	31.9-60.8	50.9-64.6	69.0-94.6	51.9-79.5	51.0-78.4
Childress	29.8-55.7	48.7-75.9	68.9-94.1	49.9-76.1	49.4-75.6
College Station	42.5-62.6	58.6-78.8	73.9-94.3	60.1-81.0	58.9-79.2
Corpus Christi	48.7-68.5	63.1-81.4	74.5-92.8	64.3-83.5	62.7-81.6
Corsicana	36.3-59.0	53.8-75.8	72.0-93.1	55.3-78.7	54.4-76.6
Dalhart	20.4-49.5	38.3-68.3	60.6-89.4	41.6-71.6	40.3-69.8
Dallas	37.3-57.9	55.3-76.0	73.9-94.4	56.8-77.9	55.9-76.6
Del Rio	42.0-65.4	59.9-83.2	74.6-96.1	60.1-81.7	59.2-81.7
Eagle Pass	42.8-66.5	60.0-84.6	74.5-97.7	60.7-83.6	59.6-83.2
El Paso	34.0-59.2	51.2-78.9	69.5-94.2	51.8-77.3	51.7-77.5
Fort Stockton	37.1-63.5	53.4-81.9	69.2-93.8	54.3-79.3	53.6-79.7
Fort Worth	36.6-57.8	54.4-75.6	73.2-94.0	56.1-77.4	55.2-76.3
Galveston	50.1-63.3	64.5-76.3	78.9-89.4	67.5-79.9	65.3-77.3
Hereford	23.6-51.6	40.8-71.6	62.4-89.9	43.3-71.7	42.6-71.3
Houston	46.8-64.5	61.3-78.9	75.1-91.6	62.9-80.7	61.6-79.0
Junction	34.0-62.5	53.0-79.3	69.5-93.5	52.6-78.9	52.4-78.6
Kerrville	35.5-61.5	53.3-77.2	69.0-91.8	53.9-78.7	53.0-77.4
Killeen	36.8-60.6	53.9-76.8	70.7-93.9	55.7-79.3	54.4-77.7
Laredo	47.7-68.8	64.2-86.9	76.5-99.1	64.4-85.4	63.3-85.1
Longview	37.3-59.1	54.0-76.3	71.5-92.4	54.5-77.7	54.4-76.5
Lubbock	27.8-55.6	46.2-75.3	66.2-91.6	47.5-74.4	47.0-74.3
Lufkin	39.7-61.5	55.5-78.1	71.2-92.6	56.2-79.3	55.7-77.9
Midland	31.8-59.2	49.9-79.0	68.6-93.8	51.0-77.1	50.4-77.4

Pampa	24.4-49.9	41.8-69.5	63.9-89.4	44.9-71.2	43.8-70.1
Paris	24.4-49.9	41.8-69.5	63.9-89.4	44.9-71.2	43.8-70.1
Perryton	20.4-49.0	38.4-69.4	61.3-90.1	41.5-71.1	40.5-70.0
Pine Springs	32.3-53.1	48.3-73.1	64.3-87.5	49.5-70.9	48.7-71.2
Plainview	27.0-52.5	44.8-72.0	65.3-89.5	46.7-72.3	46.0-71.6
Port Arthur	44.8-63.6	59.4-78.2	73.7-91.2	60.7-80.2	59.7-78.4
Presidio	36.3-69.7	55.7-89.4	74.1-100.5	56.9-86.7	55.8-86.7
San Angelo	34.6-60.9	52.7-79.5	70.2-94.0	53.2-78.3	52.8-78.2
San Antonio	42.1-64.5	58.6-80.3	74.0-94.3	59.8-81.6	58.7-80.3
Sanderson	33.1-62.0	51.8-80.1	69.1-92.0	51.8-78.3	51.5-78.2
Sherman	34.7-53.6	52.6-72.2	71.5-90.8	54.5-74.1	53.4-72.7
Sonora	30.5-61.6	50.5-79.3	68.8-93.6	50.9-78.8	50.3-78.4
Texarkana	34.8-55.9	52.3-74.4	71.6-91.8	53.6-75.8	53.2-74.6
Tyler	38.7-58.0	54.9-74.7	72.4-91.3	56.1-76.5	55.6-75.2
Van Horn	29.9-59.8	46.7-78.4	65.2-92.2	48.0-77.2	47.5-77.0
Victoria	46.8-65.7	61.7-79.9	75.1-93.3	62.6-83.1	61.6-80.6
Waco	37.7-59.6	55.2-77.3	72.9-95.0	56.5-79.4	55.7-77.9
Wichita Falls	31.3-55.6	50.1-75.5	70.3-95.0	51.9-76.8	51.0-75.8
Wink	30.3-62.2	49.2-82.1	69.1-96.5	50.1-80.0	49.8-80.3

[1] Seasonal averages are based on daily observations for the 30-year period 1981-2010.

APPENDIX 8
Temperature Extremes at Selected Locations

	Coldest ever observed		Hottest ever observed	
LOCATION	°F	DATE	°F	DATE
Abilene	–9	Jan 4, 1947	111	Aug 3, 1943
Alice	12	Dec 23, 1989	111	Jun 16, 1998[1]
Alpine	–3	Dec 29, 1983	108	Jun 6, 2014
Amarillo	–16	Feb 12, 1899	108	Jun 24, 1953
Angleton	7	Dec 24, 1989	107	Jul 19, 2013
Austin	–2	Jan 31, 1949	114	Jul 4, 1894
Beeville	8	Dec 25, 1983	111	Jul 9, 1939
Big Bend NP	–3	Jan 30, 1949	103	Jun 28, 1972
Big Spring	–7	Feb 8, 1933	114	Jun 28, 1994
Brownsville	2	Dec 25, 2004	106	Mar 27, 1984
Brownwood	–6	Dec 23, 1989	113	Jul 19, 1925
Childress	–5	Dec 23, 1989	117	Jun 26, 2011[1]
College Station	–3	Jan 31, 1949	112	Sep 4, 2000
Corpus Christi	11	Feb 12, 1899	105	Jul 24, 1934
Corsicana	–7	Feb 12, 1899	113	Jul 26, 1954
Dalhart	–21	Jan 4, 1959	110	Sep 7, 1907
Dallas-Fort Worth	–8	Feb 12, 1899	113	Jun 27, 1980[1]
Del Rio	11	Feb 2, 1951	111	Jul 30, 1960
Eagle Pass	7	Feb 12, 1899	115	Jul 25, 1944[1]
El Paso	–8	Jan 11, 1962	112	Jul 10, 1979
Fort Stockton	–7	Jan 3, 1911	114	Jun 17, 1924
Galveston	8	Feb 12, 1899	101	Jul 16, 1932
Hereford	–17	Feb 1, 1951	111	Jun 8, 1910
Houston	5	Jan 23, 1940	107	Aug 23, 1980
Junction	–11	Dec 22, 1929	112	Aug 2, 2011
Kerrville	–7	Jan 31, 1949	110	Jul 27, 1954
Killeen	–2	Dec 24, 1989	112	Sep 6, 2000
Laredo	16	Dec 21, 1973	115	Jun 11, 1942
Longview	–7	Feb 12, 1899	113	Aug 10, 1936
Lubbock	–17	Feb 8, 1933	114	Jun 27, 1994

Lufkin	–2	Feb 2, 1951[1]	110	Sep 4, 2000[1]
Marfa	–2	Jan 5, 1972	106	Jun 28, 1994[1]
Midland	–11	Feb 8, 1933	116	Jun 27, 1994
Pampa	–12	Jan 11, 1962	111	Jun 25, 1980
Paris	–13	Feb 12, 1899	115	Aug 10, 1936
Perryton	–17	Jan 7, 1988	113	Jun 26, 2011
Pine Springs	–3	Feb 3, 2011	105	Jun 28, 1994
Plainview	–8	Feb 8, 1933	112	Jun 27, 2011
Port Arthur	11	Jan 18, 1930	108	Aug 31, 2000
Presidio	4	Jan 12, 1962	117	Jun 18, 1960[1]
San Angelo	1	Feb 2, 1951[1]	111	Jul 29, 1960
San Antonio	0	Jan 31, 1949	111	Sep 5, 2000
Sanderson	3	Dec 22, 1989	113	Jun 12, 2014
Sherman	–2	Jan 31, 1949	113	Aug 10, 1936
Sonora	–8	Feb 2, 1951	109	Jun 28, 1980
Temple	–4	Feb 12, 1899	112	Aug 11, 1947
Texarkana	–6	Dec 23, 1989	112	Aug 4, 2011
Tyler	–8	Feb 12, 1899	110	Aug 3, 2011
Uvalde	6	Feb 2, 1951	114	Jun 9, 1910
Van Horn	–7	Jan 11, 1962	112	Jun 25, 1969
Victoria	9	Jan 18, 1930	110	Sep 6, 2000
Waco	–5	Jan 31, 1949	112	Aug 11, 1969
Wichita Falls	–12	Jan 4, 1947	117	Jun 28, 1980
Wink	–14	Jan 11, 1962	117	Jun 27, 1994

[1] Also on dates occurring earlier in the historical record for that station.

APPENDIX 9
Average and Extreme Number of Days of 100°F and Hotter

	Average								Most in any year	
LOCATION	APR	MAY	JUN	JUL	AUG	SEP	OCT	TOTAL	NUMBER	YEAR
Abilene		0.5	1.3	3.6	3.6	0.5		9.5	81	2011
Alpine		0.2	1.0	0.4				1.6	31	2015[1]
Amarillo		0.2	1.7	1.7	0.7	0.3		4.6	50	2011
Austin		0.2	1.6	5.1	7.9	1.0		15.8	90	2011
Big Bend NP								0.0	3	1972
Brownsville	0.1	0.2	0.2	0.2				0.7	9	1918
Childress	1.1	3.6	7.5	7.1	1.4	0.1		20.9	99	2011
College Station		0.1	0.9	3.5	6.6	0.9		12.0	69	2011
Corpus Christi		0.1	0.1	0.2	0.8	0.4		1.7	28	2012
Dallas-Fort Worth		0.1	0.7	4.8	8.0	1.0		14.6	71	2011
Del Rio	0.3	2.1	4.5	8.1	8.7	1.2		24.9	85	2011
El Paso		0.6	6.7	5.1	1.5	0.1		14.0	62	1994
Fort Stockton	0.1	2.8	5.4	4.3	1.4	0.6		14.6	93	1934
Houston			0.3	1.1	1.7	0.4		3.5	18	2011
Junction	0.2	0.7	1.0	4.7	4.1	0.8		11.5	79	2011
Laredo	1.3	5.0	10.6	14.8	17.2	4.4	0.2	53.8	145	2011
Longview			0.5	3.3	2.9	0.5		7.2	73	2011
Lubbock		0.9	2.8	2.8	0.8	0.1		7.4	48	2011
Lufkin			0.4	1.5	2.3	0.4		4.6	63	2011
Midland	0.1	2.2	4.6	4.5	2.9	0.7		15.0	65	2011
Port Arthur			0.1	0.1	0.4	0.2		0.8	12	1962
Presidio	1.1	10.6	21.3	18.3	16.0	5.5	0.2	73.0	123	2011
San Angelo	0.1	1.5	3.1	4.9	4.7	0.7		15.0	100	2011
San Antonio		0.2	1.3	3.1	3.1	0.8		8.5	59	2009
Texarkana			0.3	2.0	3.8	0.5		6.6	60	2011
Tyler			0.4	1.8	1.9	0.5		4.6	81	2011
Van Horn		0.6	3.9	2.1	1.2	0.1		7.9	71	1969
Victoria			0.3	2.1	1.6	1.2		5.2	42	1912
Waco			1.1	6.0	8.8	1.1		17.0	90	2011
Wichita Falls	0.1	0.7	2.2	9.3	10.7	1.7		24.7	100	2011

Note: Monthly averages are based on daily observations for the 30-year period 1981-2010. Monthly totals, when added, may differ from the annual total because of rounding.

[1] Also on dates occurring earlier in the historical record for that station.

APPENDIX 10

Average Seasonal Precipitation (Inches and Percent of Annual Total) in Selected Locations

	Winter		Spring		Summer		Autumn		Annual
LOCATION	INCHES	%	INCHES	%	INCHES	%	INCHES	%	INCHES
Abilene	3.61	15	6.56	26	8.02	32	6.63	27	24.82
Alice	4.21	15	6.76	24	8.35	29	9.11	32	28.43
Alpine	1.70	10	2.54	15	8.29	49	4.47	26	17.00
Amarillo	1.99	10	5.08	25	8.91	44	4.38	22	20.36
Angleton	11.16	22	10.03	20	13.86	27	15.81	31	50.86
Austin	6.64	19	9.29	27	8.56	25	9.83	29	34.32
Beeville	4.91	15	8.27	25	9.80	30	9.98	30	32.96
Big Spring	2.21	11	4.79	25	6.88	35	5.62	29	19.50
Brownsville	3.50	13	5.41	20	7.05	26	11.48	42	27.44
Brownwood	5.27	17	8.74	29	8.74	29	7.68	25	30.43
Childress	2.69	11	6.79	28	8.52	36	5.92	25	23.92
Chisos Basin	1.96	10	2.92	15	9.79	51	4.69	24	19.36
College Station	9.32	23	10.16	25	9.27	23	11.31	28	40.06
Corpus Christi	5.30	17	6.80	21	9.07	29	10.59	33	31.76
Corsicana	9.54	24	11.15	28	8.40	21	11.08	28	40.17
Dalhart	1.46	8	4.49	26	7.94	45	3.70	21	17.59
Dallas-Fort Worth	7.34	20	11.46	32	7.86	22	9.48	26	36.14
Del Rio	2.25	12	5.60	29	6.31	32	5.36	27	19.52
Eagle Pass	2.57	13	5.44	27	6.27	31	6.13	30	20.41
El Paso	1.64	17	0.96	10	4.50	46	2.61	27	9.71
Fort Stockton	1.83	12	2.77	19	5.90	40	4.27	29	14.77
Galveston	10.29	20	10.53	21	13.88	27	16.06	32	50.76
Hereford	2.12	11	4.31	22	9.13	46	4.49	22	20.05
Houston	10.32	21	11.81	24	13.48	27	14.16	28	49.77
Junction	3.65	14	7.82	29	7.90	29	7.61	28	26.98
Kerrville	5.25	16	8.58	27	8.48	26	9.74	30	32.05
Killeen	6.92	21	9.34	28	7.85	24	8.97	27	33.08
Laredo	2.72	13	5.03	25	6.12	30	6.33	31	20.20
Longview	11.85	25	12.37	26	10.92	23	12.41	26	47.55
Lubbock	2.16	11	4.81	25	6.86	36	5.29	28	19.12

Lufkin	12.49	26	11.47	23	11.07	23	13.92	28	48.95
Marfa	1.63	11	2.18	14	7.64	50	3.93	26	15.38
Midland	1.87	13	2.99	20	5.46	37	4.28	29	14.60
Pampa	2.27	10	6.66	29	9.13	39	5.13	22	23.19
Paris	9.97	21	13.41	28	10.07	21	13.62	29	47.07
Perryton	1.93	9	6.53	30	9.07	41	4.57	21	22.10
Pine Springs	1.57	12	2.08	16	5.94	45	3.75	28	13.34
Plainview	2.15	11	5.60	27	7.87	38	4.83	24	20.45
Port Arthur	14.13	23	11.97	20	18.42	30	15.95	26	60.47
Presidio	1.37	14	1.15	12	4.66	48	2.48	26	9.66
San Angelo	3.13	15	5.74	27	6.05	28	6.33	30	21.25
San Antonio	5.46	17	8.42	26	8.97	28	9.42	29	32.27
Sanderson	1.70	12	3.06	21	5.89	40	4.07	28	14.72
Sherman	8.55	20	12.79	29	9.68	22	12.58	29	43.60
Sonora	3.22	14	5.88	26	7.13	31	6.80	30	23.03
Temple	7.54	21	9.71	27	8.80	24	10.06	28	36.11
Texarkana	13.45	26	13.94	27	10.74	21	13.83	27	51.96
Tyler	11.11	24	12.06	26	10.33	23	12.29	27	45.79
Uvalde	3.52	14	6.50	26	7.57	31	7.01	28	24.60
Van Horn	1.49	13	1.05	9	5.74	50	3.30	29	11.58
Victoria	7.16	18	10.05	25	11.13	28	11.75	29	40.09
Waco	7.50	22	10.14	29	7.27	21	9.78	28	34.69
Wichita Falls	4.51	16	8.60	30	8.24	28	7.57	26	28.92
Wink	1.55	12	2.96	23	5.08	39	3.50	27	13.09

Note: Seasonal totals, when added, may differ from the annual total because of rounding. Averages are based on records for 1981-2010.

APPENDIX 11

Greatest One-Day, One-Month, and One-Year Precipitation (Inches) for Selected Locations

	Day		Month		Year	
LOCATION[1]	INCHES	DATE	INCHES	DATE	INCHES	YEAR
Abilene (1885)	8.26	Jul 7, 2015	15.70	Aug 1914	48.77	1941
Alice (1893)	13.21	Sep 13, 1951	18.78	Sep 1967	51.11	1919
Alpine (1900)	3.92	Aug 14, 2005	11.15	Sep 1974	33.09	1941
Alvin (1898)	25.75	Jul 26, 1979	35.70	July 1979	102.58	1979
Amarillo (1892)	5.74	Jul 7, 2010	10.73	Jun 1965	39.75	1923
Angleton (1895)	14.36	Jul 26, 1979	22.13	Jul 1979	100.21	1973
Athens (1903)	10.38	Oct 24, 2015	19.52	Oct 1954	71.87	2015
Austin (1891)	15.00	Sep 9, 1921	20.78	Sep 1921	65.31	1919
Beeville (1945)	11.55	Jul 16, 1990	20.93	Sep 1971	44.08	1981
Big Spring (1948)	5.34	Sep 6, 1962	14.22	Sep 1980	33.88	2004
Brownsville (1898)	12.09	Sep 20, 1967	24.20	Feb 1947	47.51	1958
Childress (1893)	5.32	Oct 20, 1983	13.21	May 2015	50.02	1941
Chisos Basin (1943)	4.29	Oct 5, 1966	10.71	Aug 1980	33.68	1986
College Station (1951)	13.39	Oct 16, 1994	21.02	Aug 2017	61.04	1968
Corpus Christi (1887)	9.86	Jul 2, 2007	20.33	Sep 1967	48.16	1888
Corsicana (1893)	16.35	Oct 23, 2015	25.16	Oct 2015	69.11	2015
Dalhart (1946)	4.52	Aug 2, 1985	9.77	Aug 1981	28.03	1985
Dallas (1897)	6.90	Mar 19, 2006	16.05	Oct 1981	62.89	2015
Del Rio (1905)	17.03	Aug 23, 1998	20.93	Aug 1998	37.75	1914
Eagle Pass (1891)	15.60	Jun 29, 1936	17.37	Jun 2013	44.44	1900
El Paso (1879)	6.60	Jul 17, 1947	8.18	Jul 1881	18.29	1884
Fort Stockton (1940)	5.52	Oct 5, 1986	10.09	Sep 1980	28.14	1941
Fort Worth (1940)	5.21	Jun 28, 1992	16.97	Apr 1942	53.97	2015
Galveston (1871)	13.93	Oct 8, 1901	26.67	Aug 2017	78.38	1900
Hereford (1905)	5.30	Aug 3, 1976	11.77	Oct 1941	38.95	1941
Houston (1883)	16.07	Aug 27, 2017	39.11	Aug 2017	83.02	1979
Junction (1897)	6.10	Sep 8, 1980	13.70	Aug 1974	44.77	1919
Kerrville (1897)	8.25	Jun 23, 1965	19.94	Sep 1936	57.57	1919
Killeen (1912)	8.92	May 16, 1965	16.16	Jul 1971	54.53	1957
Laredo (1915)	6.48	Sep 12, 1971	12.29	Jun 1973	42.28	1971

Longview (1902)	8.70	Mar 29, 1989	16.43	May 1944	72.87	1957
Lubbock (1911)	7.46	Sep 11, 2008	13.93	Sep 1936	40.55	1941
Lufkin (1906)	7.47	Oct 16, 1994	21.12	Nov 1940	79.04	2004
Marfa (1958)	4.88	Jul 31, 2007	8.81	Sep 1990	27.47	1990
Midland (1894)	11.26	Apr 12, 1894	13.59	Sep 1980	27.86	1986
Pampa (1908)	4.88	Jul 19, 1953	11.71	Apr 1997	38.99	2015
Paris (1896)	7.61	Jun 24, 1928	15.15	May 1982	75.65	1957
Perryton (1893)	7.11	May 17, 1989	13.49	Jul 1950	32.76	2015
Pine Springs (1939)	3.97	Sep 12, 2013	14.74	Jun 1941	42.47	1941
Plainview (1908)	7.00	Jul 8, 1960	13.24	May 2015	38.10	1926
Port Arthur (1911)	26.03	Aug 29, 2017	54.74	Aug 2017	81.55	1991
Presidio (1927)	3.30	Apr 17, 1979	7.29	Jul 1993	23.43	1941
San Angelo (1907)	11.75	Sep 15, 1936	27.65	Sep 1936	40.88	1919
San Antonio (1942)	11.26	Oct 17, 1998	18.07	Oct 1998	52.28	1973
Sanderson (1897)	5.35	Jun 11, 1965	11.28	Jul 2010	27.54	2004
Sherman (1897)	8.40	Aug 28, 1920	22.83	Oct 1981	70.69	2015
Sonora (1902)	7.92	Sep 1, 1976	18.87	Sep 1993	42.11	2004
Temple (1893)	9.62	Oct 17, 1998	19.79	Jul 1902	53.42	1902
Texarkana (1892)	9.29	Oct 10, 1926	18.28	Oct 1919	78.21	2009
Tyler (1883)	8.15	Jun 10, 2010	17.85	Aug 1888	66.02	1990
Uvalde (1905)	13.53	Jul 2, 1932	21.01	Jul 1932	46.04	1976
Van Horn (1939)	7.00	Aug 22, 1966	9.86	Sep 1978	27.27	1941
Victoria (1953)	9.87	Apr 5, 1991	20.34	Jul 2007	73.65	2004
Waco (1883)	7.98	Dec 20, 1997	15.19	Oct 2015	59.48	2004
Wichita Falls (1897)	6.19	Sep 27, 1980	17.00	May 2015	46.58	1915
Wink (1938)	5.64	Oct 11, 1940	9.07	Sep 1980	26.81	1941

[1] First year of record keeping is in parentheses.

APPENDIX 12

Driest and Wettest (Inches Precipitation) Locations, 1950–2016

	Least annual totals		Greatest annual totals	
YEAR	LOCATION	INCHES	LOCATION	INCHES
1994	Presidio	5.40	Corrigan	82.82
1995	Fort Hancock	3.98	Orange 9N[1]	79.83
1996	Fort Hancock	5.10	Beaumont	62.63
1997	Fort Hancock	5.84	Houston Heights	80.57
1998	Fort Hancock	4.29	Orange	76.41
1999	Presidio	2.44	Sam Rayburn Dam	61.31
2000	Wink	5.26	Sulphur Springs	69.63
2001	Boquillas	3.37	Houston Heights	92.88
2002	Fort Hancock	5.47	Port Arthur	90.76
2003	El Paso	4.21	Beaumont	66.45
2004	El Paso	12.09	Town Bluff Dam	83.01
2005	Heath Canyon	7.40	Sam Rayburn Dam	54.83
2006	Langtry	7.61	Kountze	98.03
2007	La Tuna	7.12	Houston-Westbury	75.80
2008	Kermit	8.50	Baytown	65.44
2009	Tornillo	5.53	New Boston	81.87
2010	Agua Fria	4.71	Houston NWSO[2]	55.15
2011	Terlingua	1.30	DeKalb	47.23
2012	Lake Ament	4.92	Orange 9N[1]	65.92
2013	Crane	6.44	Orange	66.16
2014	Kermit	6.80	Baytown	60.88
2015	Tornillo	9.29	Baytown	101.33
2016	Dell City	7.48	Lumberton	81.39

[1] Observations were made 9 miles north of the city.

[2] National Weather Service Office between Houston and Galveston.

APPENDIX 13

Extremes in Yearly Precipitation Amounts (Inches), 1873-2015

Greatest annual totals

INCHES	LOCATION (COUNTY)	YEAR
109.38	Clarksville (Red River)	1973
106.44	Freeport (Brazoria)	1979
102.58	Alvin (Brazoria)	1979
101.33	Baytown (Harris)	2015
101.24	Boxelder (Red River)	2015
100.21	Angleton (Brazoria)	1973
98.08	Anahuac (Chambers)	1946
98.03	Kountze (Hardin)	2006
97.54	Clarksville (Red River)	2015
95.28	Beaumont (Jefferson)	1923
94.79	Liberty (Liberty)	2015
92.88	Houston Heights (Harris)	2001
92.62	Cypress (Harris)	1973
91.72	Anahuac (Chambers)	2001
90.76	Port Arthur (Jefferson)	2002
90.62	Beaumont (Jefferson)	2001
89.88	Houston-Deer Park (Harris)	2001
89.50	Port Arthur (Jefferson)	1979
89.38	Cleveland (Liberty)	1973

Least annual totals[1]

INCHES	LOCATION (COUNTY)	YEAR
1.30	Terlingua (Brewster)	2011
1.55	Terlingua Ranch (Brewster)	2011
1.64	Presidio (Presidio)[2]	1956
1.70	McCamey (Upton)	2011
1.76	Wink (Winkler)	1956
1.91	Grandfalls (Ward)	2011
1.94	Wink (Winkler)	2011
1.95	Imperial (Pecos)[3]	1953
2.00	Fowlerton (LaSalle)[3]	1917
2.01	Pecos 8W (Reeves)	2011
2.17	Fort Stockton (Pecos)	2011
2.33	Rio Grande Village (Brewster)	2011
2.36	Pecos (Reeves)	1956
2.44	Presidio (Presidio)	1999
2.45	Fabens (El Paso)	1959
2.48	Lajitas (Presidio)	2001

[1] Several weather stations operated by the Galveston, Harrisburg, and San Antonio Railroad registered less than 1 inch of rainfall in 1910 (including Ysleta, 0.7 inch; Marathon, 0.8; and Maxon, 0.9) and little more than 1 inch in 1909 (including Watkins in Terrell County, 1.1 inches); two other stations in El Paso County in 1909 and six stations elsewhere in the Trans Pecos in 1910 recorded less than 2 inches.

[2] An estimate was made for the April amount that year.

[3] An estimate was made for three months in that year.

APPENDIX 14

Greatest One-Day and One-Month Precipitation Totals, 1880–2017

One-day totals[1]

INCHES	LOCATION (COUNTY)	DATE
29.05	Albany (Shackelford)	Aug 4, 1978
26.03	Port Arthur (Jefferson)	Aug 29, 2017
25.75	Alvin (Brazoria)	Jul 26, 1979
25.00	Dayton (Liberty)	Aug 27, 2017
23.11	Taylor (Williamson)	Sep 9-10, 1921
21.62	Bacliff (Galveston)	Aug 27, 2017
21.02	Kaffie Ranch (Jim Hogg)	Sep 12, 1971
20.70	Hye (Blanco)	Sep 11, 1952
20.60	Montell (Uvalde)	Jun 27, 1913
	Deweyville (Orange)	Sep 18, 1963
20.50	Brenham (Washington)	May 27, 2016
19.58	Houston Heights (Harris)	Jun 9, 2001
19.38	Santa Fe (Galveston)	Aug 27, 2017
19.29	Danevang (Wharton)	Aug 27-28, 1945
19.20	Benavides (Duval)	Sep 11, 1971
19.03	Austin (Travis)	Sep 9-10, 1921
18.50	Liberty (Liberty)	Oct 18, 1994
18.40	Port of Houston (Harris)	Jun 9, 2001
18.00	Fort Clark (Kinney)	Jun 14-15, 1899
17.83	Taylor Ranch (San Saba)	Jul 3, 1976
17.76	Port Arthur (Jefferson)	Jul 27-28, 1943
17.58	Edna (Jackson)	Oct 18, 1994
17.50	Pineland (Sabine)	Oct 17, 1994
17.47	Blanco (Blanco)	Sep 11, 1952
16.72	Freeport (Brazoria)	Jul 26, 1979
16.31	Gonzales (Gonzales)	Aug 31, 1981
16.08	Dickinson (Galveston)	Aug 27, 2017
16.07	Houston (Harris)	Aug 27, 2017
16.05	Smithville (Bastrop)	Jun 30, 1940
16.02	Hills Ranch (Travis)	Sep 10, 1921
	Pandale (Val Verde)	Jun 27, 1954
16.00	Hempstead (Waller)	Nov 24, 1940

[1] Does not include the unofficial total of more than 38 inches reported at a point near Thrall on September 9-10, 1921.

One-month totals

INCHES	LOCATION (COUNTY)	DATE
54.74	Port Arthur (Jefferson)	Aug 2017
52.07	Baytown (Harris)	Aug 2017
47.68	Dickinson (Galveston)	Aug 2017
41.42	Port of Houston (Harris)	Jun 2001
40.97	Beaumont (Jefferson)	Aug 2017
39.11	Houston-Bush (Harris)	Aug 2017
38.87	Houston-Hobby (Harris)	Aug 2017
38.66	Houston-Clover (Harris)	Aug 2017
35.70	Alvin (Brazoria)	Jul 1979
34.85	McKinney (Collin)	May 1881
34.65	Richmond (Fort Bend)	Aug 2017
34.14	Beaumont (Jefferson)	Jun 2001
33.67	Camp Verde (Kerr)	Jul 2002
33.27	Houston-Hooks (Harris)	Aug 2017
32.78	Falfurrias (Brooks)	Sep 1967
32.56	Comfort (Kendall)	Jul 2002
32.03	Kountze (Hardin)	Oct 2006
31.61	Freeport (Brazoria)	Sep 1979
31.26	Houston Heights (Harris)	Jun 2001
31.19	Albany (Shackelford)	Aug 1978
31.05	Sisterdale (Kendall)	Jul 2002
30.95	Freeport (Brazoria)	Sep 1979
30.57	Brownsville (Cameron)	Sep 1886
30.30	Pilot Point (Denton)	May 1982
29.99	Sugar Land (Fort Bend)	Aug 2017
29.76	Port Lavaca (Calhoun)	Jun 1960
29.59	Liberty (Liberty)	Oct 1994
29.49	Brenham (Washington)	May 2016
29.22	Aransas Pass (San Patricio)	Sep 1967
29.19	Whitsett (Live Oak)	Sep 1967
28.96	Deweyville (Orange)	Oct 1970
28.90	Gainesville (Cooke)	May 2015
28.43	Boerne (Kendall)	Jul 2002
27.94	Weatherford (Parker)	May 1884
27.92	Silsbee (Hardin)	Oct 2006

One-month totals

INCHES	LOCATION (COUNTY)	DATE
27.89	Kaffie Ranch (Jim Hogg)	Sep 1971
27.72	Baytown (Harris)	Oct 1994
27.65	San Angelo (Tom Green)	Sep 1936
27.47	Boyd (Wise)	Oct 1981
27.37	Kendalia (Kendall)	Jul 2002
27.16	Midway (Madison)	Oct 1984
27.02	Kountze (Hardin)	Oct 1994
26.86	Port Arthur (Jefferson)	Jul 1979
26.50	Wildwood (Tyler)	Oct 2006
26.44	Bankersmith (Kendall)	Jul 2002
26.42	Matagorda (Calhoun)	Jul 2007

APPENDIX 15

Driest Year and Greatest Consecutive Rainless Days

LOCATION	TOTAL INCHES	YEAR	NUMBER DAYS	DATES
Abilene	9.78	1956	73	Jun 2-Aug 13, 1970
	10.85	1917	72	Jul 2-Sep 11, 2000
	13.41	1934	66	Nov 17, 1886-Jan 21, 1887
Amarillo	7.01	2011	75	Oct 21, 1956-Jan 3, 1957
	9.56	1970	74	Oct 22, 1945-Jan 3, 1946
	9.94	1956	69	Nov 1, 1903-Jan 8, 1904
Austin	11.42	1954	65	Jun 27-Aug 30, 1993
	14.69	1893	61	Nov 1-Dec 31, 1894
	15.41	1956	56	Jul 12-Sep 5, 1921
Brownsville	11.59	1953	142	Jan 3-May 24, 1901
	12.15	1917	70	Nov 22, 1901-Jan 30, 1902
	14.41	2005	66	Mar 9-May 13, 1920
				Oct 17-Dec 21, 1903
Corpus Christi	5.38	1917	60	Jun 27-Aug 25, 1993
	12.06	2011	56	Jun 24-Aug 18, 1957
	14.10	1909	56	Jun 23-Aug 17, 1895
			54	Jun 1-Jul 24, 1915

Dallas	17.52	1963	85	Jul 1-Sep 23, 2000
	18.57	2005	53	Jul 11-Sep 1, 1999
	18.63	1909	52	Jun 22-Aug 12, 2011
El Paso	2.22	1891	136	Feb 7-Jun 22, 1910
	2.73	1934	128	Feb 6-Jun 13, 2002
	4.03	1910	126	Feb 25-Jun 29, 1896
Houston	25.39	2011	58	Mar 15-May 11, 2011
	26.65	1988	46	Sep 21-Nov 5, 1978
	28.32	1956	44	Sep 22-Nov 4, 1952
Laredo	6.65	2011	116	Jan 16-May 11, 2011
	9.43	2012	106	Oct 13, 1921-Jan 26, 1922
	9.61	1955	105	Sep 26, 2010-Jan 8, 2011
Lubbock	5.86	2011	98	Oct 28, 2005-Feb 2, 2006
	8.81	2003	76	Feb 12-Apr 27, 1972
	10.83	1956	76	Nov 8, 1955-Jan 22, 1956
Midland	4.60	1951	135	Oct 8, 1966-Feb 19, 1967
	5.14	1998	127	Sep 27, 2010-Jan 31, 2011
	5.47	2011	112	Jan 17-May 8, 1946
San Angelo	7.41	1956	116	Oct 18, 1966-Feb 10, 1967
	8.29	1917	100	Oct 21, 1950-Jan 28, 1951
	8.57	1933	74	Oct 17-Dec 29, 1970
San Antonio	10.11	1917	63	Jun 27-Aug 28, 1993
	13.70	1954	60	Dec 31, 1995-Feb 28, 1996
	14.92	1909	54	Jul 2-Aug 24, 1962
Texarkana	22.48	1896	48	Jul 6-Aug 22, 2011
	27.02	1903	44	Sep 18-Oct 31, 1963
	27.50	2005	44	Dec 4, 1955-Jan 16, 1956
Waco	13.39	1917	83	Jun 5-Aug 26, 1901
	14.92	1954	70	Jun 23-Aug 31, 1924
	15.15	1956	64	Nov 19, 1922-Jan 21, 1923
Wichita Falls	12.97	2011	75	Dec 19, 1913-Mar 3, 1914; Jan 2-Mar 6, 1996
	16.07	1970	72	May 31-Aug 10, 2001
	16.36	1952	71	Nov 1, 1904-Jan 10, 1905

APPENDIX 16

Average Number of Days with Precipitation of 0.10 Inch or More

LOCATION	JAN	FEB	MAR	APR	MAY	JUN	JUL	AUG	SEP	OCT	NOV	DEC	YEAR
Abilene	2.2	2.9	3.4	3.1	4.6	4.7	3.3	3.8	3.5	4.5	2.5	2.5	41.0
Alpine	1.4	1.5	1.1	1.6	3.3	5.2	5.3	5.9	4.6	2.7	1.4	1.5	35.5
Amarillo	1.7	1.4	3.2	2.9	4.4	5.4	4.0	5.3	3.8	3.1	2.1	1.9	39.2
Austin	3.8	3.9	5.1	3.6	5.1	5.6	3.5	3.2	4.1	4.9	4.0	3.9	50.7
Beeville	3.8	3.6	2.5	3.3	5.3	4.9	4.4	3.4	5.0	4.5	2.9	3.0	46.6
Big Bend NP	2.0	1.5	1.2	1.7	3.4	4.7	5.8	6.0	3.8	3.3	1.4	1.4	36.2
Big Spring	1.5	2.2	2.0	2.1	3.6	4.1	2.8	4.0	3.3	2.8	1.4	1.6	31.4
Brownsville	2.7	2.2	1.9	2.1	2.6	3.6	2.9	4.1	6.6	4.7	2.9	2.6	38.9
Brownwood	3.1	3.4	3.9	3.3	5.3	5.2	2.9	3.2	3.6	4.1	2.9	2.8	43.7
Childress	1.8	2.6	3.0	3.8	5.1	5.9	3.6	3.9	3.6	3.3	2.3	1.8	40.7
College Station	4.9	4.3	4.9	3.6	5.6	6.0	3.6	3.7	4.4	5.1	4.7	5.1	55.9
Corpus Christi	3.2	2.5	2.7	2.3	4.0	4.7	3.5	4.0	6.2	3.9	2.9	2.8	42.7
Dalhart	1.2	1.2	2.5	2.5	3.9	4.7	4.9	5.1	3.1	2.6	1.3	1.6	34.6
Dallas-Fort Worth	3.7	4.3	5.1	4.3	6.2	5.8	3.1	2.9	3.7	4.9	4.4	4.2	52.6
Del Rio	1.6	1.8	2.4	2.6	3.8	3.0	2.5	2.3	3.1	2.8	1.9	1.7	29.5
Eagle Pass	2.2	2.0	2.0	2.9	3.7	3.7	2.7	2.6	4.0	3.2	1.8	1.9	32.7
El Paso	1.5	1.3	0.7	0.8	1.3	2.1	3.6	4.1	2.9	2.0	1.5	2.3	24.1
Hereford	1.4	1.9	2.9	2.5	4.0	5.8	4.1	5.3	3.4	2.7	2.1	1.9	38.0
Houston	5.4	5.2	4.8	3.9	5.1	6.9	5.6	5.6	5.4	5.3	5.3	5.7	64.2
Kerrville	3.3	3.3	4.3	3.5	5.2	4.8	3.5	2.6	4.5	4.8	3.7	3.2	46.7
Killeen	3.7	3.9	5.1	3.3	6.0	5.2	3.1	2.7	3.9	4.8	4.7	4.4	50.8
Laredo	2.2	1.9	1.9	2.5	3.2	3.1	2.8	2.8	4.3	2.6	2.2	1.7	31.2
Lubbock	1.5	2.0	2.3	2.5	4.1	5.2	3.5	3.8	3.6	3.0	1.7	2.1	35.3
Lufkin	5.5	5.7	5.6	4.0	6.2	6.7	5.0	4.9	4.5	5.3	5.6	6.3	65.3
Marfa	1.3	1.2	1.0	1.6	2.8	3.8	5.6	5.3	4.3	2.7	1.1	1.8	32.5
Midland	1.4	1.8	1.5	1.6	2.9	3.0	2.9	3.2	3.3	2.7	1.5	1.5	27.3
Pampa	1.5	1.9	3.5	3.5	5.4	5.7	4.6	5.3	3.9	3.0	2.4	2.1	42.8
Paris	4.9	5.0	5.9	5.2	7.1	6.1	4.0	3.7	4.9	5.6	5.3	5.3	63.0
Perryton	1.3	1.7	3.6	3.3	4.3	4.8	4.4	4.7	3.4	3.0	1.9	2.0	38.4

Plainview	1.6	1.8	2.4	2.8	4.6	5.8	3.6	4.1	3.8	3.3	2.0	2.0	37.8
Port Arthur	6.7	5.2	4.9	4.0	4.7	7.5	7.5	6.9	6.9	5.2	5.6	6.0	71.1
Presidio	1.3	0.8	0.5	0.8	1.6	2.6	3.7	3.2	2.8	1.9	0.8	1.0	21.0
San Angelo	2.0	2.7	3.0	2.3	4.5	4.1	2.4	3.2	3.2	4.3	2.2	1.9	35.8
San Antonio	3.7	3.4	4.3	3.2	4.8	5.1	3.4	3.1	4.1	4.5	3.4	3.3	46.3
Sanderson	1.3	1.7	1.3	1.4	2.3	3.4	2.5	2.7	2.7	2.9	1.3	1.2	24.7
Sherman	4.2	4.8	5.5	5.0	7.2	6.1	3.8	3.6	4.7	6.1	4.8	4.7	60.5
Sonora	2.2	2.4	2.7	2.7	3.8	4.2	2.7	3.8	3.1	3.8	2.5	1.8	35.7
Temple	4.5	3.8	4.6	3.5	5.5	5.7	2.6	2.7	4.3	4.8	4.4	4.7	51.1
Texarkana	6.0	6.1	6.5	5.6	7.1	6.0	4.7	3.9	4.2	6.3	6.0	6.4	68.8
Uvalde	2.5	3.7	3.2	3.0	3.7	4.3	2.6	2.7	4.4	4.1	2.9	3.5	40.6
Van Horn	1.7	1.4	0.8	1.0	1.5	2.6	4.8	4.9	3.4	2.5	1.5	1.6	27.7
Waco	4.1	4.1	4.8	3.8	5.2	5.3	2.9	3.0	3.9	4.7	4.5	4.0	50.3
Wichita Falls	2.3	3.5	3.7	3.9	5.3	5.1	2.9	3.9	3.7	4.3	3.0	2.9	44.5
Wink	1.5	1.5	1.5	1.4	2.6	3.3	3.3	2.9	2.6	2.5	1.5	1.4	26.0

Note: Monthly totals, when added, may differ from the annual total because of rounding. Averages are based on records for 1981-2010.

APPENDIX 17

Average Monthly Snowfall Accumulations (Inches)

REGION AND LOCATION	OCT	NOV	DEC	JAN	FEB	MAR	APR	TOTAL
High Plains								
Amarillo	0.2	2.5	3.7	4.7	2.9	2.9	0.7	17.8
Borger	0.2	2.1	4.7	4.8	4.1	3.5	0.9	20.3
Dalhart	0.6	1.3	4.3	4.3	3.0	4.2	1.2	18.9
Lubbock		0.9	2.3	2.6	1.6	0.6	0.2	8.2
Midland		0.5	1.6	2.0	0.5	0.2	0.1	4.9
Muleshoe		1.1	3.4	2.2	1.4	0.9	0.2	9.2
Perryton	0.3	1.0	4.0	3.8	4.1	4.3	0.8	18.3
Plainview		1.2	3.0	3.5	1.9	0.9	0.2	10.7
Seminole		0.8	1.4	3.0	2.0	0.4	0.4	8.0
Low Rolling Plains								
Abilene		0.7	1.1	1.5	0.8	0.3	0.3	4.7
Childress	0.2	0.7	1.7	2.7	1.1	0.4	0.2	7.0
Clarendon		0.3	1.0	1.6	0.7	0.9	0.3	4.8
Wichita Falls		0.3	1.0	1.4	0.7	0.5		3.5
North Central								
Brownwood		0.1	0.2	0.5	0.2		0.1	1.1
Dallas-Fort Worth			0.3	0.3	0.4	0.2		1.2
Paris			0.4	0.4	0.1			0.9
Sherman		0.2	0.1	0.3	0.5			1.1
Waco		0.1		0.3	0.5	0.1	0.2	1.2
East								
Center					0.2	0.4		0.6
Longview			0.3	0.3	0.3			0.9
Lufkin				0.1				0.1
Trans Pecos								
El Paso		0.8	3.1	1.3	0.6	0.3	0.8	6.9
Marfa		0.1	0.5	0.4	0.3			1.3
Pecos			1.5	2.3	0.4	0.1	0.1	4.5
Edwards Plateau								
Del Rio				1.2				1.2
San Angelo		0.3	0.3	1.2	0.3	0.1		2.2

Note: Monthly totals, when added, may differ from the annual total because of rounding. Averages are based on records for 1981-2010.

APPENDIX 18

Average Relative Humidity (Percent)

	January				April				July				October			
LOCATION	6AM	12M	6PM	12PM	6AM	12M	6PM	12PM	6AM	12M	6PM	12PM	6AM	12M	6PM	12PM
Abilene	73	53	49	67	73	45	39	63	74	46	39	60	77	52	48	68
Amarillo	72	51	49	67	71	39	33	59	76	42	38	63	75	45	44	67
Austin	79	61	57	73	83	56	52	74	89	52	48	76	85	57	55	76
Beaumont-Port Arthur	88	68	75	85	90	61	68	87	95	66	72	93	92	59	74	89
Brownsville	89	66	74	88	89	60	68	87	92	55	63	87	91	60	71	88
Corpus Christi	87	67	70	84	90	62	67	86	94	56	63	89	90	59	69	86
Dallas-Fort Worth	80	61	59	74	81	55	51	71	81	49	45	67	83	55	55	73
El Paso	44	35	56	66	23	18	30	42	37	29	48	64	39	31	53	65
Houston	86	64	67	82	89	58	60	85	93	57	62	86	91	57	68	88
Lubbock	73	50	45	65	68	37	29	53	74	46	38	61	79	47	43	68
Midland-Odessa	72	47	42	65	67	33	27	53	73	42	35	58	80	47	44	70
San Angelo	78	53	48	70	75	43	35	63	79	44	37	62	83	52	50	74
San Antonio	80	57	55	75	82	55	49	75	87	53	46	75	85	55	53	78
Victoria	88	65	69	85	89	59	62	85	93	55	60	89	91	58	67	88
Waco	84	64	62	78	85	57	53	77	85	49	46	71	86	56	57	77
Wichita Falls	80	56	57	73	80	49	46	72	78	44	40	66	84	52	54	74

Source: Based on data from US Department of Commerce, Local Climatological Data, 2015.

Note: All times are local standard. 12M is midday, and 12PM is midnight. Averages are based on observations from 1981-2010.

Acknowledgments

The indispensable help of others made possible this effort to describe the attributes, subtleties, and idiosyncrasies of Texas weather, past and present. The initiative shown by Casey Kittrell at the University of Texas Press was a catalyst, given that it has been over 30 years since the Press published my original book devoted to Texas weather. His patience and encouragement when I sputtered in my writing on occasion were indispensable to crossing the finish line. Robert Kimzey and others on the staff of the University of Texas Press supplied the expertise necessary to get this new volume in print. I am grateful to Eva Silverfine for her skillful and insightful editing of the manuscript and Elli Puffe for her meticulous proofreading.

A keen awareness of the vagaries of Texas's weather, shared by Jon Zeitler of the National Weather Service and Bob Rose of the Lower Colorado River Authority, sharpened the focus of this book, allowing me to expound on the challenges of anticipating and recognizing the kinds of adverse weather that pose a threat to Texans somewhere in virtually every week of the year. The last chapter in this book is the first-ever substantive treatment to be published of efforts in Texas to modify the weather for the benefit of all Texans, so I extend a heartfelt thank you to C. E. Williams, the late Tommy Shearrer, Dale Bates, the late Wayne Wyatt, Ed Walker, Craig Funke, Mike Mahoney, and other groundwater district leaders for their tireless efforts in applying cloud-seeding technologies to bring more freshwater to a thirsty Texas, especially in those inevitable spells of drought. I am indebted to William Kuntz, longtime executive director of the Texas Department of Licensing and Regulation, for his vision in affording invaluable state support of research to demonstrate the efficacy of cloud seeding, and to Brian Francis, George Ferrie, and Randolph Nesbitt, colleagues of mine at TDLR, for their interest in and support for my participation in weather modification activities throughout the Lone Star State. I am very thankful to

Gary Walker and the Seeding Operations and Atmospheric Research (SOAR) Program for our many collaborative efforts to refine approaches for successful seeding of thunderstorms—and for the imagery used in chapter 11.

I am forever grateful to my wife, Judy, and daughter-in-law, Ashleigh Bomar, for their discerning eyes in helping me proofread the manuscript one final time.

Weather Terminology

absolute humidity: the ratio of the mass of water vapor present in moist air to the volume occupied by the mixture; usually expressed in grams of water vapor per cubic meter (gm/m^3).

accretion: the growth of a precipitation particle by the collision of a frozen particle (ice crystal or snowflake) with a supercooled liquid droplet, which freezes on contact.

acre-foot: the volume of water required to cover 1 acre to a depth of 1 foot (i.e., 43,560 cubic feet).

advection: the transport of a property (such as temperature or moisture) solely by the motion of the atmosphere.

advection fog: a type of fog caused by the advection of moist air over a cold surface and the subsequent cooling of that air below its dew point.

air mass: a widespread body of air that is approximately homogeneous in its horizontal extent, especially with respect to temperature and moisture.

albedo: the ratio of the amount of radiation reflected by a body to the amount of radiation incident upon that body.

altocumulus: a type of middle-level cloud, white or gray in color, that occurs as a layer or patch with a waved aspect.

altostratus: a type of middle-level cloud that appears in the form of a gray or bluish sheet or layer of striated, fibrous, or uniform cloud elements.

anemometer: an instrument designed to measure the speed of the wind.

aneroid barometer: an instrument, containing no liquid, that measures atmospheric pressure.

anticyclone: a weather system having an anticyclonic (or clockwise in the Northern Hemisphere) circulation pattern; also known as a high-pressure cell.

atmosphere: the envelope of air surrounding Earth and confined next to Earth resulting largely from Earth's gravitational influence.

atmospheric pressure: the pressure exerted by the atmosphere as a result of gravitational attraction imposed upon a "column" of air lying directly over the point in question.

autumnal equinox: the time (approximately September 22) when the sun's noon rays are directly overhead at the Equator and when the sun approaches the Southern Hemisphere; the official beginning of autumn.

bar: a unit of pressure equal to 1 million dynes per square centimeter (10 dynes/cm^2), or 29.53 inches of mercury.

barometer: an instrument for measuring atmospheric pressure.
barometric pressure: see atmospheric pressure.
Bermuda high: semipermanent subtropical high-pressure cell in the North Atlantic; its circulation pattern is largely responsible for the warm and humid conditions that prevail in Texas in summer.
black frost: a killing dry freeze, with respect to its effect upon vegetation.
blizzard: a severe wintry condition typified by cold temperatures and strong winds (with speeds at least 35 miles per hour) bearing a great amount of snow.
blowing dust: dust particles picked up from Earth's surface and blown about by the wind as clouds or sheets.
blowing snow: snow lifted from Earth's surface by the wind to a height of 6 feet or more and blown about to such an extent that horizontal visibility is restricted at or above that level.
breeze: a light wind (with speeds ranging from 4 to 27 knots, or 4 to 31 miles per hour).
ceiling: the height ascribed to the lowest layer of clouds or other phenomenon (such as fog or smoke) that obscures visibility.
Celsius: a temperature scale (formerly known as centigrade) whose ice point is 0° and boiling point is 100°.
cirrocumulus: a type of high-level cloud that appears as a thin, white patch of cloud without shadows and is composed of very small elements in the form of grains or ripples.
cirrostratus: a type of high-level cloud that appears as a whitish veil, usually fibrous but sometimes smooth, and sometimes produces the halo phenomenon around the sun or moon.
cirrus: a type of high-level cloud consisting of elements in the form of white, delicate filaments, white patches, or narrow bands.
clear: a sky condition when clouds are absent or when the cloud cover is less than 10 percent.
climatology: the scientific study of climate, or the long-term manifestations of the weather.
cloud: a visible aggregate of minute water, ice particles, or both in the atmosphere above Earth's surface.
cloud base: the lowest level in the atmosphere at which the air contains a perceptible quantity of cloud.
cloud seeding: a technique performed to add to a cloud a certain amount of particles that will alter the natural development of that cloud.
cloudy: a sky condition in which clouds cover about 70 percent or more of the sky.
coalescence: the merging of two water drops into a single larger drop.
cold front: the leading edge of an advancing air mass that replaces a warmer air mass.
cold wave: a rapid fall in temperature within 24 hours that necessitates substantially increased protection to agriculture, industry, commerce, and social activities.
condensation: the process by which a vapor becomes a liquid or a solid.
condensation nucleus: a solid or liquid particle upon which condensation of water vapor begins in the atmosphere.
continental air: a type of air whose characteristics are developed over a large land area and that is often marked by a low moisture content.
convection: motion within the atmosphere that results in the transport and mixing of certain properties of the atmosphere (e.g., moisture).
convective cloud: a cloud that owes its vertical development to currents of convection.
cooperative observer: an unpaid volunteer weather observer who maintains a weather station for the National Weather Service.
Coriolis force: an apparent force exerted on moving particles that stems from the rotation of Earth on its axis.
corona: one or more prismatically colored rings that concentrically surround the sun or moon when veiled by a thin cloud layer.
cumulonimbus: a principal cloud type that appears as mountains or huge towers and often produces heavy rain of a showery nature; its popular name is thundercloud or thunderhead.
cumulus: a type of low-level cloud, made up of individual, detached elements that generally are dense, that develops vertically as rising mounds, domes, or towers.

cut-off low: a low-pressure cell that becomes displaced from the basic westerly current in the midlatitudes.

cyclogenesis: the development or intensification of a cyclonic circulation pattern (e.g., a low-pressure cell).

cyclone: any weather system having a closed counterclockwise circulation pattern in the Northern Hemisphere.

deepening: a decrease (or intensification) in the central pressure of a weather system (such as a low).

degree day: a measure of the departure of the mean daily temperature from a given standard (most often 65°F or 19°C).

density: the ratio of the mass of any substance to the volume occupied by it; usually expressed in grams per cubic centimeter (gm/cm^3).

depression: an area of low pressure; also known as a low or trough.

dew: water condensed onto grass and other objects near the ground whose temperatures have fallen below the dew point of the layer of air next to Earth's surface but is still above freezing (if temperature is below freezing, hoarfrost occurs; if temperature falls below freezing after dew has formed, the frozen dew is called white dew).

dew point: the temperature to which the air must be cooled in order for it to become saturated (assuming pressure and moisture content remain constant).

diurnal: daily, particularly with reference to processes that are completed within 24 hours and that recur every 24 hours.

dog days: period of greatest heat in summer, usually from mid-July to the end of August.

downrush: the strong downward-flowing current of air associated with a dissipating thunderstorm.

downwind: the direction toward which the wind is blowing.

drifting snow: snow raised by the wind from Earth's surface to a height of less than 6 feet above the surface and then deposited behind obstacles and irregularities of the surface in heaps referred to as snow drifts.

drizzle: very small, numerous, and uniformly dispersed water drops that may appear to float and that fall to the ground; classifications include very light drizzle, which does not completely wet an exposed surface, regardless of duration; light drizzle, the rate of fall ranging from a trace to 0.01 inch per hour; moderate drizzle, 0.01 to 0.02 inch per hour; and heavy drizzle, more than 0.02 inch per hour.

drought: a period of abnormally dry weather of sufficient length to cause a serious hydrologic imbalance (e.g., crop damage, water-supply shortage).

dry freeze: freezing of soil and objects on the ground resulting from a lowering in temperature when the air does not contain enough moisture for hoarfrost to form; with reference to vegetation, it is known as black frost.

dry snow: powdery snow from which a snowball cannot easily be made.

dust: solid materials suspended in the atmosphere that give a tannish or grayish hue to distant objects.

Dust Bowl: a region of the United States, including the Texas High and Low Rolling Plains, afflicted by extreme drought and dust storms in the decade of the 1930s.

dust devil: a small, vigorous, well-developed whirlwind rendered visible by the dust, sand, or other debris picked up from the ground.

dust storm: a severe weather condition marked by strong winds and dust-filled air that reduces visibilities to ⅝ mile or less (if lowered to $1/16$ mile, a severe dust storm).

easterly wave: a migratory disturbance, imbedded within the broad easterly current that moves from east to west across the tropics, that occasionally evolves into a tropical cyclone.

echo: the appearance on a radar indicator of radio energy reflected or scattered back from a radar target.

effective precipitation: the portion of precipitation that reaches stream channels as runoff or that remains in the soil and is available for consumptive use.

effective temperature: the temperature at which motionless, saturated air would induce, in a sedentary worker wearing ordinary indoor clothing, the same sensation of comfort as that brought about by the actual conditions of temperature, humidity, and air movement.

elevation: a measure of the height of a point on Earth's surface above a reference plane (most often, mean sea level); usually expressed in feet (ft.) or meters (m).

equinox: the moment at which the sun passes directly above Earth's Equator (see also autumnal equinox and vernal equinox).

evaporation: the process by which a liquid is transformed to the gaseous state; the opposite of condensation.

evapotranspiration: the combined processes by which water is transferred from Earth's surface to the atmosphere through evaporation of liquid or solid water plus transpiration from plants.

extratropical: typical of weather events that occur poleward of the belt of tropical easterlies.

eye: the roughly circular area of comparatively light winds and fair skies found at the center of an intense tropical cyclone (such as a tropical storm or a hurricane).

Fahrenheit: a temperature scale whose freezing point is 32° and boiling point is 212°.

fair: a term generally descriptive of pleasant weather; it implies no precipitation, less than 40 percent sky cover of low clouds, and no other extreme conditions of cloudiness, visibility, or wind.

first-order station: any weather-observing facility staffed in whole or in part by National Weather Service personnel; there are 10 such installations in Texas.

flash flood: a flood that rises or falls quite rapidly with little or no advance warning, most often as a result of high-intensity rainfall over relatively small areas.

flood: the condition of water overflowing the natural or artificial confines of a stream or other water body; also the accumulation by drainage of water in low-lying areas.

fog: a visible aggregate of minute water droplets suspended in the atmosphere near Earth's surface (see also advection fog, frontal fog, ground fog, radiational fog, sea fog, steam fog, upslope fog).

freeze: the condition in which air temperature remains below freezing (32°F or 0°C) over a widespread area; if it cuts short a growing season, it is termed a killing freeze; if it is sufficiently cold and prolonged, it is known as a hard freeze, a phenomenon recognized by the destruction of seasonal vegetation, a ground surface frozen solid underfoot, and heavy ice on small water surfaces such as puddles.

freezing drizzle: drizzle that falls in liquid form but freezes upon contact with an object to form a coating of glaze.

freezing level: the lowest altitude in the atmosphere, over a given location, at which the air temperature is 32°F or 0°C.

freezing rain: rain that falls in liquid form but freezes upon impact to form a coating of glaze on the ground and other exposed objects.

front: the interface or transition zone between two air masses having differing densities; also referred to as frontal surface, frontal system, and frontal zone.

frontal fog: fog associated with frontal surface and frontal passages; prefrontal fog results from rain falling through a cold stable air mass and raising its dew-point temperature, whereas frontal-passage fog stems from the mixture of warm and cold air within the frontal zone.

frost: a deposit of interlocking ice crystals on Earth's surface and earthbound objects when the temperature of the surface and those objects falls below freezing.

gale: an unusually strong wind, categorized as follows: moderate gale, 28–33 knots (32–38 miles per hour [mph]); fresh gale, 34–40 knots (39–46 mph); strong gale, 41–47 knots (47–54 mph); and whole gale, 48–55 knots (55–63 mph).

gale warning: a storm warning for marine interests of impending winds with speeds from 28 to 47 knots (32–54 miles per hour).

gamma ray: electromagnetic radiation having extremely short wavelength (between X-rays and cosmic rays) that contributes to the ionization of the atmosphere, one manifestation of which is lightning.

glaze: a coating of ice formed on exposed objects by the freezing of a film of water deposited by rain, drizzle, fog, or even supercooled water vapor.

greenhouse effect: the effect of heating exerted by the atmosphere upon Earth as a result of the absorption and reemission of radiation by the atmosphere.

ground clutter: a type of radar echo that stems from the reflection of a radar signal by fixed ground targets (such as tall buildings).

ground fog: a fog that hides less than 60 percent of the sky and that does not extend to the base of any clouds that may be above it.

growing season: the period of the year when the temperature of cultivated vegetation remains sufficiently high to allow plant growth.

gust: a sudden brief increase in the speed of the wind; it is reported when peak wind speed reaches at least 16 knots (18 miles per hour) and the variation in speed between peaks and lulls is at least 9 knots (10 miles per hour); its duration is usually less than 20 seconds.

haboob: a strong wind stirring up sand and/or dust into a dense whirling wall that may be several thousand feet high.

hail: precipitation in the form of balls or irregular lumps of ice always produced by convective clouds (such as thunderstorms).

halo: an atmospheric optical phenomenon that appears as colored or whitish rings and arcs around the sun or moon when seen through a layer or cloud of ice crystals.

hard freeze: a condition when seasonal vegetation is destroyed, the ground surface is frozen solid underfoot, and heavy ice is formed on small containers of water.

haze: dust or salt particles, so small they cannot be felt or seen individually with the human eye, that diminish horizontal visibility and give the atmosphere an opalescent appearance.

heat: a form of energy transferred between systems as a result of a difference in temperature.

heat wave: a period of abnormally and uncomfortably hot and usually humid weather.

heating degree day: a popular indicator of fuel consumption; one heating degree day is assigned for each degree that the daily mean temperature departs below the base of 65°F (19°C).

high: an expression for an area of "high" pressure, which refers to a maximum of atmospheric pressure.

hoarfrost: a deposit of interlocking ice crystals formed by direct sublimation on objects, most often those freely exposed to the air (e.g., tree branches, wires, poles, plant stems).

humidity: a measure of the water-vapor content of air (see also relative humidity).

hurricane: a severe tropical cyclone in the North Atlantic Ocean, having a sustained wind speed of 64 knots (74 miles per hour [mph]) or greater; classifications include a major hurricane, when winds of 101–135 mph (88–117 knots) and a minimum central pressure of 28.01–29.00 inches mercury (Hg) (711–737 millimeters Hg or 948.5–982.0 millibars [mb]) are observed, and an extreme hurricane, when maximum winds of 136 mph (118 knots) or higher and a minimum central pressure of 28.00 inches Hg (711 millimeters Hg or 948.5 mb) or less are noted.

hurricane warning: an advisory of impending winds of hurricane force.

hurricane watch: an announcement for a specific area that hurricane conditions pose a threat.

hydrologic cycle: the composite picture of the interchange of water substances among Earth, its atmosphere, and the seas.

hygrometer: an instrument that measures the humidity, or water-vapor content, of the atmosphere.

ice pellets: a type of precipitation consisting of transparent or translucent fragments of ice, 0.2 inch (5 millimeters) or less in diameter, that bounce when hitting hard ground and make a sound upon impact; commonly known as sleet.

ice storm: a weather event characterized by the fall of freezing precipitation, which creates hazardous conditions by causing glaze to form on terrestrial objects.

infrared radiation: electromagnetic energy having a wavelength from about 0.8 micrometers to an indefinite upper boundary; bounded on its lower limit by visible radiation and on its upper limit by microwave radiation.

insolation: solar radiation received at Earth's surface.

instability: an atmospheric condition in which certain disturbances, when introduced into the steady state, will increase in magnitude.

intertropical convergence zone (ITCZ): the broad trade-wind current of the tropics; the dividing line between the southeast and northeast trade winds.

inversion: a deviation from the usual decrease or increase with altitude of the value of an atmospheric property (e.g., temperature or moisture).

ionosphere: the layer of the upper atmosphere characterized by a high ion density, having a base at about 43–50 miles (70–80 kilometers) and a ceiling of indefinite height.

isallobar: a line of equal change in atmospheric pressure for a specific time interval.

isallotherm: a line connecting points of equal change in temperature for a given time period.

isobar: a line of equal or constant pressure; on a weather map, a line drawn through all points having the same atmospheric pressure.

isohyet: A line connecting ponts having equal precipitation.

isotherm: a line of equal or constant temperature.

jet stream: a concentration of relatively strong winds within a narrow stream of Earth's atmosphere; commonly referred to as a current of maximum winds imbedded in the upper atmosphere within the midlatitude westerlies.

killing freeze: a condition in which the surface temperature of the air remains below 32°F (0°C) for a sufficiently long time to destroy all but the hardiest herbaceous crops and to shorten the growing season.

knot: a unit of speed in the nautical system; equal to 1 nautical mile per hour, which equals 1.1508 statute mile per hour (or 0.5144 meters per second).

land breeze: a coastal breeze blowing from land to sea, set up by a difference in temperature when the sea surface is warmer than the adjacent land surface; usually occurs at night.

lapse rate: the decrease of an atmospheric variable (most often temperature) with height.

leader: the streamer of electrical charge that initiates the first phase of each stroke of a lightning discharge.

light freeze: the condition when the surface air temperature drops to below freezing (32°F or 0°C) for a short time period, such that only the tenderest plants and vines are harmed.

lightning: any and all forms of visible electrical discharge produced by thunderstorms.

lightning rod: a grounded metallic conductor with its upper extremity extending above the structure that is to be protected from damage due to lightning.

long wave: a wave in the major belt of westerly winds high in the atmosphere that is characterized by large length and significant amplitude.

low: an expression for an area of "low" pressure, which refers to a minimum of atmospheric pressure.

major trough: a long-wave upper atmospheric low-pressure area.

Marfa front: a transition zone between moist air to the east and desert-like air to the west that oscillates eastward in daytime and westward at night across the Trans Pecos region of Texas; it is so named because a weather station at Marfa transmits data hourly that allow forecasters to monitor its movement.

maritime air: a type of air whose characteristics are developed over an extensive water body; customarily high in moisture content, at least in its lowest levels.

mean sea level: the average height of the sea surface, based upon hourly observations of the height of tides for all stages over a 19-year period.

mesopause: the boundary between the mesosphere and the thermosphere; at an altitude of about 50 miles (80 kilometers), it is usually marked by a sudden change in the rate at which temperature drops with height.

mesosphere: that portion of the atmosphere extending from the top of the stratosphere to the mesopause; ranging in altitude between 12 miles (20 kilometers [km]) and 50 miles (80 km), it is characterized by a broad temperature maximum at about 30 miles (50 km).

meteorology: the science that deals with the phenomena of the atmosphere.

millibar: a measure of atmospheric pressure; equal to about 0.03 inch of mercury, or 33.86 millibars equal 1.0 inch.

minor trough: an atmospheric pressure area having a scale smaller than a major, or long-wave, trough; usually moves rapidly.

mist: an aggregate of microscopic water droplets suspended in the atmosphere that produces, generally, a thin, grayish veil over the landscape; intermediate between haze and fog.

moist air: air that is a mixture of dry air and any amount of water vapor.

moisture: a general term referring to the water vapor content, or total water substance, in a given volume of air.

nautical mile: the distance unit in the nautical system; its value is 1,852 meters (6,076 feet or 1.1508 statute miles).

nimbostratus: a type of middle-level cloud that is gray colored and often dark, rendered diffuse by falling rain, snow, or sleet.

normal: the average value of a meteorological element over a fixed period of time (customarily 30 years) that is recognized as standard for the area and element concerned.

norther: a strong cold wind, from between the northwest and northeast, that accompanies a cold-air outbreak; characteristically a rushing blast that brings a sudden drop of temperature of as much as 25°F in 1 hour or 50°F in a 3-hour period; a phenomenon most often observed from November to April.

nucleus: a particle of any nature (e.g., salt, sand, soil) upon which molecules of water or ice accumulate as a result of a phase change to a more condensed state.

occluded front: a composite of two fronts, formed when a cold front overtakes a warm or quasi-stationary front; a common process in the late stages of the development of a strong surface low-pressure area.

overcast: a sky condition in which the sky cover is solid and at least a portion of the sky cover is attributable to clouds or some other obscuring phenomenon.

overrunning: a condition when an air mass is in motion aloft above another air mass of greater density at the surface; a common circumstance in Texas's coastal plain when moist Gulf air pours up over a denser dome of cool polar or Arctic air.

ozone: a nearly colorless gaseous form of oxygen that occurs in trace quantities in Earth's atmosphere, primarily in the stratosphere, where it results from photochemical processes involving ultraviolet radiation.

partly cloudy: a sky condition typified by an average cloudiness from 40 to 70 percent for a 24-hour period; popularly regarded as the condition when clouds are conspicuously present but do not completely dull the day or the sky at any moment.

peak gust: the highest "instantaneous" wind speed recorded at a weather station for a specific time period (usually a 24-hour period).

persistence: the tendency for the occurrence of a specific weather event to be more probable, at a given time, if that same event has occurred in the immediately preceding time period.

point rainfall: the rainfall during a given time interval measured in a rain gauge.

polar air: the type of air whose traits are developed over high latitudes, especially within the subpolar regions (e.g., northern Canada).

potential evapotranspiration: the amount of moisture that, if available, would be withdrawn from a given land area by the process of evapotranspiration; often determined in dry regions by the amount of irrigation water used.

precipitable water: the total amount of water vapor contained in a vertical column of atmosphere (of unit cross-sectional area) between any two specified levels in the atmosphere.

precipitation: any and all forms of water particles, whether liquid or solid, that fall from the atmosphere and reach Earth's surface.

prefrontal squall line: a line of squalls, about 50 to 200 miles (80–320 kilometers) in advance of a cold front, that moves in about the same path as the cold front.

pressure: see atmospheric pressure.

prevailing wind direction: the wind direction most frequently observed during a given time interval.

probability of precipitation: the forecast likelihood that a precipitation event (e.g., rain, snow, sleet) will occur at a particular point during a given interval of time (for instance, a probability of 30 percent implies that, in 100 similar weather situations, any point within the local forecast area should observe measurable precipitation 30 times).

quasi-stationary front: a front that is stationary or nearly so; one whose speed of movement is less than about 5 knots (6 miles per hour).

radar: an electronic instrument used for the detection and ranging of distant objects having a composition that scatters or reflects radio waves.

radar echo: see echo.

radiation: the process by which electromagnetic radiation is propagated through free space by joint variations in the electric and magnetic fields.

radiational cooling: the cooling of Earth's surface and nearby air that results when the surface sustains a net loss of heat.

radiational fog: a major type of fog that results over a land area when radiational cooling drops the air temperature to or below its dew point.

radiosonde: an instrument, borne by a balloon, used for simultaneously measuring and transmitting meteorological data.

radome: a dome-shaped covering that houses the antenna assembly of a radar to protect it from wind and other foul weather.

rain: a kind of precipitation consisting of liquid water drops having a diameter larger than 0.02 inch (0.5 millimeter [mm]) or, if widely scattered, even smaller than that; classifications of rainfall intensity include very light rain, when scattered drops do not wet an exposed surface completely, regardless of duration; light rain, the rate varying between a trace and 0.10 inch (2.5 mm) per hour, with the maximum rate of fall amounting to no more than 0.01 inch (0.25 mm) in 6 minutes; moderate rain, from 0.11 inch (2.8 mm) to 0.30 inch (7.5 mm) per hour, the maximum rate being no more than 0.03 inch (0.8 mm) in 6 minutes; and heavy rain, over 0.30 inch per hour or more than 0.03 inch in 6 minutes.

rainbow: one of a family of circular arcs consisting of concentric colored bands, with red on the inside to violet on the outside, that may be seen on a "sheet" of water drops (such as rain, fog, or spray).

rain day: a 24-hour period having measurable precipitation, with 0.01 inch (0.25 millimeter) the most often used minimum threshold amount.

rain gauge: an instrument designed to measure the amount of precipitation that has fallen. The device provides "ground truth" measurement of rainfall amounts useful to researchers.

rainmaking: a common term referring to all activities designed to increase, through any of an assortment of artificial means, the amount of precipitation released from a cloud.

rawinsonde: a method of observing upper-atmospheric weather conditions—notably wind speed and direction, temperature, pressure, and moisture content—by means of a balloon-borne radiosonde tracked by a radar or other electronic finding device.

reflectivity: a measure of the portion of the total amount of radiation reflected by a given surface.

refraction: the process in which the direction of energy propagation is changed owing to a change in density within the propagating medium.

relative humidity: the ratio (usually expressed as a percentage) of the actual vapor pressure of the air to the vapor pressure of the air when saturated; a popular measure of the amount of moisture in the air.

ridge: an elongated area of relatively high atmospheric pressure; the opposite of a ridge is a trough.

rime: a white or milky and opaque deposit of ice formed by the rapid freezing of supercooled water drops as they impinge upon an exposed cold object; it is lighter, softer, and less transparent than glaze but denser and harder than hoarfrost.

sandstorm: a severe weather condition marked by strong winds carrying sand through the air that reduces visibilities to ⅝ mile or less (if lowered to 5⁄16 mile, a severe sandstorm); usually confined to lowest 10 feet and rarely rises more than 50 feet above the ground.

saturation: a condition of the air in which any increase in the amount of water vapor will initiate within the air a change to a more condensed state.

scattering: the process by which small particles suspended in a medium diffuse a portion of the incident radiation in all directions.

scud: rugged low clouds, usually seen moving rapidly beneath a layer of nimbostratus clouds or a base of a thunderstorm.

sea breeze: a coastal breeze blowing from sea to land, caused by the temperature difference that exists when the sea surface is colder than the adjacent land.

sea fog: a type of advection fog formed when air lying over a warm water surface is carried over a colder surface.

sea level: see mean sea level.

sea-level pressure: the atmospheric pressure at mean sea level.

semi-arid climate: a type of climate for which plant life consists of short, drought-resistant grasses; regions having this type of climate are highly susceptible to severe drought.

severe storm: generally any destructive storm, but often used to describe intense thunderstorms that produce heavy rain, hail, tornadoes, strong winds, or a combination of these events.

shear: most often used in meteorology to describe the variation of wind speed and direction with height above the surface of Earth.

short wave: a progressive wave in the horizontal pattern of air motion within Earth's atmosphere.

shower: a precipitation event characterized by a suddenness with which it starts and stops, by rapid changes in intensity, and usually by rapid changes in sky appearance.

sleet: see ice pellets.

small-craft warning: an advisory to marine interests warning them of impending winds up to 28 knots (32 miles per hour).

smog: a natural fog contaminated by industrial pollutants (i.e., a mixture of smoke and fog).

smoke: foreign particulate matter in the atmosphere resulting from combustion processes.

snow: precipitation consisting of white or translucent ice crystals, often agglomerated into snowflakes; classifications of intensity include very light snow, when scattered flakes do not cover or wet an exposed surface completely, regardless of duration; light snow, when visibility is ⅝ mile or more; moderate snow, when the visibility is less than ⅝ mile but more than 5/16 mile; and heavy snow, when the visibility is less than 5/16 mile.

snowfall accumulation: the actual depth of snow on the ground at any instant during a snowstorm or after any storm or series of storms.

solstice: popularly regarded as the time at which the sun is farthest north or south (see also summer solstice and winter solstice).

spring equinox: same as vernal equinox.

squall: a strong wind typified by sudden onset, a duration on the order of minutes, and a sudden decrease in speed; a sustained wind speed of 16 knots (18 miles per hour) or higher for at least 2 minutes.

squall line: a line or narrow band of active thunderstorms, not associated with a front.

stability: an atmospheric condition in which a displaced parcel of air is subjected to a buoyant force opposite to its displacement.

standard atmosphere: a hypothetical vertical distribution of temperature, pressure, and density that is regarded as representative of the atmosphere for calibration, for example, of equipment and aircraft design.

stationary front: same as quasi-stationary front.

steam fog: a type of fog that forms when very cold air drifts across relatively warm water by which water vapor is added to the air.

stepped leader: the initial streamer of a lightning discharge.

storm: any disturbed state of the atmosphere that strongly implies destructive or otherwise unpleasant weather.

storm surge: an abnormal rise of the sea along a shore as a result, mostly, of the winds of a storm; also known as storm tide.

storm warning: a specially worded forecast of severe weather, intended to alert the public to impending dangers.

stratocumulus: a type of low-level cloud in the form of a gray or whitish (or both) layer or patch, which nearly always has dark parts and is nonfibrous; composed of small water droplets.

stratosphere: the layer of the atmosphere above the troposphere and below the mesosphere, from an altitude of about 5–7 miles (8–11 kilometers) up to about 15–18 miles (24–29 kilometers).

stratus: a type of low-level cloud in the form of a gray layer with a rather uniform base; usually does not produce precipitation of consequence.

sublimation: the transition of a substance from the solid phase to the vapor phase.

subsidence: the descending motion of air in the atmosphere.

subtropical high: one of the semipermanent high-pressure cells that lie over the Atlantic and Pacific Oceans and have a profound effect on Texas weather, especially in summer; also called a subtropical ridge.

subtropics: the belt in each hemisphere between the tropics and the temperate zones, or roughly 35–40° north and south.

sultry: an oppressively uncomfortable state of the weather that stems from the simultaneous occurrence of high temperatures and high humidities; some lower limits are 95°F (35°C) and 25 percent humidity, 86°F (30°C) and 40 percent humidity, and 77°F (25°C) and 65 percent humidity.

summer solstice: the time (approximately June 21) when the sun's noon rays are directly overhead the point at 23.5°N latitude; the official beginning of summer.

sunrise: the phenomenon of the sun's daily appearance when the upper limb of the sun first is seen on the sea-level horizon.

sunset: the phenomenon of the sun's daily disappearance; when the upper limb of the sun just vanishes below the sea-level horizon.

sunspot: a relatively dark area on the surface of the sun; usually occurs in pairs with a lifetime from a few days to several months.

supercooled water: liquid water drops whose temperature is reduced below their nominal freezing point without a change of status.

synoptic: affording an overall view; used with reference to weather data obtained simultaneously over a wide area for the purpose of presenting a comprehensive and nearly instantaneous picture of the state of the atmosphere.

temperate climate: the climate of the "middle latitudes," between the extremes of the tropics and the polar regions.

temperature: the degree of hotness or coldness as measured on some definite temperature scale.

thermometer: an instrument for measuring temperature.

thunder: the sound emitted by rapidly expanding gases along the channel of a lightning discharge.

thunderhead: a popular term for the cloud mass of a thunderstorm, or cumulonimbus cloud; also called a thundercloud.

thunderstorm: a local storm invariably produced by a cumulonimbus cloud and always accompanied by lightning and thunder and usually accompanied by strong wind gusts and heavy rain.

thunderstorm day: an observational day during which thunder is heard (precipitation need not have fallen).

tide: the periodic rising and falling of Earth's oceans and atmosphere.

tornado: a violently rotating column of air, pendant from a cumulonimbus cloud; the most destructive of all local atmospheric phenomena.

trace: a precipitation amount of less than 0.005 inch (0.125 millimeters).

trade wind: the current of air that is a major component of the general circulation of the atmosphere; it blows from the subtropical highs toward the equatorial trough and is northeasterly in the North Atlantic.

transpiration: the process by which water in plants is transferred as water vapor to the atmosphere.

tropical air: the type of air whose traits are developed over low latitudes; maritime tropical air is generated over tropical and subtropical seas and is therefore very warm and humid, and continental tropical air is produced over subtropical arid regions and is consequently hot and very dry.

tropical cyclone: a weather system in the Northern Hemisphere having a closed counterclockwise circulation that originates over the tropical oceans; includes tropical depressions, tropical storms, and hurricanes.

tropical depression: a tropical cyclone having a sustained wind speed not greater than 34 knots (39 miles per hour) and usually appearing, on a weather map, with one or more closed isobars.

tropical disturbance: a tropical cyclone with only a slight surface wind circulation and appearing on a weather map with only one closed isobar or none at all.

tropical storm: a tropical cyclone with a sustained wind speed of 34 knots (39 miles per hour) to 63 knots (72 miles per hour).

tropopause: the boundary between the troposphere and the stratosphere, usually marked by a sudden change in the rate at which temperature drops with height.

troposphere: the portion of the atmosphere between Earth's surface and the tropopause, or the lowest 6 to 13 miles (10–20 kilometers) of the atmosphere.

trough: an elongated area of relatively low atmospheric pressure; often used to describe a surface front or an upper-atmospheric storm system; its axis is known as a trough line.

twister: a colloquial term for tornado.

typhoon: a severe tropical cyclone (including a hurricane) in the Pacific Ocean; its counterpart in the Atlantic is the hurricane.

ultraviolet radiation: electromagnetic energy having a wavelength shorter than visible radiation but longer than X-rays.

upper air: generally the portion of Earth's atmosphere above 850 millibars (or about 5,000 feet above mean sea level).

upslope fog: a type of fog formed when air flows upward over rising terrain and is cooled to or below its dew point.

vapor pressure: the partial pressure of water vapor in the atmosphere.

veering wind: a change in wind direction in a clockwise sense (in the Northern Hemisphere).

vernal equinox: the time (approximately March 21) when the sun's noon rays are directly overhead at the Equator and when the sun approaches the Northern Hemisphere; the official beginning of spring.

virga: wisps or streaks of water or ice particles falling out of a cloud but evaporating before reaching Earth's surface as precipitation.

visibility: the greatest distance in a given direction at which it is just possible to see and identify with the unaided eye (a) in the daytime, a prominent dark object against the sky at the horizon, and, (b) at night, a known, preferably unfocused, moderately intense light source.

warm front: any nonoccluded front that moves in such a way that warmer air replaces colder air.

waterspout: a tornado or lesser whirlwind occurring over water.

water vapor: water substance in the form of a vapor.

weather: the state of the atmosphere, mainly with respect to its effects upon life and human activities.

weather modification: any effort to alter artificially the natural phenomena of the atmosphere (e.g., rainmaking, fog dissipation, frost prevention).

wet-bulb temperature: the temperature an air parcel would have if cooled to saturation (at constant pressure) by evaporating water into it.

white dew: dew frozen as a result of the temperature falling below the freezing level after the dew originally formed.

white frost: a relatively heavy coating of hoarfrost.

wind: air in motion relative to Earth's surface.

windchill: that part of the total cooling of a body caused by air motion.

wind direction: the direction from which the wind is blowing.

wind vane: an instrument used to indicate wind direction.

winter solstice: the time (approximately December 22) when the sun's noon rays are directly overhead the point at 23.5°S latitude; the official beginning of winter.

X-ray: electromagnetic energy of very short wavelength, lying between the wavelength interval of 0.1 and 1.5 angstroms, or between gamma rays and ultraviolet radiation.

zonal flow: the flow of air along a latitude circle (essentially a westerly or easterly wind).

Suggested Reading

Aguado, Edward, and James E. Burt. *Understanding Weather and Climate*. Upper Saddle River, NJ: Prentice-Hall, 1999.

Ahrens, C. Donald. *Meteorology Today: An Introduction to Weather, Climate, and the Environment*. Pacific Grove, CA: Brooks/Cole, 2000.

Arya, S. Paul. *Introduction to Micrometeorology*. San Diego: Academic Press, 1988.

Barnett, Cynthia. *Rain: A Natural and Cultural History*. New York: Crown Publishers, 2015.

Bluestein, Howard B. *Tornado Alley*. New York: Oxford University Press, 1999.

Burnett, Jonathan. *Flash Floods in Texas*. College Station: Texas A&M University Press, 2008.

Burroughs, William J., Bob Crowder, Ted Robertson, Eleanor Vallier-Talbot, and Richard Whitaker. *Weather Watching*. San Francisco: Fog City Press, 1996.

Burt, Christopher C. *Extreme Weather*. New York: W. W. Norton & Company, 2007.

Caviedes, Cesar N. *El Niño in History*. Gainesville: University of Florida Press, 2001.

Challoner, Jack. *Amazing Weather*. New York: Chartwell Books, 2012.

Cox, John D. *Storm Watchers*. Hoboken, NJ: John Wiley & Sons, 2002.

Cox, Mike. *Texas Disasters: True Stories of Tragedy and Survival*. Lanham, MD: Rowman & Littlefield, 2015.

Douglas, Paul. *Restless Skies*. New York: Barnes & Noble, 2004.

Dow, Kirstin, and Thomas E. Downing. *The Atlas of Climate Change*. Berkeley: University of California Press, 2006.

Estaville, Lawrence E., and Richard A. Earl. *Texas Water Atlas*. College Station: Texas A&M University Press, 2008.

Gibson, Christine. *Extreme Natural Disasters*. New York: Harper Collins, 2007.

Libbrecht, Kenneth, and Patricia Rasmussen. *The Snowflake: Winter's Secret Beauty*. Stillwater, MN: Voyageur Press, 2003.

Lloyd, Julie. *Weather: The Forces of Nature That Shape Our World*. London: Parragon Publishing, 2007.

Lynas, Mark. *Six Degrees: Our Future on a Hotter Planet*. Washington, DC: National Geographic Society, 2008.

Lynch, John. *The Weather*. Toronto: Firefly Books, 2002.

Mason, B. J. *Clouds, Rain, and Rainmaking*. Cambridge, UK: Cambridge University Press, 1975.

Mogil, H. Michael. *Extreme Weather*. New York: Black Dog & Leventhal Publishers, 2007.

Moore, Peter. *The Weather Experiment: The Pioneers Who Sought to See the Future*. New York: Farrar, Straus and Giroux, 2015.

North, Gerald, Jurgen Schmandt, and Judith Clarkson. *The Impact of Global Warming on Texas*. Austin: University of Texas Press, 1995.

Norwine, Jim, John R. Giardino, Gerald R. North, and Juan B. Valdes. *The Changing Climate of Texas: Predictability and Implications for the Future*. College Station: Texas A&M University, 1995.

Parzybok, Tye W. *Weather Extremes in the West*. Missoula, MT: Mountain Press Publishing, 2005.

Phillips, David, Michael Parfit, and Suzanne Chisholm. *Blame It on the Weather*. San Diego: Portable Press, 2002.

Schmidt, Gavin, and Joshua Wolfe. *Climate Change: Picturing the Science*. New York: W. W. Norton & Company, 2008.

Williams, Jack. *The Weather Book*. New York: Vintage Books, 1992.

Index

Note: Page numbers in *italics* refer to charts, graphs, or illustrations.